THE PAINFUL TRUTH ABOUT HUNGER IN AMERICA

FOOD, HEALTH, AND THE ENVIRONMENT
Series Editors: Robert Gottlieb, Henry R. Luce Professor of Urban and Environmental Policy, Occidental College
Nevin Cohen, Associate Professor, City University of New York (CUNY) Graduate School of Public Health

THE PAINFUL TRUTH ABOUT HUNGER IN AMERICA

Why We Must Unlearn Everything We Think We Know—and Start Again

MARIANA CHILTON

The MIT Press
Cambridge, Massachusetts
London, England

The MIT Press would like to thank the anonymous peer reviewers who provided comments on drafts of this book. The generous work of academic experts is essential for establishing the authority and quality of our publications. We acknowledge with gratitude the contributions of these otherwise uncredited readers.

This book was set in Adobe Garamond and Berthold Akzidenz Grotesk by Jen Jackowitz. Printed and bound in the United States of America.

Library of Congress Cataloging-in-Publication Data

Names: Chilton, Mariana, author.
Title: The painful truth about hunger in America : why we must unlearn
    everything we think we know—and start again / Mariana Chilton.
Description: Cambridge, Massachusetts : The MIT Press, [2024] |
    Series: Food, health, and the environment | Includes bibliographical
    references and index.
Identifiers: LCCN 2023046312 (print) | LCCN 2023046313 (ebook) |
    ISBN 9780262048309 (hardcover) | ISBN 9780262375672 (epub) |
    ISBN 9780262375665 (pdf)
Subjects: LCSH: Hunger—United States. | Food relief—United States. | Food
    security—United States. | Social justice—United States.
Classification: LCC HV696.F6 C4925 2024 (print) | LCC HV696.F6 (ebook) |
    DDC 363.80973—dc23/eng/20240309
LC record available at https://lccn.loc.gov/2023046312
LC ebook record available at https://lccn.loc.gov/2023046313

10 9 8 7 6 5 4 3 2 1

For all people who
have struggled to buy food.
May you be loved,
may you be happy,
may you have
wealth and good health,
and may you and your families
eat well and flourish.

Contents

Series Foreword

The Painful Truth about Hunger in America is the twenty-third book in the Food, Health, and the Environment series. The series explores the global and local dimensions of food systems and the issues of access, social, environmental and food justice, and community well-being. Books in the series focus on how and where food is grown, manufactured, distributed, sold, and consumed. They address questions of power and control, social movements and organizing strategies, and the health, environmental, social, and economic factors embedded in food-system choices and outcomes. As this book demonstrates, the focus is not only on food security and well-being but also on economic, political, and cultural factors and regional, state, national, and international policy decisions. Food, Health, and the Environment books therefore provide a window into the public debates, alternative and existing discourses, and multidisciplinary perspectives that have made food systems and their connections to health and the environment critically important subjects of study and for social and policy change.

Robert Gottlieb, Occidental College
Nevin Cohen, City University of New York (CUNY)
Graduate School of Public Health

Notes on Reading This Book

Names. Most names have been changed to protect confidentiality and privacy.

Transcription. In the tradition of celebrating artistry in communication, it is important to portray the cadence and timing of verbal expression in dialogue and storytelling. I use a different format for active dialogue or narrative that was shared with me in oral form, most of which was recorded in research studies. The line breaks suggest a pause, long breath, or difference in cadence. Ellipses ". . ." signify a brief utterance that has been removed or replaced for clarity.

Terminology. Food insecurity is an official term utilized by the US Department of Agriculture (USDA) and many researchers. The formal definition is "lack of access to enough food for an active and healthy life due to economic circumstances." I use the term food insecurity when I talk about specific research. *Hunger* has many definitions. Some people say the term hunger only signifies the "painful sensation in the stomach" due to lack of food because a person does not have enough money for food. I take a much broader view of hunger. Most of the time I use hunger as my shorthand to indicate the injustice of not having enough money for food to the point where it deeply impacts one's ability to flourish. Throughout these pages, you will see that hunger is broader than people think, and its solutions go way beyond food. Lastly, a brief note on demographic terminology: where I discuss statistics from research that uses different terminology than my general preference, such as "Hispanic" rather than "Latinx," or "LGBT" rather than "LGBTQIA+," I follow the publication's usage for accuracy in reporting results.

Caution. This book covers what lurks underneath hunger. What is underneath is unfair, unjust, and deeply disturbing. Ahead there are descriptions of rape, sexual assault, family violence, enslavement, colonialism, racism, misogyny, white supremacy, systemic oppression, and indifference to human suffering. Please take good care of yourself while reading. Ways of navigating this book are reading in brief doses, skipping pages, reading with a human or animal friend nearby, or occasionally looking out the window or at the horizon to remember how much joy and beauty there is in the world. It may also be helpful to read this book with a group of people, such as in a book club or classroom, so several people can support you and you can support them. As you will learn ahead, belonging to a group of your choice promotes healing and solidarity. I lend you encouragement and care. Take it slow.

Prologue

Welcome, dear reader!

I'm grateful you opened this book. It means you care about the world and your place in it.

Before we begin, I'll ask, "How are you feeling today?"

This is the first question we ask each other in our "community meeting" at the Center for Hunger-Free Communities, which I founded twenty years ago at Drexel University's School of Public Health in Philadelphia, Pennsylvania. The center is a place where staff and program members deeply care about each other and ending hunger. As an expression of that care, before we start our meetings, we ask each other "How are you feeling?" Not "How you doin'?" as many say in Philadelphia, but "How are you feeling in your emotional landscape or your own body?"

As responses, we hope for more than "fine," "good," or "OK." Those are answers that people use to bypass their bodies or emotions they may not want to touch. Or they don't say more because they assume people don't want to know. Or they are concerned for their safety. But addressing emotions is built into our structure, so we take the time to say how we are feeling; we take the time to listen to and sense one another. This is where the true work of solidarity begins.

Me? I'm brokenhearted. I'm brokenhearted because learning about people's experiences with hunger tore me apart, challenging my ability to make sense of the world and find my place in it. I also feel joyful. Surprisingly, joy can emerge from pain and grief. I didn't come to joy easily. This book invites you along with me to understand the pain and injustice of hunger, and find ways to overcome it through transformative policy change, building solidarity, and, yes, generating joy.

Since you've read this far, chances are you might be brokenhearted too. Clearly you care about hunger and suffering or you wouldn't be here.

If you are willing, put your hand over your heart. Feel the comings and goings of your blood in your own body. Feel your own warmth? This is where the action is.

Perhaps we agree: the reality that millions of people in the United States do not have enough food to eat for an active healthy life fills us with grief. Let us consider this potential shared grief to be the grounding of this book. Grief is an important emotion to feel and acknowledge; in doing so, we can understand many other emotions such as anger, rage, and despair that are contained within grief. If we feel grief, we know that there is a felt sense of what was, what is, and what could be. Grief can be an acknowledgment of loss for someone we love or something (an idea, dream, job, and so on) that we have loved. So where there is grief, there is evidence of love. Love for a person, for people, love for a feeling, a sense of connection and belonging, and a sensation that all is well. Where there is love, there is gratitude. And out of gratitude the possibility for joy can blossom.[1]

This brings me to the second question we ask each other in our community meeting. We ask, "What is your goal?" We ask this to help people articulate what they hope to get out of the meeting; this way, we can understand each other's expectations and stay focused on the task at hand without getting bogged down in our emotions. Perhaps your goal is to learn more about the experience of hunger or find some new ways of doing. My goal is to help you with that and to help you feel that you belong in here so you can share in the relationships with the people I have met over the past twenty-five years. Perhaps you might take comfort in knowing you are not alone. Many people are in here with you and me. I'm hoping you can learn alongside them. We are in good company.

Perhaps you work in an organization, run programs, or do research or make policy in response to hunger and food insecurity. Maybe we engage in the same circles. I'm a professor of public health and health policy. I am an ethnographer (meaning I work alongside people and participate in their lives while also learning and observing to understand their worldview and experiences) and epidemiologist (meaning I'm interested to understand how health and flourishing are distributed across large groups of people or a population). Twenty-five years of research and engagement alongside thousands of people who shared their experiences and wisdom with me supposedly makes me an "expert." I've testified before Congress to try to convince policymakers to invest in families and communities and ensure everyone is nourished. I've been quoted in hundreds of news articles and appeared on television and the radio talking about hunger in the United States and what to do. I've led research studies and created programs that address and treat hunger at its roots. I was the cochair of the National Commission on Hunger, which was created to advise the US Congress and secretary of the US Department of Agriculture on ways to eliminate hunger. An "expert" knows the facts, advances the truth, and helps identify solutions.

But don't be fooled. In my position, as an upper-middle-class white woman who has never experienced hunger and deprivation, I am an unexpert. I'm a beginner and always will be. To be a beginner is a wonderful stance; it keeps all of your options open and helps you keep learning.

People who have experienced hunger are true experts. They know hunger in their bodies, their histories, and their families. It was for this reason I started the program Witnesses to Hunger in 2008. I wanted to create the infrastructure for the true experts on hunger to speak directly to members of Congress, the press, and the public. For twelve years, we did just that. Members of Witnesses to Hunger visited the White House and Congress to speak directly to legislators. They talked to the press, appeared on television, and spoke on the radio as experts. It was the people in this program that instilled courage in me. They also taught me that it was a courageous act to admit you don't know. They didn't have the all the answers or expect me to have all the answers. We could explore them together and learn from one another on how to create collaborative solutions. What was most important to members of Witnesses to Hunger was to be in good relationship with each other. To show up. To be a good friend. To generate joy. To express love. In loving relationships, everything is possible.

My goal is that, by reading this book, you too can gain courage to enter a place of unknowing, become aware of the trauma underneath hunger, and be unafraid to plunge into the depths of that suffering to help heal it.

When I started talking about the violence underneath hunger, many advocates, researchers, and agency administrators asked me to stay quiet about this. People were worried that it would detract from actions to reduce hunger such as the multibillion-dollar policy fights in Congress regarding Supplemental Nutrition Assistance Program benefits. But it's time to stop pretending we're doing the right thing and pay deep attention. Once and for all, let's listen to the people in this book, most of whom are Black women, women of color, and other marginalized women who, for generations, have been expressing their pain in hopes of inspiring the world to change and make opportunities to feel and express joy. If we stay with the pain long enough to understand and transform it, our work could provide grounding for social, cultural, political, and economic revolution. Only then can we say we are seeking to end hunger in America.

Perhaps you are a student or lifelong learner whose goal is social, political, cultural, and economic transformation. You may be studying in the disciplines of history, public health, medicine, social work, nutrition, anthropology, economics, political science, and beyond. Maybe you are on the road to creating your own organization or preparing to write policy. Hopefully this book inspires you to be honest, take courage, and stay with your resolve. I invite you to not rely solely on your intellect. I hope you take time to know your body, emotions, and spirit. When addressing hunger, having a strong and tender heart, sense of body sovereignty, and meaningful spiritual practice are just as important as having a sharp and disciplined mind.

This is no textbook nor standard journey through simple quick fixes. What's ahead is an attempt to dissolve stale ideas that keep regenerating in the antihunger and social justice spaces. In this book, I rely on four strategies. First, I ground this book in the wisdom and lived experiences of hundreds of people who know hunger firsthand. Second, I describe what I learned through working with my team, partners, and colleagues over the last twenty-five years. This includes what I learned through my work with Indigenous people, primarily the Southern Cheyenne and Arapaho nations in my early career, and then with Black and Latinx people to create programming and take action through participatory advocacy. Third, I root my analysis of hunger in the generations-long scholarship of Black and Indigenous people who have been engaging with the possibilities of abolition and decolonization by tapping into wisdom traditions more than five hundred years in the making. Finally, I outline the potential for nourishment from perspectives I gained through reading, listening, and practicing alongside monastics and laypeople engaged in the Plum Village spiritual tradition of Zen Buddhism—a tradition that taps wisdom developed over twenty-six hundred years.

I was driven to write this book because I see many people in the antihunger and social justice spaces who sincerely care but have yet to engage with the deep and violent roots of hunger. This book serves as my invitation to plunge the depths of despair in oneself and others, and to tap into wisdom traditions deep enough to support the goal of ending hunger.

This brings us to the final question we ask each other: "Who will you ask for help?" This is an important aspect of starting a meeting because it indicates that we cannot do the work and achieve our goals alone. Dominant culture in the United States makes us feel like we cannot ask for help, that it is a sign of weakness or place of unknowing. But asking for help is healthy. It is a way of acknowledging and building our sense of community as well as the reality of our interconnectedness. Ahead I show that public assistance programs seek to separate and isolate us from each other. Through isolation we become lonely, we lack creativity, and lose our power. Alone we are vulnerable. Together we have more power to make the changes we want to see in the world. In our community meeting, we ask a person or people who are in the meeting for help (not someone outside the circle we are in). So I'm hoping the people you meet in this book can help you. I, too, will do my best to help you stay interested and go deeper page by page. I hope you can also help me by attending to the wisdom of the people herein.

Yes, it's a little rough going ahead, but I hope I can help you to take courage. So if you please, hold your heart, look to the horizon, and feel free to gently turn the page.

INTRODUCTION

GRAND OPENING OF THE EAT CAFÉ

I was in my office fiddling with the giant scissors we bought to cut the big red ribbon for the next day's grand opening.

Ring! Ring!

Slinging the scissors up over my shoulder, I looked at the caller ID. It was the chef manager of the EAT Café.

> Hey, uh . . .
> The toilet in the basement
> burst.
> There's sewage running all over the basement floor.
> We need a plumber,
> ASAP.
> It stinks!

It was the end of our workday, and we were finalizing plans for the next morning's grand opening. For our team, opening the EAT Café signified the culmination of decades of painstaking work on hunger. After years of careful study and research, successful programming, and deliberate and well-thought-out political action, we were going to try something new. It felt as if our team was at the precipice of a great achievement.

The name EAT Café stands for **E**veryone **A**t the **T**able. Regardless of people's ability to pay, we welcomed everyone to join in and enjoy a three-course meal served directly to their table just like they do at a full-service restaurant.

This was the vision: People who do not have enough money can enjoy a meal made from scratch served with care to their table. Wealthy people would come to the EAT Café because not only was the food delicious but they would feel happy and satisfied supporting the mission as well. The EAT Café was based on the idea that people who can afford to pay would pay extra money to supplement the cost of meals for those who could not afford to pay. Everyone orders from the same menu and shares the same energy in this joyous, colorful, and communal place without privilege or marginalization, without separation of rich and poor, Black people and white people, immigrant and citizen, professor and sex worker. Everyone is welcome, equal, celebrated, and nourished.

When a person is hungry, they just want to sit down and eat. They don't want to wait in line to be served food cafeteria-style like they are in school, the military, or prison. Instead, people should be able to enjoy good food, soothing music, and lovely colors, and receive food without having to prove their worth.

For a person to show that they are "worthy" of getting food at a soup kitchen, food cupboard, food pantry, or food shelf (terms vary by locale), they usually have to show ID or provide proof of residency with their utility bill or some other piece of paper that demonstrates they are "in need." Often, they sense a side-eye from volunteers for the way they look. Maybe they look pitiful or maybe they look too good—too good to get leftovers or food otherwise headed to the landfill. People must show their worth to get food stamps, or what is now called the Supplemental Nutrition Assistance Program (SNAP). They must wait in line for hours at a county assistance office and suffer the stare down from the caseworker who does not trust them to tell the truth. If they succeed, they will get SNAP in such low amounts that the best way to stretch their dollar might be with a dry package of ramen noodles, hot dogs, and a Coke. When people don't have enough money for food, they often have no social connections to ask for help. They cannot call a neighbor or show up at a friend's house and hope to get a meal. Hunger is a sign of disbelonging.

We built the EAT Café as an antidote to all of this stress, isolation, and bad food. It was meant to greet the urgency, judgment, and depressing state of affairs with a healing embrace. To walk through the door of the EAT

Café would be an opportunity to join community, be nourished, and be welcomed home.

I hung up the phone and emerged from my office dragging the scissors across the floor.

As our team cleaned up the watery sewage in the basement, we debated what to do. If we immediately called off the grand opening, it would raise alarm with the community stakeholders with whom we had worked for three years, not to mention the mayor's office, city council, and press. Plus the EAT Café staff had been cooking for days. Everything was ready.

A plumber came, we helped clean up, and agreed to wait until the next morning to decide what to do. Our biggest worry? The stench.

After a fitful sleep, the next morning we teamed up to sniff around the café. "Hmmm. . . . *Sniff.* Not too bad."

"Let's do this!" we agreed.

The television cameras arrived. People offered heartfelt words of communion. Many hands grasped the big scissors, and we cut the red ribbon. It was a grand opening.

This is where I begin: the beauty, joy, communion, community, and shit exploding underneath.

This is what working on hunger is like. Most initiatives to address hunger in the United States are working on the surface. On the surface, people concern themselves with food and community. Everyone knows the shit is there underneath, but they work hard to hide it, ignore it, pretend it's not there, or overpower its stink with Lysol, sage, or the smell of corn bread. Our approaches aren't working.

GOING BEYOND FOOD

Most people think hunger has to do with food. Of course, this is true to some extent. But lack of food is only a symptom of hunger, not the cause and certainly not the solution. Because people think hunger has to do with food, and food only, they spend enormous amounts of energy, money, and time trying to help people get food. Researchers and policymakers focus on SNAP and the health consequences of hunger. Advocates focus on promoting more SNAP and emergency food. Others insist the answer is community gardens. The agricultural industry pretends to solve hunger by selling seeds that grow plants that secrete pesticides or that can withstand their overuse, and by doping animals with antibiotics so they will stay healthy enough to gain weight faster to make more burgers and chicken nuggets. Well-meaning people spend their creativity and money trying to get leftover, unharvested, or wasted food, or food that is out of date from farms, universities, grocery stores, restaurants, and hotels, to people whom they deem "hungry." Grocery stores raise money for hunger relief at the checkout counter while their own employees make so little that their salaries are supplemented with SNAP and Medicaid (government-funded health care). All the while, philanthropists take pleasure in being celebrated for donating their money to such charitable causes.

While engaging in these activities, few people ask, "Who is paying the low wages that keep people impoverished?" or "Who is overproducing so much food that creates so much waste?" or "How is it that US government policies allow people who are disabled to struggle for money?" or "Why are women and children, Black, Indigenous, Latinx, and immigrant people, more likely than men and white people to be hungry? Why are lesbian, gay, bisexual, transgender, intersex, asexual, or nonbinary people (LGBTQIA+) more likely to experience hunger than people who are heterosexual?"

Important fact: there are millions more white people than Black, Indigenous, and Latinx people who experience hunger. For instance, in 2021, a little over 6 million white households reported food insecurity, while 3.3 million Black and 3.1 million Hispanic households reported they were food insecure. But when you break out the rates by *percentage* of each population, you see that Black and Latinx people have rates that are two to three times higher than white people. Almost 20 percent of Black households and 16.2 percent of Hispanic ones reported food insecurity, while only 7 percent of white households reported food insecurity.[1] So the burden on Black and Hispanic communities is far greater than it is for white communities. Worse still, the greatest burden is among Indigenous communities, which have rates ranging between 25 to 90 percent depending on nation, group, and region. To address these inequities, it is necessary to focus on the experiences of people who have the highest rates of food insecurity to learn more about their expertise in navigating toward health and well-being. When we construct a world where those most marginalized can get the supports they need, everyone flourishes. This is standard public health practice to focus on programs for people who have been made vulnerable by oppression and discrimination. By doing so, *everyone* benefits. A concrete example of this process is in how sidewalks are constructed. Thanks to the advocacy by people who use wheelchairs, sidewalks have dips on many street corners so that people with wheelchairs, walkers, and canes can get to where they are going. It turns out this helps everyone, especially people who use strollers for their infants and toddlers, movers that use dollies for moving large equipment and furniture, and people who tend to shuffle their feet. The people who struggle with the way the world is have the best ideas for ways to improve it to make it more inclusive and supportive. This is why I unapologetically side with people who are the most marginalized. They have the central wisdom that can help us all.

HUNGER IS CREATED BY PEOPLE IN POWER

In 1952, Brazilian scholar Josué de Castro, chair of the Executive Council of the International Food and Agriculture Organization, made his blunt assessment: hunger is man-made. That is, people who are wealthy and greedy take more food, resources, and money for themselves, and leave others to suffer and struggle. Long before that, Pëtr Kropotkin in his 1892 book *The Conquest of Bread* explained how the wealthy seek out the destitute and starving and pay them a paltry wage. In doing so, elites keep people with low incomes in a perpetual state of precarity and suffering so they will be forced to work for low wages. In other words, elites keep people on the verge of hunger to magnify their own wealth. Responsibility for hunger in America lands in the wallets, laps, hearts, and minds of the wealthy, who create inequality for their own profit. To solve it, we have to focus on ending inequality. This is not breaking news; 125 years ago, Kropotkin asserted, "In solving the question of bread, we must accept the principle of equality, which will force itself upon us to the exclusion of every other solution."[2]

Across more than a century since Kropotkin's treatise, it is rare to hear nonprofit leaders and government officials admit to hunger's shameful, man-made beginnings. Even fewer talk about working toward equality. Most people working on hunger refuse to point their finger at the people who generate hunger in the United States and around the world. Even fewer attempt to change our social structures to ensure that no one goes hungry.

In the following pages, I introduce you to hunger's underbelly: collective and individual violence caused by unchecked capitalism along with America's history of genocide, slavery, colonization, white supremacy, patriarchy, and the intentional abuse and neglect of women and children. In short, hunger is a manifestation of our lack of love for each other, ourselves, and the planet. Hunger exists because our relationships with our families and communities, ourselves, food, and the natural world are dysfunctional or broken altogether.

To address hunger, we must talk about our relationships through the lens of power and control.

Amartya Sen, internationally revered scholar and Nobel prizewinner in economics, started his career by studying famines in India. He recognized that during the great Bengal Famine of 1943, when over three million people died and corpses piled up in the streets, India was experiencing a year of abundant harvests. There was plenty of food in the country—more than enough to feed everyone. Where was the food and money? The English royals, administrators, and businesspeople were stealing and hoarding it.

The stage was set for this massacre by starvation at least fifty years earlier. Mike Davis, in his book *The Late Victorian Holocausts: El Niño Famines and the Making of the Third World*, explains that from 1870 to 1914, the British and Americans profited off the mega droughts and monsoons that resulted in crop failure. The worst-hit areas were regions of India, China, and Brazil. Though people in nearby regions could readily and willingly transport food to areas affected by droughts and storms, British companies and elites restricted the transport of desperately needed food, resulting in starvation killings of over thirty million people. Davis showed how a handful of elites controlling the London-centered world economy sucked away people's food, resources, and livelihoods. "Millions died not outside the modern world system," he said, "but in the very process of being forcibly incorporated into its economic and political structures. They died in the golden age of Liberal

Capitalism; indeed, many were murdered by the powerful elites' adoption of the economic and political philosophy of free-market capitalism."[3]

Hoarding food and resources also occurs within countries. The United States is no exception. During the dust bowl of the 1930s and the Great Depression, while so many people were starving, growers with ample crops dumped truckloads of oranges and other produce into heaps and sprayed them with kerosene to destroy the food because no one could afford to buy it. All the while, children starved or were born with a low birth weight, and many people suffered and died from diseases associated with malnutrition.

Starvation amid plenty is *not* a paradox. As Janet Poppendieck observes in her book *Breadlines Knee-Deep in Wheat: Food Assistance in the Great Depression*, keeping people hungry is a coordinated and systemic effort by the wealthy to increase profits. Hoarding food and sequestering it from large swaths of society makes food seem scarce, so the wealthy can then put a hefty price tag on it and leave those who can't pay to suffer the consequences. Poppendieck also demonstrates how the New Deal nutrition assistance efforts failed to help people in poverty. People who were hungry were an afterthought—after the elite, the economy, big agriculture, and big business.[4]

SOLVING HUNGER DEMANDS MORE THAN FOOD

Jean Drèze and Sen, in their seminal work *Hunger and Public Action*, insist that the focus on food to solve hunger is rooted in conceptual confusion. Focusing on food alone obstructs effective action and policymaking because it ignores the harmful dynamics of deep inequality that cause hunger.[5]

The magnitude of our conceptual confusion can be exemplified by hyped-up media coverage of miles-long car lines of people waiting to secure food at food banks throughout the United States during spring and summer 2020 when the COVID-19 emergency forced shelter-in-place orders. Emergency food providers seemed like heroes.

But what was really happening?

In the United States, there was no shortage of food or profits for food companies.[6] During the months of the COVID-19 pandemic-related shelter-in-place orders, hundreds of thousands of people lost their jobs and main sources of income while members of Congress hesitated and debated about what to do. Simultaneously, food hardship skyrocketed in April and May 2020. Scientists at the US Census Bureau quickly attempted to capture levels of hardship in the Household Pulse Survey. The rate of food insufficiency among families with children tripled from pre-COVID-19 rates of 2019. Additionally, despite increases in SNAP use and amounts, people's reliance on charitable food increased from 2019 rates by 50 percent. At the same time that the COVID-19 disease was disproportionately affecting Black, Brown, and Indigenous communities, which saw higher rates of infection and death compared to white communities, the same injustices were seen in rates of food and housing hardship. Black and Hispanic families had two and three times the rate of food hardship compared to white families.[7]

While these racial and social inequities in suffering, pain, and death hit the national consciousness in 2020, none of these injustices are new. Before the COVID-19 pandemic in the United States, the rate of food insecurity— lack of access to enough food for an active and healthy life—was already astronomical at 10.5 percent of households (35.2 million people). Since the start of the formal measure by the US government in 1995, rates of food insecurity have never been lower than this. Food insecurity peaked during the Great Recession that started in 2008, when 14.9 percent of households (41 million people) experienced food insecurity. When we break the statistics down by race, ethnicity, gender, and ability, we see the patterns that give clues to the truth of what is happening in the United States. Since the beginning of the national measure of food security, single woman–headed households have always experienced food insecurity at extremely high rates (currently 23.4 percent) compared to all other households with children (12.5 percent). The rate for single woman–headed households is more than three times higher than two-person-headed households (7.4 percent). LGBT people also have a greater proportion of their population reporting food insecurity compared to national rates. Results from the Pulse Survey carried out during the COVID-19 pandemic show that among LGBT people the rate of food insufficiency was 12.7 percent compared to 7.8 percent of those who are non-LGBT. Food insufficiency was three times worse for LGBT people of color, whose rate was 17.3 percent compared to 5.6 percent of

LGBT white people.[8] Finally, one-third of people with disabilities report food insecurity.[9]

What you see here is a pattern of power relations—populations with less power have higher rates of hunger than people who have more power to control their circumstances to meet their basic needs.

Trying to get people to think beyond food, Drèze and Sen call hunger a manifestation of "entitlement failure." Entitlements are access to basic necessities to which everyone has a right. These rights are access to food, water, housing, health care, social services, a job that pays a living wage, and—in the event of illness, disability, age, or other circumstances—financial and other supports that can help people pay for and acquire resources to meet basic needs. Again, when there is widespread hunger, there is a clear indication that the powerful are withholding and restricting people's rights and "entitlements."

Through this lens, reasons for hunger in the United States are glaringly obvious. Historic, systemic, and ongoing discrimination is at its core.

Knowing that most people get food by buying it, we must pay attention to money and how people make it. The federal minimum wage of $7.25 per hour has not been raised in over thirteen years, nor has it been indexed to inflation. If the minimum wage were indexed to inflation and kept up with productivity since 1973, when the poverty rate in the United States was at its lowest at 11.1 percent, it would currently be over $24.00 per hour. Today, meeting basic needs is no longer a guarantee if someone is working. Public assistance benefit calculations are based on outdated ideas about the real cost of food, housing, and health care. Despite expansion of health insurance through the 2010 Affordable Care Act (ACA), millions of people still have no health insurance, and medical expenses are the prevailing reason for bankruptcy.[10] Childcare and quality education are accessible only for those who can pay. Disability benefits are almost impossible to get, and do not meet the true cost of self-care and need. For seniors, Social Security payments are notoriously low. Overall, adequate entitlements have never been established for the majority of people in the United States.

But people are distracted by the generations-old conceptual confusion that hunger has something to do with food. In the meantime, the social structures and political processes stay the same, and hunger is regenerated. Hunger is by design. It is as American as apple pie.

These dynamics at play today are products of systems and processes in the United States that are hundreds of years old. Ahead I show how the history of genocide, enslavement, and capitalism are just a few of the seeds that allow hunger to flourish today. These seeds are also at the root of our climate crisis, which is causing global catastrophic destruction of our food and water. But these violent seeds have yet to be fully named and recognized as a trauma that needs to be addressed, touched, or described in our education, health care, and welfare systems, the media, the US nonprofit and philanthropy world, and even among those of us who do research on food insecurity. Nor has there been a nationwide effort to create opportunities for healing, remediation, reparations, and decolonization.

Most people know this violence lies deep in their bones, but in trying to solve hunger and poverty, they are doing the same old thing with tiny steps within the same systems we have in place now. There are many recommendations for solving hunger that thousands of people are already working on. You can read those solutions on any major antihunger organization website. Or you could go to the cybercemetery and exhume the recommendations from the National Commission on Hunger, on which I served as the cochair. Some approaches are on the Biden-Harris administration website as a result of a months-long call for recommendations by advocates, researchers, and experts through lived experience in preparation for a highly disappointing White House Conference on Hunger in September 2022 where many pundits expressed concern but made few promises and took even fewer actions to end hunger. These initiatives will not suffice. So with the intent to transform approaches to hunger, I'm inviting you to recognize the violence and trauma underneath hunger. Only by facing the violence can new opportunities to heal the wounds of hunger emerge.

WOUNDS THAT CAUSE HUNGER: GENOCIDE, SLAVERY, CAPITALISM, AND PATRIARCHY

People of Indigenous nations in the United States have the highest rates of food insecurity compared to all other groups. This is due to state-supported impoverishment and genocide carried out by white people over the past five hundred years. No Indigenous nation was spared US government–backed massacres, forced removal, exploitation, war, child abductions to boarding schools, plundered lands, religious conversion, and cultural and economic genocide. If Indigenous people did not die of hunger, disease, or murder, they were often starved into submission.

For instance, after the Southern Cheyenne were forced to walk from Colorado to a small region in Oklahoma, then called "Indian territory," the US government promised to provide food rations. But it would do so only if Cheyenne parents and grandparents gave up their children to be sent far away to government "boarding schools," which were more like child labor camps. Here, the children were stripped of their language, heritage, and sense of belonging. Oftentimes they were physically, emotionally, and sexually abused. Others were neglected to death.

"That was the way the Cheyenne people gave in to the United States government," explained Willie Fletcher, chair of the Cheyenne and Arapaho Health Board and spiritual leader, in 1995. "It was through forced starvation." In other words, the US government weaponized food assistance, using it as an act of war. When the US government did supply food rations, it sent flour and many other unrecognizable, rancid, or low-quality items that were never part of the Cheyenne traditional diet.

As a result of this exploitation, violence, and food provision today, it is no wonder but rather *by design* that Indigenous people have the highest rates of food insecurity and diabetes in the United States. Contemporary food insecurity is maintained by long-standing land theft, active racism, and restricted access to affordable, nutritious foods for the 50 percent of Indigenous people who live in cities, as well as the Indigenous people living in their traditional homelands or reservations onto which they were forced and who must travel long distances to a grocery store.

There are so many examples of extreme rates of household food insecurity among Indigenous nations that it causes overwhelm, so I cite just a few. Among the Diné (Navajo), for example, rates of food insecurity are around 80 percent.[11] In the Klamath River Basin, the area of Southern Oregon and Northern California that is home to the Karuk, Yurok, Hoopa, and Klamath peoples, rates of food insecurity are at 92 percent, and over half report very low food security, the severest form of struggles with hunger. People interviewed insist that in addition to poverty, lack of jobs, and low income, the combined effects of land loss, loss of salmon due to polluted waters, and overkilling of doe by white people have caused food insecurity.[12]

Hold these atrocities in one hand, and with the other consider 250 years of enslavement of Africans and their descendants. Even with the supposed abolition of slavery, white people continued to exploit and abuse Black people through Black codes (laws that restricted Black people from working for fair wages, or punishing and imprisoning them for being unemployed), convict leasing, Jim Crow laws, lynching, housing discrimination, mass incarceration, debtors' prison, and police brutality, which still keep many African American people in a state of precarity, disenfranchised, and unsafe today. This ongoing subjugation of Black people is evidence of what historian and cultural scholar Saidiya Hartman refers to as the "nonevent of emancipation," when white people and their lawmakers simply found new ways to subjugate and limit the flourishing of Black people.[13] Black families have suffered generations of residential segregation and historically racist policies that exploit communities of color. White homeowners and politicians were complicit in harnessing local and national laws to exclude, exploit, and marginalize Black, Brown, and Indigenous people.[14] Residential segregation concentrates economic and social disadvantage and simply encourages systemic neglect of key infrastructure that helps people build wealth and stay healthy. These disinvestments result in poorer housing quality, inadequate school funding, increased exposure to environmental toxins, and lower access to affordable, healthy foods. The fact that African Americans also have rates of food insecurity that are more than twice the national rate and almost three times that of white people is a symptom of this ongoing discrimination by white people, who are the lawmakers, agency heads, schoolteachers, and the like.

A similar fate affects immigrants, especially those from the Caribbean, Mexico, and Central America. My colleagues and I found that among 19,275 mothers of children under age four, children of immigrants experience a rate of food insecurity that is twice as high as for children of US-born mothers.[15]

After the introduction of legislation that barred noncitizen participation in SNAP in 1996, the rate of food insecurity among children of noncitizens became much higher compared with children of citizens.[16] Such injustices are simultaneously national and hyperlocal. Among immigrant farmworkers in Georgia, undocumented workers are nearly three times as likely to be food insecure compared with documented workers.[17] The rate of food insecurity among families that migrated from Mexico is five times that of the general US population.[18]

These disparate rates of food insecurity are the result of clear policy choices rooted in colonization, racism, and imperialism.

Theft of land—about 2.5 billion acres—is also the theft of Indigenous people's lifeways, waterways, spiritual depth, tens of thousands of years of history, *and* access to food. Second, 30 million Africans were ripped away from their lands, and those who survived (and their descendants) were not allowed to "own" land or work it for their own livelihood. When they were "allowed" to own it, their land was often stolen or swindled by white people armed with guns and white supremacist laws. Indigenous and Black people have almost no access to land. With no land sovereignty, access to food becomes extremely challenging.

Going deeper, the primary way in which bodies and lands were stolen and exploited was through rape. Sarah Deer, a Muscogee lawyer and professor who works to support Indigenous rape victims, explains that rape, as a violent act as well as metaphor for subjugation and exploitation, is the primary way through which colonization was enacted. She insists that to decolonize the United States and end the domination, we must end rape culture, which perpetuates the oppression of Indigenous people.[19] In similar fashion, Hartman asserts that enforced Blackness (or racialization) built into the institution of slavery and carried out through today's times is a "perpetual condition of ravishment."[20] That is, again, until we grapple with how our social, cultural, and political systems promote and allow the rape and domination of women, especially Indigenous and Black women, we cannot understand the power dynamics that allow poverty and hunger to persist. Simply put, with no body sovereignty, one cannot even enjoy nor absorb the food provided or bought. Nor can one function to earn money.

This mega exploitation, domination, and theft is central to understanding hunger in America.

These threads of heteronormative, patriarchal, white domination hold together the US political, economic, and cultural institutions and shape our relationships. They influence how people succumb to greed and the desire to own (land, people, and even ideas), dominate, surveil, control, diminish, or murder. Cultural critic and sociologist bell hooks described these characteristics as a "culture of domination."[21] This culture of domination is woven into all US systems—the justice system, child welfare system, and public assistance programs, including those providing nutrition assistance. These systems have a major impact on our health, well-being, and belonging. In her recent book *America Goddam*, Treva Lindsey describes these intersecting systems as a "death-dealing superstructure" that generates food insecurity.[22]

When the structures of domination are so huge, penetrating our institutions and the ways of organizing ourselves, we have to look for ways to completely transform our society, dismantle the institutions grounded in enslavement and genocide, and build a new world based on values of care and equanimity.

ACKNOWLEDGING AND HEALING THE WOUNDS OF DOMINATION

There are three interconnected ways of transforming our society and healing hunger. They are personal, political, and spiritual. These domains overlap. If you wanted to, you could find a scrap of paper and make a standard Venn diagram with three overlapping circles to identify each, find their overlaps, and perhaps create your own atlas for self-discovery and action. First, it takes deep personal work to undo racism, white supremacy, and patriarchy. This personal work requires us to self-reflect and engage with friends and family. Second, it takes political work to change our policies and economic systems. Political systems penetrate our bodies, enter our bloodstream, and influence the way we think, feel, and do. The personal and political each feed off each other. So third, to build the strength necessary to transform our society, one needs to build spiritual depth that includes a willingness to express love for ourselves, each other, and the world. The work to end hunger demands our whole body, mind, and spirit in order to revolutionize the structures we develop to care for each other. It's a daunting task.

To build the courage and resilience necessary requires recognition of the truth underneath hunger. The best way to do this is to acknowledge and understand that we are in a trauma-organized society that allows for hunger to persist. Understanding trauma gives us good grounding for the hard work ahead.

THE PERSONAL: COURAGE TO FACE TRAUMA AND INDIFFERENCE

The first half of this book is devoted to describing how underneath hunger is a violence that causes trauma-related responses in our body, beliefs, emotions, and behavioral practices. I learned about the trauma of hunger directly from the people I talked to about their experiences. While I began our discussions speaking about food, money, or social systems, the conversations often landed on the most important challenges they wanted to talk about: having been traumatized by rape, sexual assault, child abuse, and emotional neglect. As a result, I was forced to learn about trauma.

Trauma is not only a critical physical insult. It is a *response* to an insult. Trauma can be a psychological and emotional response to a severely and deeply distressing incident, or a series of chronic or recurring extremely stressful situations. Among adults, such incidents that cause trauma are experiences on the battlefield—many are familiar with this already: post-traumatic stress syndrome. Exposure to murder, witnessing killings, killing other people, torture, and many other outrageous, soul-shattering experiences can cause a person to have distressing flashbacks, physical responses such as adrenaline rushes, lack of sleep, depression and anxiety, fragmented personality, dissociation or loss of emotion, and "loss of self." These same experiences are also reported by people who have experienced rape, assault, sexual violence, emotional abuse, economic abuse, and racial and ethnic discrimination. Historical trauma is a trauma response to genocide and enslavement that has reverberated throughout a people's history. This includes a response to the traumatic devastation of a people along with their culture, family ties, and economic and social systems, thereby generating major biological, psychological, and social responses that pass on through successive generations. This collective trauma can manifest in unresolved grief, which has a major impact on health and well-being, and can influence parenting and other social practices.[23] Among Indigenous people, there is an understanding that the trauma of genocide and colonization is a deep wound to the soul, a shattering of spirit.[24] Scholars and health practitioners addressing trauma among descendants of enslaved Africans also recognize that unaddressed trauma of the torture and terror of enslavement in their families has been passed down through the generations over four hundred years.[25]

To separate, dominate, exploit, violate, and rape based on the lie of racial difference is called *racialized trauma*. It is not just Indigenous and Black people and people of color who suffer from the racist legacies of the United States but white people, too, are long traumatized by genocide and enslavement. This trauma is hardly noticeable compared to the magnitude of suffering that Black and Indigenous people have experienced. Because US society maintains a culture of whiteness, and white people have more power and privilege, the trauma manifests very differently. It is important to remember that perpetrators of violence are traumatized by the violence they inflict; they just might not have the depth of emotion and maturity to be aware of it. As well, people who hurt others have likely been traumatized themselves. In the healing professions, the saying goes, "hurt people hurt people." Violence and trauma regenerate if they are not processed and healed. Racialized trauma lands in our bodies, changes our neurons, and affects the way we carry our bodies and express our emotions. Resmaa Menakem, an expert on racialized trauma, suggests that Europeans were deeply traumatized by the plague, massive famines, and, between the fourteenth and seventeenth centuries, the torturing, hanging, and burning of tens of thousands of women because they refused to comply with male-dominated social norms and the newly advancing economic systems. Identified as potentially thwarting the burgeoning new world order, most people identified as "witches" were women. This practice was then exported to the Americas and became a type of weapon of colonization.[26] To cope with or project their pain and unresolved trauma from these terrifying and painful collective ordeals, people from Europe violently harmed Indigenous people of the Americas and Africa. This unbearable trauma of genocide, enslavement, and unbridled violence against women is handed down across the generations and manifests in many people's behaviors today. Over time, Menakem explains, the original traumas are forgotten, and the way people have adapted to the trauma and behaved "starts to look like culture."[27]

I can attest to this as a white woman. Because I regularly absorbed and utilized a culture of "whiteness" and internalized sexism, I considered the way I behaved as the norm. I was taught to keep my emotions tucked away, shoved deep down inside. Menakem underscores that this cultural pattern of a white-bodied person like me leads to an inability to deeply feel our emotions, especially unprocessed grief. This makes us seem frozen in mind, body, and heart. Such iciness is what trauma specialists refer to as dissociation, or a turning off of one's emotions, one's sense of being whole. A dissociative response to trauma can be taken as the way things are or should be. So many of us, millions in fact, can get caught up living lives devoid of emotional and spiritual depth. Spiritual leader and psychologist Larry Ward, a Buddhist teacher in the Plum Village tradition of Zen Master Thich Nhat Hanh, ventures to diagnose this emotional numbness as an American pathology.

Nesting within that icy pathology is America's tolerance for hunger.

In summary, trauma—the cognitive, physical, emotional, and spiritual response to extreme violence and suffering (whether from the perspective of the victim, perpetrator, witness, or bystander)—fragments the mind and heart, truncates our thinking, and limits our capacity to feel and express emotional breadth and depth. If the trauma resulting from enslavement and genocide, murder, abuse, torture, rape, and exploitation is unattended, then that original cause of trauma can often be forgotten or obscured. Our emotional responses to original traumas land and stay in our bodies. They are there but unnamed and unidentified. No wonder we are so confused!

Another word for emotional numbness is indifference. Indifference is the incapacity to deeply feel or express emotions such as grief, empathy, and compassion. It is a lack of feeling for people and complex or disturbing social situations; indifference is a demonstration of lack of concern, care, interest, or curiosity. It is a dulling of the mind, heart, and gut. Ward explains, "This is the wizardry of America's racial karma passed from generation to generation through the actions of thinking, speaking, and physical behaviors. Our very constitutional history contrives it, our lived suffering testifies to it, and our cultural indifference gives permission for the retribution to continue."[28]

So what do we do? We have to address our collective trauma. To do so requires that we reveal the truth and open up the wounds that cause hunger, no matter how painful. This helps us to heal the wounds and transform them into a source of strength.

To do this work, one must be willing to see what has always been there, but that most people ignore or shove away. We must deal with our dissociation due to physical, social, political, and economic violence at an individual, family, organizational, community, systems, and societal level. Looking in the wrong place to solve hunger is a part of this dissociation. It's as if anti-hunger advocates know something is there but refuse to address it.

To heal the trauma that goes back in time and manifests today, we have to allow ourselves to feel the grief caused by generations of oppression, early death, and murder. Our avoidance of grief is deeply entrenched in the psyches of many people in the Americas. Part of the way to avoid the experience of grief is to either stay indifferent or seek constant pleasure in dominating and controlling the world around us. The pleasure of domination is derived from objectifying or viewing people as "things" that can be owned, manipulated, or exploited. Hartman observes that this pleasure typifies the sensations of white people's enslavement of Africans and all the ensuing practices of racially motivated domination of Black people. Hartman's work builds on that of sociologist W. E. B. Du Bois, especially his book *Black Reconstruction*, where he outlines how the subjugation and exploitation of Black people was directly tied to southern whites' penchant for ownership and grand living.[29] Racism and sexism have roots in the pleasure of domination, allowing it to be entrenched in everyday behavior and thought.[30] The emotional pleasure of domination also allows capitalism to flourish through the commodification of people and the natural world (including food) as things that can be bought, sold, and owned.[31] The idea that people and land can be owned and controlled through a racialized, gendered hierarchy is backed by European and US legal systems. It is the basis for capitalism.[32]

So what are we avoiding? Do we know how to feel and express grief? Can we truly empathize with people and join with them in solidarity? Or do we follow the endless dopamine hit of pleasure and quick fixes we can click, buy, own, and sell? Or do we numb our emotions and become indifferent altogether? These are good starter questions for the personal work.

THE POLITICAL: COURAGE TO ABOLISH SYSTEMS AND CREATE NEW ONES

For all the exploitation, forced disappearances, and abuse in US history, Indigenous nations and communities that currently struggle with comparatively high rates of food insecurity and hunger have enacted as well as maintained an equally long history of subversion and resistance to survive violence and hunger. These traditions of resilience and resistance have kept generations of people alive and fighting for their right to live and be healthy. Indigenous people have fought for their sovereignty through self-defense, the courts, intellectual and spiritual engagement, stealth hunting, fishing, gathering, their own governance, businesses, and courageous resistance in the present day. Their resistance to the Dakota Access Pipeline and Line 3, for instance, have been noticed worldwide. While many times Indigenous activists and lawyers get violently overruled, their actions have kept one-quarter of the potential emissions in the United States in the ground.[33] Their resilience and resistance should embolden the rest of the people in the United States to do the same.

Demands for Indigenous sovereignty have also fueled the food sovereignty movement. While food sovereignty is not always related to Indigenous sovereignty, food sovereignty from pluralistic Indigenous perspectives from the Global South and North can be understood to be grounded in the principles that land is sacred and that sovereignty is not based on the ownership and domination of land. Rather, it is people's *relationships* with land, water, and wildlife that allow for mutual benefit for all humans and more-than-humans.[34] Additionally, developed by many Indigenous peoples and global organizations such as Via Campesina, the food sovereignty movement merges deep reverence and respect for land, plants, and animals with actions for securing rights for farmworkers, laborers, and small farmers.

Resilience and self-reliance have a long tradition in Black communities ranging from times people were enslaved up through the present day, explains ethnographer Ashanté Reese. In her analysis of the history of food acquisition in the Washington, DC, area, she describes how African Americans have built up communities of self-reliance parallel to and in spite of white supremacy. This has involved long-standing traditions of mutuality and adaptation that support growing, getting, preparing, and sharing food.[35] In the midst of enslavement, enslaved people held secret gardens, started mutual aid efforts, and established other types of solidarity economies.[36] Maroon communities built by fugitives, people formerly enslaved, and many communities of the Gullah Geechie tradition in the low country of North and South Carolina, Florida, and Georgia have taken care of each other as well as stewarded their land and syncretic lifeways up through today. Many from those traditions migrated north too, including the family of Valerie Erwin, chef and manager of the EAT Café. That wisdom of food growing, preparation, sharing, and mutual aid continues to thrive.[37]

Beyond the focus on food, seed, and cultural heritage, both traditions have a long history of insisting on decolonization and abolition. Though decolonization seems impossible, bold attempts to decolonize can take many forms, such as through the Land Back movement, actions of the Indigenous Environmental Network, and "Red Power" movements like the takeover of Alcatraz, the American Indian Movement, and collective resistance against the Dakota Access Pipeline and Line 3.[38] Such ongoing and relentless resistance makes plain that the United States is an illegitimate state power.[39] Additionally, calls from the Black Panther Party to end police brutality and for reparations in the 1960s helped provide some grounding for the modern and robust Black Lives Matter movement.[40]

Movements for abolition, fought for and sharpened over hundreds of years, are still very much alive. Building on the tradition of abolishing slavery, contemporary calls for the abolition of police and prisons along with an overhaul of all programs for families in poverty were strengthened with support from Black queer feminism, which coalesced with the Combahee River Collective in the 1970s. It asserted that sexism, racism, heteronormativity, and imperialism collide in the vast majority of US systems.[41] This coalesced again in the abolitionist work shared widely by many. This can be found in learning and action collectives such as Critical Resistance, Project Nia, and Black Lives Matter.[42] Once people see the "death-dealing superstructure" in the United States and learn about Indigenous and Black practices of resistance, counterresurgence, and fugitivity, a way forward is to do political work to dismantle the superstructure while caring for and supporting people harmed by it, and collaborating with each other to build structures that are life-giving and equanimous.

Following abolitionist approaches in the living footsteps of the Combahee River Collective, Angela Davis, Ruth Wilson Gilmore, Mariame Kaba, Andrea Ritchie, Dorothy Roberts, and many others, I demonstrate ahead how the systems that are meant to address food insecurity and poverty are working as designed: to subdue Black, Brown, and Indigenous people.[43] By extension, these systems also harm millions of white people. If the systems do not destroy, they keep people subjugated. Hungry.

How do we incline toward abolition? In the words of Gilmore, a geographer and abolitionist, to solve today's problems, we have to "change just *one* thing." That is, "*everything*."[44]

To do this takes political will and action, and personal and spiritual growth.

I did not come to abolition easily. As an upper-middle-class white woman, I was miseducated by my family, community, schools, and universities. I was hardly ever introduced to the truth of how the United States began or maintains itself or invited to question its political and social infrastructure or learn about transformative alternatives. I came to abolition through listening deeply to Indigenous people in my early career, and then from listening to Black women, people who are Latinx, and white women too—almost all of whom experienced food insecurity, trauma, and hunger, and who experienced the challenges of public assistance programs like SNAP and the Special Supplemental Nutrition Program for Women, Infants, and Children (WIC), housing subsidies, energy assistance, and Medicaid. They brought me straight to the root of hunger. Thanks to listening to their wisdom, I became radicalized.

Radical is another word for foundation or root. It is a place of beginning. To be radical is rational and practical. We cannot SNAP or WIC our way out of hunger in America. Yes, these programs are important, but the way they were built and sustained relies on the status quo. As long as we try to simply tweak these programs, we may make it easier for people to withstand racism, sexism, and colonialism. But the same injustices will still be here thirty years down the road while the slow genocide continues. You and I will be listening to the same old conversations about why there is hunger in America and what to do about it. We'll be sitting in the back of the room rolling our eyes thinking, "We've been here before," and our hearts will be crushed.

I felt this recently as I participated in the White House Conference on Hunger that occurred in September 2022. It was the first time the White House hosted a conference on hunger in over fifty years. But the solutions offered were few and limited while deeply entangled with for-profit companies that contribute to the problem. Meanwhile, the administration was getting ready to end COVID-era universal free meals in schools and cut the SNAP program for millions. It was a shameless display of self-importance that diverted attention from addressing ongoing harms enabled by the US government.

Neither of us want to be involved in this charade. So to change course, let's break through this deceitful status quo and start again by working with the truth, however painful.

THE SPIRITUAL: COURAGE TO FEEL AND EXPRESS LOVE

The people I interviewed about hunger not only talked about food insecurity but also reported problems of rape, neglect, abuse, racism, misogyny, and unrelenting systemic violence. As I carried out my research, I used to think the people I interviewed had all the problems with trauma and that I did not. I thought I was healthy and they were not. What a racist I was—thinking that Black, Brown, and Indigenous people had all the problems, and I was learning how to fix the problems as if I was not somehow complicit as a white person and had no problems myself. Many people call this the "white savior complex." The antihunger world is filled with white people thinking they are there to solve other people's problems—problems that many white people created and maintain.[45] I thought I was working hard, hard to the bone. In truth, I was just floating along as I enjoyed all the privileges of the systems founded on keeping white people in a dominant position (I'm a professor), and thinking that who I was and what I was doing were the norm (doing research and policy work without trying to transform the systems). With each interview those "layers of nonsense," as Regina Jackson and Saira Rao refer to white women's racism, began to shred, tear, and rip off.[46] While I have thousands more layers to dissolve, my heart, mind, and gut have become more exposed in ways that allowed me to soften enough to look at myself in the mirror. And I mean really look at the tyranny in my skin, body, and ways of thinking and being. I talk more about this in part III. Since I began my work, I've been keeping at least one eyeball on myself and how I show up, how I utilize "whiteness" or "white culture." What I see is not pretty. Throughout this book, white supremacy culture, the culture based on five hundred years of racist and sexist ideas about how the world should be, will be a constant theme. Many white people unconsciously use the tools, thoughts, and ideas of white supremacy culture, but all kinds of people can use it to survive and thrive in schools, universities, workplaces, and health systems as well as on playgrounds. I invite you to join me and keep at least one eyeball on yourself; that's primarily part of the personal work. This includes spiritual work too.

Back to my own layers of nonsense. The horrors that the people I interviewed experienced started to become my horrors. Their harrowing experiences began to draw out deep experiences of pain from within myself that I couldn't seem to understand or identify. I became deeply unsettled. Some may call this secondary trauma. That is, by hearing about other people's traumatic experiences, the listener can start to manifest trauma-related symptoms.

But no, it goes deeper than that. It forced me to reckon with myself along with my family, politics, and spiritual understanding of how I move through the world.

After reading Menakem's book, I was encouraged to acknowledge that, as a white person, I too suffer from racialized trauma. I began to recognize that I and my people developed a way of being as if we had been frozen into a place of dissociation and disconnection from the pain of others. This means that we were also disconnected from the pain in ourselves in response to violence inflicted on Black and Indigenous peoples through their bodies, lands, and lifeways. These ongoing trauma responses to the original violences of America and the political, social, and economic world order keep us fragmented and alienated from one another. And they keep us alienated from ourselves. People in the antihunger community, academia, and the political and nonprofit realms often have this kind of trouble, which we refuse to name or discuss. To address our emotions about it all is taboo.

But breaking taboo can help us evolve. According to Ward, to evolve, we need to become "whole" and recover, or emerge from our social despair rooted in "the absence of genuine connection."[47]

In the midst of the climate catastrophe, the urgency to change our ways to be resilient in the years ahead demands our evolution. We will not evolve through our intellect alone. We need a lot of guts, intuition, and a deep understanding of our own bodies. Our bodies are a form of land. Part of the technology of the human body is our capacity to feel deep emotion, our ability to recognize ourselves in each other, and our ability to seek solidarity with each other to survive and thrive.

Love, that ability to seek and experience communion with each other, is also the glue that holds together cultural, social, political, and economic movements. You and I both know this focus on love is nothing new. But it bears repeating. Reverend Martin Luther King Jr. insisted that love be at the root of nonviolent struggles. He said love is not a weak sentiment. Instead, it is an ethos of powerful action "that does something to the hearts and souls of those committed to it. It gives them new self-respect. It calls up resources of strength and courage that they did not know they had."[48] Writer James Baldwin agreed. All of us, he insisted, need to get wise and courageous to turn this country around. We cannot reduce ourselves and our world to simplified concepts, ideas, and answers. It takes appreciation for complexity and love. "Love," he said, "is the only key to our maturity."[49] In her trilogy on love, hooks explained that an "ethic of love" is the antidote to the US culture of domination. She described love as "the will to nurture our own and another's spiritual growth." By "spiritual," hooks means where the body and spirit are experienced as one, where the principle of the self (the life-force) can be more fully self-actualized. It is the ability to engage in communion with the world around us.[50] Additionally, hooks embraced the teachings of Zen Buddhism in the tradition of Thich Nhat Hanh, who has shared his wisdom with millions through his retreats, books, and the ongoing teachings of the monastics, lay teachers, and practitioners committed to holding the space for people to experience and generate peace in the world. Thich Nhat Hanh describes four facets of love that emerge from Buddhist traditions. They are understanding, compassion, joy, and equanimity.[51]

Most scholars and academics I know start to squirm when I talk about love or spirituality. That squirming indicates discomfort as it threatens the supremacy of the intellect that we have all toiled so hard to sharpen so we can dominate and control the narrative in education and policy as well as on the media airwaves. To survive and be taken seriously as an academic and advocate, I used to be pretty quiet about love. But now I want to make it plain, I want to shout it out across the crevasse that separates so many of us. Loving openly and fully can help us heal. Love should be a central tenet of promoting public health and human flourishing.

Now that that's clear, I want to take things a step further. I invite us into the energy of the erotic, as writer and poet Audre Lorde comes to it. She explains that *erotic* comes from the Greek root *eros*, or the "personification of love" as a creative life force. This can be a deep source of power, especially for women, who have been deprived of their own power to be fully satisfied, and fully seen, heard, and valued. Women's erotic power threatens all that is rooted in patriarchal capitalism. This is because it is a source of deep satisfaction, spirituality, excellence, fulfillment, and creativity, and it doesn't need men, nor the male gaze. It is deeply sourced and transcends boundaries. Lorde asserts, "The dichotomy between the spiritual and the political is also false, resulting from an incomplete attention to our erotic knowledge. For the bridge which connects them is formed by the erotic—the sensual—those physical, emotional, and psychic expressions of what is deepest and strongest and richest within each of us, being shared: the passions of love in its deepest meanings."[52]

Further, Lorde insists that the connection to the erotic functions as an open and fearless underlining of "capacity for joy." This occurs when one has a deep connection with oneself; to know that oneself is "capable of feeling." This is what makes so many people fear the erotic and try to relegate it only to the bedroom or, worse, to press it down to a useless nub that blunts human potential. When the erotic is fully expressed, we can feel deeply all the aspects of our lives, ensuring that our life pursuits are in accordance with joy. "This is a grave responsibility," she says, "projected from within each of us, not to settle for the convenient, the shoddy, the conventionally expected, nor the merely safe."[53]

She, too, maintains that focusing only on the "outside" systems of oppression without attention to what is within us reduces us to self-negation and numbness. "Our acts against oppression become integral with self, motivated and empowered from within." Because "recognizing the power of the erotic within our lives can give us the energy to pursue genuine change in the world, rather than merely settling for a shift of characters in the same weary drama."[54]

So if the personal, political, and spiritual were a Venn diagram, then body sovereignty, deep emotion, complete satisfaction, and extraordinary potential might just land at its center—that gorgeous place where all three overlap.

I invite you to get close to your feelings. Crack them open and see what's there in your own soil. Your soil is the source of all the change that's possible.

HOW THIS BOOK IS ORGANIZED

This book is comprised of three parts. In part I, "The Trauma of Hunger," I demonstrate how racism, colonialism, enslavement, rape culture, and capitalism are visible in every aspect of the experience of hunger. Hunger is a trauma to the body, mind, and spirit. It is also a sign that, despite their tremendous resilience and ability to survive, the people who are the true hunger experts have been neglected and disrespected. It consists of four chapters. Starting with Juleen's experiences and the gift that emerged from our connection, I provide an overview of food insecurity in the United States and review the social, political, and economic context for why there are inequities in rates of hunger. I introduce you to the brilliant Black, Latinx, and white women whom I met in Philadelphia, and what they have to teach us about different ways of understanding the hunger experience. I describe how those who have known poverty and hunger help reveal violence, discrimination, and lack of love as root causes. So you know what to expect, I bring you to the taproot: rape. Rape in the family, rape in the community, rape in US history of enslavement and colonization, and state-sanctioned rape of people's land and ecosystems. I also demonstrate that there are many ways to heal trauma, including through healing-centered peer support coupled with financial empowerment to build wealth.

Part II, "Reconsider Everything," explores the personal experiences of members of Witnesses to Hunger and the Building Wealth and Health Network (programs we developed at the Center for Hunger-Free Communities) as they navigate public assistance. Through their experiences and my work on nutrition assistance policy, I lift the veil on the programs to show how most public assistance programs meant to address food and economic insecurity uphold racist, sexist, and capitalist structures that pry children away from their parents, and actively separate us from each other.

I demonstrate how a parallel process is at play in our public assistance and emergency food systems. This parallel process is the mechanism through which our systems inadvertently recapitulate the very experiences that have proven to be so traumatic for people who need help. Just as the lives of people exposed to repetitive and chronic abuse and maltreatment become organized around the traumatic experience, so too can entire systems become organized around regenerating trauma by pathologizing, penalizing, surveilling, and dominating people, and separating them from each other.

I also expose the toxicity of the emergency food system that is dominated by Feeding America, Walmart, Coca-Cola, and, sadly, your child's third grade teacher. I show that well-meaning people often cause harm through disempowering and humiliating people living in poverty.

Part III, "Nourishing Our World," offers a way forward through personal, political, and spiritual lenses. To begin with the personal, part III relies on the centrality of enslavement and genocide to demonstrate the harms of white supremacy, patriarchy, and capitalism in the United States that generate poverty and hunger, and then launches into the political importance of reparations, rematriation, and universal programs. I also offer up transformative policy approaches such as universal basic income (UBI), universal health care, prison abolition, and solidarity economies. I then describe how to advance human rights, build on the rights of nature, support Indigenous sovereignty, and engage in reciprocity. Finally, I show how it is possible to address the painful truth about hunger through friendship, love, joy, and equanimity. Awakening this loving approach can help us to begin anew and promote the flourishing of future generations.

I THE TRAUMA OF HUNGER

1 WHEN YOU CAN'T LAY WITH YOURSELF COMFORTABLE

THE GIFT OF CONNECTION

In 2002, I began learning in earnest about the experience of hunger from women in Philadelphia who utilize food pantries. Food pantries or food cupboards are places where families get free groceries. Pantries are often hosted in a church basement, a community center, or sometimes a gym after school. There are about seven hundred pantries throughout the Philadelphia region. I volunteered at several pantries in order to recruit over thirty women into my first study in Philadelphia. I paid participants $50 per interview, and then $50 again in follow-up focus groups to get their feedback on themes emerging in the interviews and to give feedback on the analysis. It was this first group of women that unveiled the violence of hunger.

Juleen was a little over five feet tall, wiry, with a piercing look of the ancients. Her commanding presence demanded I give our brief relationship all I had. In that first three-hour interview we dialogued about love, hunger, dignity, affection, drug addiction, desperation, and redemption. Juleen told me she wanted to be an artist. She was sad it never came to be. When she was sober, she would sometimes teach kids art in an after-school program. "Those were some of the few times I ever felt happy," she said.

A year after those original interviews and focus groups, and while I was analyzing the data, I took some time out from work to pack groceries and connect with people at the food pantry of Zion Baptist Church.[1] Juleen was there again. She waited until other people got their groceries before she came to talk to me.

"Hey, remember me? I can do another interview. Do you need another interview?"

"Yes, I do! Hi Juleen! I'd love to, but that study is over," I said. "I'm just analyzing data now."

"Oh." She replied, "Well, I'm needing some money. My son just got out of prison, and I need some money to help him out."

"Sorry," I said, "I've got no cash on me. But if you are willing to come to my office tomorrow, I have some cash there." I gave her my address. "I'd also love to share some ideas about what I have learned from all the interviews. I hope you can correct me if I'm going astray."

Juleen ambled into my office the next day. "I brought you a present," she said.

> I painted it this morning and I want to give it to you.
> I was thinking about our interview about hunger and dignity.
> It reminded me
> that even during the times I had nothing,
> even the nothing I had was falling apart.

In thick Sharpie, she had lettered an adaptation of a saying often attributed to Benjamin Franklin—ending in "involve me I learn." She had also painted an image of a barrel, pasting a cutout on it from her Bible from Mathew 7:9–11, which reads,

> What man is there among you who,
> if his son shall ask for bread,
> would give him a stone?

Beneath it was a well-known reading called the blessing of unanswered prayers. It begins like this:

> *I asked for strength that I might achieve;*
> *I was made weak that I might learn humbly to obey.*
> *I asked for health that I might do greater things;*
> *I was given infirmity that I might do better things.*

She pointed to this passage and told me, "This Bible reading reminds me that through my suffering, I have learned so much about the world, about other people, and myself."

"Who is this person?" I asked pointing to the figure in the barrel.

"This is me," she said. "When I had nothing. See the nail coming out? Even the nothing I had was falling apart."

We talked at length, going back over the themes she described in our interview a year earlier. I told her the isolation, despair, and violence she had portrayed were coming up in many other interviews; that violence was a central concern connected to food and money. "Makes sense," she said. "You are on the right track."

I gave her the leftover cash from that study that was still in my office. She counted it and smiled.

"Thank you."

"No, thank *you*. I will cherish this painting and keep it with me always."

That's good.
Talking with you brought up a lot of things
I had tried to forget.
Now I realize
it was important for me to remember them.
I think this painting will help you
to explain to the world
what it's like,
what's really going on with people.

"By the way," she laughed, "I glued this onto the back of a poster advertisement of my favorite wine coolers." She showed me the front of the poster: "St. Ides, Special Brew, Malt Liquor."

I hung Juleen's painting on my office wall immediately, and it's been there since.

Through her painting, Juleen looks at me every day. You will notice that no matter how far away you pull your head back or to the side of this book, she's also still looking at you.

Figure 1.1
Juleen's painting of when she had nothing, and even the nothing she had was falling apart.
Reprinted by permission.

Just like she watches you, she watches me. She's always asking, listening, considering, and preaching.

Juleen's painting contains almost everything you need to know about hunger in America. I'm still listening to Juleen and still learning from her gift. I'll start us off with a few of the lessons.

Let's begin with this: "What man is there among you? . . ." can be restated as, "If you do not offer someone food who needs it, then you are not a human being." In other words, to share food or break bread together is to recognize our shared humanity.

Second, one-way teaching is limited. Instead of teaching, you should engage with people and involve them. Join together with neighbors and new friends in solidarity. This way, everyone will understand.

Third, Juleen explained that she wanted people to know this: "When you're hungry," she said, "it means everything around you has been reduced to nothing. So hunger also means you don't have a safe place to live. It's like you are naked, you are cut down to nothing, and you're in the street."

Fourth, Juleen's painting shows that the stress of this deprivation is overwhelming and permeates the entire body. Though the painting is reprinted here in black and white, the original shows her body in neon orange and green; her eyes and the barrel are neon yellow. Here, the stress infuses the body with electrified discomfort. It is just as important to heal the stress of impoverishment as it is the money, food, and housing situation.

"I felt totally, totally alone." Juleen underscored. "I felt like I was beyond help." The fifth lesson is, if a person is hungry and homeless, they are isolated and abandoned.

The sixth lesson, goes beyond both Juleen and me. This is the lesson of shared connection.

The experience of receiving Juleen's pain in gift form was almost overwhelming. Disturbing. She got into me, and so did the injustice. Her experiences and willingness to share them with me became my story to bear. I am obligated to tell it far beyond the tape recording, the walls of the office, and our own lifetimes.

It has taken me years to absorb, metabolize, and understand people's experiences along with their descriptions of food insecurity and hunger.

Throughout my time learning about hunger, providing testimony, taking action, and helping others to take action on issues of poverty, hunger, and trauma, I have cherished Juleen's painting. It is a way of keeping myself in companionship with her. I invite you, too, to stay in companionship with her. She is looking at you. Maybe she's reading *you*.

What does she say? What does she want? What does she need? How did she get to this point? Who allowed this to happen? What is expected of you and me?

As Juleen connected with me, in this book, she also connects to you. This connection is a gift. There is a tie—a social bond—between all of us now. The gift demands attention. I will return to it several times throughout this book. You may want to return to it too, even if I don't mention it.

What does she ask of you?

HUMILITY AND DEEP LISTENING

When a researcher is interviewing people, there is always a complicated power dynamic. The interviewer is likely (but not always) to be highly educated with economic power, as they have social status and grant money to pay people for their time. People may agree to participate not because they want to help or are interested in the subject matter but rather because they need the money. Indeed the second time around, and maybe the first, Juleen asked if she could do an interview because she needed some money to help her son. The desperate need for money can create a dynamic where the interviewee just goes through the motions with no incentive to tell the truth, deeply engage, or care for the outcome. They may be trying to tolerate the interview just long enough to get the cash. This keeps the researcher at a great distance and never close to the truth. There are many problematic dynamics in research across race, ethnicity, and class that have been written about at length, and demand attention to research processes that avoid mere extraction of information. There are many ways to do so, such as grounding approaches in abolitionist techniques and Indigenous methods that demand mutuality and reciprocity on multiple levels.[2] This is why many researchers and community groups do action research or community-based participatory action work that has a built-in structure of solidarity between people who have the wisdom (the researched) and people who hope to share in that wisdom (the researcher).[3]

In my case, as an upper-middle-class white person, because of my focus on food insecurity and hunger, I'm generally interviewing Black, Indigenous, Latinx, or immigrant people, thus making the entire scenario feel exploitative and reminiscent of extractive, colonialist processes. Though that power dynamic and tension are almost always there, I did everything to acknowledge the dynamics and sought to flatten the significance of our differences. I often did this through ensuring people involved in the research could engage in shaping the research, and developing the questions I ask and the processes of engagement. This also includes participating in the analysis and dissemination, such as with publishing, writing reports, media engagement, testimonies, and exhibits. At the grounding or beginning of an interview, I always came from a place of not knowing, of being a beginner.

Before I started the work in Philadelphia, the people of the Southern Cheyenne and Arapaho nations taught me an ethic of humility. They demonstrated that to engage in science involving people, the researcher must come from a place love, solidarity, and mutuality. Otherwise, you are just a colonizer, coercing and extracting wisdom and expertise for your own benefit. Many Cheyenne elders and friends taught me that love, spiritual connection, solidarity, and deep reverence and respect for human and non-human relations are central to all attempts to learn more about the world. To avoid any offense that can emerge from transactional exchange, they taught me to bring and share gifts that indicate reciprocity and care. Most of the time this took the form of groceries, as sharing food is a primary way relationships are generated, solidified, and maintained. It also required a gift of tobacco to create a grounding in spiritual connection and transmission. I have carried this ethos of humility and reciprocity throughout my work.

Once we got started in our first interview, it felt to me that Juleen recognized my humility and genuine warmth. With humility comes many gifts of connection. To do a good interview demands a person be willing to drop down into an earthly awareness that allows for deep listening. Listening is not a passive action. Listening demands the entire body, mind, and spirit. It demands our full presence. People can sense when you are truly listening and attempting to understand. They feel your empathy and humanity, and if you care. They know if you are teachable and if they can be nourished from your presence. Such a bond demands that you be willing to share yourself, show emotion, and respond—not in terms of the information shared, but in the humanity you both share. A great interview is never a one-way experience. Rather, it is a shared energy and vulnerability. Through the vulnerability, a bond is generated. For a good interview, both people allow themselves to be cognitively, emotionally, and spiritually available to each other. It does not mean that Juleen is interviewing me; it just means that when Juleen was talking to me for more than three hours about her struggle with drug addiction and her family, I responded as a fully present human being with corresponding physical and spiritual emotions, such as sadness, grief, and kindness.

Juleen shed a lot of tears in her interview. We also laughed together. She admonished me because she could see how little I knew about what it means to struggle. Many things came out, she said, that she had told no one else. This was the case with many of the interviews my team and I carried out over the years. There is sometimes comfort in talking with a stranger; there is no prior relationship, no history, and little possibility of seeing each other again. People told my team and me things that happened to them that they had been keeping hidden from their intimate partners, parents, and children. Many times, they said, no one ever asked them about their experiences. Or they didn't feel safe to reveal them with their family. Sometimes when they explained their own surprise at telling me things they kept hidden, people would laugh with relief or sigh with recognition that what they shared just needed to come out. There was no judgment, no consequences; just a deep abiding commitment to educate the world.

In a good interview, a sense of resonance and affection can emerge. It is as if when two musical notes are played simultaneously, they bring into being a third overtone, a type of harmonic connecting sound wave. It is a transcendent experience. Perhaps this is a form of empathy and understanding that a person can feel not just in the mind but in the body and spirit too. As the person you interview describes their experiences, what they lived through can seep into your consciousness, lift up aspects of your spirit, and help it to resettle, or unsettle, in new ways. It can settle into unnameable places that then well up through our emotions. Sometimes, there is no language to describe the suffering. Instead, a deep sense of connection emerges between speaker and listener.

Juleen and I seemed to have a similar experience with each other. Her painting was a testament to that original shared experience one year earlier. Her gift also demands I share it with you.

HOW IT FEELS TO BE SO HUNGRY

Juleen described her experiences with hunger in the midst of her interview while she was talking about the struggle of taking care of herself and her young son. In jail, her husband was unable to help her, and she was on her own. She worked long hours at White Tower, a burger chain modeled after White Castle, and had other low-paying jobs to feed herself and her son. Her income went up and down as she went in and out of jobs. She tried to supplement her income with food stamps, but getting and losing jobs also triggered a loss of food assistance. Sometimes, she was completely destitute and hungry, unable to be comfortable. Here's how she depicted it.

> I know how it feels to be so hungry
> until you feel like you can't walk,
> you can't sit
> you can't lay with yourself comfortable.
> And I know how it also feels to be so hungry
> you feel like you'd eat just about anything.

As you might imagine, there was a lot more going on in her experience of "not being able to lay with herself comfortable."

But I'll just start here in the discomfort to bring us toward the experience of hunger.

Celeste, a five-foot-tall Black woman with a bubbly laugh and a seriousness that seared to the gut, also used the Zion Baptist Church food pantry.

The day of her interview, we met at Zion. She wore a bright-pink T-shirt, and her loose braids were tied back in a low bun. In her friendly way, she invited me back to her home, where she had planned to do her interview alone so she could be candid. When she and I arrived at her doorstep—both of us a little sweaty from walking in the summer heat with groceries—her mother was in the kitchen. As we unloaded the food, her mother insisted on staying for the recorded conversation. Celeste seemed a little displeased but was respectful as her mother launched into her experience of meeting Rosa Parks when she visited Philadelphia. The stories kept coming while we sat at the kitchen table. Each one deepening with storms and more struggles. Mother and daughter riffed off each other as if they were a mirror to each other's lives. Celeste tried to get a few words in as her mother dominated the conversation. Halfway through our interview, Celeste butted in on her mother, and won herself three minutes uninterrupted.

> Now listen to this.
> Now, I'm gonna tell you how I was living
> when I was pregnant with my daughter
> three years ago.
> I remember when I was pregnant with my daughter,
> I was living without water for six months.
> I used to eat chicken wings and hoagies every day.[4]
> So I know the meaning of struggling.
>
> I was living on the streets
> in the snow and sleet and rain and sleeping on the benches.
> Pregnant.
> Yeah.
>
> I had slept in this one room.
> It was more cold in there than it was outside.
> I wanted to go back outside and sleep because it was
> more warm outside than it was in there.
> I was pregnant.
> And half the days I didn't eat and the other half of the days I did.

So I know the meaning of being hungry and wanting food
and being without lights
and being without water
and being without gas.

I know the struggling parts of wanting nourishment and substance
    in your body.
I know the importance of it.
I know that it's not how much you have.
You don't have to have steak every day.
If you have potatoes and a frying pan and a stove,
cut them potatoes up
and make that potato.
You got to dice them a little thin, but then you eating.

I know the importance of food,
and why you need it and what it's supposed to do.
For number one, food will give your body energy.
And without the food and the water, your body can't function.
You just waste away.
So you got to have water to keep your body going.
For number one, because if you don't,
your body gets dehydrated,
you'll get dizzy and pass out and stuff like that.
So your body needs food so you can be able to move.
You got to be able to move.
If you ain't got no food, you just weak.
I mean, you out of it.
You may be able to go a week or two weeks without eating.
But you can't go a long, long period of time without eating
because you'll just waste away.

Celeste explained that hunger is intermittent and interwoven with many
other kinds of suffering. It is not a daily constant for months at a time but
instead is sporadic ("half the days I didn't eat and the other half of the days

I did"). It can affect one's health and well-being ("food will give your body energy. And without the food and the water, your body can't function. You just waste away.") If you only have a little, you can make do, even if it's not enough ("cut them potatoes up and make that potato. You got to dice them a little thin, but then you eating.") But the quality won't be good—chicken wings and hoagies, or a single potato.

Not having food coalesces with not having a safe place to live and not being able to pay for water and electricity. Feeling cold. Dizzy. Dehydrated.

The way Celeste described it, hunger was so much more than not having food; it was a cascade of troubles and trade-offs ("I know the meaning of being hungry and wanting food and being without lights and being without water and being without gas.") One cannot be in a nice house with nice things, able to pay for heat, air-conditioning, and gas for the car and go hungry. By the time you are food insecure, you have made hard decisions about paying for rent versus food, utilities versus food, childcare versus food, or medicine versus food.

So remember, while we call it food insecurity, it is not simply a measure of not having enough money for food. It is an indication that people have made often-impossible choices between paying for food and paying for other basic needs.

HOW THE SCIENTISTS MEASURE HUNGER AND FOOD INSECURITY

Food is important to the equation, though, and not having enough or the right kinds has major health consequences. We know this and can keep track because, over thirty years ago, social scientists, economists, and others developed a way to measure food insecurity and match it up against health outcomes and other indicators of well-being.

As President Ronald Reagan's 1980s' administration cut back social spending on food stamps and other supports, advocates and legislators expressed concerns about growing hardship in the United States. In response, the Reagan administration created a task force to identify the magnitude of hunger in the early 1980s. Simultaneously, a group of researchers at Cornell

University were uncovering experiences of hunger, poor nutrition, and hardship in upstate New York. Interview results revealed that hunger was not only about lack of food due to lack of money; it was a broader experience that included worry, anxiety, and reducing meal quality. The results from these interviews inspired the USDA to create a measure of hunger.

In 1992, the USDA reviewed the literature on measuring food insecurity, and then hosted a conference in 1994 that brought together academic experts, researchers, and federal agency staff to identify the appropriate conceptual basis for a national measure. Taking an expansive view of hunger, their consensus report stated, "*Hunger*, as a recurrent and involuntary lack of access to food which may produce malnutrition over time, *is discussed as food insecurity in this report*" (emphasis added). That is, food insecurity and hunger were considered to be one and the same, with some identification of varying levels of severity.[5]

This conference inspired what would become the USDA Economic Research Service's (ERS) eighteen-item survey, the US Household Food Security Survey Module (HFSSM). For the past twenty-five years, it has been considered the gold standard survey measure of the severity and depth of food insecurity in the United States. The ERS defines *food security* as "access by all people at all times to enough food for an active, healthy life." By contrast, *food insecurity* is having inadequate economic resources to have consistent access to safe, adequate, and nutritious food to support an active and healthy life for all household members.

Two important concepts are "enough food at all times" and "for active and healthy life." Enough food at all times is what the general public might think of as the threshold below which someone experiences hunger, or "not having enough." Integrating a component of active and healthy life helps expand the concept of hunger to include wellness.

To take some of the pressure off answering direct questions, the survey questions ask about people's experiences in comparison to what other people do rather than directly asking the respondent, "What do *you* do?" As well, it focuses on the *household*, not the individual. Here are the preamble and first two questions:

Now I'm going to read you several statements that people have made about their food situation. For these statements, please tell me whether the statement was OFTEN true, SOMETIMES true, or NEVER true for your household in the last twelve months.[6]

1. "We worried whether our food would run out before we got money to buy more." Was that OFTEN, SOMETIMES, or NEVER true for you in the last twelve months?
2. "The food that we bought just didn't last, and we didn't have money to get more." Was that OFTEN, SOMETIMES, or NEVER true for you in the last twelve months?

In the early years of the survey's use, there were two levels of food insecurity. Those who answered between three and seven questions in the affirmative indicated a household that was "food insecure *without* hunger." Those answering affirmative to eight or more questions indicated a household that was "food insecure *with* hunger." I outline the characteristics of these experiences included in the measure and the levels of food insecurity they depict in appendix 1.

Every year since 1998, researchers at the ERS release the food insecurity numbers. When I was starting out as an assistant professor in the early 2000s, the ERS put the report on its website, and the media hardly covered it.

That is, until 2006.

Under the George W. Bush administration, the ERS undersecretary insisted on changing the food security terminology. Conservative legislators in Texas with federal influence had doubts about recent ERS reports on hunger. As a result, a new expert panel was identified and convened by the Committee on National Statistics to review the food security measure. After a thorough review, it suggested the two main categories, *food security* and *food insecurity*, stay the same. But *hunger*, the committee insisted, should no longer be considered the same thing as food insecurity. This is in contradiction to the consensus report of 1995, where they were considered one and the same. The new panel recommended that the two levels of food insecurity (food insecurity *without* and *with hunger*) be renamed. Additionally, it proposed to remove the term *hunger* from the measure altogether. Reflecting the committee's assessment that hunger is a subjective measure with various meanings, the committee maintained that the Food Security Supplement did not "objectively" measure hunger.

In my conversations with some members of this committee, I learned that from their perspective, to be "objective" would entail a doctor or lab report from a blood draw or some other lab-based identification of micronutrient deficiency. According to these expert panelists, most of whom were statisticians, only a doctor or scientist would be able to "verify" if a person was hungry. Reporting about one's own feelings of hunger or not having enough food to eat was not considered viable.

If one follows this faulty logic, it seems odd, then, that they did not think to throw out self-assessment of one's finances as well. Why would we trust someone who said they worried they did not have enough money to buy food? Following the panel's train of thought, that should be verified by the bank, an employer, or the Internal Revenue Service.

This review committee sought input from scientists; it did not, however, seek insight from people who experienced food insecurity firsthand, nor did it engage qualitative researchers who have spoken with many people who experienced food insecurity.

Here's the good news: the measure is solid, committee scientists insisted. So the terms "food security" and "food insecurity" remained.

Here's the bad news: the general public's understanding of food insecurity was already questionable. This new terminology simply magnified the confusion. After considering the committee's uncertainty on the use of the term hunger, the USDA undersecretary suggested a new terminology for indicating severity. Food insecurity "without hunger" would convert to "low food security" and food insecurity *with* hunger converted to "very low food security." That is, *within* a category called food *in*security, there are two categories: low food *security* and very low food *security*.

Not until the USDA changed the name and extracted *hunger* altogether did the media take notice of the annual food security report. The media attention backfired. In 2006, Mark Nord, the chief analyst who released the reports each year, was deemed by MSNBC's Keith Olbermann to be the "Worst Person in the World."

Here's Olbermann's reporting:

Nobody goes to bed hungry in America anymore? Hallelujah. Would that that were true. The Ag Department did not eliminate the condition we know as hunger, just the word. The 35 million Americans who could not put food on the table all or part of last year are now described by Mr. Nord as experiencing "very low food security."

Mr. Nord would appear to be experiencing very low honesty security.[7]

When the committee changed the terminology, it took the only shadow of clarity out of the term and made it even more confusing. On the other hand, my research colleagues did not seem so upset about it. They suggested, "We don't have to worry too much, as the actual measure itself held up, despite the terminology shift."

But the reality of hunger was obscured. Scientists and government administrators just broadened the crevasse of misunderstanding between themselves and the true experts, those who know hunger in their bodies and minds. My kind of science is the work of staying close to people like Juleen and Celeste who know the truth.

CHILDREN'S HEALTHWATCH

There is an adage among those of us who work on health policy and disease prevention. There are many doctors and other do-gooders "downriver" who pull drowning babies out of the water in order to save them. Then there are others who do that but also take the time to whack the bushes and tramp upriver to stop the jerks who are throwing those babies in the river. Deborah Frank does both: she "pulls the babies out of the water" through her clinical care for children with failure to thrive (severe malnutrition), and she "tramps upriver" and uses the evidence of her research to stop members of Congress from doing more harm.

She's a five-foot-tall powerhouse pediatrician in a skirt that hangs below the knees. Frank wears sneakers, has a brilliant wit, and her glasses are often tilted. For decades, she tended to the babies living in poverty, and sounded the alarm that America's families were struggling due to new federally mandated work requirements and other welfare reform changes in 1996. Policies that barred families from receiving life-sustaining financial support were making babies sick.

Due to the major changes in welfare under the Clinton administration, known as the 1996 Personal Responsibility and Work Opportunity Act (PRWORA), many families were getting kicked off welfare. As a result, they were having a hard time paying for housing and food. Strict work requirements and stricter family punishments were created without consideration of the health of children and their parents. Many families thus had their welfare benefits cut off or were "sanctioned," meaning that they were no longer eligible to receive support or only their children could receive support (with less money) for a certain period. The outcome was sicker babies and more children in the hospital.[8]

Those outcomes came from the research group I later joined in 2004 called the Children's Sentinel Nutrition Assistance Program (C-SNAP). It monitored the health of children and their caregivers in Boston, Washington, DC, Baltimore, Minneapolis, Little Rock, and Los Angeles. What I liked about the work of Frank and colleagues was the ability to link child health outcomes to federal-state policy change. As Frank liked to say, the punitive nature of welfare "is inscribed onto the bodies and brains of kids," and the public needed to know.

I visited Frank and asked if I could join the science team with a site in Philadelphia. She introduced me to a potential funder, and I received my first major grant to join C-SNAP in 2004. This was also the founding grant of the Center for Hunger-Free Communities. Our first interviews in Philadelphia started in January 2005 at St. Christopher's Hospital for Children, a large hospital located in one of the poorest zip codes in the country that sees over fifty thousand children per year in the emergency room.

I started the research with a graduate student. We practiced the interview together, working with Gabi, my youngest child, who was then six months old—all wiggly and pudgy—in order to practice measuring a child's height. The survey asked parents or caregivers (foster parent, auntie, grandma, or other guardian) of young children about their health and well-being as well as their child's health. Then we asked questions from the HFSSM and others about paying rent and utilities. After that, we would weigh and measure the height of their baby.

Since January 2005, our Philadelphia-based team has interviewed over twelve thousand families (about a thousand families per year), and measured the height and weight of almost as many infants and toddlers. These were not open-ended qualitative interviews like I described earlier. The interviews are closed ended with only a numbered response (not narrative experiences) about being able to pay for rent, food, housing, and childcare, and about their child's health and their own. Each interview takes between twenty to forty minutes depending on people's answers. To avoid any confusion with the name change of food stamps to SNAP, our research network changed the name of the research collaborative from C-SNAP to Children's HealthWatch. Since 1998, Children's HealthWatch researchers have cumulatively interviewed over eighty-five thousand families at all sites.

FOOD INSECURITY, HOUSING INSECURITY, AND DEPRESSION

Here is what we know from that research. Celeste and her daughter (long before she was born) were headed toward greater hardships. Food insecurity during pregnancy is associated with increased risk for child hospitalization and poor child development. If a pregnant person is homeless while pregnant, the risk of their child being at greater odds for low birth weight increases by over 40 percent.[9] Birth weight sets a baseline from which a child can grow and develop; hence it is an important indicator of child health.

Even if we know nothing else about what happens during pregnancy, if a young child is in a household that is food insecure, both mother and child will experience negative health consequences. Inadequate or interrupted food intake, even for a short time, can cause long-lasting health problems. This is because a child is growing so fast. Their brain is growing seven hundred neurons a second. Anything that interrupts or truncates that lightning speed development affects a child's chances of full flourishing. Among infants and toddlers under four years old, food insecurity is associated with increased hospitalization, poor health status, and iron deficiency anemia.[10] Young children living in food insecure households have a high probability of being at emotional, social, and cognitive risk, which has strong implications for a child's school readiness and subsequent well-being later in life. Developmental risk experienced during early childhood indicates a twelvefold increase in the risk of being disabled as an adult.[11] The impacts in young children can be so severe that Frank often refers to hunger as a brain injury.

Children's HealthWatch also found that food insecurity and homelessness are harmful to the caregiver's physical and mental health. What we do not know is which comes first, depression or economic deprivation. Our research from Children's HealthWatch is cross-sectional. Cross-sectional research operates like taking a snapshot in which everything is reported at the same interview time. This does not allow for us to identify cause and effect. It only allows us to see associations.

Since the days of the early studies on starvation that found serious affective disorders and depression associated with malnutrition (such as the Minnesota starvation study, where thirty-six men were intentionally starved during World War II to study the impact of starvation and protocols for bringing the men back to health), research that follows people over time has been unable to help researchers disentangle the directionality of relationships between depression and food insecurity.[12] Poor and low nutrition can cause depression and emotional distress, and vice versa. Is a person depressed because they have no food? Or are they food insecure because they are depressed? If a person is depressed, it could mean that in addition to feeling down or "blue" for more than a few days a week, they have little energy to find or keep a job where they can make enough money for housing and food, nor will they reach out to friends, neighbors, and acquaintances. Some insist that if we treat depression, food and housing insecurity will go away. Some think that if we provide food, mental health will improve. As Juleen knows, providing food without attending to the depression and stress is also inadequate.

The depression and food insecurity relationship is even harder to disentangle than that, as depressive symptoms and food insecurity may be reciprocal; each exacerbates the other. Mothers who report depressive symptoms experience more employment difficulties that may be related to financial hardship, and this impacts housing and food insecurity. When mothers have to skip meals so they can feed their kids with the little money they have, and therefore eat low-quality food for days to save money, their mood can change for the worse. Lack of food, or eating the same low-nutrient foods repetitively, can alter the gut's microbiome, cognitive functioning, and over-all well-being too.

MEET JOANNA, SUPERWOMAN

I met Joanna in summer 2008. She was an early member of Witnesses to Hunger, the program I tell you about in future chapters. She is a supercreative mother of three children (though when I met her, she had two children, aged six and two). She's a white-presenting Latina woman, with short hair that was sometimes dyed orange. Her wit and humor defy all categories. The way she dressed? Tight T-shirt and leggings to fit her curves. I love to think of the outfit she wore to a live interview at the local public radio station: skintight red leggings and a superman shirt with an *S* on the front. Consider her the superhero of this book (along with Juleen), as she taught me so much with her everyday wisdom, cutting tone, and easy laughter.

Joanna was not homeless like Celeste. She lived with her two children and their father in the same home in which she grew up. But they were living rough—without running water and gas. Worse still, there was sewage coming up in the basement, and they had no money to fix the pipes. The kitchen ceiling leaked when it rained.

According to Joanna, her life was "really depressing." When she started out with Witnesses to Hunger, Joanna took a picture of her kitchen. But she was ashamed of her circumstances, so she gave the photo to her neighbor, another member of Witnesses to Hunger, to hide her identity.

Many years later, Joanna described her situation with hindsight in our shared article on food insecurity and poor health.

> When I look at pictures of myself from the time when I lived in that house,
> I look completely unhealthy.

Figure 1.2
Joanna's kitchen. "When things get this bad, your kids can go hungry." (The feet to the left are part of a doll.) Reprinted by permission.

I look like the stress was getting to me.
Look at me now, compared to how I look then.
My hair was falling out,
I was skinny,
I was pale.
I wasn't healthy at all.
But there was nothing doctors could really do about it
if they weren't changing my situation.
They can pump you up full of a bunch of pills
to keep you from being so depressed
and to calm you down,
but they're not changing what the problem is.
My problem is that I don't have food.
You can give me all the Xanax in the world,

but it's still not changing what I'm going through.
I don't want to go to the doctor for being depressed because I don't
    have any food.
Unless you're giving me groceries,
you're not doing anything for me.
So, you can give those pills to somebody else.[13]

This is an important warning. To address hunger, we cannot treat just one thing. Remember, food alone could not solve the pain that Juleen and Celeste were feeling. They needed a safe home with heat and a place to cook. Similarly, treatment for depression was not going to solve Joanna's depression. She needed food. She needed water. She needed her plumbing fixed. She could not cook until she could pay for consistent gas and electricity. To fix the plumbing and get the gas on, she needed thousands of dollars. As a result, she was stuck in a dangerous situation with shit burbling up through her basement floor.

Almost every week, she said, she brought her daughters to the emergency room with colds, ear infections, and skin rashes because of her circumstances.

What can the family doctor do? What's the point of their training? Doctors can treat the cold, rash, or ear infection, but they cannot solve the issues once and for all. Joanna's kids will return soon enough, sick again for the same reasons.

FOOD INSECURITY, DISABILITY, AND FAMILY STRESS

Joanna's debilitating depression was related to the stress of not having food, having no running water or gas, and trying to raise two small children. No pill can cure that stress, and children absorb it. Additionally, one childhood illness can set off a cascade of challenges, especially when children have special health care needs or disabilities. Low employment rates and high health care costs constrain the economic resources of people with disabilities. This can lead to food insecurity. In a nationally representative study of over 420,000 adults, those with disabilities were 2.6 times as likely to be food insecure compared with adults without disabilities. Among households reporting very low food security, the most severe form of food insecurity, 38 percent include an adult with a disability.[14] As a reminder, disability includes depression. Food insecurity can make coping with a disability difficult and dangerous. One-third of chronically ill adults cannot afford both food and medicine, and when people cannot take their medicine, their challenges can be exacerbated.[15] Or if they take their medicine without food, the medicine may cause problematic side effects or not work as well.

Food insecurity is associated with poor academic performance along with poor cognitive and social development among school-age children and adolescents. Compared to low-income school-age children living in food secure households, children in food insecure households are more likely to have challenging social relationships and lower math and reading scores, and to need to repeat a grade.[16] Children who live in homes experiencing food insufficiency are more likely than their food secure counterparts to receive special education services or mental health counseling as well as exhibit behavioral problems.[17] Among adolescents and children, poor mental health and food insecurity are also strongly linked. For example, family food insufficiency is positively associated with depression, suicidal ideation, and suicide attempts among adolescents.[18]

Some researchers talk to kids without their parents to try to understand their experiences. School-age children are often aware of food insecurity, despite their parents' attempts to protect them from this knowledge.[19] Children and adolescents ages nine to sixteen reported they managed immediate food resources for themselves and their parents, worried about their parents' level of stress, and felt angry and helpless when their families did not have enough food.

Most parents feel desperately guilty about this. Yet they will rarely admit the food insecurity and hardship to anyone, especially a doctor.

Joanna described how awful she felt that her kids were struggling. Deeply afraid that the Department of Human Services (DHS) (the city-run child welfare agency) would find out about her living conditions and take away her children, she made her older daughter swear to never tell anyone about how they were living without running water and gas for heat.

Aside from the father of her girls, and her friend and confidante Maria, who lived across the street, I was one of the few people who knew about Joanna's situation.

We developed a mutual sense of affection. Her oldest daughter was the same age as my daughter Zora, and we often talked and laughed about the struggles and joys of parenting.

I could hardly sleep for thinking about her situation and pain. I worried about what I was supposed to do. Joanna is loving, kind, and caring with her children. She is a doting mom. But her circumstances were unbearable for any human being. She and her kids were really suffering. I shared my concern with her. She knew it was bad. She said she would work on it. I provided her with ideas about different programs, gave her referral phone numbers, and offered up the unthinkable.

"Maybe," I said, "take yourself and your kids to a shelter?"

At the time, this was the fastest way in Philadelphia to get subsidized housing for women and children. Otherwise, it was a ten-year wait to get subsidized housing through the Philadelphia Housing Authority. If a person was demonstrably homeless, they had a higher chance of getting housing support. But everyone knew the Eliza Shirley House run by the Salvation Army, the singular place through which homeless families could legitimately enter the city's shelter system, was a place of hell.

To enter the shelter system, it is best to show up to Eliza Shirley House in the early morning, and then wait in line outside with your kids in strollers and all of your paperwork stuffed in the diaper bag. After you complete a long intake and suffer the indignity of people asking all manner of personal questions, the shelter staff decide if they will let you stay the night. Then you must leave for the full day and only return at night to sleep. Moms and kids are everywhere. Moms are so stressed that they yell at their children or worse, according to some witnesses. One mother I spoke with described a valid fear of bedbugs, which have made a comeback in the big US cities. There is also the threat of people with good sleight of hand who can steal your money, clothes, and baby's diapers.

Joanna refused to subject herself and her children to that. She was afraid to tell anyone else of her circumstances or ask for help. She knew that if she shared information with anyone, the authorities would not only condemn her house but take away her children too. The thought was unbearable. This is why she kept a pit bull in the house. His name was Caesar.

"I'm afraid of Caesar," I told Joanna.

"Good. You're supposed to be," said Joanna. "To us he's a sweet puppy. But he scares all the neighbors and anyone who comes near. He's useful to us."

"How is he useful?"

"This way, if L&I [the Philadelphia office of licensing and inspection—which condemns places as uninhabitable] comes by, they won't come in. And they won't report me to DHS. Caesar is our protector."

This was the opening I was looking for. "Your situation is quite awful. You need to get out. It's not safe for the kids."

"I know that, Mariana, better than anyone."

"I hate to say this, but you telling me about your situation is putting me in a terrible position. I'm a mandated reporter. As a university employee, I'm required by law to make a report to social services if I learn about children being in harm's way. But I don't want to report you. You should not be reported. This is outrageous!"

"Yep. I agree."

Silence.

"Do what you gotta do, Mariana."

"Come on, Joanna. Can you please just get out? I've given you so many phone numbers of places to call for help. You need some help."

"I told you, I will."

I would call every few days to check on her. Many times, she would not answer. Several months after she had moved out of that house, she admitted she avoided my calls.

Though a few people I confided in encouraged me to do so, I never called DHS. It was six months before she got out. During this time, I could not sleep well. I was unable to lay with myself comfortable. The situation defied all rational actions, despite the many ways I tried to think of a way out. I would imagine Joanna awake at night too. I would picture her needing to go to the bathroom. Or her little children needing to do the same. I thought of her menstruating and not having a place to clean up. I thought of everyone desperate to wash their hands.

MORE THAN ONE POT

After Joanna spoke on a synagogue panel about her experiences through an event with Witnesses to Hunger, a member of the synagogue sent a huge box of brand-new pots and pans to our offices as a gift for her. When she came by to pick them up, she asked,

"Are these all for me? What am I supposed to do with all these pots?"

"Use them for cooking," I said.

"But I don't need them. I just use one pot."

"Wait, what?"

Joanna looked at me blankly. "How do you use more than one pot?"

Well, you know, when you have the pot of spaghetti on one burner, it allows you to have a second pot for heating up your sauce, and another pot for string beans or something." I explained.

"Is that how you do your cooking, Mariana?"

"Well, I'm not a great cook, but yes. I use multiple pots at the same time when I cook. I use different pots for differing kinds of foods and cooking methods."

"Oh."

"Please, Joanna," I said after a long pause, "don't tell me you've only ever used one pot. Even now that you're in a different house with a working stove, electricity, water, and everything."

"Nope. Never did."

"Do you mind if I ask you why you've only had one pot all this time?"

"To tell you the truth, Mariana, I never thought I was worth more than one pot."

Through being so demeaned, Joanna absorbed society's imposed low value for her. Nothing about what Joanna was going through was her own problem. Her low esteem was tangled up in the web of generations of residential segregation and social exclusion based on race and ethnicity, and the low value society afforded to her as a woman who was impoverished.

In other words, the magnitude of food insecurity in the United States is a measure of how much the wealthy, professional, and powerful view the worth of others.

The United States is the only Western country that does not provide paid family leave when someone has a child. Many other countries also offer universal preschool and kindergarten. But the United States does not provide such support. Parents, medical professionals, members of Congress, and government administrators know that early childhood nutrition and parental attachment are so fundamental to human health and well-being. But in spite of this knowledge, the US government and employers do not value young children and their families.

For low-income families, staying home without pay to take care of a child is not financially viable. But working at low wages and taking care of a child is not viable either. Most women in low-wage work are sole breadwinners. Black and Latina workers are also more likely to experience discrimination in terms of hiring, wages, and career advancement.[20] Desperate for jobs to pay for food, housing, childcare, heat, and transportation, women are often forced to take jobs that are part-time, unstable, or seasonal. Such jobs offer few opportunities for career advancement, and are less likely to provide work supports such as health insurance, paid sick time, or family leave. These seasonal and fluctuating jobs are associated with income instability or sharp income fluctuations, which in turn exacerbate food insecurity. Low-wage work and seasonal fluctuations affect eligibility for income supports and food assistance such as SNAP. As a result, gig, seasonal, and part-time workers are far more likely than people who have stable employment to be food insecure.[21]

Contrary to commonly expressed opinions, work does not protect against food insecurity. According to the USDA, in 2022 55 percent of people who reported household food insecurity were working full time.[22] Consider this: during 2020 when the COVID-19 pandemic was at its height, states that had minimum wage levels set to less than $8 per hour saw rates of household food insufficiency to be 16.6 percent among households with children and with adults under the age of 65, while states that had minimum wage levels set to at least $12 per hour had rates of household food insufficiency at 13.8 percent.[23] Forty-two percent of all US workers make less than $15 per hour. More than half of African American workers and almost 60 percent of Latinx workers make less than $15 per hour.[24] Eighty percent of the lowest-wage workers earning less than $10 per hour are women. Black and Latina women are more likely than white women to hold these kinds of jobs.[25] Remember, Juleen was earning poverty wages at White Tower when she experienced hunger. Public assistance could not make up the difference.

MEASURING RACIAL AND ETHNIC DISCRIMINATION

As I explained in the introduction, inequities in food insecurity follow patterns of historic and contemporary racial, ethnic, and gender discrimination. Even though we knew that discrimination was at the core, my colleagues at Children's HealthWatch were reluctant to focus on discrimination. Some in our group insisted we stay centered on improving public assistance programs because they are tied to specific policies that have proximal effects on health. Racism is everywhere, on the other hand, and its impact is supposedly "indirect." Despite my colleagues' reticence, I was eager to figure out how to assess ways in which discrimination factored in.

In 2015, at the Children's HealthWatch Philadelphia site, we integrated a measure of experiences of racial/ethnic discrimination in settings such as the justice system, schools, and employment.[26] The survey includes a preamble followed by different social settings. Here's the survey instrument:

> "Discrimination" includes experiences of being prevented from doing something, being hassled, or being made to feel inferior in any of the following situations because of your race, ethnicity, or color. How many times have you experienced discrimination . . .
>
> At school?
> While getting hired or getting a job?
> At work?
> While getting housing?
> While getting medical care?
> While getting services in a store or restaurant?

While getting credit, bank loans, or a mortgage?

While on the street or in a public setting?

By the police or in courts?

After two years of collecting data with almost fourteen hundred mothers, we found what should be obvious by now. When compared to mothers who did not experience interpersonal discrimination from police/courts and in workplaces, those who did experience it were 1.5 to 2 times as likely to report household food insecurity.

We also accounted for whether participation in SNAP, WIC, and cash welfare mitigated the association between discrimination and food insecurity. Our results showed that receiving public assistance was not associated with reductions in the strength of the association between discrimination and food insecurity.[27]

Many people believe that SNAP can solve the problem of hunger, but when it does not reduce the relationship between racism and food insecurity, then we must start asking much harder questions. I get to these in part II.

There are many pathways between discrimination and food insecurity. Discrimination by police and courts is linked to higher incarceration rates, which negatively impact income, food security, and health. Even when people return to society after serving time in prison, they are far more likely than people with the same income to experience food insecurity. In one study, 80 percent of people returning from prison reported household food insecurity.[28] Workplace discrimination based on race, ethnicity, and gender can affect wages, job security, and the ability to be promoted. In turn, this affects income and mental health.[29] Additionally, discrimination in schools is associated with differences in disciplinary actions that affect school performance, thereby affecting adolescent mental health and income later in life.[30]

I hope it is clear by now that food insecurity cannot be solved with food alone. It demands attention to *all* basic needs, including one's ability to earn a living wage. And it demands we pay deep attention to discrimination.

2 HUNGER IN MIND AND BODY

LEARNING THROUGH A DIALOGIC PROCESS

Before I started working with my colleagues at Children's HealthWatch, I sought to understand the experience of hunger from women who use the food pantries. I focused in on women because they have the highest rates of food insecurity and the least power to do something about it; they are less likely to become elected officials, run companies, and be asked to speak to the press and public about their experiences. I wanted to ground my understanding of hunger in their lived expertise. So years before founding the Center for Hunger-Free Communities, I launched that qualitative study with thirty-four women, including Juleen and Celeste.

Here's a summary from my interview protocol:

1. What is it like to get groceries and food for you and your family?
2. What are challenges you face in getting food?
3. What do you like or dislike about getting food from a pantry?
4. How does what you eat influence your health and the way you feel?
5. Do you participate in food stamps or WIC? What is this experience like?
6. Do you think that access to food is a basic human right?
7. What is dignity and how do you know?
8. What else should I know?

In open-ended qualitative interviews, if the story the interviewee is telling you seems relevant to them and your questions, you follow their lead and ask clarifying questions throughout the interview. After a while, you return to another planned question.

I audio recorded our interviews and had them typed verbatim. Then I analyzed the transcripts. Analyzing a transcript includes looking for themes, ideas, and concepts along with how they relate. Put simply, this means you ask people a lot of questions, transfer their responses into data, look across the data of many people, and then ask questions of the data itself. You can create comparison groups to look at differences between those who reported food insecurity and those who did not. You can circle, color code, and identify patterns across many interviews. Or as I did, you can use a software program that allows you to select pieces of transcript or stories to create a code or overarching theme to categorize narrative segments, search for relationships between themes and codes, or capture tone of voice that indicates emphasis or trepidation.

There are several different qualitative lenses through which to analyze data. I took a reflexive, phenomenological approach, where analysis begins without preconceived notions of relationships or themes. To do this, you allow the intricacies of the themes to emerge from the people, not from hypotheses, frameworks, strict ideas, and definitions. With a reflexive approach, you dialogue with participants to seek their feedback on what you are learning and how you are interpreting what you are learning from their interviews. This is different from most other forms of qualitative research, which tend to be one-way interactions where the researcher asks questions and extracts experiences and stories from people without circling back to dialogue with participants about what they are learning, and without concern for how their interpretations are perceived by the people interviewed.

Alternatively, in a reflexive approach the research participants ground, correct, redirect, or even fool you, potentially throwing you off course or, more likely, allowing you to understand them more deeply. You double check to ensure that what you think you are finding makes sense to them. Of course, you will influence the interpretation, just as your participants influence your interpretation. The analyses are mutually explored and generated.

In talking with many people, you can start to hear and see patterns in what they choose to describe. Then once you have a feeling of "saturation" with themes coming up in interviews (this usually happens after about eight to ten interviews), where the same themes begin to recur in a variety of itera-tions, you start to shift the quality and timing of questions. Once you have a hunch of some important themes, it is crucial to go back to the participants and ask for their feedback. You also ask questions about things you do not understand.

As part of this reflexive process, I invited the women I had already interviewed individually to convene for focus groups in combinations of six to eight people at a time. In these groups, I explained some of the themes that came out in the individual interviews. This iterative process creates conditions for the group to give feedback, provide more context, or disagree. The longer you are at it, the better and more informed your ques-tions are, the more insight you gain, and the more you are trusted. In these interviews, people began to tell me experiences that they had never shared with others. It was in these interviews of my earliest study on food insecurity that gender-based violence overpowered people's narratives about finding and buying food. In my collaborations with the women I interviewed, we explored what was going on during the times when people experienced hunger. These explorations led me to their most profound and harrowing experiences.

FROM GROCERY SHOPPING TO RAPE

Tinisha, a Black mother of two young girls, was a slight and reserved woman. She had a blue tint in the whites of her eyes. I'd seen that among several women I interviewed. Reading about it later, I learned it can indicate a variety of health problems, including anemia, which means low iron, and can be a sign of poor nutritional intake that causes exhaustion and many other resulting struggles.

She had little furniture in the house, so we sat on the floor of her ground-level apartment in North Philadelphia. Tinisha seemed tense as we participated in small talk and worked through the consent process. As we were easing up beyond the stiffness of strangers and warmed to each other, I started the audio recorder. This was my opening question: "Can you please describe what it's like to get groceries and food for you and your family?"

Tinisha: Well, I don't like going to the store. And I don't go to the Pathmark near here.

Me: Why not?

Tinisha: Because a few years ago, I had a really bad experience.

Me: Are you willing to explain what happened?

Tinisha: I didn't have anyone to take care of my kids—they were toddlers—
but I needed groceries, and it's really hard to travel to the store and shop
with them.
So I left them home alone,
and took the bus to the Pathmark grocery store to get food.
After I shopped, I needed a ride home with all my groceries.
I was in a hurry to get back to my kids.
In the parking lot, there was a guy waiting outside his white van.
He said, "Need a hack?"[1]

I got into the front seat with my groceries.

Well, there were about five or six guys hiding
waiting in the back of that van.
And
they drove me to an abandoned parking lot,
bound up my arms and legs, and gang raped me.

After that they actually drove me home
and put my groceries on the front steps.
They threatened to kill me if I told the cops.
And reminded me
they knew where I lived.

It took me a long time before I could eat food
because [what they did to me] was all I could think about.
I think I went down to about ninety-eight pounds or something.
Looked like I was dying.
Because every time I go to eat
or swallow something,
I just thought about what they did.

Tinisha's experience was the most horrifying of this study. But it was not an outlier. What she and so many others described was an undeniable pattern of violence and abuse mixed in with the everyday experience of getting groceries, cooking, and eating food.

Most women I spoke with described some form of violence intermixed with everyday matters. Here are some examples. One woman's husband locked her inside their house for several years. She was not allowed to grocery shop for food because he hoarded all their money and never allowed her to leave. Another was repeatedly raped by a former boyfriend, affecting her ability to make money for food and rent. Celeste, who clearly described the mechanics of hunger in the previous chapter, was raped at age nine by her grandfather, who began his sadism by penetrating her with a sausage. Bringing diapers for their baby, Celeste's ex-boyfriend and the baby's father would demand sex in return. Desperate for diapers, she explained she felt she had no other choice. Another woman had to take part in violent self-defense such as throwing lye on an attacker (because she was always being threatened in her home by acquaintances and friends of friends). Women described self-harm through self-cutting or attempted suicide. One woman's method? Intentionally starving herself. This grandmother noted how she became so weak and delirious with intentional malnutrition that she had to be pried off the sofa and taken to the hospital in an ambulance.

The majority of the women I met in 2002 in the food pantries talked about experiencing deep depression or sadness. This included emotional and physical responses to experiences of rape by family members, child abuse, and cops kicking down the doors of their homes in the middle of the night. Violence seemed to blanket almost every story about food and health.[2]

I was not looking for these harrowing experiences, nor did I know that I should be looking for them. I was simply asking open-ended questions about where people go for food, what happens when there isn't enough money for food, or what are some ways in which a person gets money for food. Through follow-up questions and requests for clarifying examples as well as listening deeply, women responded with descriptions of violence and gender-based terror.

After I did those individual interviews, I analyzed the data, came up with general themes, and checked back with the original interviewees in focus groups. As I became more adept with more interviews and learned what might be going on underneath, I began to ask follow-up questions about experiences such as social isolation and depression. Many insisted that isolation and interpersonal violence were everyday occurrences that got in the way of making enough money for food, paying for utilities, and carrying out activities of daily living.

Or the depression was simply crushing. Deadening.

STRUGGLES DEEPER STILL

In the previous chapter, I introduced you to Juleen, who described feelings of hunger and not being able to lay with herself "comfortable." To introduce you to the initial concept of hunger and food insecurity as well as demonstrate how it dovetails with existing science, I extracted her depiction of hunger from the other parts of the story. But hunger was a side effect of what she considered the more important story.

Underneath her descriptions of trying to make ends meet through work, food stamps, and odd jobs was a struggle deeper still.

When my son was a year old,
his father stuck a needle [heroin] in my arm.
I remember his friends saying to him,
"She's pretty! Why did you ever stick a needle in her arm?"
And he said,
"Because I really believe that's the only way I can keep her."
He started mainlining me with heroine
and then we would mix it with cocaine.
Speedballing.
So then,
for years,
—yes, years—,
I injected heroin and cocaine into my body.
I got physically sick.
And he went to jail.
He went to jail a lot.

From selling drugs.
So sometimes I had help and he was there,
and a lot of times
he wasn't.

Soon after her husband went to prison for the first time, her husband's father visited her house to see how she and her infant son were doing. While her son was asleep upstairs in the crib and at the end of their visit, her father-in-law hugged her to say goodbye. Then he grabbed her, pushed her down onto the living room sofa, and raped her. She had a small build. Her father-in-law was a large, heavy, and strong man. Though she tried mightily, she couldn't fight him off. After that happened, she felt she could tell no one.

Imagine if I told my husband
(who was in jail)
what had happened?
What could he do?

That was the first time that I got raped.
I couldn't eat and I couldn't sleep.
That feeling was like I went to sleep,
and I woke up,
and all my feelings were gone.
I couldn't laugh.
I couldn't cry.
I couldn't smile.
I was like looking at myself in a dream.
That's the only way I can explain.
I just had no emotions.

Juleen described her rational and quite common response to overwhelming violence. She shut down all emotions and feeling.

Though I did not know it at the time, this rape and emotional muffling was a key that Juleen provided to help me, my team, and now hopefully you to understand the depths we need to go to recognize the roots of hunger.

HUNGER IN BODY AND MIND

One of the well-known insights among those of us who do ethnographic and qualitative work is that what bothers an interviewer, or rather, what stumps them, is likely a key that opens a door to deeper understanding, insight, and revelation.

In addition to violence, there were several perplexing issues emerging from the interviews. First, there were multiple reports of intentionally not eating, even when a person had money and food. Second, at least one-third of the people interviewed reported gastric problems and loss of appetite. Third, there was persistent, ever-present deep emotional pain. If pain and sadness were not explicitly described, there was an eerie numbness. I could feel that there was a connection, but I did not understand how emotional sadness, deadening, or emotional crisis was related to the experience of hunger.

When I had an opportunity to run the first focus group as a follow-up to a series of individual interviews, I spoke of my puzzlement. I said, "I can understand that people don't have enough money to eat and can experience hunger. But what does it mean when a person has food or money, and they *still* won't eat? They cannot eat or refuse to eat. What is this experience?"

A focus group member said, "What you're talking about is a kind of hunger of the mind."

The room erupted as the women jumped to agree and offer similar insights. After several minutes of discussion with people talking over each other, the group came to a consensus.

There are two kinds of hunger. Hunger of the body is when you feel physically weak or have a pain in your stomach and feel faint. Or as Juleen puts it, "You can't lay with yourself comfortable." These painful physical sensations include lack of concentration or low work capacity. Hunger of the mind is different. As a focus group member summarized, "It is when you are suffering so much that your mind and emotions make you stop eating."

People sat back and nodded, sensing a group-generated revelation. We were all basking in it, and I glanced (as I always do) at the tape recorder to ensure it was running. There was a rich lull of acceptance and connection.

"That happened to me," said Noreen, a Black woman who was remaining mostly quiet until she burst through the silence. "I've done that. I was so depressed. I thought that by not eating, I could kill myself faster."

When I had previously interviewed her at her home, Noreen seemed to have it all together despite her ripped T-shirt and the sofa shredded at the edges. She was kind and worldly. She appeared relaxed despite the hardships she described. Perhaps that was because her house was on a tree-lined street and a gentle breeze was blowing through the window screens. The shade and breeze were a vivid memory, I understand now, because she had been talking about how she had been raped several times by people she knew. We both were looking through the screens at the trees and trying to tune our bodies on the breeze coming through. It was as if the hyperfocus on the breeze could keep us upright throughout the interview.

Back to the focus group. After Noreen's outburst, there was a lengthy, visceral discussion where several women jumped from their chairs with excitement. They talked through tears and gave each other reprimands for not speaking out sooner. It was clear they were becoming fast friends, and the experience ended in a group hug with promises to get together again. That emotional magic goes far beyond words, but I'll do my best to summarize the insight that Noreen sparked in the group.

According to Noreen, the pairing of deep depression and social isolation sears itself into the body, mind, heart, and emotions. The impact is so great that it can make a person try to harm themselves in an effort to feel, divert, or stem the pain. Additionally, the depression, stress, and loneliness were related to lack of money for food.

How Noreen portrayed this stress and emotional pain was echoed in many individual interviews that came before the focus group as well as multiple interviews that came afterward. Not only did these interviews help that explanation to emerge, but these themes are reflective of the qualitative and quantitative work of others where depression and hunger co-occur and intermingle. Anthropologist Nancy Scheper-Hughes explained how the women she interviewed in Bahia, Brazil, would describe *nervos* (nerves) and *fome* (hunger) as if they were one and the same.[3] When attempting to understand the difference, she found that nervos were depicted as a response to an anxious sensation of having little money and feeling weak. The weakness was often characterized as being related to not having enough food because of scarce resources, whereas hunger was an experience in the belly that was caused by lack of food (fome). Scheper-Hughes typified nervos and fome as everyday forms of violence caused by systematic and chaotic experiences ranging from violence within their own households to police brutality, petty administrators, and doctors who prescribed antidepressants instead of helping families get money for food. She linked these to systematic discrimination and abuse by the state that ignored the suffering of women and children in the slums. Violence interwoven into examples of hunger and emotional anguish in Brazil is similar to the experiences of hunger depicted by Juleen, Celeste, Tinisha, Noreen, and the majority of women I interviewed.

LISTENING WITH THE GUT

Vera walked up to the porch outside her front door a few minutes after I did—just in time for our midday interview. She was a tall and lanky Black woman in a deep-purple blazer and black pants. As she climbed the steps, she was sluggish and perhaps a little high. As she opened the door for the two of us, she sighed, pulled off her wig, and apologized for being tired because she had been up all night. As I followed her into her living room, Vera said she had been with a friend, and when she spends time with him, he gives her money she needs. It occurred to me she did sex work.

As she slumped down into a chair at her dining room table, she gestured for me to sit across from her. The table was neatly appointed with a white lace tablecloth covered by a glass top. As she leaned her head up against her hand, she answered my simple questions about groceries, food, and health.

"I can't really eat," she said, closing her eyes and drifting her head beyond her hand.

Pause. She opened her eyes again,

"Well, I can't eat most things 'cuz my stomach's always hurting . . ."

I asked, "What does that mean you can't eat most things?"

Without responding, she laid her head down on her arm, which was stretched out over the glass and tablecloth, and fell asleep.

I waited.

And waited.

"Oh my god!" I thought to myself, "is this interview that boring?"

I waited some more.

I could feel her exhaustion. With the tape recorder running, I just sat there.

Though Vera was clearly asleep, I continued to sit quietly, slumping over my elbows with my chin resting on my hands, staring at the flowery patterns in the tablecloth.

I began to enjoy the silence.

Bluo——ooah.

Rr——rrr——ggggg, ggggroooop.

Pluah!

Her stomach gurgled. Loud, low, and deep. The sound woke her up.

She gave me a questioning look, as if I had said something.

We both laughed.

"How long was I asleep?"

"Not sure. Maybe about ten minutes? Maybe you should get something to eat, eh?" I looked at the bag of apples, orange juice, and other groceries I had brought for her.

"Yeah. Give me a sec."

She took the bags into her kitchen. After some time, she came back with a big glass of orange juice. I pressed record again on the tape recorder, and we continued.

"Just orange juice?"

"Yeah, 'cuz I can't really eat."

"Why is that?"

"As I said, I always have indigestion. I don't eat food."

"Do you have some kind of illness?"

"The doctor said maybe it's irritable bowel syndrome."

Around that time in the early 2000s, many health professionals were learning more about emerging research on depression, mental illness, and gut bacteria. Depression, attention deficit hyperactivity syndrome, and autism were linked to the quality of food people eat and how it is digested.

Scientists refer to the site of intestines as the microbiome, an entire ecosystem inhabited by trillions of bacteria, over five hundred million nerve cells, and a hundred million neurons comprised of twenty different types. These neurons connect through the vagus nerve to the brain. Hence the gut has an influence over the limbic and emotional systems, breathing, inflammation, heart rate and blood pressure, and recognizing fear. The gut acts as an "adviser" to the brain. Or as some scientists say, our guts are our second brain.[4]

Indigestion, irritable bowel syndrome, and an inability to eat are linked to anxiety and depression.[5] But the directionality is unclear. It is plausible that a lack of money for food diminishes the quality of the food one eats, and the sporadic eating that is dependent on times when there is money for food can confuse or alter one's metabolism.[6] This creates more gas and the buildup of problematic bacteria that create an imbalance. Or one may eat outdated or unsafe foods that exacerbate problems in the gut. In turn, this affects mood and creates anxiety, worry, depression, and other mental illness. Additionally, as it was described to me by several women in this initial study, it is possible to suppress feelings of hunger altogether. In other words, we can mentally override our body's hunger signals.

But where does this leave Tinisha? The reason she could not eat was because eating triggered memories of what those men did to her in the back of the van. She had to drink beer to ease the way for the food. The assault by a group of men and its effects are a clear override of her microbiome.

The ongoing interviews surfaced more questions. Beyond lack of food, what is hunger? Is it a lack of money? Lack of a good job? Being homeless and lacking heat? Oppression and abuse by men? Drug addiction? Inadequate support systems? Exploitation on the job? Abusive families? Discrimination? Depression, despair, indigestion, and irritable bowels?

From the silence at her dining room table, Vera's stomach and intestines provided the insight. Hunger of the body (physical) and hunger of the mind (emotional) belong to each other. These are the two sides, the front and back, the top and bottom, of a singular condition. Body or mind, there is no distinction. Hunger or violence, no distinction.

Juleen's painting started to make sense. Her painting shows green and orange stress pathways throughout the body. In the experience of violent stress, that stress becomes hunger.

WITNESSES TO HUNGER

I testified for the first time in front of Congress in 2006 to defend the SNAP program by explaining how important the program is for the health and well-being of America's families. But I was deeply disappointed in the feeling I received after testifying. That is, I could tell that the legislators could not relate to nor feel the brilliance and wisdom of the women I met. They could not relate to the experience of surviving exploitation and roughing the streets of North Philadelphia to get to the variety of food pantries so they could feed themselves and their kids.

I wanted to find some way to get legislators into the kitchens and living rooms where I had been. In awe of the women I met, it felt necessary to get congresspeople to feel their pain and directly listen to their insights. I wanted them to meet people like Juleen, Celeste, Noreen, Tinisha, and Vera. I searched for ways to help policymakers walk in their sneakers. If they could do this, I thought, then surely they would pass better policies that would lift minimum wage, increase SNAP benefits, and increase supports for families with disabilities. I thought that the way to do that would be either to invite them to Philadelphia and plan a whole series of in-person meetings, or literally place them there through some experiential mechanism. Knowing that the first option was impossible, I went for photos, videos, and audio recordings in ways that could stop legislators in their tracks by witnessing the truth. I wanted them to feel what the women talked about from their gut.

The hell of the women's experiences with not having enough money for food had entered my guts. The women were working on me, especially Juleen.

Juleen's painting had another teaching: "**INVOLVE ME, I REMEMBER, I UNDERSTAND.**"

Taking Juleen's instructions, I launched a new program in 2008 called Witnesses to Hunger. We called it Witnesses for short. It is a program meant to ensure that people who know the experience of poverty in their bodies can and should participate in as well as lead the national dialogue on hunger.

Witnesses is a participatory action program, which means that everyone involved in the study is supported in taking action to address the challenges they identify. We also integrated a methodology called *photovoice*. This is a process by which people use cameras to take photographs of images they deem important to the topics at hand, and then use those photos and the stories behind them to speak to key community leaders to influence policy change. In 1992, Caroline Wang, then at the University of Michigan, and Mary Ann Burris, program officer for Women's Health at the Ford Foundation in Beijing, China, built the concept of photovoice based on the influences of documentary photography, empowerment, and feminist theory.[7] In photovoice methodology, the participants themselves define what is important and what should be addressed, not the researchers. The participants identify their own research questions and solutions; they take control over the inquiry through their photographs and narratives.

So much research on food insecurity and hunger silences the very people who have the most to say. One of the ways this is done is by relying only on quantitative data, where every person is reduced to a number. Their experiences are numbered and then all those numbers are crunched through statistical computations to make assumptions and tell a single-number story the length of a ratio of odds. I was interested in hunger and nutrition policy. But having learned from the quantitative research of Children's HealthWatch and my previous qualitative studies that exposure to violence, lack of community resources, inadequate public assistance supports, and gender-based violence were important to the equation, I was open to what the members of Witnesses would bring forth. Witnesses was meant to provide a platform for the true experts to speak on their own behalf in their own words, and from physically being in social settings where hunger is discussed. It was also an opportunity to create a sense of belonging and group membership. This is why the people of Witnesses were "members" of a collective. Members of Witnesses began to feel a sense of group, to belong to each other.[8]

Witnesses became a platform to express what members considered most important to communicate to policymakers about their experiences with trying to break out of poverty and be healthy. We invited legislative officials and community leaders to exhibits to see their photos and discuss them directly with members. The exhibits and other activities, such as meeting with elected officials and agency administrators, were meant to establish social connections between the people who make major policy and economic decisions and those who are directly impacted by such decisions.

I had read the work of Irvin Staub, a psychologist who sought to understand the roots of state-supported violence, especially mass killings, genocide, and terrorism. Staub's research demonstrated that people who have the capacity to kill, crush, and maim others do not see the people they harm as part of the human family. To prevent this violence, he says, people should have strong and friendly social bonds between each other.[9] I envisioned that this might be possible between legislators and people like Juleen, Celeste, and Tinisha. What was needed, I thought, was a platform for meaningful social bonds to get created.

This, too, is why I'm directly writing to you, dear reader. So that you and I might have a bond, and so that I can facilitate a bond between you and the people I have come to know and love, many of whom appear here in this book in your hands.

What a gift for both of us.

THINGS LOOK GOOD ON THE OUTSIDE

From the ongoing Children's HealthWatch study, we had developed an outreach database. The people we interviewed provided their addresses if they wanted information about public assistance, jobs, or child development. We sent a flyer to parents we interviewed that stated, "You are invited to join Witnesses to Hunger. This is a research study. You have all the experience you need. Free digital camera (value $200). Fifty dollars per interview."

When I get a formal-looking letter in the mail that is not a bill, I immediately throw it away without thinking. Trying to avoid this fate for the recruitment flyers, I hand addressed the envelopes. I drew flowers on each envelope and stuck on a colorful LOVE stamp with a pink and red heart that was popular in 2008. As I pushed 150 envelopes into the blue mailbox at my local post office, I muttered a small prayer: "Please open me, please say yes."

The following week, my phone was constantly ringing. People wanted to join Witnesses.

Once people agreed to meet, I would make a time for a graduate student or staff assistant to join me on a home interview. We went in pairs most of the time. Nadea, a public health master's student, and Judy, fresh out of college, took turns going with me to people's homes for the interviews. Not everyone had homes, or sometimes they chose to do the interviews at our offices, the local library, or just sitting in my car in a parking lot in their neighborhood. We asked members to respond to a survey similar to Children's HealthWatch and explained how to use the Canon Powershot digital camera, which was theirs to keep.

We said, "Consider this camera as your friend. Use it as your voice to teach the public and policymakers about what's important to you and express your ideas for change." Then over the course of a few weeks, one of us would call to see how things were going with the camera. After two to three weeks, we would return to their house, or a location they preferred, and download the digital photos. We then audio recorded our interview based on their photos. Following the original methodology of photovoice, we asked three main questions for each photo: "Why did you take this photo?" "What do you want people to see?" and "What do you want people to do?"

At age nineteen, Maria was one of the first participants. She had brown wavy hair that she sealed close to her head with gel, going to the back of her head to a ponytail that she let poof freely down her back. As a young and curvy mixed-race Latina woman, she speaks English and Spanish, and has an inviting confidence. When she regards you, you feel fully seen and accepted. She's immediately friendly and kind. You just can't help but love her right away. That's how Judy and I felt the moment we met her. We could hardly wait to return to her house for the second time to talk about her photos. We felt as if we were visiting with an old friend.

Things got deep as soon as we downloaded the photos, and she leaned over the top of my laptop to point to the first photograph in the queue.

It was a picture of a kitchen. You have already seen this photo in chapter 1. It was taken by Joanna, but we did not know it at the time.

"Why did you take this photo?" I asked.

Maria responded, "Well. I didn't take this photo. I gave my camera to a friend, and I asked her to take it. It's a picture of her kitchen."

"What did you want people to see?" I followed up.

Maria explained:

I wanted to show that
just because the house might look nice on the outside,
doesn't mean that there isn't trouble on the inside.
So that's why I felt as though I should get her to take those pictures,
because you never know what goes on behind closed doors.
So I thought,
some people need to know exactly how we're living
—being single moms,
being that we're on our own—
and we don't have that many opportunities.
When situations like that happen,
that something in the house breaks, or
you know, it gets in bad condition,
or maybe you bought the house in bad condition and
just being that you're a single mom, you have limited income.
And it's really hard to try to get everything fixed.

Being in a situation like that, your kids can stay hungry.

I guess it depends on the mom and how far she will go for her children.
I felt as though it was really important to show something like that.
Because, like I said,
just because you see people with happy faces doesn't mean anything,
and you can go to welfare and show them things like that
—and a lot of people don't because they're afraid, you know—
that they're gonna call DHS,
And their kids are gonna be taken away from them.

At our first exhibit months later, this photo remained anonymous. Maria took credit for it by having us include the photo's title "My Neighbor's Kitchen." Its next appearance was in Washington, DC, at the formal exhibit in the rotunda of the Russell Senate Office Building in 2009.

Maria showed us a series of photos of her and Joanna's houses. She showed us pictures of a flooded basement, mold on a ceiling, rusted pipes, and doors falling off their hinges. This photo series brought us to a discussion of how Maria herself had lived without heat for the winter, and her kids were constantly sick and hospitalized because of it.

The story is long. Here is the short version.

Some days Maria's mother never got out of bed because she suffered bouts of severe depression. During her childhood and teenage years, Maria's father spent ten years in jail. Maria was going to school to try to get a nursing assistant degree. The father of Maria's kids took care of the children when she went to school. After she came home from school in the afternoon, he would go to work. The previous fall, Maria's mother got help from someone to call the gas company to request they turn off the gas. Maria is unclear why her mother did this. But she thinks it is because her mother was trying to force Maria, her boyfriend, and her kids out of the house. But Maria had no money for a rental deposit, nor to pay rent. Maria's kids were always getting sick due to the lack of heat. Then Maria found out that it was her brother's girlfriend who helped her mother turn off the gas. Maria confronted her brother's girlfriend, and the two of them got into a loud argument that wended its way outside.

Maria's boyfriend and her brother heard the two women and joined. Things heated up. Maria explained to me how both men are tall and large. So she backed away from between them. Maria's boyfriend, angry at how Maria's brother was talking to Maria, hit her brother so hard that he broke his jaw. Maria's brother pressed charges, and Maria's boyfriend was sent to jail for aggravated assault. Then Maria had to drop out of school because there was no one to help take care of the kids and she had no more money coming in because her boyfriend, who had agreed to work to support them, was in prison. She was ashamed and embarrassed to go to the welfare office, and so was trying to find a job by herself.

When her boyfriend was in jail and Maria had quit school to stay home with the kids, she had no money for food. Remember, this is a similar scenario to that of Juleen whose husband was in jail while she was trying to take care of her baby son. To stave off the hunger pangs, Maria explained, she would look at the pizza menus and colorful food advertisements that came to the door. She stared at pictures of pizzas trying to convince herself that she had eaten them and was full.

At the time of our interview, which was several months after this incident, Maria had been assaulted and bruised by her mother. We know because she showed us a photo (that she took with the same camera we gave her) of the bruises and scratches on her shoulder. Additionally, the back door to their kitchen was broken off the hinges, and she was afraid that someone would bust into her house to harm her and her children. She felt threats from both inside her house (from her mother and brother) and people in the neighborhood.

Nadea, Judy, and I interviewed forty-two people that summer, and then two more a few years later in Philadelphia. It was not the same pattern for everyone. But the issues were similar. In some cases, they were far worse.

One mom of twin toddlers described how when she was around seven years old, she was being groomed by her mother to be sexually assaulted by her mother's own brother. Her mother would lock her in the bathroom, give the uncle the key, and then walk out of the house. The uncle used the key to enter the bathroom and sexually assault her on a regular basis for years. Several others talked about terrible, harrowing relationships with their own mothers who refused to believe that their mothers' husband or boyfriends were raping members of Witnesses when they were ages five, six, and seven. They described how, when they were kids, they were afraid to tell their mothers.

Some told, and some did not. In some cases when they told their mothers, their moms would then respond by beating their own children for telling them. In several instances, members of Witnesses described running away from home at ages thirteen, fourteen, or fifteen because they were being repeatedly raped, neglected, or abused, or their own parents kicked them out for becoming pregnant, for how they were behaving, or for their gender expression. Several members did sex work to pay for food and shelter.

Aretha was a young Black woman with a slight frame, huge laugh, and talent for writing songs and poetry. In her first interview with us, Aretha explained that her father, who was a "big-time" drug dealer, was murdered when she was little. She and her mother argued incessantly. Primarily, her mother disapproved of Aretha's bisexuality. According to Aretha, her mother also detested Aretha's behavior of staying out late and being "disrespectful" to her. When they argued, a common refrain her mother used to say to Aretha was, "Why don't you just commit suicide!"

After telling or writing a hard story, Aretha's common refrain was, "I just laugh to keep from cryin'."

RAGE

In the same way I integrated focus groups or talking circles as a part of the research to elicit feedback and insight in my first study in Philadelphia, I integrated them in Witnesses to Hunger to ensure that members identified primary themes, selected photos for the exhibit, and generated ideas for engagement with policymakers, the press, and the public. Members of Witnesses reviewed each other's themes during a series of focus groups, where they shared each other's photos and experiences.

More than food, more than economic hardship, the theme that members of Witnesses talked about the most was safety. They wanted to talk about how they felt unsafe in their relationships, homes, communities, and everyday society. They also felt that the policies and programs such as SNAP (food stamps), Medicaid, and Section 8 housing subsidies seemed to chop up their lives through chaotic and disjointed eligibility criteria along with punitive rules of engagement. They would have to go to different offices to fill out unique paperwork for each program, each of which had different eligibility criteria, and almost always, the caseworkers were mean and judgmental.

Because of these violences, many said they were angry.

Enraged.

Members of Witnesses took photo after photo of people showing their middle finger to the camera. If it wasn't the middle finger, sometimes it was "deuces," sometimes described as peace. When I asked about the photos with middle fingers in one of our focus groups, some of the members explained how their middle finger was a judgment about how they were feeling—how they hated their jobs or their homelives where they were mistreated, or how much they loathed their own neighborhoods. They enjoyed being at our office because it felt peaceful. They could forget about their worries or the gangs of women who would watch for them from their windows, looking for a way to beat them up.

Aretha was one of those women. She was part of a "gang of girls" who would look for "chickens"—that is, "girls who were alone and looked weak." If they spotted someone, they would attack them. She and her friends made up matching tattoos for their left hands using the stylized letters *MHB*: Most Hated Bitches.

In a focus group, Ester, a quiet and friendly Black mother of two, described being attacked by women—most of whom she knew to be other mothers in the neighborhood. One time they broke her windows from the outside by throwing bricks and rocks. In response, she came outside to join a group argument and physical fight. She hated every minute of it, yet felt she had no other option but to fight back, lest the women think she was a chicken.

In a separate focus group, Sarafina, a brilliant and commanding Black woman and mother of two boys, explained that when a person is so badly hurt and keeps their emotions bottled up, it feels good to hurt someone in return. She stood up to use her booming voice and large body to demonstrate herself strangling someone.

She said,

Like right here, this is my own mother.
(*She clasped her hands around the air in front of her.*)
If I could, I'd just choke her and
slam her head against the ground.
I want to kill her!
It would feel so good.

Knowing her story, her enactment of hurting her mother felt justified, as Sarafina had suffered ongoing rape from her father while her mother did little to stop it despite her knowledge of it. Sarafina spent over a year living in a car in order to escape both her parents. According to her, doing so helped her survive and stay safe enough to become a track star in high school.

The further and deeper the focus groups went, the more harrowing the stories, the more we uncovered what was underneath the laughter and behind the doorways.

When I reflected that back to the group, they responded almost in unison: "Violence and trauma should be at the center of the photo exhibit, Mariana."

Within six months of our first interviews with Maria, we mounted the exhibit.

We found a professional exhibitor, who built a video booth with three sets of headphones and a bench to sit on for viewing three videos: "Violence and Trauma," "Anger," and "Imagine." The "Imagine" video was a tribute to the joy of having children, and to the dreams the mothers had for their children. Around the periphery of the videos were exhibit walls showing photos grouped among themes of health, housing, public assistance, education, opportunity, and "breaking the cycle."

"Breaking the cycle" was filled with ideas and glimmers of hope for finding a way out.

SLOWING DOWN

We'll get to breaking the cycle. But I need us to slow down a little to explore the violence and associated trauma. Though a part of me wants to speed past it, I've learned that it is important to slow down, way down, to give time to understand the implications.

After our first exhibit in December 2008, members of Witnesses hosted many exhibits in city halls and statehouses on the East Coast as well as exhibits in the US Senate and US House of Representatives. People who came to the exhibits or read the news stories about them could understand housing, health, public assistance, education, and opportunity. But many had a hard time with the trauma-focused center of the exhibit. Some people asked, What does violence have to do with poverty and hunger? Aretha, Sarafina, Maria, and others tried to explain. In return, we received blank stares or a shift in the direction of questioning. Most people learning about Witnesses just wanted to talk about nutrition. Maybe you, too, want me to move on to the nutrition. To food. To farming. To anything except the violence in the middle.

But it is important to take time to clarify.

The physical, cognitive, social, and emotional consequences of coping with and trying to deal with terror and violence are related to hunger. When a person is attempting to cope with exposure to overwhelming violence throughout their lifetime, it can take a serious toll on one's health, relationships, and school and job performance. If a person has experienced traumatic physical, social, emotional, and moral violence, they may have hypervigilant tendencies and may be quick to anger. This can create conflict in working with managers and coworkers over seemingly small slights and unthreatening yet stressful situations. Alternatively, a person may emotionally, cognitively, or physically shut down on the job, create discord among coworkers, or be unable to show up to work due to a debilitating anxiety attack or stress-induced flare-up of heightened mental states such as agoraphobia. This affects earnings and therefore one's ability to afford enough food.

These trauma responses could also affect how well the police treat you, how social workers talk with you, and how social services providers interact with you and your baby. Members of Witnesses would talk about "stepping out of character" at the welfare office. Or they described how they might yell at their boss or a coworker and, as a result, lose their job. The outcome was a humiliating return to the welfare office. Or they would describe debilitating depression that kept them in bed or in a daze, feeling confused, scattered, or unable to keep it together. Sometimes the adversity and mistreatment would lead to sleeplessness, lack of trust in family and friends, panic attacks, or low self-esteem.

Irritable bowel syndrome, self-harm, suicide attempts, and the other behaviors and experiences of the women I interviewed in the early 2000s along with the stories of the members of Witnesses were not theory. They were real, lived experiences, real emotions and behaviors in living color shared by wonderful, brilliant women with so much potential to do greater things.

I was following the members of Witnesses where they wanted to lead me. They led me down a path where all of my preconceived notions about what I thought was important had to die.

3 KNOWING AND NOT KNOWING

The hunger, the pain, the depression—it always comes back.
It's like a bird nesting in your head.

        —CASSIE, TWENTY-TWO-YEAR-OLD MOTHER OF ONE CHILD

HOW TRAUMA CHANGES MIND, BODY, AND RELATIONSHIPS

Trauma is not only a critical physical insult. It is a *response* to an insult, as I explained in the introduction. Trauma can be a biological, psychological, and emotional response to a severely distressing incident, or a series of chronic or recurring deeply stressful situations such as rape, abuse, shootings, and stabbings. It can also be a physiological and psychological response to emotional neglect, racism, and misogyny. These trauma responses can fragment one's sense of self. Again, violence can cause trauma responses in both the victim and perpetrator. It can cause a trauma response among people who witness the violence too.

Trauma is infectious, as people who hear about trauma or witness its effects can feel a type of empathic engagement with people who experience trauma called *vicarious trauma*. Research shows that up to 25 percent of therapists working with traumatized populations and up to 50 percent of child welfare workers have a high risk of secondary traumatic stress or related conditions of post-traumatic stress syndrome.[1]

Among children, traumatic experiences are sometimes referred to as *toxic stress*, which can be a type of overwhelming stress related to homelessness, hunger, neglect, abuse (sexual, physical, or emotional), or witnessing violence or drug addiction in the home or community.[2] In the world of public health, there is an array of recognized experiences during childhood that are referred to as adverse childhood experiences (ACEs). ACEs can include exposure to physical, emotional, and sexual abuse as well as household adversity such as witnessing violence in the home, having someone in the family who attempted/completed suicide, or having a parent who was sent to prison. These experiences are associated with many major public health problems such as depression, anxiety, cardiovascular disease, diabetes, sexual risk-taking, and early death.[3]

Nadine Burke Harris, the first surgeon general of California and a pediatrician in the San Francisco Bay area, helped bring ACEs to greater awareness and understanding. Through her work as a pediatrician, she began to connect the dots of family trauma and societal trauma and how they affected children, their families, and communities. She explains the science in straightforward terms for how childhood exposure to violence, neglect, abuse, and family strife have a deep and lasting impact on a child's nervous system, organs, and immune function through the stress response. This stress response manifests in what is commonly known as fight, flight, or freeze. These responses, when utilized beyond the original threat or ignited due to ongoing threat, wreak havoc in our bodies and in our society.[4]

Most nutrition and food security researchers ignore this research primarily because they focus on food and nutrition, without regard to people's social contexts. They might be surprised to know that Vincent Felitti, who started the widespread use of the ACEs measure in 1998, learned about the importance of childhood sexual abuse in his clinic to treat obesity, a nutrition-related disease. Felitti found that there was a unique group of people who were initially successful at losing weight through his program but then tended to drop out and gain most of their weight back. On further investigation, when he compared those who regained weight fast to their counterparts who stayed in the program, the people who dropped out were far more likely to report childhood sexual abuse and related traumas. They explained their weight gain was a result of trying to cope with stress and depression, and also a form of protection against perpetrators. Felitti's first study was small, but after he convinced researchers at the Centers for

Disease Control and Kaiser Permanente to consider childhood adversity, they launched a study with over seventeen thousand people, the vast majority of whom were white and middle class. They found that ACEs were linked to every major chronic disease such as diabetes, being overweight, and cardiovascular disease as well as depression, alcoholism, and substance use.[5] Since then, hundreds of studies have corroborated their results among many kinds of people.

I want to point it out again, so you do not skip the message: weight issues, diabetes, and cardiovascular disease are commonly thought of as *diet*-related diseases. But there is more to the story, much of it related to trauma.

Trauma affects health and well-being through physical, emotional, and cognitive responses to extreme danger. Our *physical response* to danger is an automatic, without thought, whole-body reaction to a threat that manifests through numerous neurotransmitters and hormone production reaching every organ system. The brain sends messages to the adrenal glands, which then release adrenaline that speeds up heart, blood pressure, and respiratory rates to increase alertness, vigilance, and strength. The message also goes straight to the groin and hips, thereby stimulating a response to flee, fight, or freeze. Simultaneously, in a terrifying incident, an opioid-like substance called dopamine is released to relieve pain. These are essential to survival in the moment of threat.

But if these biological processes continue beyond the threat, or if they are triggered even without a threat to a person who has previously experienced trauma, they can create major health problems. A lingering affect of trauma is *chronic hyperarousal*, meaning one is always on high alert, despite the level of threat. This is why sometimes people become very agitated over a small perceived threat. *Triggering* is a term that indicates the kind of experience that can be benign and unthreatening but can cause someone who has been previously traumatized to feel threatened. A trigger can be a sound, smell, or phrase, or the way a person looks at you, thus releasing a fight, flight, or freeze response in the body.

Usually, once a person is aware of their triggers—certain smells, words, or sensations—they can learn to recover from them and calibrate their response. If at a young age, however, a child has experienced sexual abuse or chronic abuse and violence, this adversity can have serious consequences over the life course because a child's brain and limbic system are not yet developed in order to modulate arousal. Children without a soothing and trusted adult may, in fact, never gain the skills to be able to soothe themselves.

According to Bruce Perry, an internationally renowned childhood trauma specialist, this heightened unmodulated arousal can have lasting effects on brain and body functions and cause many medical and psychiatric conditions. Trauma can limit immune function and make someone more susceptible to infectious diseases. As well, trauma responses can create toxins in the organs that lead to depression, uncontrolled anger, cardiovascular disease, and poor nervous system function. In response, someone might self-medicate with alcohol, tobacco, and drugs. Such patterns of behavior pass down in the family through behavior and biology.

At the biological level, this transfer across generations is referred to as *epigenetics*, meaning the dynamics of environment and gene interaction. Genes that cause diseases and other health states can turn on and off depending on environmental conditions. In this way, memories, behaviors, illnesses, and reflexes are passed on through our genetic codes across generations. Some describe this as ancestral pain or memories in the body. Research among children of World War II–era Holocaust survivors has shown this biological transfer of trauma responses to be incontrovertible.[6]

But this focus on biological processes in response to an unspecific environment diverts attention away from the truth of the ongoing violence of our social structures and political systems. So I concentrate on behavioral responses to social, economic, and political structures. Focusing solely on biological reasons for children's experiences discounts the influences of history as well as relationships with parents, neighborhoods, communities, and institutions. Trauma is rooted in relationships. Trauma responses are mirrored in our families, community, and society through systems of education, medicine, urban planning, social welfare, religion, charity, philanthropy, government functioning, and research.

Two other common trauma responses that help people survive threats are *appease* and *dissociate*. To appease is to protect oneself by pacifying, placating, or making oneself smaller to appear nonthreatening. This can become standard practice and a way of holding or recoiling one's body. To dissociate is a form of self-protection where one can find ways to disconnect oneself from their emotions and physical sensations when escape is impossible. This dissociative response is literal, not metaphoric. Survivors of childhood sexual abuse have explained that to survive assault, they could leave their bodies and "go elsewhere." Again, this is another practical gift of evolution.

Yet as Staci Haines observes in her book *The Politics of Trauma: Somatics, Healing, and Social Justice*, if this strategy becomes automatic despite the threat not being present, it can have long-term negative effects. Primarily it can "leave us compartmentalized and disconnected." In Haines's words, these trauma reactions are a way to help us "not feel the things we cannot tolerate."[7] As an extension, dissociation can cause us to close off so we have no feelings at all, as it did for Juleen after her father-in-law raped her.

But remember, for her self-portrait, Juleen painted her body with bright orange and green. That stress and terror were still running through her veins. This running in the veins is there regardless of Juleen's expression of emotion. These trauma responses make their way into our bodies and can nest there, affecting our postures, organs, psyches, and relationships. They shape the way we interact with the world around us. They are, however, not limited at all to a single body, singular family, or even singular lineage. As Burke Harris argues, "Trauma is endemic of many communities, it isn't just handed down from parent to child and encoded in the epigenome; it is passed from person to person, becoming embedded in the DNA of the society."[8]

INTERPERSONAL VIOLENCE REFLECTS STRUCTURAL VIOLENCE

As a reminder, racism is an ACE, and is associated with cardiovascular disease, depression, anxiety, and food insecurity.[9] What goes on in our homes, relationships, and bodies reflects what occurs in society. Historical and contemporary housing discrimination and systemic violence such as school funding policies, which ensure that schools in Black and low-income neighborhoods receive far less money per child than schools in white and affluent neighborhoods, create environments that facilitate the emergence of interpersonal, family, and community violence.[10] This phenomenon is what Wendy Ellis and William Dietz call the "Pair of ACEs."[11] The pair is adversity in our society (adverse community experiences) and ACEs in the home. They use an image of a tree of adversity that has branches showing hardships such as homelessness, addiction, abuse, and food insecurity. The tree's roots are in the soil of discrimination, poor housing, community violence, and limitations on opportunities to build careers and wealth.

The tree is a metaphor. But the true site of this intersection of ACEs and societal violence is in the body. In his book *The Body Keeps the Score*, Bessel van de Kolk describes how trauma reorganizes the way the mind manages our perceptions and ability to think. Our reactions in response to severe stress and danger manifest in our physical bodies, cognitive responses, emotional reactions, social relationships, and behaviors. Trauma fragments our thinking. It makes it difficult to stay healthy, have positive social relationships, perform well in school and on the job, earn enough money, and even absorb our food.[12] When we recognize that US policy and societal disfunction also generate adverse community environments, we can see how our bodies keep the score.

By extension, the fabric of our society also keeps the score. Examples are police brutality, punitive educational environments, and soul-sucking public assistance programs. These systems make their way into our bodies, or *soma*, in a continuous feedback loop. Our soma is a way of understanding that our bodies are the medium through which we interact with our environments along with the ways we carry our history, relationships, and sense of well-being. Hence trauma is a somatic experience.[13]

I hope you can understand, now, what I had a hard time understanding at the outset of my research in Philadelphia. Violence travels from a societal level to the family one; it penetrates our soma, where we may want to harm ourselves (suicide or self-cutting), or even starve ourselves or harm others. To see violence at the root of hunger helps us remember that when a person admits to not having enough money for food, it is a sure sign that they have been deeply disrespected by our society and people around them. That disrespect can take the form of neglect, abuse, and indifference. They feel it in their bodies because it penetrates the bloodstream, immune system, and gut.

After blank stares from colleagues in response to my growing attention to the relationship between violence and food insecurity, I felt compelled to start categorizing and counting. I thought data in numeric form rather than as narrative based on qualitative interviews would convince scientists and policymakers to take these connections seriously. Perhaps the numbers could be sharp enough to penetrate scientific numbness to the pain of hunger.

To quantify and characterize different forms of violence, we set up a second round to the original study of Witnesses to Hunger in Philadelphia. We returned to as many members of Witnesses as possible and asked about exposure to ACEs (something we could measure on a scale of zero to ten) and other forms of violence. We quantified levels of violence in relation to food security and depressive symptoms. Here are the results: most members of Witnesses reporting *very low food security* also reported extreme forms of violence such as rape and assault with a gun or knife. In contrast, those who reported food security rarely reported such violence.[14]

A few published studies, however, do not establish hard truths in the world of scientific research. Additionally, we only had forty-four people in the Philadelphia Witnesses group. This is a small sample. For a scientific finding to be broadly accepted, results have to be proven many times in different types of settings with large sample sizes.

One of the strengths of Witnesses was our shared relationships with each other. We heard about when a family's SNAP benefits were cut or their Medicaid benefits had fallen through. We learned about their family relationships. We celebrated their birthdays, weddings, and pregnancies. We helped them access abortions and attended funerals with them. We were there when they reached out with suicidal intent, when their kids got a 100 percent on a test, when their Section 8 housing was approved, or when they were evicted. We were learning depth, breadth, and nuance as members of Witnesses navigated social services, education, health care, and other systems as well as how they interacted with loan sharks, neighborhood drug dealers, and nasty caseworkers at the county assistance offices. But to scientists who clung to their big sample sizes and "normal distributions" in large datasets collected by big research corporations, the fact that we had meaningful and heartfelt relationships with members of Witnesses was considered a weakness. There is a common understanding that as a person responds to a survey, they may be trying to please, hide from, or tell the researcher what they think they're expecting to find. This is referred to as *responder bias*.

Trying to reduce that bias, we set up two other studies.

Knowing it would take years to accumulate a large enough sample, we added ACEs to the existing Children's Healthwatch survey as an add-on at the end of the standard battery of questions. But because everything is reduced to numbers without context, the content still stays on the surface. Most of the time, the *why* and social context of an experience cannot be captured by the numbers. To ensure we had contextual understanding, we set up another simultaneous study where we recruited thirty-one new people who reported household food insecurity in the Children's Healthwatch survey. In this smaller sample, we carried out qualitative and quantitative interviews (mixed methods) to learn more about child hunger. As you will recall from earlier chapters, parents will do almost anything to protect their children from these experiences, and if they cannot protect their children, they are unlikely to reveal this unless there is some modicum of trust and patience.

CHILD HUNGER

Part of the household food security measure assesses the depth of hardship among the children from the primary caregiver's point of view. If a family with at least one child agreed only to a few questions indicating their child's nutrition suffered, the reference child was considered "food secure" (even if they were in a household where the caregiver themselves had indicated the household was "low food secure"—remember that is *food insecure*). If the parent said "yes" to more than three of the child-focused questions about their children's nutrition, including to a question indicating their "child did not eat for a whole day," then the child was considered to be "low food secure" (that is, *food insecure* at the child level). Reports at this level are rare for many of the reasons I outlined in chapter 2: parents protect their kids as much as they can, and also fear that if they admit they cannot feed their child, the people from protective services will take away their children. The national rate of child "low food security" in 2020 was at 6.8 percent; "very low food security" was at 0.8 percent.[15]

To set up the mixed-method study, we recruited from families unknown to us. If a parent, foster parent, or grandparent indicated their household was *food insecure*, our team looked more closely to ensure we recruited an equivalent number of people who reported child hunger versus those who were similar *without* reports of child hunger. We kept our recruiters and the follow-up interviewers separated. This ensured that, when we interviewed a parent, the in-home interviewers did not know whether the family reported their child was food insecure or not. We only knew they were eligible for the study because, at the household level, they were "food insecure." This would reduce any tendency to ask leading questions as well as reduce interviewer bias.

We asked about memorable life events across the life span. Those who study trauma and human development understand that when violence occurs at certain developmental stages (such as before age five, before language is fully formed and the brain is still growing and trimming neurons, or during early adolescence, a time of even more body and brain growth along with changing self-awareness), it can have devastating consequences that last a lifetime. If trauma occurs at other times when a person is not in a major complex stage of development, the violent experiences may not be as devastating.

We sought to understand how the type of violence and timing of it might be related to the severity of food insecurity. To do this, we interviewed people in their homes or at other locations they chose. We asked about life-long trajectories, and the relationships between food insecurity and violence among previous generations. Holding our clipboards with paper surveys, we asked questions from the formalized measures on food security, housing security, and public assistance participation, knowing these were repeat questions that the interviewee had already answered in the hospital emergency room. This repetition helped corroborate the original interview and situate their economic experiences during the survey. Then we asked questions from the ACEs questionnaire. See appendix 2.

At the survey's end, we put down the clipboard and pressed record on the audio equipment to do a semistructured interview around a time line of lived experience. With a pencil on a blank piece of paper we drew out a time line that started at age zero and went up to their current age with a notch for every five years. We began asking questions based on their responses to the food security and ACEs measure. For instance, if they previously said "yes" to the emotional neglect question:

> Did you often or very often feel that . . . no one in your family loved you or thought you were important or special? Or your family didn't look out for each other, feel close to each other, or support each other?

During the audio-recorded session, we would then ask,

> In the survey, you answered "yes" to the question about whether people made you feel as if you were not loved. How old were you when you felt this, and what was going on in the household during that time?

As we listened, we would draw lines with key words in the areas across their life span. This was a mutual process between us (the interviewers) and the interviewee. These jointly created diagrams indicate who the story was about, the other people who were involved, from which generation in the family, and at which time points they occurred across the life span. We would learn about the caregiver's childhood and could then draw lines to their mother, grandparents, or their own children as they described their experiences with each generation.

People brought us to their earliest memories.

As we filled out the diagrams, listened to the interviews, and transcribed the audio files, it became clear that hunger was not a single incident that had occurred in the previous twelve months as the survey questions indicate. Rather, it was like a chronic, menacing experience that had repercussions rippling back in time across generations and went far beyond nutritional deprivation.[16]

Jocelyn, a twenty-year-old Black woman and mother of one child who reported household "very low food security," "child low food security," and an ACE score of nine (very high), described her early experiences of hunger as being related to her childhood when her parents struggled with drug addiction:[17]

> We barely had food.
> I don't even know if food stamps existed.
> They probably did, but my mom worked at [a fast-food restaurant]
> —not to mention the fact that she was still getting high. . . .
> We was always hungry.
> The only time I've learned really eating
> is when my dad used to drop us off at this lady's house down the street.
> She used to babysit us.
> That's the only time we really ate. . . .
> In the morning we had to have oatmeal.
> Before she sent us back with our dad,
> we used to have cut-up hot dogs and baked beans.
> So that's the only time we would eat.

Jocelyn was a slight woman. As she talked, she sat at the edge of the sofa in her dark living room. She never took off her down coat and hugged her arms around herself as she talked. Hunger was compounded by other types of challenges.

> When I was really little,
> I was so hungry
> That I couldn't help myself
> I actually ate the giant paint chips
> off all the windowsills.
> (*She swept her arm across her and above her head in front of her to portray herself as a young child reaching to the windowsills and pulling off the paint chips.*)
> It was so bad I got lead poisoning.

She related lead poisoning to her struggles in school, where she often got into fights, including one involving the police. Out of frustration over this incident at her school, her mother sent her to live with Jocelyn's father and stepmother. In her words, this is how it went:

When I was around ten, she got tired of me.
She kept saying I was, like, bad;
something was wrong with me.
So she just finally sent me to my dad
and while I was there, I got a stepbrother.
Basically, it started with him touching me
and then he had sex with me.
I was still ten,
but it was like two months into me being there.
A month later I just, like, said that I didn't want to do nothing.
I just started acting out.
But besides [my stepbrother], that was the best part of my life,
like besides everything else,
I got taken care of.
I always had something to eat.

Afraid to tell her father and stepmother about being raped by her stepbrother, Jocelyn chose to go back to her mother's house, where she continued to be abused and neglected. She eventually told her mother and a counselor that she had been raped and was hospitalized for suicidal depression at age thirteen.

Similar devastating patterns occurred among almost half the participants who reported *very low food security* and indicated their child was experiencing *child food insecurity*, whereas those who reported low food security, the milder form, had significantly less reports of rape and abuse.

Cassie, a self-assured and highly reflective Black woman who reported food insecurity for her young child, explained how depression, pain, and hunger nested in her head. I asked her to share how violence and hunger are related. She reprimanded me:

You cannot ask a person,
"Why are you *stressing*?"
You cannot ask a person,
"Why is there so much *violence* here?"
You cannot ask a person,

"Why are you *hungry*?"
All three go together. . . .

I could be here like,
"Okay, I'm *stressing* because I don't have no *food*,
and it's *violent* because I'm fighting my husband
because we need money."

Shrugging her shoulders, Cassie insisted that hunger, stress, and violence are equivalent.

IF A PERSON SAYS YOU'RE NOTHING, YOU'RE NOTHING

Remi was a twenty-two-year-old Black woman who gave slow and thoughtful responses while her toddler sat on her lap and patted her chest, neck, and hair. As she answered the household food security questions, my heart sank. Her "yes" without qualifications to each question indicated her household was *very low food secure*, and, by the end, that her child was *low food secure*. Her ACE score was nine.

She became more animated as we drew out her time line. She explained she was abandoned by her mother at age five. She was raped at age six by members of the family with whom she was left, and was emotionally and physically abused by her grandmother, who took her in at age seven. Remi attempted suicide during childhood. She suffered from depression and had difficulty managing her anger. At age fifteen, her grandmother kicked her out of the house. Ever since, she was living "house to house." Despite these experiences, she was able to graduate from high school at age twenty-one. "But," she said, "it's a struggle to find work." She described the effects of childhood experiences on her self-esteem and job prospects, and therefore on her ability to provide for her daughter:

If a person always says you're nothing;
you're nothing.
Then for a while, I used to think I'm not anything.
So maybe that's how I don't have a job,

because I'm thinking I'm nothing.
I'm not ever going to have a job.
I'm "not going to be shit,"
like my grandma said.
So it's like maybe that's a part of how I don't have a job
or I couldn't finish school. . . .
Because I can't find a job, I cannot feed my daughter.
How am I supposed to?
I cannot buy her what she needs.

Remi explained how abuse affected her behavior in school, getting her into trouble as well as making school and life circumstances throughout adolescence extremely challenging. She traced her difficulties in school and inability to find or maintain a job to being mistreated.

[My grandmother would] be like,
    "You can't come downstairs to eat.
    You only can eat when I say so."
And I'd be, like,
"Grandma, I'm hungry."
    "You heard what I said!"
And then she'll try beating me or she'll throw something at me.
Or when I had gotten of age,
she put me out.
You don't put anybody that you love out.
I've been on my own since I was fifteen
—sleeping outside,
not knowing if I'm going to wake up tomorrow,
not knowing anything.

Remi portrayed a life of chronic homelessness coupled with hunger and deep depression.

In most interviews, we learned about four generations: the mother's child, the mom we interviewed, the mom's parent(s), and her grandparent(s). This generational piece is important as most research on food insecurity only provides evidence of household food insecurity as if it occurred in the last thirty days or one year. We found that current reports of food insecurity stemmed from previous hardship during the caregivers' childhood, suggesting hardship of their parents. Their hardship was rooted in their childhoods and thus *their parents*, and so on.[18] To see a graphic depiction, see appendix 3.

This depth of experience that people described helps us begin to see that violence across the generations is associated also with historical, social, and political experiences, which I address in following chapters.

VIOLENCE IN NUMBERS

Simultaneous to analyzing transcripts of interviews on child hunger two to three hours long, four to six days a week, the center's Philadelphia Children's HealthWatch team interviewed people in the emergency room. The setting at St. Christopher's Hospital is context rich, but the survey contains "yes" or "no" questions, or "how many," "how much," or "when." So people's responses are reduced to a number: zero, one, or two. Often, full stories emerge; sometimes there are tears—mom's tears or the baby's—but the survey instrument is a tight mesh sieve, straining out anything quantitative researchers consider extraneous, tears included.

More than two years had passed since we added the ACEs questionnaire to the dry sieve of the Children's HealthWatch survey, and we finally had enough data from 1,255 caregivers. A doctoral student in epidemiology and member of our research team mathematically accounted for whether a person was more likely to be food insecure if they were depressed *and* had high ACEs. If you have read everything in order so far, this should seem like common sense to you. But we performed the statistical tests with the large sample to assess whether the associations were beyond "chance."

We found that mothers reporting depressive symptoms and at least four ACEs were more than twelve times as likely to report *low food security* and almost thirty times as likely to report *very low food security* when compared to those who had no depression and zero ACEs.[19] These results demonstrate that the odds of food insecurity are astronomically high for those reporting depression and high ACEs when compared with people who have low to no ACEs and no depression.

We added another dimension to our statistical inquiry. We asked of the data, Does nutrition assistance from SNAP or WIC make the relationship between depression, food insecurity, and ACEs less severe? We found that *even when families participated in SNAP or WIC*, the strong relationships between childhood adversity and food insecurity persisted.

To repeat, ACEs, depression, and food insecurity are linked. This does not mean that *everyone* who reported *low food security* had high ACEs and depression; it just means they were more likely to report it. It also means that SNAP and WIC benefits do not change the relationships between violence, depression, and food insecurity.

LACK OF LOVE

I glossed over what each specific ACE shows us. My science mind jumped right over a dark hole of pain and sorrow. It is common practice among scientists to dissociate, or bypass context, to make a "scientific" case. Sometimes we feel that if we can prove something by numbers, it will make more sense, be more accepted, and establish credibility. It cuts out complexity.

But reviewing the outcomes of the statistical tests between ACEs and food insecurity was a gut punch.

To slow this down, I show you how each ACE was associated with food security severity.[20] Figure 3.1 shows rates of food security for each ACE reported. Mothers reporting *low food secure* and *very low food secure* show increased percentages for each ACE when compared to mothers who reported they were food secure.

This question captures emotional neglect: "Did you often or very often feel that no one in your family loved you or thought you were important or special?" You will see that 56 percent of the people who reported emotional neglect were *very low food secure*. This is an extremely high prevalence compared to the original Centers for Disease Control and Kaiser study among over seventeen thousand people in which the prevalence rate for emotional neglect was about 15 percent.[21]

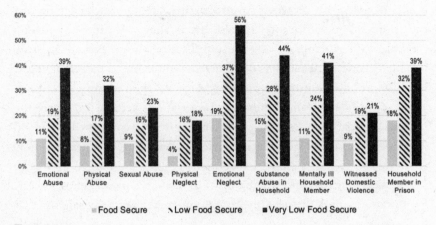

Figure 3.1

Prevalence of ACEs by food security status (n = 1,255). Data drawn from Jing Sun et al., "Childhood Adversity and Adult Reports of Food Insecurity among Households with Children," *American Journal of Preventive Medicine* 50, no. 5 (May 2016): 566, https://doi.org/10.1016/j.amepre.2015.09.024.

Seeing lack of love in numeric form should bring us closer to understanding this: household food insecurity in its severest form is an indication that a person was more likely to be neglected, mistreated, and exposed to severe hardship—lack of love included.

We cannot ignore this lack of love right in the middle of the data.

SEARCH BEYOND THE LIGHT

Our group was not the only one whose research was showing clear lines between violence and food insecurity. In the early 2000s, Cheryl Wehler and colleagues found that mothers who experienced sexual assault in childhood were over four times as likely to report food insecurity than women who had not been assaulted.[22] Others demonstrated that child hunger was more prevalent in households in which mothers reported higher odds of post-traumatic stress syndrome and substance use. Another study found mothers in persistently food insecure homes had significantly higher rates of depression and/or a psychotic spectrum syndrome, or had experienced domestic violence.[23] Yet when most researchers attempt to characterize the causes of food insecurity and its health effects, they rarely, if ever, touch on the published evidence of violence and discrimination. Perhaps it is too painful, chaotic, or demanding of a different type of attention. Perhaps most scientists are unwilling or incapable of understanding or addressing violence.

If scientific results have proven the association over and again, why are most scientific articles describing the overall causes and consequences of food insecurity ignoring solid evidence of violence? Why don't more people know about this relationship and try to act on it?

It takes time for concepts that upset the standard paradigm to emerge. For instance, it took the scientific community many years to recognize that post-traumatic stress syndrome was treatable. It took psychiatrists a long time to understand that child abuse was real, and had devastating health consequences in the immediate and long term.

Sometimes when people talk about scientific confusion, they describe the "streetlight effect" or "drunkard's search." This is a kind of bias that happens when people search for answers in the easier places. To make this plain, I'll use a story. Stories about misguided approaches to solving problems appear in many cultures and traditions; let's take one from Sufism, a mystic tradition of Islam.[24] There is a fool who looks for things only in places where there is light—perhaps under a streetlight—even though the seeker knows what they are seeking can only be found in the dark. Here's a modern-day version:

It's nighttime, you're driving along on the highway, but you're feeling a bit sleepy and need to stretch. You arrive at a rest stop and see a person looking for something. You stop and inquire.

"Do you need some help finding something?"

"Yes!" the person says, "I lost my keys to my car!"

So you help them look around.

You look for a while in silence.

After no success, you say, "Can you describe again where you think you lost them?"

"Yes," they say, pointing toward the forest at the side of the road. "It happened when I was walking my dog over there, in the woods."

"So," you ask, "why are you looking here, if you know the keys are in the woods?"

The person answers, "Well, there's light here and it's all dark over there."

This allegory describes most of us working on food insecurity. We know that societal dysfunction and historical discrimination are key to understanding food insecurity, but many refuse to study or acknowledge these dynamics—because it is dark out there! Not only does darkness make it hard to see, but many of us are afraid of the dark. I gently insist, however, that in the darkness there is wisdom. Let's stay in the darkness as it may hold the key to our ability to evolve.[25]

KNOWING AND NOT KNOWING

Dissociation is an adaptive coping instinct and skill for when one cannot fight or flee violence. One dissociates from overwhelming emotions and bodily sensations. It is a type of fragmentation that can later be associated with amnesia or forgetting. In contemporary terms, it is a form of compartmentalizing or ignoring. This is what Dori Laub and Nanette Auerhahn, psychologists who worked with survivors of the World War II Holocaust, called "knowing and not knowing." It is a type of split in our consciousness. They depict this process of dissociation as a "massive trauma that cannot be grasped because there are neither words nor categories of thought adequate to its representation. Knowledge of trauma is also fiercely defended against, as it poses a momentous threat to psychic integrity."[26]

So to survive, we deceive ourselves.

This dissociative trauma travels from mother to child, to the children's children, and throughout generations. We embody these traumas individually, in our families and communities, and through conditioning from our cultures and social relations.

Resmaa Menakem explains that among entire populations such as descendants of people who were enslaved *and* descendants of enslavers, the specifics of the original traumas are forgotten. Though the original trauma experiences may be forgotten, they still have intergenerational effects. As a result, our trauma responses—that is, our behaviors, beliefs, and practices that are linked to the original traumas—are still present and real today. As I explained in the introduction, traumas can be so deeply somaticized that they escape cognitive attention. As a result, our trauma responses get mistaken for culture.[27]

If trauma is unaddressed, it festers and haunts in ways that are sometimes visible, and at other times not. It becomes a type of amnesia or worse. Larry Ward argues that "we have spent the last five hundred years becoming so skillful in denying our atrocities and projecting the shadows of America's racial karma onto the bodies of nonwhites that we are like people suffering from traumatic brain injuries and amnesia."[28]

In the United States, many communities are operating with this dissociative engine of knowing and not knowing. This means that our historical trauma of genocide, land theft, and hundreds of years of colonization, enslavement, and cultural, social, and bodily destruction comes back to haunt *all* of us in the day-to-day.

4 BREAKING THE CHAIN

What path are you going to take?
How do you walk around and not look depressed?
How do you walk around and not look angry?
And be able to hold your head up?
And you have to realize that your child is growing.
They're going to have to do the same thing.
You got to break the chain somewhere.
You got to break it.

—JEWELL, WITNESSES TO HUNGER

Jewell described her mental health as poor because she had been raped many times. The first time at age five. With conviction, she said, "Just because that happened to me doesn't mean I have to let that define me." The "chain" of the intergenerational transfer of violence, she insisted, can be broken.

Many mothers we spoke to are fierce advocates for themselves and their children. No one wants to be defined by poverty, adversity, violence, or trauma. A person and a people are far greater than their traumas and oppression. They can resist societal forces, break the chain, choose life, plan, generate joy, and imagine a future.

Though some get lucky and have superhuman powers to overcome trauma and systems of oppression against all odds, it is wrong to think that people should be expected to break the chain by themselves. Millions of others are left behind, dragged down, mowed over, kidnapped, or pushed down by US government systems, white terrorists, and everyday people who harness racism in big and small ways, such as calling police for some imagined slight by a Black person, or excluding Black people from particular jobs, neighborhoods, and other public spaces. Instead, we must set the conditions to break the chains so that all people can flourish.

To do this, one must be willing to see what has always been there, but that most people ignore or shove away. This means that as a society, we must deal with our "dissociation" at an individual, family, organizational, community, and systems level that is due to physical, social, political, and economic violence.

THE HEALING POWER OF SOLIDARITY

Faith and Carla are long-standing members of Witnesses. I met them both when they were in their late twenties. Faith is currently a mother of three children, though when we met, she had two young boys. Carla is the mother of four children, although when we first met, she had three. Both are kind and soulful Black women who have experienced a lot of hardship. Faith has an occasional edge of hostility while Carla is always kind and full of humor. Both suffer no fools.

It was morning, and I had met up with a few staff members of a US legislator to visit Carla at her house in North Philadelphia in spring 2010. On the same afternoon, the staff of Witnesses were going to host a meeting with these staff members and many members of Witnesses and prepare themes and photos for a traveling exhibit across the state. It was a big moment for Witnesses and signified a new chapter in our collective work.

My cell phone buzzed with a text. It was Faith.

"Mariana, I'm getting ready to kill myself."

I immediately stepped away from the conversation and called her.

"What's wrong, Faith?"

"I just can't do this anymore. I just can't."

"Please don't, Faith!" I said, heart pounding. "You are wonderful and beautiful and I love you. Also, we are counting on you to come to our meeting this afternoon. We're all looking forward to seeing you."

"I can't, Mariana. I just want it to end."

My professional training kicked in. I asked tentatively, "Do you have a plan?"

"Yes, I got the gun right here, and I'm going do it here in the basement laundry room because it has a drain, so the mess won't be too bad."

"Oh my god, Faith. Please don't."

"No, Mariana. I don't fucking matter. No one gives a fuck. I don't give a fuck."

I saw the conversation between the visitors and Carla was in a pause. Knowing I was out of my depth, I asked Carla to talk to Faith. Carla took the phone from me, manifesting her warm, kind spirit, and said, "Come on to the meeting, honey, and let's talk about it."

During their conversation, I texted other members of Witnesses asking them to reach out to Faith to encourage her to come to the afternoon meeting. They texted to encourage her too, expressing their care and support.

None of us were sure if she would show up to the afternoon meeting.

When she did, the whole group stood up to embrace her.

But she did not really feel like being in the meeting. Things were dire. She agreed she ought to be hospitalized.

While Carla sat with Faith in my office and held her hand, I worked the phones with the emergency room across the street. After a time, she willingly walked across the street with Witnesses staff.

After being hospitalized for a week and taking medications to stabilize, Faith said she felt better. Years later, Faith still has her ups and downs. But she is generally well. She had another baby who is full of laughter and growing up loving the world.

What saved Faith was her ability to reach out for help. Second, the group reached out to her to express their care and remind Faith of her belonging. Several members of Witnesses had started to form strong social bonds they referred to as a sisterhood. When people came to meetings to talk about their photos or plan an exhibit, they would talk about how they felt seen, heard, and recognized.

When members of Witnesses spoke in public about why they joined the program, they explained it was mostly because they wanted the camera. They also wanted the money for doing the interviews.[1] Once they started coming together in the groups to design the exhibit, they noted, everything deepened, and the social bonds kept them together and provided each other support for many years.

THOUGHT FOR OTHERS

When Audrey and I met, she was the mother of six children. She was one of the few white non-Latina women who joined Witnesses. Her intermittent partner and father of several of her kids was an undocumented immigrant from Mexico. Her life was difficult and complicated. She was a loving mother when she could be and stayed in touch with one family that was fostering several of her children. Due to her hardscrabble life, the Department of Human Services later removed all of her children.

She contributed several photos, and joined our meetings when she could. Audrey explained what Witnesses meant to her:

> I needed food.
> I needed money to take care of my children.
> But in the process of it, I became more involved,
> and I felt like I was fighting for something
> that could help not just myself and my kids
> but a lot of other people as well.
>
> Becoming a part of something helps people grow.
> It helps them change their outlook on life
> and helps people find different things that make them happy in life.
> And it helped me grow.
>
> Before, I was not thinking of anybody but myself and my family.
> But now I have an acquired thought for others,
> and how I can be a voice for them in any way I can.

Other members explained, "It felt good to get my story out." As they did that, they felt connected with others, or simply felt relieved and more at ease.

Witnesses meetings always had ebullient energy as we collaborated to prepare for conferences, hearings, and exhibits in both the US House of

Representatives and US Senate, ran our own events, hosted a national conference, and grew the program to other cities and invited in new members. We hosted panel discussions on housing, child development, and violence to accompany the exhibits in city halls and state households in Boston, New Haven (CT), Camden (NJ), Harrisburg (PA), Scranton (PA), Johnstown (PA), Philadelphia, Washington (DC), and Providence. While we celebrated these public appearances, the most joyful experiences were in our social gatherings.

Jack Saul, founder of the International Trauma Studies Program, explains that trauma is more than one person can bear. We need others to acknowledge and provide support for us to bear the trauma. According to Saul, the most important work of addressing trauma is to do it with other people. You need the support of a peer group so you are not "confined in your own story." Peer group support is known to help reduce anxiety. It helps heal loneliness and improves mental health.[2]

Some have declared social isolation and loneliness to be America's number one public health problem.[3] Those who experience social isolation are more likely to report household food insecurity.[4] Lonely people are also more likely to report depression, have complications from heart disease, diabetes, and being overweight, and die an early death. According to a 2020 study, among all generations from baby boomers to Gen Z, 47 percent of people in the United States feel alone, left out, and lacking in meaningful connection with others.[5] Some scientists declare that this isolation is causing "deaths of despair" such as suicide and opioid overdose.[6] Even the surgeon general has released a report on the public health crisis of loneliness and the need to establish social connection and community.[7]

A FUTURE THROUGH HEALING

How can we start to heal?

Express solidarity. Join a group. Love one another across racialized and class lines, ethnicities, and nationalities.[8]

Knowing the group was eager to see her, Faith remembered she belonged. Being part of the group helped save her life. This gave her purpose and interrupted her intended suicide. But the group experience alone was not enough to help her heal. In her crisis state, she needed professional and intensive clinical care. There are multiple forms of care that help to prevent people in Faith's situation from escalating. This includes peer group experiences integrated with trauma-informed practice.

Trauma-informed care used in clinical settings or *trauma-informed practice* used in other organizational settings are umbrella terms encompassing practices and values that recognize how interpersonal violence and victimization impact health, well-being, and social relationships. They are organizational and treatment practices rooted in establishing safety, recovery, and resilience. Healing and recovery are primary trauma-informed care and practice goals. Such approaches are meant to build individual agency and collective efficacy. Collective efficacy is a group's shared belief in its joint capability to organize and execute a course of action for group achievement. Individual agency is a person's ability to take charge of their life; specifically, to have conscious choice and control over their own actions.[9] Since fear and helplessness are legacies of victimization, empowerment in safe environments with healthy relationships can go a long way to help people find and harness their dignity, purpose, and power. Trauma-informed practices focus on healing, empowerment, self-control, and resilience, rather than mandating specific behaviors, demanding compliance, or implementing outright punishment (such as kicking a person out of the program or isolating them from the group).

When organizations are set up to serve or help people, they are also implicated in how interpersonal relationships play out between professional and client as well as among staff themselves. So how an organization is set up and structured in the day-to-day becomes important. An example of an organization's ability to potentially retraumatize someone is when a welfare office (where people apply for public assistance) is set up in such a way as to resemble the waiting room of a prison.

Put yourself in the winter boots of a woman who needs to apply for SNAP. When you enter the Philadelphia county assistance office, there is a security officer with a gun waiting for you to sign in at the door. Though most assistance programs serve families with young children, there are no child-size chairs and toys, nor decorations on the wall or plants. There are, however, pitiful black-and-white photocopied flyers taped to the walls with signs that shout

NO FOOD

NO TALKING

NO CELL PHONE USE

The guard could trigger emotions or sensations of previous encounters with police. In West Philadelphia, one office has all the chairs facing the back wall of the waiting room, away from the cubicles where the social workers and frontline staff sit with their computers. A person sits there for hours at a time, facing backward, and waits for their number to be called—like they are a criminal to be controlled and called to account.

A more severe example of traumatizing organizational practices is what happens in residential treatment facilities where they may use restraints on a child who might be having a mental health crisis. This can push a child into reexperiencing the same symptoms and signs of duress as a traumatic episode that caused them to be placed in the residential treatment facility in the first place.

Sandy Bloom, an internationally renowned psychiatrist based in Philadelphia, created the Sanctuary Model, a trauma-informed approach that extends beyond the boundaries of interpersonal relationships to create patterns of working that organizations can adopt to ensure that people and processes within organizations themselves do not retraumatize clients and their staff.[10] Based on years of research and experience with colleagues in mental health care services, Bloom and her team developed everyday practices to ensure that people who struggle with exposure to violence and adversity (including staff) have opportunities for healing. Organizations can transform their processes and spaces into healing environments, and adopt organizational practices that support growth, care, and community. The model and ethos of trauma-informed practice helps clinicians, social workers, and frontline staff to redirect their thinking from concepts such as *What's wrong with you?* and change it to *What happened to you?*

But this is not enough. Shawn Ginwright, a professor of education at San Francisco State University who works with African American youths, implores us to look beyond the pain. Let's move, he says, from *What happened to you?* to *What's right with you?*[11] This places healing at the center. Echoing these sentiments of the people in Ginwright's youth programs, members of Witnesses insist, "I cannot let what happened to me define me." Ginwright adds that sometimes, trauma-informed work stays at the individual or group level while ignoring the historical, social, and political context. Ongoing political consciousness-raising and community engagement are fundamental to the healing. It opens space for people to explore and stake a claim to their desired place in the world.

LEARNING TO CREATE SANCTUARY

In the early years of Witnesses, I was experiencing trauma-related symptoms such as hypervigilance, lack of sleep, depression, and misplaced anger. I became more demanding of people's time as well as more impatient with staff, students, and colleagues. I was trying to urgently implement processes that could not tolerate flexibility. The staff, too, were starting to feel the strain on our ability to communicate well and support each other to stay healthy.

As I became more familiar with trauma theory, I could see that not only was I experiencing secondary trauma but our organizational practices such as intolerance for ambiguity, lack of flexibility, misplaced urgency, and hyper-arousal over the slightest organizational hiccup were also starting to mirror the same trauma-related behaviors I was learning about from members of Witnesses. We needed a reset and deeper training to help us stay healthy. We sought training in the Sanctuary Model, which consisted of a five-day residential experience along with ongoing coaching and group assessment.

Since we received our original trainings in 2010, the center's staff, members of Witnesses, and members of our new Building Wealth and Health Network program have been using healing-centered techniques and strategies to create opportunities for healing and resilience. Any new staff member who joins the center also participates in healing-centered trainings. The practice tools have become so much a part of our everyday grounding that

I couldn't help but use "community meeting," one of the Sanctuary Model tools, to start this book. This tool supports opportunities for all to be seen, recognized, heard, and valued, to acknowledge our emotions, ground ourselves in a goal, and ensure we can ask for and provide support for each other.

THE BUILDING WEALTH AND HEALTH NETWORK

Continuing the work with Witnesses, and building on the immense power of solidarity with a group and utilizing the sanctuary ethos, our team launched a new program in 2014. Tired of the same old dominant stories about scarcity and poverty, we wanted to focus energy on the positives of human potential. We concentrated on creating abundance and well-being. This is why we called it the Building Wealth and Health Network (or for short, the Network).

We developed the Network as a program to treat and prevent isolation, depression, and food insecurity for people with high ACEs. The Network is a healing-centered peer support program that integrates financial education and matched savings accounts. Inspired by the resilience of Faith, Audrey, Carla, and so many others, the goal is to support parents of young children who are participating in Temporary Assistance for Needy Families (TANF) to get help from peers to improve their health and build wealth. This would, of course, aid the participants in being able to pay for food *and* heal from trauma by helping them develop social relationships and build collective efficacy that could mitigate depression while building financial security.

Members of the Network help each other face their experiences with trauma and deep poverty, and learn financial strategies to save money and build wealth. The Network members share their needs and struggles with their peers, who are eager to help and offer understanding. Members of the group almost always offer up resources and assist with problem-solving; consequently, the role of the coaches recedes to the background. The coaches merely hold the space, and on occasion, provide one-on-one support after class. In addition to basic and creative financial strategies and emotional wellness, the curriculum includes political education, which is a way of deepening everyone's understanding of how structural racism and capitalism work and influence our lives. Everyone gets an opportunity to open a savings account, and we match their savings.

We started out the program as a randomized controlled trial, a type of research study set up to compare health and well-being among different groups of people randomly assigned to each group. Random assignment ensures there is no obvious "selection bias" that facilitates people's self-selection into a particular group. This way you know you are comparing groups that are relatively equal or have the same variability of people within each group. When people signed up for the Network, they agreed to be randomly selected to one of the three groups. Two were "intervention groups," and one was the "control group." A control group receives nothing extra, just the currently accepted standard of care, which in this case was TANF programming as supplied by the state. In doing so, one can find out if the proposed program or "treatment" works—that is, if one sees a positive difference in the intervention groups in comparison to the control.

Peer support healing circles coupled with financial empowerment education and matched savings was the full intervention. We compared it with the partial intervention, which consisted of financial education and matched savings but lacked the trauma-informed approach to building community and healing. Finally, we compared these two groups to the control group, which received regular TANF assistance with no peer support healing circle, no financial education programming, and no matches for savings.

We followed each group over fifteen months, and each person anonymously filled out surveys every three months on the computer with audio prompts. Each participant answered a series of questions related to health, well-being, financial skills, and practices. We added our old standards: ACEs, depression, and household food insecurity. The results showed that the group that had the greatest reductions in depression, food insecurity, and housing insecurity was the group that had both financial empowerment training and the trauma-informed group approach. Not only did it help in terms of caregivers' health and financial well-being, but the trauma-informed financial empowerment approach helped protect their children from developmental risk. So the Network had a two-generation impact.[12] After the original research study was completed and showed positive results, we were able to expand, adapt, and continue the program, which is still ongoing. We have worked with over three thousand people, and the program has extended outside Philadelphia to Atlantic City, NJ, and rural areas in central Pennsylvania.

Here are the results: participation in the Network reduced depression, improved rates of employment, and increased family savings.[13] We offered no medication, no direct therapy, and no job search support.

Here's the clincher: the Network reduced the odds of household food insecurity by 65 percent. There was no food involved.[14]

How did we improve mental health without pills? How did we reduce food insecurity without food?

At the outset of this book, I explained that solving hunger is not achieved through food alone. It has much to do with power and control. Through the Network, we sought to ensure that people built power and control over their own futures, had a sense of emotional sovereignty, and could make choices and take advantage of opportunities to heal from trauma. We also nurtured strong social connections where people were committed to helping each other. This is what the members of the Building Wealth and Health Network were able and eager to do. When they started our program, most members had no bank accounts, and many reported low to moderate social isolation as well as high rates of household food insecurity. By the end, the majority of people without bank accounts had opened one and started saving. Thanks to being in a community of support and solidarity, they felt happier, more capable, and healthier. Food security was significantly reduced, especially for those who had high ACEs.[15]

Currently, the Network curriculum adapts to each group that comes through the program. As an outcome of these adaptations after the original randomized controlled trial, the program has become more attuned with issues of structural racism, antiracism, and political education coupled with community advocacy. But the core of the Network has always remained. That is, we sustain the common language from the Sanctuary Model called "SELF," which stands for safety, emotions, loss, and future (or freedom).[16] This SELF-based language convention helps people take the space they need to work through their challenges. Here are questions that can help people do so:

Safety: What are issues that threaten our physical, moral, emotional, or social safety?

Emotions: What are the emotions involved? How can we effectively manage them?

Loss: What have we lost or are likely to lose? What will we have to give up in order to change?

Future: Where do we want to end up? How can we create a future where we can flourish? What can we do to generate freedom?

There is so much more to the program, but this simple framework indicates how the complexity of trauma across the life course is held in a space of wonderment, care, and solidarity.

The Network helps people deal with trauma symptoms at the individual and small-group level. It also promotes resilience against community trauma. For instance, we help people learn about and resist predatory lending, heal from toxic family relations, handle conflict on the job, and testify when called on to improve policies and social services. We help people face their emotional challenges head-on and learn about ways to improve their relationships, have a greater sense of self-worth, and find tools for self and community care. We help people strategize about saving and spending that promotes household food security along with greater access to safe, affordable housing.

The Network is a success as well as inspiration.

It does little, however, to address the epic proportions of collective and historical trauma in the United States. Even if a person can work through their personal traumas, the systems in place around them—schools, health care systems, social services, and employers—can still exacerbate trauma while regenerating inequality, racism, and sexism.

To take action at collective and historical levels, we need to reconsider everything.

II RECONSIDER EVERYTHING

In part I, I described how exposure to violence and trauma are at the root of hunger. Trauma responses to rape, racism, abuse, and neglect affect one's biology through the organs and bloodstream, one's social functioning, behaviors, and cognitive capabilities. Trauma responses are wide-ranging and include heightened awareness, dissociation, shutting down emotions, and harboring feelings of deep shame, anxiety, and depression. These can all affect one's ability to earn money, function well on the job, and have positive and lasting relationships. I also explained healing-centered approaches that consider ways to prevent the reenactment or triggering of trauma responses as well as create group-oriented experiences that support positive social, emotional, and financial functioning. These processes can help to heal deep-seated sadness, lack of self-worth, and isolation, and simultaneously reduce food insecurity. I noted, too, that this internalized response to trauma is a fractal of societal, political, and economic violence in everyday life in the United States.

In this segment, I demonstrate how most people in the United States are attempting to function in what many would call a *trauma-organized society*, meaning a society that is reenacting over and again our traumatic experiences that haunt us. The unresolved trauma creates disordered attachments, social isolation, separation from each other, and separation from our own emotions and bodies. Trauma in someone's family is a reflection of our societal, collective trauma.[1]

This kind of collective trauma is easy to understand if one traces the ways in which it is transferred. In trauma theory, one of the concepts that helps to explain this is *parallel process*. Parallel process is how two or more systems—consisting of groups or organizations—have significant relationships with one another, and tend to develop similar affects, cognition, and behaviors rooted in trauma. So the systems that are meant to support people with minimal income start to reflect the same processes as the original violences that created poverty. Organizations, if recognized as living entities comprised of many people, become trauma-organized systems. That is, they are systems organized around reenacting violence.[2] Organizations are also sites of multiple unfair inequities and reproduce them in ways that are especially harmful to women of color.[3] Many social services organizations and government agencies are part of systems that seek to regulate, control, and separate people from each other. Additionally, it seems as if the very energy that keeps the systems going is the pleasure that workers, their bosses, and agency administrators experience as a result of being on top and keeping others down.

What's ahead are a few examples. In chapter 5, I demonstrate how public assistance programs separate people from each other and have the effect of severing the most profound ties in the family, especially those between parent and child. The parent-child bond during early childhood is a fundamentally important time of development and growth, and any interruptions or severing of that attachment is a trauma.[4] Through such severing, the government and corporations can ease in and exploit people, keep families down through low wages, imprisonment or hunger, and blunt efforts to improve programs. Chapter 6 takes you into people's personal experiences to show how TANF is one of the worst offenders of the separation technique, and utilizes racist and sexist practices to achieve it. Chapter 7 takes on the sacred cow of SNAP. I say sacred cow because many people view SNAP as the number one way to address hunger in the country. But just because it's the largest and most effective does not mean it will end hunger. In fact, SNAP is used as a tool by food corporations and the American Beverage Association to profit off of people in poverty, and the US government makes this possible. Finally, I take on the beloved charity practices that so many of us engage in thinking we are doing our part to address hunger. Beware, the path that the emergency food system leads us down is the wrong way. It leads us toward a cute candy house. Yes, it's sweet on the outside, but inside is a murky energy meant to fool everyone into believing we are helping, when all we are doing is supporting the very processes that make people hungry in the first place.

What's ahead may shatter your ideas of the helping social systems. It may cause you to question everything. This is a healthy practice; it is a good time to adopt a beginner's mind.

5 PUBLIC ASSISTANCE AS DIVIDE AND CONQUER

DON'T FEED ADULTS

After two and a half years of operating the EAT Café from 2016 to 2019, having tried various forms of advertising, changing the menu, changing the prices, and improving customer service, the café was unable to bring in enough money to breakeven. Our dreams of transforming it into a worker-owned cooperative were fading.

People tried to console us. They said, "Most new restaurants close within the first six months" and "many don't make it past a year." One reason we had difficulty getting stable was that we funded the café through foundation grants that had to be administered through the university. No university should administer a restaurant, as human resources takes three months to hire people and almost a year to let someone go. That timing does not work in a restaurant. Another reason was that, unlike most restaurants, we paid well. Full-time staff received health benefits. Restaurant industry partners in Philadelphia warned us that we would never be financially viable if we paid living wages and provided sick leave.[1]

We also refused to pay tipped minimum wage ($2.25 per hour), nor did the café accept tips. Tipped wages come straight out of slavery. Immediately after Emancipation in 1865, many southern states passed "Black codes" as a continuation of enslavement. If approached and questioned by white people, Black people had to prove they were working or they would be criminal-ized, thrown in prison, and then forced to work for free. Oftentimes, Black adults were forced by white employers to sign yearly contracts. Many white employers refused to pay people who had been enslaved. To survive, Black people in the South had to find the most immediate job available—even if it did not pay—to stay out of prison. Employers frequently would not pay a Black person outright, and Black people had to depend on customer tips, an unpredictable paltry wage. Still today, corporations use tipped wages to continue the plunder that spans hundreds of years. The US government allows it. But at the EAT Café, we meant to break that chain.

After a time, the original philanthropic groups that helped us get started became tired of footing the bill. So they stopped funding us. We tried to get other foundations interested in the café, but they did not want to fund it because it wasn't "new" enough, since we had already been open for over a year. Even though we were still innovating and working on the model, it looked as if we were already successful.[2] Finally, well-paying customers stopped paying well or stopped coming altogether. We became desperate and highly dependent on a generous anonymous donor. We knew that funding model was not sustainable. All along, those who enjoyed eating for free or low cost really loved the EAT Café and invited more friends. It was not empty; we were just broke. We hated to close the EAT Café in April 2019. We also didn't want to leave the café empty while we figured out a way to pivot.

Enter summer meals for schoolchildren.

The Summer Food Service Program is a federally funded, state-administered effort that reimburses organizations who serve free meals and snacks to children and teens in low-income areas when school is not in session. It launched in 1968 as an extension of the school breakfast and lunch program. While families can rely on breakfast and lunch for their children during the school year, they struggle during summer—the season when food insecurity spikes because the kids are not receiving meals at school. In consideration of this trend, the federal government provides per child reimbursement for breakfast and/or lunch at community centers, schools, bible camps, and other locales with educational or enrichment activities.

Until 2020, only 16 percent of the children who were eligible received summer meals. Even then, they did not receive them every day nor every summer week. Summer meals distribution depends on transportation, availability and summer programming, the will of political leaders and nonprofits, and the weather. Some communities get meals delivered on school buses or by vans that become a pop-up café. Programs in other areas such as in the Anacostia neighborhood of Washington, DC, could reach up to 40 percent of children because they served meals at the public libraries.

In addition to the requirement to provide enrichment activities, these were the rules.

First, all children must be counted every day. They must be counted on paper (not by computer). Otherwise, the "provider" (those who make and deliver the food) will not receive reimbursement for supplying that child's meal. For organizations with scarce funding, that can make a big difference.

Second, all meals must be eaten on-site. No one can take home leftovers unless it is the end of the meal service time.

Finally, adults are not allowed to eat.

Let that sink in.

Nutritional Development Services is a primary sponsor in Philadelphia. It was delighted to help us set up a summer meals site at the EAT Café. We were so grateful, as it provided our team with free and enthusiastic training. But then its staff sent us flyers that we were required to place around the EAT Café as a condition of serving meals. The flyers consisted of "dos" and "don'ts." Here is one of the "don'ts," typed verbatim:

DON'T FEED ADULTS

Don't allow adults to take items from the Share

Table. This includes parents, volunteers, or any adults

from the community.

I'm sure this reminds you of similar signs in zoos and parks: "DON'T FEED DUCKS. DON'T FEED ELEPHANTS." During summer meals service, adults are clearly not part of the human family, and thus not worthy of a meal.

I emailed the coordinator at Nutritional Development Services suggesting the language was hostile. They explained in their return email that "strong language was needed" because the agency hears many reports of adults "hovering for a meal or leftovers." I disagreed with the tactic and implored the staff to change their signs. After a few weeks, they changed their poster to say, "DON'T LET THESE ITEMS GO TO WASTE."

Every summer, those in the antihunger community hear about programs that refuse to let parents share meals or take food home. According to New Mexico's chief of the Family Nutrition Bureau, Reagan Smetak, who provided testimony to the National Commission on Hunger in 2014, parents would eat parts of their child's on-site summer meal, and grandparents who accompanied their children would roll food up in a napkin and put it into their purses for later. In 2018, a Colorado summer meal program made a posting in its locale. The sign stated, "Adults MAY NOT eat off of a Child's Plate!" The flyer had a cartoon of people around a table, with three children at the table and two adults standing around. The adults each had a circle around their head with a red line drawn diagonally through it, as if to cross them out.[3]

While nonprofits and Indigenous communities scramble to find ways to feed kids in the summer (and some even try to be creative in finding ways to make sure adults don't eat), the USDA already had a proven solution to summer hunger. In 2014, it began a pilot in three communities by providing thirty dollars per child per summer month to families receiving SNAP or WIC. The program, called Summer Electronic Benefits Transfer (EBT), provided money *directly* to caregivers. Evaluations of the program found that compared to those who did not receive Summer EBT, those who did reported a 30 percent reduction in very low food security.[4] That is a profoundly positive impact.

The USDA, researchers, and advocates have known about the success of this program for years. This became important during the COVID-19 pandemic. With children suddenly out of school, thousands of people provided community meal sites as well as grab-and-go breakfasts and lunches, and the USDA finally made it possible for each state to create Pandemic EBT. This is the same concept as Summer EBT, where families whose children were receiving free/reduced meals during the school year could get extra funds on their EBT card to supplement their children's meals at home when schools were closed. Most states opted to continue providing Pandemic EBT through the summer the following two years. Additionally, the USDA offered a federal waiver to reduce reporting requirements for each child to support physical distancing.

Do you wonder why, before the pandemic, children in the United States had no opportunity to access Summer EBT, even though the federal government had evidence it reduced food insecurity by 30 percent?

Intentional design.

Herein lies the problem not solely with summer meals but instead with all public assistance programs devised in the United States. They create a false division between parent and child; they separate the wealthy from the people who are low income, the "deserving" from the "undeserving." Summer meals are for kids only, even if their parents are close by and hungry. Separating the wealthy from people with little money means that eligibility criteria is dependent on proving one's income is below a certain percentage of the federal poverty line. This last part of eligibility is ostensibly to ensure that people who make a certain amount of money over a low threshold, or, in some states, if they had a felony, should not get support that they may desperately need. This ongoing separation of groups and families from each other becomes a way to target destitution.

THE UNSETTLING TRUTH

As they try to understand the policy-related dynamics of public assistance, most researchers adhere to what is on paper or in public assistance participation data. But how public assistance programs are experienced by families and in people's bodies is the most important wisdom there is when it comes to understanding public assistance. What I describe ahead is grounded in the lived experience of people I have interviewed. Here you find out that public assistance programs can help somewhat. Yet they can simultaneously cause harm.

I was not always clear on how public assistance programs can cause harm. The epidemiology and economics research on these programs shows that they can help people be healthier, stay safe, or stabilize otherwise turbulent lives. We also saw the benefits of SNAP reflected in our Children's HealthWatch research. Children's HealthWatch was built on the idea that if there were strong public assistance programs, children's health would be better. The evidence for the positive benefits is irrefutable.[5] For instance, we found that SNAP was associated with reduced child hospitalization. WIC was associated with reductions in stress, preterm birth, and underweight issues. Housing subsidies protected children from being underweight, and energy assistance promoted children's development.

When I started Witnesses to Hunger and invited members to use their photos as their voice to advocate on their own behalf, they asked me for examples of how I advocated on poverty.

I explained, "I say things like 'Food stamps are good medicine, but the dosage is not enough.' I say, 'We need to protect SNAP.'"

Some members responded with revulsion.

No, Mariana.
That's terrible!
I don't want to be on food stamps for the rest of my life.
I want to get *off* food stamps
forever.
I want *out*
of the system.

Shirley is a tall and fashionable Black woman who loved going to hear live jazz with friends. In addition to taking many photos of her smiley children whom she adored and of nature scenes—bushes, rabbits, trees, rainbows over the nearby row homes, and ominous clouds during thunderstorms— she took one of the most iconic photos of the exhibit. It's one she wanted to highlight despite it being devoid of children and nature; it was a photo of a simple chain with a backdrop of drywall.

I took this picture of a chain
to show you that
welfare is like a chain.
It's meant to keep you down.

She was not alone. Consider the insights from Jewell. When she and I talked about how she experienced Medicaid benefits, she described it this way:

Medicaid will cover my health benefits only so much.
It's like they give you just enough,
just enough to hang yourself.

If I had not listened to members of Witnesses and absorbed their points of view, I might still be trying to advocate for public assistance programs without thought, care, or nuance.

As with everything I learned from members of Witnesses, the truth is unsettling.

IT'S NOT A NET, IT'S A CHAIN

Some people refer to public assistance—which includes many programs such as housing assistance, energy assistance, SNAP, Medicaid, and TANF—as the *safety net*. But this term is inadequate; it is not woven together like a net that catches people as they fall toward deprivation. One staff member from my team prefers to call it the *safety floor* because when you are in that system, you are close to rock bottom; there is nothing safe about it. It is inadequate at best. At worst, it is a basement floor that leaks sewage, equipped with chains to imprison women and children.

To participate in most public assistance programs, one needs to demonstrate "need" or eligibility. This is mostly achieved through proving a person has a low enough income in comparison to the criterion of the *federal poverty line*. This is a level of income that indicates whether a person is eligible for support. It is based solely on the supposed cost of food, income, and family size. The poverty line is calculated from an outdated back-of-the-napkin measure based on the cost of food from the 1960s. At that time, the average family spent one-third of its income on food. But over the years, the cost of transportation, housing, and childcare became much more important as both parents entered the workforce. These days, food is a much smaller share of family budgets compared to fifty years ago. Yet the federal government refuses to change its multiplier to match the times.

Rather than multiplying the cost of food by 3 to get the federal poverty level, the multiplier should be 7.8.[6]

Consider that in 2022, the federal poverty level for a family of two was $17,420. Multiplying the cost of food by 7.8 would calculate the federal poverty level to $45,292 if the federal government based its calculations on reality. Millions more people would be eligible to receive support, and food insecurity would be considerably lower because more people would get necessary assistance. But the US government, stuck deep in the past, insists on using the inaccurate calculation that undermines people and keeps them impoverished.

Food is a single basic need among many competing needs. One single cost is not fully relevant, nor is it adequate to calculate a family's cost of living, which should be based on local housing costs along with a combination of multiple basic needs including a cell phone and ample time for rest. Administrators know the federal poverty measure is too low, so they established a variety of thresholds for program eligibility. To be eligible for SNAP, the federal threshold is 130 percent of the federal poverty line (but states can raise the threshold); for WIC, it is 185 percent of the poverty line. Unlike SNAP and WIC, which acknowledge and support families whose incomes are higher than the federal poverty line, eligibility for TANF demands that they must have income that is *less* than half the amount of the federal poverty line. This punishing eligibility rule has not changed since 1996.

According to Shirley, once you get TANF "benefits," you regret it the same day. County assistance office caseworkers will put you through the wringer when you go to an office to apply for public assistance. In his book *Street Level Bureaucracy*, Michael Lipksy describes how frontline caseworkers often take matters into their own hands to discern whether a person is eligible for assistance. They are frontline arbiters of stigma against people with low incomes. Overworked at their jobs, they also bring in their own philosophies of what constitutes appropriate behavior.[7]

Interactions at the county assistance offices are described as stressful and humiliating. They are an assault on people's time too. Many participants have complained that caseworkers are incompetent and mean. Wanda, a participant in the 2002 study, explained her encounter:

When I was reapplying for food stamps,
I remember how I was made to feel.
Because of my working schedule
I would have to take off for the day or try to get out early;
which, of course, wasn't good work wise.
I just felt demeaned. Because, yes,
I turned in my pay stubs regularly.
But they would lose my paperwork!
They'd make me go back to the office again and again.

According to many, caseworkers act as if it is their own money they are giving out. At other times, they ask penetrating questions with unbridled judgments. Remember Joanna from chapter 1? She does not mince words.

The county assistance office is ridiculous.
Crowded.
Slow.
By the time you get seen, they've got an attitude,
and they're taking it out on you.
Or they are asking so many ridiculous questions.
One lady asked me how I was making it work with no income.
I told her,
"I pick up pennies.
I do things.
What the fuck do you want to know?
How many little squares of toilet paper I use to wipe my butt?!"

Public assistance program participants are required to provide documentation justifying how they use benefits and demonstrating their efforts to find work. Collecting and presenting that evidence can be a barrier, forcing some people off the programs that were helping them in the first place.

Pennsylvania caregivers that use TANF assistance to purchase a weekly public transportation pass must prove they did so by providing a paper photocopy of a paper receipt. If they do not have access to a photocopy machine, they must go to a copy store and pay for the photocopy. That receipt must be personally brought to the office or sent by fax to a county assistance office staff person. This fax, too, costs money. It is not clear if the person at the county assistance office meant to document and maintain evidence of the receipt ever finds it or enters the receipt into the data systems. In response, people hoard their receipts deep in their purses as if they are gold because they know they will be called on to prove the fax was sent, the purchase was made, the place was visited, and pennies were spent.

To receive TANF benefits in Pennsylvania, most parents must prove they are looking for work by documenting every hour of their search. They are required to submit a form that describes with whom they spoke, the number they called, and the outcome. That record must then be scanned and entered into a database by a county assistance staff person every week. If a person does not do this—or if there is an error by the staff person—the state may, yet again, send them a bill in ALL CAPITAL LETTERS saying they owe the state money. They will then take those dollars out of the next month's grant. Or the caregiver might get their TANF benefits cut off, potentially leaving them and their kids hungry, unable to pay rent, or, worse, homeless.

If one fails to comply or cannot provide evidence of "work activity," they are "terminated" or "termed." Yes, I've seen it with my own eyes. That is the language used in the database and in indelible ink on yellow Post-it notes stuck to state-owned file cabinets.

Systemic discrimination is embedded in the structure of the TANF "benefit" itself. Welfare offices require people to take low-wage jobs without health benefits or sick leave. These jobs also have unpredictable hours and provide little opportunity for career advancement. The reason people are forced into taking the first available job is the federal government mandates that a certain number of people receiving TANF must enter the formal workforce every month. If contractors working with states cannot show they pushed people into jobs, they risk losing their state funding. So they circle their pool of TANF participants and work hard to either get them into a job—*any job regardless of pay or quality*—or force them out of TANF altogether so they do not detract from the ever-important work participation rate. If TANF beneficiaries cannot find a job within about twelve weeks, they must do *unpaid* "community service" for twenty hours a week to keep receiving their meager financial grant.

In Pennsylvania, this fake community service can be filing papers for social services agencies like Joanna had to do or cleaning toilets like Faith was required to do at Comcast, the Philadelphia-based multibillion-dollar telecommunications conglomerate.

Let me make this plain: Comcast does not pay the worker; it is the state of Pennsylvania that pays the recipient the paltry TANF grant amount, which does not correspond to an hourly wage, nor is it considered a wage with any worker's rights. So to continue to receive TANF support, Faith continues to show up to work on behalf of the contract cleaning company without evidence of an earned wage and at a rate far below the federal minimum wage. The contractor is not paying for her work either. You and I are, through our tax dollars and the state systems. That means your tax dollars are going toward forcing people to clean toilets at the Comcast high-rise at around $4 an hour (less than the minimum wage and with no tips), without health insurance or sick leave. Consider the other side of this sad little coin: Brian Roberts, the president and chair of the board of Comcast, made $36,370,200 in 2021.[8] That is $17,485 an hour, or 4,300 times higher than the Black women cleaning his toilets. Note that Roberts's *hourly wage* is about the same as the *annual income* for a family of two at the federal poverty level.

BIPARTISAN KNOCKOUT

Republican leaders who want to dismantle the safety net for people living in poverty would be pleased to hear these expressions of disdain for the programs. Democrats, on the other hand, tense up at the idea and say, "It's true the programs don't work well enough. But if you bring these problems into the open, all you're doing is giving Republicans more ideas for getting rid of the programs altogether." It is as if the Democrats, think tanks, and advocacy organizations hold up SNAP and summer meals like shiny armor to protect "the vulnerable." They do so in public. But behind closed doors, they complain about their inadequacy. This is another variation on knowing and not knowing as I mentioned in chapter 4.

During the Obama administration, in 2013, after Congress cut the SNAP program by over five billion dollars in favor of adding six cents per meal to the school lunch program to improve the quality, Congress threw a conciliatory crumb to those of us who balked at cutting SNAP in favor of minuscule improvements to school meals. It created a National Commission on Hunger. One million dollars was designated to establish a "bi-partisan commission to advise Congress and the Secretary of the USDA on how to address hunger in America."[9] Five members were nominated from the House of Representatives and five from the US Senate with an even split between nominations from legislators of both parties.

When I was selected and then chosen to be the cochair, I had no idea of the headaches ahead.

From the start, the commission was doomed. According to the legislative language, the recommendations the commission could consider had to be made using "existing programs." The existing programs we have in the United States are inadequate at best, and death dealing at worst. Yet we were restricted to existing programs—the same programs that sometimes created *more* problems.

With the contracted help of the Research Triangle Institute, the commission was able to travel to several states to make site visits and hold hearings. With fifteen months of targeted research and support from RTI, we held eight formal hearings with over two hundred testimony submissions to contribute to the unanimous bipartisan report with thirty recommendations. In the report *Freedom from Hunger: An Achievable Goal for the United States*, we proposed ways to improve SNAP and other nutrition programs.[10] All the commissioners agreed: the existing public assistance programs needed overhauls. SNAP and WIC, however, got a positive nod from everyone, though we had many recommendations for improvement. For transformative change, we recommended the development of a national plan to end hunger.

It was a challenge to accommodate disparate beliefs, politics, and expertise. But we managed to do so by staying focused on families, veterans, people with disabilities, and immigrants.

To improve the systems in a way that made sense would be almost impossible given the current mechanisms for program funding. Medicaid is funded through the Department of Health and Human Services, and states must match half the funding. SNAP is an entitlement program funded through the USDA, and TANF is funded through the Agency for Children and Families in the Department of Health and Human Services and has strict work requirements. People who work at these agencies are territorial about their funds as they fight to receive them from Congress annually or every five to six years. Additionally, because of legal requirements for releasing funds to states, federal law disallows funding from one program to be mixed with another.

This inability of our systems to truly help families in crisis was the fodder that Congressman Paul Ryan and House members were using to rationalize the dismantling of SNAP. Elected Republicans sought to turn SNAP into a "block grant" to provide more "flexibility." This may sound reasonable on the surface. But this would have also cut $40 billion from SNAP, thereby dismantling the SNAP program and eliminating its entitlement structure. As an entitlement, everyone who is eligible has the right to receive the benefit. But without that entitlement, even if a person is eligible, they may not be able to receive support as it might depend on funds available or some other behavioral barrier that a state may want to put into place. In doing so, SNAP would run the risk of becoming an atrophied program like TANF that no longer responds to national economic downturns and financial crises among families. Remember that in the introduction, I described how the existence of hunger is due to entitlement failure. Several of us knew that the loss of entitlements would inevitably create more trouble.

Several commissioners felt pressure from legislative staffers, politicians, and advocates on the Left and Right to include specific recommendations with precise words for how to make recommendations. The language Republicans used to justify block granting SNAP included terms such as *merging funding streams* or *program flexibility*. They were naming the "shit" and calling in their own cleanup crew without drawing attention to where the shit came from—low wages, poor infrastructure, racism, discrimination, and social violence. Democratic lawmakers were back on their heels trying to defend the programs as they are, desperate to keep the crumbs for people who are struggling. Democratic agency heads were instead working quietly to find work-arounds to braid and merge funding streams. But they offered no new language to the commissioners and refused to give credence to the fact that public assistance programs were a scattershot, poorly informed effort to assist people.

In the same vein as collective trauma, where people "know but don't know," the Democrats knew but refused to name the harm and address it. Republicans knew and were poised to reenact more trauma by making people potentially more desperate as well as susceptible to more surveillance and control.

All the commissioners agreed that the programs should be improved or restructured. To do so would demand some dismantling and merging of program rules and funding streams. Here's the conundrum: How could we stay true to what we knew was right to help people get more supports without triggering the evisceration of SNAP (which would create more hunger)? Of course, those with Republican leanings were not as concerned the language was going to trigger support for dismantling SNAP's entitlement status. They said they saw no harm in using the term *flexibility*. On the other hand, those who lived through the travesty of welfare reform and leaned Democrat were concerned the Republican Party would have another reason to dismantle SNAP. Without careful language, some of us thought all the building blocks of SNAP could be broken up through block granting. We understood that, in politics, there is no room for subtlety, nuance, and grace.

As we were finalizing the report, the presidential campaigns were heating up. People were taking Donald Trump seriously—including some members of the Hunger Commission. Others on the commission were edging toward Bernie Sanders. Our alignment was fraying, and we were losing each other's trust. Everyone was on edge.

Each word carefully crafted, we managed to hold our consensus together and deliver the written report to every member of Congress along with the secretary of the USDA, Tom Vilsak, and Food and Nutrition Service undersecretary Kevin Concannon. The report was an example of how hunger could be addressed through bipartisan fashion.

But it became clear that other members of Congress and the USDA were mostly interested in squashing the report to minimize any potential news coverage, especially about our recommendations to increase the SNAP allotment, incentivize the purchase of fruits and vegetables, and restrict the purchase of sugar-sweetened beverages. At the end of our work, no member of Congress publicly supported the recommendations with any fervor. We had reached the end of the commission's tenure. With no funding left, and without USDA and congressional support, we could do little to drum up media interest. The USDA, which was entrusted with overseeing the contracting process, ensured that all the money was spent out and any more staff time would be stopped on cue, on January 1, 2016. Our press release was set for a few days afterward on January 4, 2016.

Just to dig in the message that our endeavor was useless, the USDA decided to house the report, testimonies, and commission minutes and notes on a time-honored government website called the "cybercemetery."

The report was dead on arrival.

It felt like getting hit from multiple directions. We dodged left, then right, then left, then over the unbelieving trolls of the think tanks and national organizations, and delivered the report to its own tombstone.

I was knocked out by the experience.

Concussed.

Such a star-spangled clash makes you want to reconsider everything. Our political systems are clearly not meant to help people living in poverty. Policymakers and those with some say in the matter can be so dysfunctional as to knock you out cold.

TO SEPARATE, SURVEIL, AND CONTROL

Under the guise of "helping," public assistance programs have administrative and procedural structures meant to separate, surveil, and control.

As if a magnified echo of the summer meal program that throws parents to the side, the American horror of separating children from their parents at the border has become commonplace. Over the past several years—and yes, even in the Obama administration—the US government has been separating infants, toddlers, preschoolers, school-age kids, and teenagers from their caregivers with whom they were traveling. Under the Trump administration, border patrol and immigration officers were not just separating children from families but also putting the kids in cages or giant warehouses with no beds. The children were forced to sleep on cement floors without blankets; they were provided no soap, toothpaste, and other matters of basic hygiene, including diapers. Worse, some were left to die from flu or COVID-19.[11]

Over thirty thousand children were separated from their parents and caregivers during the Trump administration. Several thousand children were "lost" in the system. The Agency for Children and Families, the government agency meant to care for these children, the same one that funds the foster care system and TANF, could not seem to find their parents.[12]

Some might think these are unprecedented times. This traumatizing separation has been standard US policy since our founding, however. The US government separates children from parents to "save" the children and punish the parents.

A clear example is the separation of Indigenous children from their parents. The US government forced families to relinquish their children to boarding schools run by the Department of Interior between 1819 and 1969. Boarding school is a misnomer. Many such "schools," including the infamous Carlisle Indian Industrial School in Pennsylvania, where they are still rematriating the remains of Indigenous children who died while there, are better known as work camps and acts of war against Indigenous people. The schools were meant to "get rid of the Indian and save the child." The forced separation of children from their parents was an official government policy that attempted to weaken and destroy Indigenous cultures as well as force assimilation into white society and thus into the capitalism that keeps the US government running.[13] It was also an act of warfare over land and resources; it was slavery for the children and yet another form of starvation for their parents.

While Canada has begun to reckon with its history through a yearslong truth and reconciliation process, the United States has yet to acknowledge and repair the massive damage done. Family separation simply continues. Take, for instance, the foster care systems in South Dakota. The Lakota Child Rescue Project found that the state government of South Dakota is financially incentivized to take Lakota children away from Lakota caregivers and place them into the state foster care system, which allows for adoption by non-Indigenous people. South Dakota receives $12,000 for every child it moves into non-Indigenous adoption.[14] This is in direct violation of the 1978 federal law called the Indian Child Welfare Act, which is meant to ensure that Indigenous children, if they must be removed from their current home, stay with kin among the same nation.

Removing children from parents, especially among Black and Brown families, happens in a quiet, highly systematized fashion through the US foster care system. Most social workers working in child protective services are white women. Their record is not good. Based on reviews over many decades of an increasingly punitive foster care system, almost two-thirds of child removals are because a family lives in deep poverty. Most children removed from their homes are children of color. Dorothy Roberts, in her book *Shattered Bonds: The Color of Child Welfare*, describes the foster care system as an attempt at social control, where "social problems that are rooted in poverty and discrimination become interpreted as parents' mental depravity and inadequacy."[15] In the early 2000s, it was common practice for welfare caseworkers to knock on the door in the middle of the night in New York City to inspect children's bodies for bruises and interrogate children.[16]

Some children do die at the hands of their parents and can suffer terrible abuse, as is clear from the previous chapters. But even more clear is the damage done to children and families because of the systematic tendency to remove children without first helping the parents with health care, mental health therapy, food, housing, clothing, and social supports.

Mental health professionals insist that one of the most important things a person can do when they are in distress or feel overwhelmed is to ask for help. Yet in our public assistance programs, the very act of caring for oneself and one's child—that is, asking for help—is not viewed as a wonderfully positive form of care and concern. Rather, it becomes a liability—a reason to take a child away.

In our child hunger study, we talked with Cassie, who told us what happened to her when she asked for support at the county assistance office as she reapplied for SNAP.

I went to the welfare office.

I explained my refrigerator was broken.

I was afraid to admit that.

But I was desperate.

Instead of helping me with emergency funds,

the caseworker said,

"If you don't have a refrigerator,

Maybe you shouldn't have your kids."

THE COUNTY ASSISTANCE OFFICE AS CHIEF SEPARATOR

It is a common complaint among public assistance participants that case-workers either do not care or have an attitude. Consider the Google ratings for a county assistance office in West Philadelphia. In 2019, its star rating was 1.8 (out of 5). Here's a smattering of comments:[17]

- "Horrible Service, I promise. Trash Service is guaranteed 100%."
- "They never answer the phone. I want their jobs."
- "Met with Ms. Charles twice.[18] Once in April, once in June, and both times her personality was horrible. I should call Fox News and tell them to investigate this office."

Charles is a commanding woman who was the administrative director at the local county assistance office in West Philadelphia. When we were recruiting for the Building Wealth and Health Network, Charles allowed us to use one of the many empty cubicles there. Each cubicle had a desk, swivel chair on the inside of the desk, and straight metal folding chair on the other side.

Ruth, a doctoral-trained social worker, was the first director of the Build-ing Wealth and Health Network. In summer 2014, she was recruiting new members for the Network at the county assistance office. Hoping to establish a warm connection with potential members, Ruth moved the swivel chair to the outside of the desk so she could be on the same side and not "profes-sionally separated" from the potential members showing up for recruitment.

Charles saw this and became immediately incensed.

Charles: What are you doing?!

Ruth: I'm just putting the chair on the same side of the desk.

Seems more pleasant that way.

Charles: You have no idea what you are doing!

You better not do that.

That's stupid.

Put that office chair back

on the right side of the desk.

Ruth: Well,

I'd like to try it this way.

Charles: No you won't!

Put the chair back on the other side of the desk!

Ruth did so. But once Charles was out of sight, she moved the chair out to the front again—because as she and I agree, the other way is just wrong.

People were happy to be asked to join our program, mostly because we treated people with respect. One member of the Network explained why she joined. "It's how you talk to us," she said. "You don't talk to us like we're servants or something." Another member observed that the regular county assistance staff "belittle you so bad, it gives you that mindset that anyone who might hire you is thinking the same way."

Not only do caseworkers take it on themselves to be the arbiters of eligibility and propriety, but the entire welfare system is built on enacting surveillance, compliance, separation, punishment, and, for effect, humiliation.

WELFARE REFORM, AN AMERICAN DISASTER

TANF used to be Aid to Families with Dependent Children (AFDC). AFDC was a federal assistance program in effect from 1935 to 1996 created by the Social Security Act. It was created especially for white widows, and later for all caregivers of children who had very low incomes. AFDC was an entitlement program, meaning that anyone who was eligible could participate. Then in 1996 during the Clinton administration and under the leadership of Republican Speaker of the House Newt Gingrich, Congress decimated the program by turning it into a block grant, instituting stringent work requirements, time limits, and severe sanctions. This change is referred to as the Personal Responsibility and Work Opportunity Reconciliation Act (PRWORA) of 1996. In President Bill Clinton's words, it was the "end of welfare as we know it."

The PRWORA also proposed the new goals of TANF: "Provide assistance to needy families so that children can be cared for in their own homes or in the homes of relatives; End the dependence of needy parents on government benefits by promoting job preparation, work, and marriage; Prevent and reduce the incidence of out-of-wedlock pregnancies; Encourage the formation and maintenance of two-parent families." Note the dominance of heteronormative social control along with the absence of a commitment to poverty alleviation or improvement in women's wages. The result was deeply destructive to families. More money was invested in patriarchal "responsible fatherhood" programs to the detriment of supporting the mothers who were actively caring for the kids, and promoting marriage when, much of the time, women were single by choice. Public money was siphoned from state coffers to companies that promoted marriage. Pat Gowens, the head of a Wisconsin-based advocacy program called Welfare Warriors, referred to the organizations that capitalized on this program as "marriage poverty pimps," who would "earn living wages to teach us poor folks how to stay with our batterers and abandoners."[19]

Additionally, with the PROWRA, welfare participants were no longer able to attend a university, community college, or technical school for any meaningful length of time (beyond one year). So opportunities for educating oneself to get better wages for the long term were decimated.

Funding for TANF was no longer tied to fluctuations in the national economy nor to a person's need for support. Rather, TANF funds were locked into the amounts of AFDC that each state spent in 1996. Since then, TANF has lost more than 40 percent of its value in the financial support provided to families. Additionally, states were given the freedom to spend their TANF money as they saw fit. In some states, this included diverting money to childcare, transportation supports, abstinence miseducation, unrelated infrastructure, and "abortion prevention."

Stop to consider that states diverted money away from mothers living in poverty in order to fund antiabortion or private religious-based "crisis pregnancy" companies, which spread misinformation about pregnancy and abortion *as well as* encourage people to put their children up for adoption.[20] If you remember how I started this chapter, you see the pattern of parent-child separation.

In Pennsylvania, the TANF grant amount has not changed for over twenty-five years. The 1996 TANF grant amount for a mother with one child was $330 per month. A few years later, Pennsylvania state administrators reduced it to $306, and it has not been indexed for inflation since. To index for inflation is to increase funding to match the increase in the cost of living. If an amount is not indexed for inflation, then the dollar amount loses much of its value over time. For instance, if the TANF benefit had been indexed to inflation since the PRWORA, the current Pennsylvania rate would be $683.77 per month, or more than double what it is today. Instead, a mother with one child who currently participates in TANF receives $306 on their EBT card, split up into two payments across the month.

For the mother of a toddler in Pennsylvania, the benefit is equivalent to $3 or $4 an hour for a twenty-hour workweek—about half the paltry federal minimum wage of $7.25. If the mother gets a job and starts making more than 50 percent of the federal poverty line, or $8,230 per year, they are cut off from their TANF benefits and may lose their childcare support.

Alongside many other advocacy organizations in the state of Pennsylvania, members of the Building Wealth and Health Network have spoken out to improve the TANF grant amount. They encourage Pennsylvania to catch up to other states such as Massachusetts and California to increase the grant amount. But the Pennsylvania legislature refuses to budge.

Another challenge with the PRWORA was the administrative separation of food stamps (SNAP), Medicaid, and TANF. Before welfare reform, if a person was eligible for one of those programs, they were automatically enrolled in the others. After 1996, families were no longer able to apply for all three programs simultaneously but instead had to fill out a separate application for each program, oftentimes at three different moments in time with different eligibility criteria and documentation, despite the fact they were likely eligible for all three programs.

These changes created confusion not only among families but also among frontline caseworker staff and administrators themselves. In turn, this created administrative mistakes, hurdles, and headaches for everyone involved. This was matched by longer and more convoluted rulebooks.[21] If a TANF participant mistakenly crosses the line of the rules, such as earning a few extra dollars on the side through their own ingenuity and entrepreneurship, they may be charged for defrauding the system. This means the state takes away money from people with little to no money to punish them.

The result? Poor health.[22]

Here is how it worked: People lost program eligibility for "failing to show up for appointments." This was often an excuse for the state to "sanction" people or throw them off the program. It resulted in more caregivers showing up with their kids to emergency rooms with infections, colds, and behavioral problems because their families were suddenly destitute—unable to buy food, pay rent, or heat their homes.[23] The Children's Healthwatch research owes its existence to this massive influx of kids to emergency rooms and the horrified doctors who treated them.

Welfare reform also caused a spike in incidents of domestic violence and intimate partner violence. Mothers returned to abusive boyfriends and husbands because they were desperate for money and had no other means of subsistence.[24] Despite the provision for family violence where a mom could receive support without having to work, most would not admit they were getting beaten up by their partners. Additionally, caseworkers were ill prepared, if at all, to ask about it. This had chilling effects all around.

Gingrich was almost able to implement something even worse. He and others in the Republican Party wanted to exclude teen mothers from accessing TANF. Instead, they were planning on simply taking away their children. As Representative Bill Archer (R-TX) said, "We'll help you with foster care, we'll help you with orphanages, we'll help you with adoption."[25] In other words, if you have little to no income, we cannot help you with money or other supports. But we have no problem "helping" you by taking away your child. Archer added, "If you lose your welfare benefits and if the children cannot be supported by you, they have to be put into foster homes." Luckily this child-snatching policy did not get put into place, but it was one of the underlying intents behind the PRWORA.

POLICE YANKING CHILDREN AWAY

Sometimes those surveillance systems harness the power of the police. Consider, for instance, Jazmine Headley. In 2019, twenty-three-year-old Headley brought her eighteen-month-old son to a county assistance office in New York City. She had to take off a day from work to address a problem she was having with her childcare voucher. Headley needed public assistance to pay for childcare so she could work. According to her attorney, the welfare office had cut off her funding without warning.

Most state systems, including New York's, do not allow a parent to go online to check the status of their coverage, send an email, or make a phone call that will get answered. Instead, Headley had to wait with her toddler for several hours to talk to someone in person.

As all parents know, no one can stand up and hold a squirming toddler for long. Young children are curious and filled with energy. Because there was no open chair in the waiting area, Headley sat on the floor with her child. Asked by the office security guard to stand up, Headley, with all rational motherly thoughts about her, refused. The armed security guards called in multiple New York City police officers. When she refused to stand up, the cops grabbed her son and tried to pull him out of her arms.

Like you and I, she would not dare let go.

Headley and several police officers had a literal tug-of-war with her screaming child that was caught on camera by horrified onlookers. Despite outrage and pleas from onlookers, the officers succeeded in pulling away her child as he screamed in terror. One officer even pointed a stun gun at the other adults and children in the county assistance office who were witnessing this.[26]

Headley was sent to Rikers Island jail for several days without bail. The charges? "Resisting arrest, acting in a manner injurious to a child, obstructing governmental administration, and trespassing."

She joined others at Rikers who had not yet been convicted of a crime. Rikers has a reputation for guard-induced violence, assaults, and abuse.[27]

What happened to Headley and witnesses present at the county assistance office is reflective of the punitive design of public assistance.[28]

6 WELFARE TO WORK MAKES YOU FREE?

The Twelve Days of Welfare
(Sung to the tune of "The Twelve Days of Christmas")

On the twelfth day of welfare, the system gave to me . . .
no childcare service,
crooks in charge of welfare,
ten angry talk shows,
"motivation" meetings,
phony-baloney job search,
Maximus38 and workfare,
one termination,
no ben-e-fits,
a five-hour wait,
no callback,
no fo-od stamps,
and a [case]worker who never did work.
—WELFARE WARRIOR PROTEST SONG, ON EVE OF 2005 REAUTHORIZATION
OF TANF, IN *WELFARE WARRIORS* BY PREMILLA NADASEN

ARBEIT MACHT FREI! IMPRISONMENT THROUGH LOW-WAGE WORK AND WELFARE

"Arbeit macht frei," which translates to "work sets you free" in English, was soldered onto the gates of multiple Nazi concentration and death camps during the World War II Holocaust. The saying was made popular by German writer Lorenz Diefenbach, who wrote a novel with this title in 1873

depicting gamblers and con artists getting "saved" through standardized work. This Prussian philosophy turned Holocaust horror has made a place in American welfare politics. It lands in places such as among clean-cut Ayn Rand aficionados like Paul Ryan and nameless trolls who write anonymous comments after a person talks about being low income in the newspaper. Those self-ascribed news commentators are usually first to anonymously shout in article comments sections, "GET A JOB!"

Even in progressive circles, one of the first recommendations for getting people out of poverty has been to help people "find work." This is why TANF still has a primary focus on getting people to work, regardless of pay, quality, convenience, or meaning. Since the mid-2000s, progressives have started pushing for living wages and family leave. Most people who can find work were already making terrible wages and still did not have enough money for food. Conservatives stick to their party line, however, that work is the way out of poverty, without ever referencing wages or quality. In the meantime, since 2009, the federal minimum wage has been stagnating at $7.25 per hour.

Almost everyone I have spoken to who works in this system—from PhD level, to director, manager, administrator, and caseworker, knows the TANF programs do not really help. They know that the TANF grant amount is criminally low and the sole purpose of TANF is to ensure people's compliance. Many have written about how it breaks families apart, and that the program is rooted in racism and misogyny.[1]

Yet the program continues.

By intentional design.

TWO SAD LITTLE TOKENS

When you are successful in getting TANF benefits, you are required to do "work participation" for at least twenty hours a week if you have at least one child under age six and thirty hours if your kids are older.

Most people in the Network participate in TANF so that they can receive support to pay for childcare. But if you do not comply with the rules and regulations—let's say you feel sick and do not show up for the work participation hours, yet still bring your child to day care—you may receive a letter in ALL CAPITAL LETTERS telling you to pay back the state for the cost. A Network member showed us the letter she received. The state took out over $80 from her biweekly TANF grant to "pay back" the state for childcare. She was expected to live on $118 for two weeks.

It gets worse. Let's say you find a job on your own. This is what Witnesses member Esther did. Esther is a deeply thoughtful Black woman with unparalleled insight into the racial and social politics of the day. In fall 2008, she got a job as a customer service agent at Comcast without help from her TANF caseworker. Comcast offered to pay Esther $11 dollars an hour. The welfare case manager said, "Good for you, you got a job! Now since you no longer qualify for TANF, we will stop paying for your childcare." In Pennsylvania in 2008, childcare cost over $40,000 annually. Low-wage workers can receive a subsidy to defray costs, but there is usually a long waiting list. When I knew Esther in 2008, that list in Pennsylvania was backed up to a three-year "wait." If Esther had waited on it, her youngest daughter would be about five years old before Esther would be eligible for childcare assistance. In the meantime, Esther struggled to find affordable childcare for her daughters. Ultimately, she could not show up to her new job at Comcast because she could not find affordable childcare. So she left a moderately low-paying job and went back to the county assistance office to reapply for TANF, with the hope of getting childcare. In doing so, she was forced to go to a lesser-wage job and begin, again, hoarding receipts.

Others participating in TANF know about this dragnet. So despite getting offered a better job, they will not take it. Because if they *do* accept a higher-paying job, they will be hungrier than they were before. This phenomenon is known as the *cliff effect*. A person receives supports to make it out of poverty. But once they start earning, the money and other supports that help people stay afloat disappear. And they are worse off than they were before.[2]

Notice the weaponization of one's children. TANF will pay for your childcare only if you take a lower-paying job with companies with which the state has contracts. Paid childcare lures parents into compliance. It also bolsters the profits of employers that refuse to pay living wages.

This dynamic is the invisible twin of previous iterations of child separation and state-sanctioned family abuse. In the late 1960s and early 1970s, African American and Indigenous women were told by state caseworkers and doctors to get sterilized to continue to receive welfare. Or they were sterilized without their consent. The sterilization of Black, Indigenous, and Puerto Rican women continued up through the 1980s.[3]

Shadows of this dynamic continue. Several states still have what is called a "family cap." This means that if a mother has another child while participating in welfare, even as their costs increase, the size of the TANF grant does not. This pushes them and their family deeper into poverty.

Joanna's experience reveals the pathology of TANF. She was living in that house you read about in chapter 1. She was receiving SNAP and TANF. Joanna used her camera to take a picture of bus tokens, and another photo of two large stacks of papers and folders.

> These, Mariana, are my two sad little tokens.
> I had to sell my last tokens for cash
> because I didn't have enough money to feed my kids.
> But then I had no way of getting to the welfare office to file their
>   papers.
> Now I am afraid they will cut me off
> for not showing up.

Joanna explained she was quite depressed. She hated her "community service" job filing people's records. For her, the photo, which consisted of the stacks of folders, was a metaphor for her poor mental health and desperate situation.

She had no money and was forced into making this trade-off: selling her tokens for a few dollars in order to feed her kids in the moment versus hanging on to the tokens and letting her kids go hungry, so she could then go to her mandated community service and receive a TANF payment weeks later. She gave me the common refrain that many members of Witnesses gave: "You're damned if you do and damned if you don't."

The state wants to make you work but not succeed. If you succeeded, who would line up for the next poor-paying job?

The "welfare" compliance machine holds you down, chains you up, separates you from your children, or forces you into compliance for fear of losing your children. In other words, it is the prison-industrial complex for mothers and children.

SIMPLE SABOTAGE: WELFARE'S CIA MANUAL

State administrators explain this differently. They are eager to get people off TANF and to stay off TANF because the state gets a "caseload reduction credit," and therefore can draw down more federal funds or be released from some reporting requirements. These are contradictory goals within the system itself. It needs TANF recipients to demonstrate the state succeeded in getting people employed, yet it wants people off the rolls. State administrators interpret this as simply making people go away.

For several years in Pennsylvania, caseworkers were not allowed to provide TANF on the spot if a person was deemed eligible. Instead, caseworkers were obligated to send people away from the county assistance office for three weeks to find a job on their own. This is called *diversion*. If a person still needed money to live after three weeks and had proof that they looked for jobs, only then were they allowed to get support. This cut down on the number of people the state counted and contributed to the state's bottom line for TANF dollars. Among Pennsylvania public assistance workers, there were millions of dollars that the state set aside from TANF for emergency funding, yet much of those funds were unused. They were not alone. A recent report from ProPublica found that states such as Hawaii, Tennessee, and Maine were hoarding TANF dollars in the state coffers. The full total withheld from families in poverty as of 2020—yes, during the pandemic—was $5.2 billion.[4]

From most TANF participant's perspectives, the systems in place are intended to frustrate and befuddle. For instance, to stay compliant, you have to rely on caseworkers who, most of the time, never pick up the phone.

Mariah, a Black member of Witnesses and mother of one-year-old twins, wanted to go back to school so she could get a higher-paying job. She showed us a childcare support flyer, which stated, "You qualify for childcare subsidies!" in about fifteen languages including Vietnamese, Russian, Mandarin, Spanish, Haitian Creole, and Cambodian. But when she called to ask about access to childcare, they said she could only get on the waiting list and there was no guarantee that anything would open up soon, even though she explained that she was planning on matriculating at Philadelphia Community College the following week. They could not give her the name of one childcare provider near her home or school.

The requirement for paperwork, lost paperwork, mean caseworkers, and inability and unwillingness of the state to adapt to the reality of people's lives is a form of sabotage. Let us consider the *CIA Sabotage Manual*. Back in the 1940s, the Central Intelligence Agency distributed this manual among operatives in areas that were occupied by allied Germany to get regular organizations and companies to undermine Nazis and their friends. Simple sabotage is a way to frustrate and undermine the "enemy." It is something that any ordinary citizen can do. Here are some forms of sabotage:

Telephone: "At office, hotel and exchange switchboards delay putting enemy calls through, give them wrong numbers, cut them off 'accidentally,' or forget to disconnect them so that the line cannot be used again."

Managers and supervisors: "To lower morale and with it, production, be pleasant to inefficient workers; give them undeserved promotions. Discriminate against efficient workers; complain unjustly about their work."

Employees: "Think out ways to increase the number of movements necessary on your job: use a light hammer instead of a heavy one, try to make a small wrench do when a big one is necessary."[5]

In relation to TANF, people with low incomes are the enemy of the state. This is why we have such robust legal services for the poor in some areas because the state is constantly inflicting bureaucratic frustrations on people who have much better things to do with their time and potential.

This is also why many refuse to participate. Nationwide, TANF serves only 30 percent of those eligible. Some call this the "TANF misery index," which consists of eligible people who do not receive TANF.[6] Participation rates vary by state. States with the highest population of people who are

Black are far less likely to be serving the majority of TANF-eligible people. Alabama only serves 8 percent of its eligible population, and Louisiana and Arkansas just about 4 percent. Each of these states has a high percentage of Black people living in poverty. On the other hand, Vermont, which has a high population of white people living in poverty, serves 54 percent.[7] Back in 1995–1996 (pre-PRWORA), most states served at least 80 percent of the eligible population. Either way, people in poverty are frustrated by the system, and the vast majority do not have access to a comprehensive, well-designed system that can help them stay afloat to meet their basic needs. The ongoing racism and misogyny in TANF is apparent at every turn. Many scholars have written of TANF's history along with the ongoing degradations of Black families through racialized political rhetoric on welfare, punitive policies, and low grant amounts.[8]

The decline in TANF participation and TANF grant amounts has resulted in a substantial increase in the number of children, especially children of color, who are suffering and stuck in deep poverty.[9]

FINANCIAL APARTHEID

As if keeping people off TANF, frustrating them, or kicking them off TANF were not enough, let us say you succeed in hanging on and getting TANF dollars. Once you are in the TANF and SNAP electronic systems, you are discouraged and often blocked from participating in the financial mainstream. Each state has its own way of referring to an EBT. The EBT card is like a cement wall between people experiencing poverty and the rest of society.

EBT does not attach to a bank account, and it houses SNAP and TANF dollars. In some states, it also includes funds for WIC-approved foods. SNAP and WIC benefits can only be redeemed at an authorized grocery store; TANF benefits are undesignated money.

Let's say you need real paper cash, perhaps to pay your landlord. So you go to a bank machine and take out cash. You get charged a bank fee—somewhere between $0.50 to $1.50. Who gets that money? JPMorgan, Wells Fargo, and Citibank do, depending on which company successfully negotiated for the state contract to run your state EBT program.

Again, the EBT is not money in the bank. It acts like a credit card but comes with none of the benefits, and you certainly cannot use Venmo or CASHApp because EBT is its own system. EBT is a handy way for JPMorgan and Wells Fargo to capitalize off people who are low income with state help. The banks get a cut both ways: via money from the state to run the system and a cut out of people's extremely low wages at the ATM machine. In the meantime, you cannot build your credit, build up a savings account, or have access to conventional banking activities with these funds.

Add to the ongoing racism and misogyny in the TANF system, and the very fabric of TANF and SNAP contribute to everyday financial apartheid.

A COMMON CRIMINAL FOR $25

It's 2009. Put yourself in Maria's worn-out pink sneakers. You are desperate to move out of your abusive mother's home and get out of the basement where she makes you sleep with your two toddlers, aged ten months and two and a half. The roof and the walls are leaking, and you would like to move out before the next big rain comes so you can get your life out of plastic bags and breathe fresh air again.

But a market rent apartment in Philadelphia is $750. Additionally, you need first and last month's rent or at least a security deposit. So you need $1,500 up front. The current Pennsylvania TANF asset limit of $1,000 (what a person can have in a savings account) makes it impossible for you to build up savings, pay a deposit, and get out of your situation. So you are stuck in the basement. You could hide a little extra money you earned from cleaning houses or selling your things right from the inside of your plastic bag. Or you could put it under your mattress—not so safe. Or in your bra—never safe.

It was Friday night at about 7:00 on a summer evening. It was still light out, and I was drawing a bath for my kids. The phone rang. It was Maria.

Mariana. I need help.
I went to the ATM to get out my rent money,
and my boyfriend [the father of her two toddlers]

was following me,
and he beat me up,
broke my ribs,
and took all of my money.

She had just taken out a few months' worth of her TANF benefits from the EBT card that she somehow managed save. She put $750 in her bra so she could pay her new landlord. Her boyfriend found her, grabbed her, and you know the rest.

Here's another. When I paid Carla $50 cash for an extra-long interview, she smiled and said, "Thanks!" She took the money out of the envelope, put it in her bra, and told me, "I'm putting this in my bank."

Me: Please tell me you have a bank account.
Carla: Yes. (*She pats her breast.*) Right here, Mariana. This is my bank.
Me: Why don't you have a bank account?
Carla: 'Cause I don't want welfare to see it.

Her welfare caseworker would consider that $50 to be reportable income, which would then trigger a reduction in her TANF check.

While it is unlikely that a caseworker would ask to see a bank account statement, most people I met would never want to get into a situation in which they would be asked to show a bank account, much less have to report such a paltry sum of $50. But anything over $25 must be reported to welfare, otherwise it is considered "fraud." Such a designation turns a mother who is struggling to feed their kids into a common criminal.

You might find this hard to believe. It's beyond reason, but it's the truth. We know this is the way it works because my team and I have worked *within* the TANF system with the Building Wealth and Health Network. Once we got a contract to run the Network in the TANF system, the state would not let us pay more than $25 per research interview. The state staff told us to keep our "gift" incentive amounts small. Because once it was over $25, we would be forced to account for it in an endless stream of paperwork. The member would have to hoard the receipt. The state would also have to account for it, demanding more paperwork.

This financial and social sabotage is why so many people we work with started their side hustles. Carla would buy food with SNAP and make dinners to sell from her porch. Shandra, a brilliant Black woman entrepreneur, did hair and nails for other people's children. It is no wonder she was popular among her neighbors. She was gorgeous and talented with her hands, which always had nails perfectly manicured. Prom weekend was a windfall; she could earn almost $200. To make a little bit of cash for necessities, Joanna would crochet, bake, and sell crafts for ridiculously small amounts.

In the Building Wealth and Health Network, we knew that more than half the members worked under the table. How many reported this paltry sporadic income to their caseworker? Less than half. Does this mean they were slumming the system? Surely not. The amount of occasional extra money is no more than $100 to $200. Remember, people in the system are simply trying to feed their families and buy diapers, tampons, sneakers, or a coat. If they have to, they will sell their tokens.

LIFTING PEOPLE OUT OF POVERTY?

Another way to forcibly move people into the workforce is to provide the Earned Income Tax Credit (EITC). The EITC is a tax credit that, at tax time, is offered to people who work low-wage jobs. Because their wages are appallingly low, millions of people on TANF and SNAP are eligible for the EITC.

Shirley explained the inanity of this system through one of her photographs. It is a photo of six women dressed in white with graduation caps with tassels. Each woman is holding at least one baby under the age of two, and there are a few other children standing with them. They had participated in a TANF-funded program to get certified for work in medical billing.

She called the photo "Graduation to the Same Poor Wages." Here is what she described:

I just graduated from medical billing school [paid for by TANF].
But I cannot get a job in my new field.
I need a job now because I need the tax refund
to pay for furniture for the kids.

My friend convinced me
to go to McDonald's
to apply.
They pay $8 an hour.
I got to do
what I got to do.

Desperate for money and eager to receive a tax credit, she stooped to apply for a job at McDonald's. Not because McDonald's was a good job, or even a safe and desirable workplace, but because if Shirley worked a low-wage job, she could get some funds through the EITC to pay her bills. Nothing felt good about it.

Legislators left, right, and center along with poverty pundits all praise the EITC. To question it is almost sacrilegious. The EITC is a tax credit that increases with each additional dollar earned by a person who works for low wages. It therefore "encourages work" (albeit low-wage work) by supplementing earnings. According to the research, the EITC is also a prescription for good health; it helps improve children's school performance and college attendance rates.[10]

The Urban Institute, a nationally renowned think tank and research institute, holds many panel discussions regarding the EITC to promote it to policymakers. Maria was invited to speak at one of those panels. The National Academies of Science also generated a report on how to reduce child poverty by 50 percent.[11] It suggested a full array of work-oriented and income supports, such as raising the minimum wage to $10.25 an hour, expanding the childcare tax credit, and expanding access to the EITC. The right-leaning 2017 American Enterprise Institute report on poverty called *A Safety Net That Works* said that in 2014, "28.5 million tax units" (yes, tax units, not human beings) received $68.3 billion from the EITC, which amounted, it said, to "lifting 7.3 million individuals above the poverty line."[12] The Center on Budget and Policy Priorities, which leans center-left, also insists that the program "lifts people out of poverty." In 2016, for instance, according to the center, the EITC "lifted 5.8 million people out of poverty."[13]

Through the EITC, advocates as well as the federal and state government can take credit for "lifting people out of poverty."

But this claim is false.

Remember you need to work low wages in order to be eligible for the "benefit." Earning low wages is a prerequisite for receiving the EITC. The EITC does not "lift" people above the poverty line. On the contrary, it forces people to dig their own ditch and stay in low-wage jobs with no career potential while large corporations profit off this because they can continue to pay low wages. These corporations are enabled by the government, which supplements wages with SNAP and Medicaid (health care for people experiencing poverty). In other words, the EITC is another tax haven for the corporations and businesses that refuse to pay higher wages.

Advocates and lawmakers on the Left and Right are complicit in this "work makes you free" system. Welfare researchers Felicia Ann Kornbluh and Gwendolyn Mink are some of the few people who call it like it is: the EITC is like putting lipstick on a pig.[14]

Lean in for a kiss.

UNCLE SAM IS A PIMP

Shirley worked at McDonald's because she needed the EITC for her family. Yet she was treated badly and paid horribly. As the largest fast-food company in the United States, McDonald's generated $23.8 billion in sales in the United States in 2021.[15] It is one of the largest private sector employers in the world.

If you read *Fast Food Nation* by Eric Schlosser, you will remember that fast-food workplaces are unsafe for workers and customers, and tend to be hostile places.[16] According to an article in *Bloomberg*, on average, every thirty-six hours, local news outlets in the United States report about workplace violence at a McDonald's, though police reports suggest rates of violence that are much higher.[17] These incidents range from angry customers throwing hot coffee at workers, to armed robbery and assault, dangers with fry grease, and sexual harassment and rape among coworkers.[18]

Shirley would much rather work in health care billing, the job for which she was trained. She felt forced to work in any kind of low-wage job so she could get a little bit of the EITC just to meet basic needs. It felt degrading and bad for her health as well as that of her children.

When we listen to women participating in TANF and other welfare programs, we see that American bosses want people to work for them at the lowest wages possible. Government assistance programs help this along. As an example, in her book *Storming Caesar's Palace* about how Ruby Duncan and many other leaders of the welfare rights movement fought against the gambling moguls in Nevada, Annelise Orleck describes how mob bosses in Las Vegas worked with state legislators in Nevada to keep welfare financial assistance so meager that people would be desperate to work for slightly higher wages in the casinos.[19] Though that was forty years ago, the same dynamics are at play today.

Our modern-day public assistance programs are forms of entrapment constructed by big companies and facilitated by US government policy. The US government is pimping women and their children to America's corporations.

WELFARE IS RACISM'S REVOLVING DOOR

Another system with this type of neglectful entrapment is Medicaid, health insurance for people who have very low income and/or disabilities, and for children who are in the foster care system. Most people participating in TANF also access health insurance through Medicaid. The states that refused to expand Medicaid were those that had the highest percentage of Black people in their populations. On the other hand, consider those states that did expand Medicaid. They saw vast reductions in health inequities between Black and white people, especially in the areas of cancer treatment.[20] States that did not expand Medicaid are seeing comparably worse health outcomes, and some states have made it almost impossible to get Medicaid coverage. In Texas, the Medicaid application is thirty-eight pages long, sixteen times longer than a 1040 tax form.[21] Not only does this make it extremely difficult to get Medicaid coverage, but it delays people months to see a generalist and even longer to see a specialist. Such red tape delays in states without Medicaid expansion are responsible for infant mortality and maternal death rates that are far higher than those in states that did expand Medicaid.[22] Additionally, the state of Texas refuses to offer immigrants any health insurance coverage. The state will pay for health care for a fetus, but not for the mother. That is, even before a child is born, Texas is separating the child from the mother—even though it is the mother's health that leads to a healthy child. See the "don't feed adults" pattern of separation?

As another example, Carla not only hid the paltry "earnings" from research and selling meals in her bra but also tried to hide from caseworkers the fact that she lived with a caring, loving partner who was the father of her children. He made very little money and always contributed his earnings to the family and household expenses. But in order to participate in TANF to get access to childcare and receive the tiny grant amount, she claimed she did not know the father of her kids. Carla claimed he was her pimp, and she did not know his identity. Otherwise, she knew that if she did identify him, the caseworker would enter him into the system and start trying to chase him down for child support made payable to the state.

If a father does not pay child support, they may get sent to prison. For instance, in North Carolina, one-eighth of the Black men in prison are jailed for not paying child support to state coffers. You might remember Walter Scott, who was murdered by North Carolina police. It was a "routine" traffic stop, but Scott ran from police, many say, because he was worried he would be imprisoned again for not paying child support. As he ran away, a white cop, Michael Slager, shot Scott in the back and killed him.

These examples demonstrate how racism and misogyny are baked into public assistance, and are funded by the government to generate revenue for large corporations that refuse to provide adequate wages and health coverage for their workers. Simultaneously, adults and children, especially those of color, get snagged up in the chains of welfare. The welfare system, labor laws, health care expenditures, and criminal justice operate a death-dealing revolving door.

This truth was explained to me by the ex-boyfriend of a member of Witnesses, a Black man who had just returned from prison. We were walking together in West Philadelphia down Market Street toward the county assistance offices under the L train at Fifty-Seventh and Market. Remarking on the row of buildings and the group of women and children outside one of the doors, and a line of men waiting at the side door of the building next door, he said,

> That's where all the people are lined up
> from the parole office,
> to the methadone clinic,
> to the welfare offices.
> It's like a revolving door for Black men and women.

Government and corporations weaponize the public assistance programs to churn Black and Brown people around and around, or stop them dead.

7 NUTRITION ASSISTANCE AS CORPORATE WELFARE

HOW SNAP AND WIC SUPPORT PUBLIC HEALTH

Up through the 1960s, before the United States had robust nutrition assistance programs, there were children in the United States that were severely malnourished; some children were dying of starvation. *Malnutrition* is a term for many nutrition-related conditions. Three forms of malnutrition are *kwashiorkor*, a form of protein deficiency; *marasmus*, a protein and calorie deficiency; and *stunting*, truncated body and brain growth. In the present day, such malnutrition is seen in war-torn areas and regions of India, Africa, and Latin America where a majority of the population is low income. Malnutrition is rare in the United States—but does show up from time to time among children who have suffered extreme abuse and neglect as well as among neglected elderly. Up through the 1960s, such malnutrition was primarily occurring in the poorest sections of African American communities, in the hollers of Appalachia, on Indigenous reservations and lands, in the Mississippi Delta, and at the US border in the colonias (unincorporated towns without running water, sewage and garbage removal, or any other municipal services). Today, thanks to modern nutrition assistance programs in the United States, we rarely see such malnutrition.

The nutrition assistance programs, SNAP and WIC, owe their existence to leaders like Marion Wright Edelman, civil rights advocate, child defender, and longtime head of the national Children's Defense Fund. A few years before she founded the Children's Defense Fund in 1973, Edelman took US senators Ted Kennedy, George McGovern, and others to areas of the

Mississippi Delta, introducing them to families that were suffering from malnutrition in the hopes of encouraging congressional leaders to take action.[1]

WIC

In the late 1960s, Senator McGovern traveled to Nevada and other locations to learn about Indigenous women who were pregnant and severely malnourished, and to understand how children being born on Indigenous reservations were dying of malnutrition. He and others in Congress also listened to the doctors and health professionals who advocated for specialized nutrition for pregnant and nursing mothers. As a result of that advocacy, WIC started with eighty thousand mothers in the late 1960s and early 1970s. Presently, WIC is the most effective nutrition assistance program in the United States. Over seven million families participate, including almost half of all newborns.[2] This magnitude of coverage shows great success in terms of reach, as WIC serves 80 to 90 percent of the families that are eligible. The fact, however, that 50 percent of newborns participate in WIC should make us deeply worried because these participation rates indicate that half the babies born in America today are born into poverty.

WIC supplements the cost of nutritious foods that are especially important for pregnant and lactating mothers and food for young children. Such items include but are not limited to whole wheat bread, peanut butter, milk, breast milk substitute (baby formula), and pureed baby foods. WIC also provides nutrition education, breastfeeding support, and referrals to social services agencies. Recommended by parents, doctors, nurses, and social workers, WIC tends to have broad support. Most members of Witnesses were positive about the program. It prevents preterm birth and infant mortality, improves growth patterns (greater height, weight, and head circumference) in infants and children, is associated with higher scores on children's cognitive and behavior tests, and decreases anemia in women, infants, and children.[3] Our children's HealthWatch study found that it also was associated with reduced stress and depression for mothers.[4]

The positive health impacts of WIC participation are undeniable. For every dollar spent on WIC, the program generates $3.13 in savings to health care costs.[5] Overall, it is considered by public health leaders to be an excellent program, in spite of the fact that in its first two decades, it failed to promote breastfeeding. WIC's breastfeeding promotion has improved. Yet WIC currently provides "pouring rights" to Abbott, Nestlé, and Mead Johnson, the major companies that make baby formula. This means anyone who participates in WIC that uses formula can only get those formulas depending on their state residency. Companies reap profits, not just with formula but with their baby food that WIC subsidizes.[6] This reliance on only a few formula companies had disastrous effects for low-income families especially when Abbott's factory proved unsafe in 2021 and there was a widespread recall on formula, which caused devastating shortages.[7]

SNAP

SNAP, formerly known as food stamps, is for food items only. Unlike WIC, it has no designated "menu." Some items that a person cannot buy with SNAP are preprepared and ready-to-eat foods such as hot pizza or rotisserie chicken. People cannot purchase alcohol or tobacco with SNAP. Nor can they buy soap, tampons, diapers, cleaning supplies, masks, or hand sanitizer.

The founding Farm Bill enacted in 1933 was meant to provide subsidies to farmers during the Great Depression and to a lesser extent help supply commodity foods to people who were impoverished. Today, the Farm Bill authorizes most federal food and agriculture programs including SNAP, which constitutes 75 percent of the total funding of the bill. Along with WIC as well as school breakfasts and lunches, SNAP is the largest nutrition program and one of the primary defenses against food insecurity.

In 2022, in any given month, an average of 42 million people participate in SNAP. This is almost 13 percent of the US population. Approximately half of all people in the United States will have been on SNAP during some part of their childhood. As an entitlement program, SNAP is responsive to economic downturns on a national, regional, and household level through supporting low-wage, unemployed, and underemployed workers. SNAP also provides support for people who cannot work such as children, people with disabilities, elderly people, and low-income veterans. Nearly half of SNAP participants are children.

SNAP participants say the best thing about the program is that there are few restrictions on the type of food one can purchase. Thomas Ptacek, one of the 1.5 million veterans who receives SNAP benefits, gave testimony in

2015 to the National Commission on Hunger at a public hearing in Portland, Maine. After he described his experiences with the trauma of war and resultant homelessness in the United States, he explained,

> The most beneficial aspect of the SNAP program is that it allows for choice in the purchase of food that can be prepared in the home. This extra piece, that I personally benefited from greatly, is the sense of normalcy and stability that comes from going to the grocery store and choosing your food.[8]

Tianna Gaines-Turner, longtime member of Witnesses, also relies on that freedom to choose:

> [SNAP] helps me to put a quality, healthy meal on the table. I can choose foods at my own liberty. This is important since three of my four children have life-threatening health issues that demand specific nutritional supports and choices.[9]

SNAP reduces food insecurity among children, improves birth weight among infants, and promotes child health while reducing child hospitalizations.[10] It has also been found to reduce problems with childhood asthma.[11] Among adults, SNAP helps people with diabetes manage their illness—at least for the first two to three weeks out of the month. Research shows that when comparing diabetes complications between SNAP participants and those who are eligible and do not participate, SNAP participants have better overall health and diabetes management.[12] Clearly, SNAP has tremendous health benefits.

But that is only half the story.

Most SNAP research before 2021 demonstrated that benefits often do not last beyond week two. In the second half of the month, diabetics show increased hospitalizations and rising levels of HbA1c, or glycated hemoglobin, a measure that assesses a person's average blood sugar levels.[13] This is because families frequently run out of SNAP funds to buy adequate food. Clearly, US policies are inscribed in the bodies and brains of children. In the case of SNAP, such policies land in the metabolism and bloodstream of adults. The result? They are more likely to lose a toe, have diminished eyesight, or die.

The calculation for how much money a person receives is based on a variety of factors. A person's current income, assets, and expenses are calculated. Then these costs are juxtaposed with a blunt instrument used to calculate the "cost of food" without attention to region (though benefits are higher for Hawaii and Alaska, and lower and slightly different in Puerto Rico and American Samoa) to create a dollar amount that potentially "supplements" income that people already have to buy food. This is where major problems occur.

A caseworker identifies how much a SNAP applicant pays for housing and other expenses. They then weigh that number against income to verify if a person earns less than a livable wage, warranting the receipt of SNAP and determining how much. In the SNAP calculation, there is a "shelter deduction" currently capped at $624 per month. But many people pay more than 50 percent of their monthly income on rent or mortgage, meaning they are rent burdened. Remember Maria's rent was $750, which at the time was market rent for a two-bedroom apartment in one of the neighborhoods with the lowest incomes in Philadelphia. So if a person's rent exceeds the cap amount, then the SNAP calculation blatantly undermines a person's true expenses (by undervaluing their housing costs). This lowers the amount of SNAP dollars a family receives.

The standardized calculation for SNAP benefits is based on the supposed cost of food in a calculation called the Thrifty Food Plan (TFP). The USDA's TFP is used as the national standard for a "nutritious diet at a minimal cost."

In summer 2021, the USDA's Food and Nutrition Services (FNS) administrators reached out to me to inquire if members of Witnesses and the Building Wealth and Health Network, almost all of whom are SNAP participants, would share insights on the TFP. Several women participated in a focus group with the FNS administrators and followed up with the SNAP collaborative report.[14] After reviewing decades of nutrition science, SNAP research, and speaking with stakeholders like members of Witnesses, the FNS increased the TFP calculation by over 20 percent, marking the most significant effort to date by the USDA to catch up to the reality of food insecurity and cost of a healthy diet. This TFP increase is an example of how administrators *can* do the right thing if they base their decisions on long-standing science and the wisdom of SNAP recipients. While hardly noticed by the news media, this improvement in the calculation was one of the greatest achievements by the FNS to address hunger and health.

I wish more positive illustrations were ahead in this book. Alas, there are still big problems with SNAP *and* our political and economic systems that sustain it.

SHAME IN SCHOOL LUNCH

Ten-year-old Zachary Maxwell, a fourth grader, made a movie in 2014 about improvements to the school lunch program soon after the Healthy, Hunger-Free Kids Act of 2010, where Congress stole funds from SNAP to add six cents per school meal. The name of the movie? *YUCK!*[15]

Improving school lunch is challenging. Parent groups and the School Nutrition Association have worked hard to undo national and local efforts to improve school lunches. Many people insisted it was impossible to improve lunches with more vegetables and less fried foods even though many school districts were already figuring it out. In 2019, the USDA unceremoniously released a study showing that, contrary to popular belief, food waste did not increase because of the changes. Also, student diets improved after the new guidelines were implemented.[16]

Compared to children who were eligible for school meals but did not participate, those who did participate had better test scores in math and reading and were more likely to stay in school.[17] So like all nutrition assistance programs, school lunch provides many improvements in health and cognition.

Universal school lunch got its start thanks to the US government's penchant for war. Just as the US government was trying to ramp up its military to enter World War II, young people reporting for the draft were emaciated and too weak for combat. School lunch was not widespread. Well-off students were the only ones able to afford school lunches. In response, the USDA made school lunches more broadly available—all the better to make kids military ready.

Currently, school nutrition programs provide meals to thirty million children every school day. There are three tiers to the school meal program:

free, reduced cost, and full price. Janet Poppendieck, in her book *Free for All*, explains how to improve the quality and administration of school meals: make it universal and free for all; there would be no means test to see whether children are worthy (or low income enough).[18] In 2024, these ideas are not so radical. After the temporary successes of free school breakfast and lunch for all children across the United States during the COVID-19 pandemic, California, Maine, and Minnesota chose to permanently offer free breakfasts and lunches for *all* children. Other states are joining in or poised to follow suit.[19]

The administrative oversight of student eligibility wastes the money and time of administrators, school lunch providers, and parents who must fill out all the forms—not to mention the kids who are waiting in line to pay. If school meals were universal, the federal and state governments would save on administrative funds, children would have more time to eat because they would not have to contend with underpaid lunch staff calculating the costs, and everyone could avoid the scourge of school *lunch shaming*, a coordinated effort to publicly call out children with school lunch debt.

More than three-quarters of school districts nationwide have some level of student meal debt.[20] Before they expanded to universal free breakfast and lunch, and in order to retrieve lost revenue, Minnesota schools made children wear wristbands to shame students and their parents into paying overdue lunch fees. In some high schools, they would not let kids graduate until their lunch debt was paid. Alabama had its own special shaming where it stamped children's hands with "I need lunch money." Lunch monitors often reported that they allowed kids to get lunch anyway because they couldn't bear telling the kids they could not eat.

This is the kindness that Philando Castile would show in Minneapolis. Castile was a lunch monitor and often helped to pay off children's debts until, one day, he was shot by a cop point-blank during a routine traffic stop while he was seated in the driver's seat with his hands on the wheel. Who was there to witnesses this? His girlfriend, her four-year-old daughter who was in the back screaming, and many people among the American public on Facebook, Twitter, and Instagram.

The cop was later acquitted.

Castile's mother, Valerie, received a settlement from the League of Minnesota Cities Insurance Trust, and in her son's name, she uses those funds to not only help victims of gun violence and police brutality but also pay off children's lunch debts in Minnesota.

In 2014–2015, people were so nervous about lunch shaming that in New Mexico, even the governor, Susanna Martinez (who was not generally a friend to people who are poor), introduced a Student's Bill of Rights to prohibit lunch shaming. More recently, the US representative from Minnesota, Ilhan Omar, proposed legislation to end lunch shaming nationally.

Meanwhile, Valerie Castile, along with many others, asks the simple question, "Why can't school lunch be free for all children everywhere?"

SCHOOL BREAKFAST, THE BLACK PANTHERS, AND THE FBI

In 1965, there was a school breakfast program for about eighty thousand children in a few places scattered throughout the United States.

The Black Panther Party (BPP), a political movement that emerged in protest to police brutality and the militarization of the police in the 1960s, focused on basic needs too. In 1967, it launched the school breakfast program in Oakland, California, and it spread to many cities across the country, including Philadelphia in 1968. Providing school breakfast was mandatory for all BPP chapters. In offering breakfast, the party knew it helped to make the kids alert and ready for school. Black Panther Eldridge Cleaver explained, "Breakfast for children pulls people out of the system and organizes them into an alternative. Black children who go to school hungry each morning have been organized into their poverty, and the Panther program liberates them, frees them from that aspect of poverty. This is liberation in practice."[21] Many forget that the modern-day USDA-funded school breakfast program emerged from this very practical approach.

But the road to get there was violent in the extreme.

Then director of the US Federal Bureau of Investigation (FBI), J. Edgar Hoover, labeled the BPP as "the greatest threat to the internal security of the country." Eager to undermine the growing influence of the Panthers, the FBI's Counterintelligence Program (COINTELPRO) sought to dismantle and discredit the Black Panthers through coordinated smear campaigns. For instance, throughout the neighborhoods where the party was serving breakfasts, the FBI spread rumors that the breakfasts were laced with sexually transmitted diseases. Despite such ridiculous claims, COINTELPRO sowed distrust. The FBI also used tactics to increase factionalism and disrupt coalitions among not only the Black Panthers but also the Nation of Islam, the women's liberation movement, the American Indian Movement, the Chicano labor movement, and the movement for Puerto Rican independence.[22] These tactics are still in use today as the FBI surveils and seeks to discredit the Black Lives Matters movement.[23]

The FBI viewed the breakfast program not as a social or community good, as it was intended, but instead as a way for the Black Panthers to spread their power (which was for community good). An FBI memo from 1969 signed by Hoover addressed to operatives in San Francisco asserted,

> You state that the bureau should not attack programs of community interest such as the BPP "Breakfast for Children Program." You have obviously missed the point. The BPP is not engaged in the program for humanitarian reasons. This program was formed by the BPP . . . to create an image of civility, assume community control of Negroes, and fill adolescent children with their insidious poison.[24]

This racist language of white violence was the trigger for coordinated state violence. Chicago was a flash point for school breakfast and BPP leadership. Panther leader Fred Hampton, chapter head in Chicago, commanded great respect and was deeply anticapitalist and anticop. The more the FBI tried to stop Hampton and others who ran the program, the more people became interested in the breakfast program. The night before the BPP was getting ready to serve its first meal, FBI operatives broke into the Chicago warehouse where the food was stored and ransacked the next morning's breakfast stash. They also urinated on the food. This put the party on notice, but only held it back a week from starting up again. Another major setback to the BPP and school breakfast happened when the FBI and Chicago police orchestrated the assassination of Hampton at 4:30 a.m. on December 4, 1969. They broke into his home and murdered him as he was sleeping in bed.[25]

Undeterred, the BPP continued the school breakfast program. By 1971, the program was in thirty-six cities. Through its success in feeding tens of thousands of children, the BPP drew attention to the widespread need for school breakfasts.

In 1975, the BPP was decimated by COINTELPRO and its propaganda tactics. It is important to note that the FBI was violent and murderous because people wanted to feed their children and their classmates breakfast so they could be nourished and learn well.

The USDA picked up the mantle for expanding and running school breakfasts. Now school breakfasts help feed over fourteen million children before school. Without the organized actions of the Black Panthers, it might never have happened.

COMMODITY CHEESE

Ha- haaaiii eeeeee
    Eeeee—— iii ahhh!
        iiii aa!

Sam, our infant daughter, screamed high-pitched as she sat up. She had been asleep in our bed between her father and me when we lived in Oklahoma. It was two in the morning in 1999, and we were exhausted from a long drive, after a ceremony and dinner with Cheyenne friends. I bolted upright at the sound. After turning on the light, I started to pick up Sam. She looked into my eyes, gave a deep groan, and threw up all over me. It was clearish liquid with little bits of commodity cheese.

What is commodity cheese?

It's about that gross. A vomitous stain on American soil.

Commodity cheese would be distributed as giant orange bricks in boxes with other nonperishable items such as canned corn, peanut butter, flour, and cans of vegetable shortening on reservations and at tailgate food distribution programs for many years. I had put some on Sam's plate that night because my friend Edwina had some in the fridge. She only used commodity cheese as a last resort. She chuckled when I asked for it. At the time, Sam only had four teeth and could not eat what the rest of us were having. I carefully ripped the cheese into little pieces. What Sam threw up several hours later was still in the same shapes and just a little paler.

My Cheyenne friends would never refer to it as "cheese." It was *commodity cheese*. Commodity cheese is the special detritus of US government–controlled dairy subsidies developed from surplus milk to help keep dairy prices from dropping. It was created under the Carter administration to provide price supports to ensure that farmers get their "fair" share of income by removing milk from the commercial market. The milk products like commodity cheese would then be redistributed through school lunches and sent to Indigenous reservations. Sometimes it would arrive moldy.

In the 1980s' Reagan era, the warehoused commodity cheese scandal came to light. While hunger was on the rise—due to Reagan administration cuts to food stamp benefits and other antipoverty programs—the federal government stockpiled over 550 million pounds of commodity cheese. Reagan officials wanted to give it away to people who would otherwise not be able to purchase cheese. But in a news article in 1981, a USDA official said it would have been more efficient to dump those millions of pounds of commodity cheese in the ocean.[26]

The dairy industry is not slowing down. Currently, 73 percent of revenue in the dairy industry comes from the US government.[27] While people are going vegan, and recognizing how eating meat and cheese harms human health and ecosystems, the US government keeps subsidizing factory farms as well as the meat and dairy industry. Now millions of pounds of cheese taken off the market are being stored in round blocks in caves in Missouri.[28]

NUTRITION ASSISTANCE AND INDIGENOUS SOVEREIGNTY

Commodity cheese serves as a noxious entrée into understanding the troubled history of food assistance among Indigenous communities. Talking about food "assistance" brings up complex emotions among people from Indigenous communities and nations, as it is fraught with the traumatic history of the relationship of domination of Indigenous nations by the US government.

Food assistance was part of the arsenal in US government warfare against Indigenous people. After the US government had stolen Indigenous-stewarded lands through massacres, forced removal, upheaval, and other forms of violence and destroyed their foodways through the mass killings of four million bison, Indigenous people were starving. This is how they could be dominated, forced off their lands, and terrorized to give up their children.

The US military would then provide rations—which often consisted of rancid beef, old bags of flour riddled with pests, and lard. Lots of lard.

This is how fry bread came to be.

Fry bread is made with flour, water, a bit of powdered milk if you have it, and some baking soda. You put spoonfuls of vegetable shortening (or Crisco), real pig fat, or other kinds of lard in your deep pan, and fry up your dough on both sides. The bread accompanies ceremonial and everyday meals among the Cheyenne and Arapaho nations in western Oklahoma. It is also common among the Tewa (Pueblo) and Diné (Navajo) nations, and can take the form of "Indian tacos"—a larger piece of fry bread covered in kidney beans, shredded cheese, iceberg lettuce, and maybe some hamburger meat. Indian tacos are frequently sold throughout the powwow dance and gathering circuit, where hundreds of powwows happen every summer throughout Indian Country.

Fry bread can be a divisive topic. Some writers call it a symbol of per-severance and survival against all kinds of horror and trouble. Others, like Nephi Craig, of the White Mountain Apache and Diné nations, say fry bread is a food born out of colonialism; to eat it is to taste "confinement and oppression."[29] Embracing both flavors at once, Dana Vantrease, who studied how commodity food is associated with Indigenous identity and bodies, explains how fry bread and many other commodity foods in Indian Country evoke simultaneous ethnic pride and deep sorrow.[30] Most people recognize that fry bread and many foods received through food assistance are associated with the long history of colonization, genocide, war, oppression, and high rates of diabetes and early death.

Indigenous people have the highest rates of food insecurity and short-est life span among all people in the United States. In this light, it seems reasonable to view the commodity food distribution program as a weapon that continues the genocide.

TRADITIONAL FOOD VERSUS BEEF WITH JUICES

Sometimes nutritionists use fry bread on the side of the plate to get people to try traditional foods such as chokecherry, bison, venison, maize, wild rice, squash, beans, turtle, and rabbit. These traditional foods are still available and utilized, though sparsely. They make appearances during ceremonies. But they are not widely available to most Indigenous people, not only because the vast majority of Indigenous peoples were forced off their ancestral lands and had their hunting, gathering, and fishing rights taken away or severely restricted, but because they have to get to work, or they live in city apartments and may have little choice but to feed their families on low budgets.

Between 25 to 80 percent of Indigenous people receive government food assistance. About half live in sparsely populated rural areas. This means that they are also hundreds of miles away from standard jobs to earn an adequate income if they cannot generate income at home. Even if they were originally forced off their own lands, Indigenous people living in rural areas or on reservations and grant lands have told USDA officials that they prefer to receive foods from the US government that they can find on their own land, or in the forests, rivers, streams, and oceans near where they live. But federal food assistance programs do not allow for that, despite decades of lobbying from Indigenous leaders and traditionalists.

American Indians and Alaskan Natives (as they are referred to by the USDA) have two major options for food assistance: SNAP or the Food Distribution Program on Indian Reservations (FDPIR). People living near grocery stores prefer SNAP because they can choose what to purchase. But tens of thousands of others who do not live close to a store, or who would have to drive many miles to an overpriced, under-resourced grocery store, prefer FDPIR because it can be delivered in bulk to Indigenous nation headquarters or community centers. The FDPIR provides about a hundred types of food, most of which are nontraditional to Indigenous peoples' heritage.

As part of the National Commission on Hunger, we visited Acoma Pueblo and learned about its experiences with food insecurity. The people there expressed a desire for more local and culturally appropriate foods in the FDPIR. Multiple USDA-funded researchers have stated that support for local and culturally appropriate foods would not only help local economies but improve health and well-being too. Yet the FDPIR remains the same.

The commission sought expert insight from Oglala Lakota communities from Pine Ridge and Sicangu Oyate of Rosebud in South Dakota. In joint testimony from Kathleen Pickering, Benjamin McShane-Jewell, Michael Brydge, Marcella Gilbert, and Linda Black Elk, they stated,

> The USDA has tremendous potential to improve food security and the relationship with health on reservations. The FDPIR and SNAP programs together represent 45 percent of the sources of food for reservation residents in Pine Ridge, South Dakota. In contrast, only 3 percent of the total food consumed is wild food, although 65 percent of households still hunt, fish, and gather wild plants. The Lakota people often mention the idea of restoring access to wild plants instead of using land for other purposes, such as leasing it for cattle production. . . .
>
> Food insecurity is a direct result of colonization. Hunting and gathering was declared illegal, and eventually it was considered a shameful act, practiced by savages and heathens. Boarding schools reinforced these ideas and served small children daily meals of bread and coffee, altering the Indigenous pallet and mindset for decades to come. Food insecurity has not just impacted us physically, but mentally, emotionally, and spiritually as well. The food industry has become a new tool of colonization, as we must contend with a lack of access to healthy foods in our grocery stores and corner gas stations. Those of us who wish to "decolonize our diets" must deal with decreased access to traditional hunting and gathering places, as well as the complete disappearance of traditional foods due to corporate agriculture, soil and water pollution, and climate change.[31]

As a part of my National Commission on Hunger work, I spoke with USDA officials who insisted that it is too expensive to support locally grown agriculture because what keeps the FDPIR affordable for the government is the utilization of several big warehouses at strategic points across the country that are easily accessible by truckers who can then deliver the commodities to the reservations, trust lands, and other locations for monthly distribution. In recent years, the USDA has minimally expanded the Local Food Purchase Assistance Cooperative Agreement Program for states, Indigenous nations, and territories, but these funds are small and quite restricted.

Additionally, the USDA spends administrative time and money ensuring that Indigenous people are not participating in both programs at the same time. Families experience confusion and frustration when they decide to go off SNAP and switch to FDPIR, or vice versa. The administration of these programs is never smooth in Indian Country, and commission members heard about people going for months without any assistance as a result. Knowing what we know about the inadequacy of SNAP, it seems more reasonable and supportive to Indigenous people to ensure that they can participate in *both* programs. But the US government spends administrative dollars for surveillance and separation. So food pantries are there to fill the gap when SNAP and the FDIPR are not enough.

When an Indigenous family runs out of food, it can sometimes rely on friends and neighbors or other nation members for support. Among the Southern Cheyenne and Arapaho nations, sharing food is culturally compulsory. It is a matter of Indigenous sovereignty and identity. Sometimes this food sharing is in the form of extra fry bread. Sometimes, families may have to rely on a food pantry, which may be located at the same site where the FDPIR is distributed, summer meals occur, and more.

Such was the case at Acoma Pueblo. Walking through its storefront and food storage area, we could see that with the FDPIR foods there was some choice among fruits, vegetables, and cereals. But it felt like an almost-empty supermarket. There were onions, generic white boxes of cornflakes, raisins, and cans with a plain white paper label with large black letters saying "PEANUT BUTTER" or "BEEF WITH JUICES."

DYNAMICS OF SNAP AND WORK

The USDA does not just control the quality of food Indigenous people eat through the FDPIR. SNAP also has compliance rules. Most SNAP participants are not meant to work to receive SNAP benefits. But people who are labeled *able-bodied adults without dependents*, meaning they have no children and are not disabled, must start working at least twenty hours a week within three months of receiving SNAP benefits. If they do not, they lose SNAP altogether. There are some exceptions for certain areas with high unemployment, as a work requirement would be impossible if there are no jobs to be had. During the Great Recession in 2008, the work requirement was loosened for many areas around the country because unemployment was high and jobs were scarce. This was the case in New Mexico, where many Indigenous and Spanish-speaking people of the colonias had no internet nor transportation to even look for a job.

In 2014, the USDA was starting to tighten its screws, however. On paper it seemed as if jobs were returning, though the recovery has been sporadic and inconsistent. New Mexico's Republican governor at the time, Susana Martinez, not only wanted to reinstate SNAP work requirements for people aged eighteen to fifty but also wanted to lower the age minimum for required work to sixteen years and expand it to adults as old as sixty. Parents with children older than six years would be required to work to receive SNAP benefits as well. At the time, New Mexico had the highest unemployment rate in the country and fourth-highest rate of child food insecurity—behind Arkansas, Maine, and Mississippi. The governor's proposed rules to reinstate and broaden work requirements did not pass. In the meantime, other states were reinstating work requirements potentially affecting over 1.2 million people.[32] In early 2020, the Trump administration succeeded in allowing the enforcement of strict work requirements for everyone despite a lack of job availability. Now many states are pushing back in class action lawsuits.

Most people who receive SNAP—that is, over two-thirds—are unable to work or not meant to work. They are children, elderly, or disabled. Among SNAP participants who *can* work, over 50 percent had worked in the same month they applied for SNAP, and 74 percent worked within the year.[33] SNAP recipients who are not disabled see SNAP as a temporary support that carries them through to a time when they might find a better job. But when a person's wages are so low, it is practically impossible to patch together the uncoordinated array of resources such as SNAP, Medicaid, housing assistance, and childcare.

As people increase their incomes, SNAP, in theory, is meant to gradually reduce until the household is no longer eligible for the program. In practice, however, this does not happen. The cutoffs and reductions have negative health effects, especially for families with children. Our Children's

HealthWatch research demonstrated that, compared to their counterparts whose benefits were untouched because they had not increased their income, families with young children whose SNAP benefits were reduced or cut off due to increased earned income were at greater risk of child hunger, poor parent and child health, child developmental delays, maternal depressive symptoms, and household and child food insecurity.[34] In our study, we showed what has been obvious to SNAP participants and food insecurity researchers for years: reductions or loss of support have negative ripple effects, despite increased earned income.

When families weigh options for improving income, they see how they can be debilitated. Simultaneously, they see how corporations benefit from both SNAP and low wages.

The grocery industry supports SNAP because families shop at its stores, contributing to grocers' income and profits. The corporate food industry is also dependent on government programs like SNAP to supplement notoriously low wages. People on SNAP understand this dynamic. The refusal by large companies such as Walmart and Kroger to pay livable wages that value skills and a person's right to meet basic needs forces parents into applying for SNAP benefits. In turn, SNAP participants get blamed for being on SNAP while companies and the rest of society appear blameless.

CORPORATE WELFARE QUEENS: WALMART AND COCA-COLA

There is a racist, sexist trope that many have heard thanks to President Reagan, who referred to women participating in welfare as "welfare queens" to stigmatize and make fun of people who needed extra help to get through hard times. This created a toxic dialogue that portrayed people participating in public assistance as slumming off the government to live the high life. In his recent book *The Queen: The Forgotten Life behind an American Myth*, Josh Levin provides background on Linda Taylor, the woman cast by Reagan as the original welfare queen. The person whom Reagan singled out in order to start a racialized and misogynist campaign against people participating in welfare turned out to be exceptionally unique. Yes, she was one of the few people who abused the welfare system through creating dozens of aliases and managed to bilk state coffers to buy herself a nice car with the money. But Levin explains that she was not at all emblematic of a pattern among welfare beneficiaries, nor was she representative of people with low incomes. Taylor was a one-of-a-kind criminal who abused many other systems in addition to the cash assistance program.[35] What was important, however, is that her case gave Reagan the fodder he and his administration needed to justify cutting welfare programs en masse and generalizing this harmful trope to refer to all people on welfare. Welfare fraud is negligible in the scheme of things, and the concept of the welfare queen is a lie.

The USDA carries out strict quality control, and the most cited fraud rate for SNAP benefits is 1.5 percent. So fraud is negligible, and SNAP is touted as the federal assistance program that has the lowest rate of fraud.[36] Frankly, the fraud lies with the large corporations that leach off such public assistance. The Farm Bill that mandates how Congress funds the SNAP program is a pact between rural white conservatives and metropolitan progressives, most of whom have many constituents in need of assistance and large populations of people who are Black and Latinx. Stakeholders seeking to protect SNAP rely on this dysfunctional marriage. People in Congress from rural counties rely on agricultural subsidies to support big agriculture and small farmers. SNAP benefits keep the grocery industry in business, especially in small towns. So the grocery industry wants to ensure it can stay afloat. This brings in the big agricultural companies along with the food and beverage giants. They are the oversized corporate welfare queens.

Queen number one: Walmart, the largest redeemer of SNAP.

Put together the next five largest supermarket chains, and Walmart's share of America's grocery budget is still larger. A few years ago, Walmart was encouraging customers to contribute food items they bought at Walmart for their employees over the holidays. This backfired, as its attempt to brag about "helping" its employees turned into an indictment that Walmart did not pay workers fair wages, which in turn kept them food insecure.[37] Walmart's average wage in 2022 was $10.50 an hour. Even at this wage, Walmart store workers, most of whom are limited to part time and therefore ineligible for health insurance, remain eligible for SNAP and Medicaid.

Lobbyists paid by Walmart walk the halls of Congress just as members of Witnesses and other antihunger advocates do. We are all seeking to defend SNAP, but for different reasons. What else do those lobbyists advocate for? To keep the minimum wage low.[38]

Here is Walmart's special: quadruple dipping.

Dip one: Walmart profits from paying its workers poor wages while benefiting from government subsidies. This means that the US government contributes to Walmart's profits by providing SNAP, Medicaid, and other subsidies to the people whom Walmart keeps impoverished.

Dip two: The people Walmart pays poorly shop at its stores with their SNAP benefits. So the money Walmart pays workers that is supplemented by the federal government goes right back into store profits.

Dip three: The Walmart Foundation gives money to antihunger organizations such as the Food Research and Action Center, New York Coalition against Hunger, Share Our Strength, and Feeding America to cleanse its bad employer profile and make people feel good about its charity. The foundation also donates food about to go bad to Feeding America. To highlight this, Walmart runs commercials about how shopping at Walmart helps "feed the hungry." In turn, this encourages more people to shop there. Andy Fisher, in his book *Big Hunger*, demonstrates that this type of funding scheme for so many hunger relief charities and organizations muffles the fight for improving wages.[39]

Dip four: Walmart's charitable giving reduces its tax burden. Additionally, according to Americans for Tax Fairness, Walmart dodges over $1 billion a year through tax loopholes. It also advocates for reducing the corporate tax rate and for keeping wages low with members of Congress. This, too, contributes to its profit margin.[40]

In 2020, the Walton family's combined wealth was $210 billion.[41] During COVID-19 and the ensuing food insecurity crisis, the Walton family, whose fortune comes from Walmart, raked in between 26 and 55 percent *more* wealth—topping off its wealth to almost $70 billion each for Alice, Jim, and Rob Walton. While it has varied a bit since then, the family's earnings are astronomical, and their hoarding is exemplary of a pathological society that celebrates them for it.

The Walmart welfare queen's ladies-in-waiting consist of the rest of the grocery industry such as Kroger, Albertsons, Stop & Shop, and Piggly Wiggly—all of which belong to C&S Wholesale Grocers Association, the tenth-largest company in the United States.

Joining into this exploitation frenzy is the American Beverage Association, which includes Coca-Cola, PepsiCo, Dr. Pepper, and Ocean Spray. PepsiCo now has profitable contracts with the USDA to run school breakfasts and summer meals. The company is an ardent supporter of keeping "choice" in the SNAP program. It has joined forces with antihunger advocates such as the Food Research and Action Center, Emerson Hunger Fellows, and others that insist that the US government should not "regulate the poor" by restricting access to sugar-sweetened beverages in the SNAP program.

I knew soda was bad, but I did not know how bad until I testified next to Kelly Brownell, director of the World Food Policy Center at Duke University, during a 2007 congressional hearing. In his testimony, he described how the liquid delivery of sugar tricks the body. Sugar is absorbed faster as a liquid than it is in food form, glutting the body's systems all at once. When that happens, the body uses the same pathways that are used with opioid addiction.[42] This suggests that Coke and Pepsi drinks have addictive properties. At that time, soda was prevalent in public schools. For years, public schools were strapped for cash, and their deals with Coke and PepsiCo to place soda and snack machines in schools brought in needed revenue. Beyond weight gain, routinely drinking sugar-loaded beverages increases the risk of type II diabetes and heart disease as well as harms the life chances of children.

As a result of the massive growth in sugary beverages, corn syrup, and many other harmful substances in the food system in the 1990s, young people showing up for military duty were overweight and incapable of training for combat. Only then did the US government become significantly concerned about the quality of food in schools.[43] Remember that during World War II, the federal government was concerned about young people showing up too emaciated for combat.

Scientists understand that sugar-sweetened beverages including soda, sports drinks, and Starbucks's syrup-laden drinks lead to premature death. It took a long time for the research to come out, as the industry was working hard to deflect attention from sugar by demonizing fat.[44] Despite this new-found knowledge, targeted advertising to Black and Brown people as well as pouring rights contracts in schools and universities continue.[45]

Through tenderfooted internal negotiations among the commissioners, the National Commission on Hunger supported restricting the purchase of sugar-sweetened beverages in SNAP if this restriction was coupled with incentivizing the purchase of fresh fruits and vegetables. Tying the two together, we used science that backed up the idea that restrictions and incentives would simultaneously work to improve health. It was a feat that we all agreed to this along with many other potential improvements to health and food security.

We heard that legislators and advocates read our recommendations with "pleasant surprise." But not one congressperson publicly endorsed the report in full. Consensus or not, the report managed to upset many members of Congress on the Left and Right, many of whom are influenced or funded by the corporate welfare queens above. Even the legislators who had been the staunchest supporters of antihunger efforts backed away when we wanted to hold the American Beverage Association to account for harms to public health.

8 POUNDS OF FOOD DO NOT FEED AMERICA

Charity douses anger with pity.
Charity reduces the receiver
and bestows upon the giver
a power and a self-righteousness
that they ought not really have.
Charity keeps the structures in place.

—ARUNDHATI ROY, "WE NEED A RECKONING"

FOOD PANTRIES ARE NOT THE SOLUTION

I came home from work several years ago to find the kitchen counter covered in cans of lentils, chicken noodle soup, black beans, chickpeas, and sweet corn.

At first, I thought, "I'm so thankful someone went shopping." But when my eight-year-old child's head lifted up out of the bottom drawer of our food cabinet with six more cans—two between their chest and forearms, and one in each hand—I knew it was something different. Gabi laboriously set the cans down. Then they let out a breath as if they had been holding it for a long time. Clearly, like me, Gabi felt they had been hard at work and groaned under the strain.

"Hi, cutie!"

"Hi, Momma!"

"What's cookin'?"

"I'm collecting cans! We're having a contest to see which class can bring in the most cans of food. If we win, we get a pizza party!"[1]

My heart dropped, but I tried to look intrigued.

"The whole third grade is doing it. Julie brought in, like, six whole grocery bags full of cans yesterday. It was so heavy! But we need more! If I bring all this in, I bet we're going to win! Did you go shopping? I need more cans. They said we could bring in dry cereal and pasta, too. But it doesn't weigh as much as cans."

There was a glint in their eye. "Get the big ones!" Gabi picked up one of the large cans of chicken soup, "What is this anyway?"

"That's . . ."

"Ah, soup! I like this kind. I'm putting it back in the cabinet."

Silence.

Gabi put the can back.

I fingered the other cans to inspect the cache.

"Can you shop tonight? Peanut butter would be good. You could get a few more jars. The deadline is Friday."

"Well, uh, this all looks like it could be pretty heavy already."

"Please?"

"What is the purpose of this can collection?"

"Ack! I just said! Were you listening?" This is a common reprimand I receive from my children.

"If we bring in the most pounds of food, we get the pizza party. We haven't had one all year."

"Think again."

Gabi sensed my tone and impending lecture.

"I know, I know. It's about hunger, Mom! It's for a good cause. Like, we're helping you with your work."

"Actually . . ."

"Momma. I know it's for a good cause. I care about that. But I admit. The reason I'm interested, really, is because I want that pizza party! Please. Just. Go. Shopping."

Gabi loaded the cans into bags to take to school the next day and backed out of the kitchen before I could ask for help making dinner.

I took two cans of black beans from Gabi's stash to make tacos.

"*Ssiiiighhhhh.*"

My kids used to comment on this long sigh. Sometimes, they would inquire. Most times not. They began to accept my usual explanation. "I'm just releasing the stress of work. No big deal," I tried to make it seem.

Over the steaming beans, my mind went straight back to the gloom of a basement food pantry where I had been a decade earlier. I had visited many food pantries over the years, but the early ones stick in the mind. This one was in a dim-lit church basement. Packed amid giant metal shelving were stacks ten cans deep and five rows high of tomato sauce, green beans, corn, chicken soup, lentil soup, beef chunks, chicken, and an occasional SpaghettiOs.

When I recruited people for the original study where I met Juleen, Celeste, and Tinisha at the Philadelphia food pantries in 2002, the first person who agreed to be interviewed was a reserved Black woman named Grace. She was about forty-five years old, and seemed tired and worn out. I helped carry her groceries home. I followed her instructions to put them on the porch stoop.

She said, "I can get them from here." She gave a long deep sigh as she said it.

Grace told me to come back the next day for the interview.

Tapping in to the food gifting I learned from people of the Cheyenne and Arapaho nation in Oklahoma, I arrived the next day with store-bought groceries. The grocery bags included a bunch of fresh red grapes. When I got there, Grace was waiting on her stoop.

"You OK with stairs?"

"Yes!"

"OK. It's kind of temporary for now. I just moved in."

We walked up three flights. It was hot, stuffy, and dark. She led me into the kitchen with a window allowing afternoon sunlight.

"You hot?"

I hesitated, "Yeah, a little."

She bent under the rickety card table in her kitchen and plugged in the window fan.

I set down the groceries on the table and unloaded them. I pulled out hamburger meat, pasta and red sauce, crackers, applesauce, and grapes.

I scanned her visible kitchen shelves to see if I had been able to supplement. But the random assortment of cans gave no clue as to dietary preferences. There were canned green beans, yellow wax beans, and pinto beans, and about ten cans of "Beef Chunks" and an equivalent amount of Peter Pan peanut butter.

I looked around for a place to sit. So did she.

She gave a nervous laugh, "I don't have any chairs. I've been sitting on this box."

"OK. Can I sit on this milk crate?" I motioned to an empty crate under her table.

"Yeah, if you don't mind."

"Not at all. This is good."

After she consented to the interview, I pushed record and began. When I asked the food insecurity questions, she said "yes" to each one, designating her as "food insecure with hunger" (this designation was still in use). In the open-ended segment, she became more conversational.

"I don't have hardly no food," she said, motioning to her shelves with cans of meat and peanut butter.

I asked naively, "Are you a vegetarian?

"No." She said, "I like meat when I can afford it. I just can't eat *that* meat. I get all that from the food pantry. But I'm diabetic."

"Type I or type II?" I interrupted.

"Type I. I take insulin every day."

She continued,

So basically, I can't eat food that comes from a can.
It has too much sodium.
I just got out of the hospital for eating all that kind of stuff.
Now my doctors told me
about the kinds of things I can't eat.
Sugar.
Sodium.
It's sad.
Most stuff I get from the food cupboard—
I bring it home and I just look at it.

Then I end up throwing it away.

Those cans are heavy too!

I don't know why I bother to bring it all home.

I got no one else who can eat it.

So it ends up in the trash.

I take it anyway because they pack it all up for me.

I think I have a lifetime supply of peanut butter.

Want some?

(*I declined.*)

Even these grapes you brought;

they're filled with sugar.

With fruit like that,

I'm allowed to have something like four grapes a day.

I do love 'em though.

(*Long pause.*)

I don't know why I go to that food pantry.

But right now,

I don't have much choice.

I got no money coming in.

And I'm so damn hungry.

The natural light from the window faded.

"Well, it's getting late. Let's stop."

"Sounds good," I said. I was feeling foggy from the long interview, heat, encroaching darkness, and Grace's suffering.

I handed her the envelope with $50 cash, which she pulled out and counted. She stooped under the table and unplugged the window fan.

"I'll walk you downstairs," she said.

"OK, thanks." I stood up slowly and, disoriented, I headed toward the door to a kitchen closet instead of the hallway.

"Heh, heh. It's this way. Follow me. I know it's kind of dark. I keep the lights off so it stays cooler." We felt our way in the darkness, sliding our fingers against the walls on either side, and slowly creaked down the steep stairwell. Finally, we stepped out into the dusk.

"Thank you so much for talking with me," I said.

"You're welcome. Thanks for the grapes."

"Oh yeah, sorry about that. I didn't know. I didn't think . . ."

"No." She said, "That's OK. I'm going to enjoy all four of them grapes tonight." She chuckled.

Then we both looked up at the darkening sky.

"Well," I said, "thanks again."

"Yeah, see yah." Grace gave a long sigh and turned to face the open maw beyond the doorway to her dark stairwell.

The next day, I stole two folding chairs from a storage closet at the school of public health. I left them on the porch outside her door. A small gift in return for the wisdom and her kindness of letting me in, turning on her fan, and explaining the obvious.

Food pantries are not the solution.

A PIE IN THE FACE

This chapter describes ways that food charities fool the public and themselves into thinking that emergency food is the solution to hunger. I demonstrate how damaging the concept of charity is because it disempowers and humiliates the people receiving the food while propping up neoliberal values and processes that generate waste, mistreat workers, and pollute the environment.

The growth of the emergency food system is in direct proportion to the commercialization of food in the United States, Reagan's policies in the 1980s that sought to dismantle the safety net, and the loss of value in wages that coincided with the dissolution of labor unions.[2] As one of the largest nonprofits in the United States, Feeding America accepts wasted/overstocked food from big food companies like Walmart and helps distribute it to two hundred food banks across the country. From there, church- and community-operated organizations pick up the food or receive delivery to stock their food cupboards, food pantries, and food shelves. In turn, they make this leftover food available to people who wait in line to prove their worth.

The emergency food system is not really a "system." A system has structure and consistency. Aside from minimal emergency preparedness for hurricanes and other types of disasters, and aside from a handful of states that have a "state food purchasing program" or the Emergency Food Program for specific emergency foods that meet dietary guidelines, most of the emergency food system is left to charity.[3] That is, even though the system sometimes relies on state and federal nutrition commodities and purchasing programs, it is comprised of inconsistent, scattershot donations of leftover food, money to purchase leftover food, off-loaded food that is out of date, donations from philanthropists and foundations, and donations from regular people like you, me, and Mrs. Peach, my child's third grade teacher. One can never count on this system in the long term as sometimes food banks run low on food, and food pantries that are run by churches and community centers often run out of food altogether and can have inconsistent, sporadic, unpredictable hours, especially because they rely on donations, availability of food, and volunteers.

Feeding America's primary measure of its impact and importance is in "pounds of food." Though its language is changing, and it increasingly advocates for SNAP access, its pounds-of-food rhetoric has become so prevalent as to seep into well-meaning hearts of third graders like Gabi and college students who are collecting leftover cafeteria food.

The local food bank in Philadelphia is called Philabundance. It is an affiliate food bank of Feeding America. To raise money, Philabundance distributed leaflets in 2019 with a tool kit on how to hold a "food drive."

Advice for companies: "Make it a competition." Track donations so different departments can get "bragging rights" on how many pounds of food they donate.

Advice for schoolchildren: Do a "big dare." Set a goal of donating five hundred pounds of food. For the classroom with kids who donate the most pounds, say, "Donate (insert pounds) and the Principal will get a pie in the face."[4]

Food corporations and grocery stores make a deal with emergency food providers to pick up food that would otherwise be sent to the landfill and for which they would be heavily taxed. Many people describe this dynamic as providing second-class food to people considered second class. Clearly, food that grocery stores donate to emergency food providers is the waste of the multinational food industry, the overflow of neoliberalism, and the cabinet orphans of well-off citizens who are tired of looking at two-year-old cans of lentils.

All the while, people in the giving position host press releases with legislators as well as go on television and radio to brag about helping others. The emergency food system—sometimes referred to as the hunger-industrial complex—plays into the hands of the wealthy and powerful, while disempowering people through the humiliation of waiting in lines for free food of questionable quality.[5]

When people who need food speak of going to food pantries, they talk of shame and humiliation in receiving free food. A *Philadelphia Inquirer* report on government workers who were not getting paid due to the government shutdown during the Trump administration read like this: "First day of emergency food for federal workers: 'Grateful' but 'humiliated.'"[6]

On top of this, research has shown that food pantry volunteers and providers misread or ignore the needs of their clients.[7] These include the need for mental health services, housing support, and legal aid. Only in 2015 did Feeding America decide to address issues of housing insecurity, access to health care, and mental health support. It worked with five food banks, out of a network of two hundred, to start piloting new programming and new types of partnerships, called Collaborating for Clients. But the pilot funding is over, and it is unclear what the outcomes were, it is difficult to find any reports about it, and there is no public information on whether Feeding America will continue it.

Only a small percentage of people who report food insecurity use food pantries. Given the way that Feeding America member food banks and the corporations involved portray their charitable works, however, you would think they were feeding *all* people who are hungry and that they were America's number one way to end hunger. But this is a lie. Emergency food accounts for only 5 to 10 percent of the total food assistance in the United States.

How does that look in Philadelphia? It looks like big white trucks painted with colorful green stripes to indicate a basket, and colorful fruits and veggies surrounding a tagline: "Philabundance: Driving hunger from our communities." In addition to the Walmart logo, its trucks also sport labels for Sunoco and Energy Transfer—companies responsible for multiple oil spills, fracking disasters, and mud spills that have polluted waterways and drinking water across the country.[8]

Despite this toxicity, Feeding America capitalizes on its ability to convince everyday people like you and me that we can also do something in an easy way. The best way to do it? **Click here** to donate. This way, you too can be a "hunger hero."

NORMALIZED DESTITUTION

The surest sign of public systems and entitlement failure is the arrival of a food pantry to the neighborhood, school, church, community organization, university, or military base. When you see a food pantry, know you are witnessing the frayed edges of our democracy and disintegrating moral fabric.

Poppendieck, in her book *Sweet Charity: Emergency Food and the End of Entitlement*, describes how, during the Reagan era, there were many cuts to public assistance, which continued through the Clinton years via welfare reform. During these long decades, the US government was releasing itself from the responsibility of protecting human welfare and the public good. Who was expected to step in? Churches and philanthropists. Poppendieck explains, "The resurgence of charity is at once a symptom and a cause of society's failure to face up to and deal with the erosion of equality."[9]

Emergency food is not really for emergencies anymore. Those traditional emergencies would be a house fire or if someone had a major health emergency and, as a result, had lost income and could no longer afford to pay hospital expenses. Not anymore. Now emergency food is considered by the public and legislators to be legitimate damage control related to society's failure to care for each other. This damage control is done without questioning the dynamics of what got us to this point in the first place. The response is, as Poppendieck said, the institutionalization of a charity culture that "normalizes destitution and legitimates personal generosity as a response to major social and economic dislocation."[10]

Big Bird has helped to normalize emergency food as well. I take some responsibility for that, as I was an adviser to *Sesame Street* for its endeavor called "Food on a Budget." As an international leader in meaningful programming that addresses children's most pressing challenges, *Sesame Street* was ready to take on household food insecurity for families with young children in 2010. At the height of the recession, one-quarter of children five years old and younger were in households that were food insecure.

I loved commenting on drafts of videos with Elmo singing along with a head of broccoli. For my review and guidance, *Sesame Street* also sent me a bilingual draft of a book about Big Bird going with his uncle and cousin to a farmers' market to redeem their WIC vouchers, and then to a food pantry. Horrified at the normalization of food banks, yet trying to keep an open mind, I asked a few members of Witnesses to review the book.

"I think it's great," Carla said. "Because I don't want my kids to feel bad about the fact that I have to use a pantry. I like this because I can see myself and my children reflected in Big Bird and his family."

"Really?" I asked, "you don't see this as problematic in any way?"

No. Not really.
Well, yes.
Things should be different.
It shouldn't have to be this way.
But I want my kids to feel like we are like anybody else's family.

Shirley was at our offices, and she came in to have a look.

I think it's great.
I just redeemed my WIC vouchers
with my kids the other day.
And if a family has to go to a pantry,
there should be no shame in that.

I incorporated the feedback from several members of Witnesses, and *Sesame Street* carried on.

But Big Bird's bilingual book—English one way, and flip it over and it is Spanish the other way—still makes me dizzy with disappointment. Yes, it helps reduce stigma, which can help families cope with hardship as well as protect children and their parents from absorbing shame. This work is what makes *Sesame Street* so profound and transformative. Yet I'd rather write a flip-book that places stigma where it belongs: with the people of corporate America and members of Congress.

In *Big Hunger: The Unholy Alliance between Corporate America and Anti-Hunger Groups*, Fisher added another dimension to the stark reality of institutionalized "emergency food" along with the lack of corporate and philanthropic accountability. He demonstrates how the emergency food industry refuses to engage with the root causes of poverty—such as corporate greed for profit and out-of-control overproduction, which are both tied to low wages and inequality—because emergency food assistance has been usurped by big corporations that actively seek to keep wages low.[11]

Here's a list of top donors to Feeding America: Coca-Cola, Conagra, Kroger, PepsiCo, Starbucks, Walmart, Albertsons, and Nestlé. Fisher describes this corporate dominance to flesh out just how entrenched this charity model is. Everyone who works in the emergency food system as well as the antihunger advocacy space, he explains, is entrapped by these corporations. They pay everyone's salaries, from the truck driver to communications staff and the food bank CEO. Corporate CEOs, most of them white men and women, sit on the boards of Feeding America and the large food banks in every state. Nonprofit dependency on funds from these corporations also prevents people who work in emergency food from advocating for increasing the minimum wage. Some food banks have tried to advocate for increasing wages with mixed results. A nonprofit can participate in lobbying as long as it does not exceed 20 percent of the nonprofit's first $500,000 in expenditures. The Community Food Bank of Arizona made a $50,000 donation to a campaign to increase the minimum wage. As this became publicized, people who had made donations ostensibly to feed people became irate that their contributions were funneled into a political campaign. As a result, the CEO stepped down, even though they were not breaking the law.[12]

It works out, doesn't it? Low wages and public assistance keep people hungry, so they resort to going to the food pantry, which gives Feeding America reason for being. Then CEOs of corporations in today's food industry, who would have been considered robber barons in the 1920s, can call themselves hunger heroes.

MECHANICS OF DISGRACE

Here is how it works. Food banks raise money to buy a warehouse and trucking fleet. Instead of paying to send food to the dump, big grocery stores invite local food banks to pick up food. They pay nothing to the food bank and count the food as a tax-deductible donation. The food banks take food back to their warehouses, where volunteers check the quality. They then prepare it to go to pantries. Not every food pantry works the same, but they have similar processes. I'll give an example from my experiences unpacking and repacking groceries at Zion food pantry, where I met Grace, Juleen, Celeste, and Tinisha.

Before I continue, I highlight that this dynamic has recently changed in Philadelphia since the COVID-19 pandemic. They no longer ask for any verification about "need" or home address. But it is not clear that these new ways of doing things will last beyond the pandemic.

Food pantries get a list of foods they can order from the food bank at low cost. A few days later, they receive it by the truckload. At the pantry, they have a few volunteers who pick through everything to sort and organize. Volunteers unload giant sacks of cucumbers, for instance, and before they bring them out to give to people, they will pick through and throw out the dead-looking cucumbers, or cut off the dead end of a cucumber, and then rebag them and get them onto a rolling cart, which in turn gets wheeled out to the basement common room.

Just outside the door to the common room, people are waiting in a line in the heat or cold with papers necessary to prove, one by one, they are worthy of food. They must have a picture ID or utility bill that proves they are from the neighborhood. They must report how many people are in the home. At some places, the volunteer at the card table asks to see proof of residency for everyone in the household, which can include asking for a birth certificate. There are frequently restrictions on how many times a person can utilize a specific food pantry. Once you have provided some form of identification, you can often be checked against a list to make sure you are not coming to the pantry too often. Common restrictions are once a month or every three months.

Then people are shown the kinds of food they can have. Behind the bread, stale pastries, canned goods, outdated boxes of cornflakes, and rebagged salvaged cucumbers is a volunteer who hands one or two packages over to each person as they walk down the line. Most of the time, there is someone standing near you, watching you, saying in a friendly voice, "You can have one loaf of bread," "You can have three cans of corn," "You may take one box of cereal," or "Only one jar of peanut butter."

Other options are "choice pantries." They turn their food items into "points," and you can select foods up to a certain number of points. Some organizations are proud of their choice pantries, saying they "provide dignity" to their customers.

A 2019 *Philadelphia Inquirer* news story explains how a foundation in the Philadelphia area gave funds to a pantry to put items online so people who were homebound could get groceries.[13] The people who came up with the scheme suggested they were providing dignity. While the news story celebrates the providers, the receivers who were interviewed said they were "grateful for the food" and even more grateful they did not have to show up to get their food in person. A participant explained, "Online ordering offers anonymity. It was embarrassing to go to the pantry."

In an interview with an elderly Black woman I met at a food pantry in 2003, I asked her why she came to the pantry that particular day. She said,

> Well, I'm out of food.
> My cupboards are totally empty.
> I don't really like coming here.
> I'd rather take care of me and mine without asking for help.
> 'Cuz I don't like getting a handout.
> I know some people who would never come here.
> But I always say, your pride can make you go hungry.
> Sometimes you got to leave your pride at the doorway.

In a pathological power dynamic, every time someone participates in providing emergency food, they heighten their sense of power. Every time someone gets food at a pantry, their power and agency are diminished. People who supply food are deemed heroes. They get accolades for donating. People receiving food are considered passive and "needy."

Big companies are unashamed to brag. Once a year, Shake Shack encourages you to buy its milkshakes so it can donate to Share Our Strength. If you purchase a Philadelphia Dunkin' Donuts coffee during its "perks" program, it will give the proceeds to Philabundance. So people who work at big companies can feel good about their charity, they pay Kinkos to make a big foam poster board of the enlarged check for the photo op where company donors and food bank CEOs smile for the camera.

This is a sacred pact of self-congratulation in which charities, corporations, and the media are entangled, especially around the holidays. Dunkin' Donuts, ABC News, and Philabundance are exemplary. Here's a tweet from @Philabundance from March 2019:

> We run on @dunkindonuts! Thanks @DunkinPhilly for a whopping $198k donation as part of @6abc's holiday food drive! TY both for helping #roasthunger #hungerheroes.[14]

Showing off becomes the way to spread the word. On social media, you can create cute food and donation puns such as "peas give" with a picture of smiling peas. Or you can say things like #beethunger and #squashhunger.

For Dunkin' Donuts, it is #roasthunger. Every donation is an opportunity to create a buzz. Never mind that in 2015, Nigel Travis, the CEO of Dunkin' Donuts, made more than $10 million a year, or over $4,800 per hour, while his workers made $9 per hour. At that rate, Dunkin' Donuts employees are eligible for SNAP and may well find themselves turning to pantries to "fill the gap." Travis has spoken out against efforts to increase the minimum wage. He said that increasing the minimum wage to $15 per hour is "absolutely outrageous."[15]

MONETIZATION OF A MEAL

Let's peal back another layer: the monetization of a meal and competition to brag about feeding people on the cheap.

Feeding America has a website called Map the Meal Gap, which helps people see rates of food insecurity in every US county. According to Feeding America, this builds food banks' capacity to say how much money they need to "fill the meal gap." By identifying this scarcity in monetary terms, without attending to the very calculations that go into modeling the calculation of food insecurity rates—wages, unemployment, and the cost of food—Feeding America and its partners use fundraising tactics that follow this logic: "We need (this amount) of money to feed (this many people) for (this number) of meals."

The emergency food industry makes it seem cheap to feed families, degrading beyond recognition the real cost of food and labor.

Share Our Strength is particularly good at this. In a 2019 Facebook post, it said,

> At our DC No Kid Hungry Dinner, we honored two #hungerheroes and raised over $680,000. That's enough to provide over 6.8 million meals for children in need. 🪁[16]

That is just ten cents per meal. This is not possible. This calculation includes either mass-produced and mass-distributed food for which Share Our Strength did not have to pay, or it means that Share Our Strength is leveraging federal funding for school breakfasts and lunches, which has a real cost that it is not including in its calculations.

No matter what, it is a lie.

When Share Our Strength says it can provide a meal with ten cents, it sends a message that helping people is cheap and easy. It also makes people wonder how it is possible that people who are poor cannot feed themselves if a meal costs ten cents. Finally, it makes it seem that when people are providing free food in other ways, such as through the EAT Café or by purchasing fresh produce to distribute through mutual aid, it involves an outrageous expense.

THE PRICELESS IMAGE OF "HELPING"

While food banks insist they keep things cheap, it is clear that legislators see food banks and pantries as an inexpensive way to generate value for themselves and their pet policies. Food bank and soup kitchen personnel are familiar with the cachet they receive from legislators. So to draw attention to food banks, food bank leaders invite elected officials to swing by and pack up some groceries. Conversely, elected officials, Republican, Democrat, and Independent, love to make a show of their ability to "give back" to their communities. The emergency food providers like it because it raises their profile so they can make more money due to the increased media attention. Legislators like it because the public visibility of their charity could lead to future political donations and votes. The press capitalizes on these opportunities to fill the news hole.

When people are running for office, they'll make sure they are seen as charity minded. This backfired, however, for Paul Ryan when he was running for president in 2012. According to witnesses, he showed up at a soup kitchen after it closed, but he still wanted the photo op. He donned a clean apron, rolled up his sleeves, and got photos of himself "washing" pans that were already clean. No one who needed food at the kitchen was present. The photo op became yet another opportunity to laugh at Ryan and his engagement on poverty—smiling for the camera, sleeves rolled up, doing nothing.

President Joe Biden has made two Martin Luther King Jr. Day appearances at Philabundance. In January 2021, before his inauguration, his appearance was a rushed scenario with photo ops of him and the First Lady packing carrots.[17] The Bidens made no official statement, and Philabundance leaders made no attempt to press the incoming president to address hunger. For the second visit in January 2022, it was the same media frenzy. At least he made a public commitment to reinstate the Child Tax Credit, which Congress had just let expire. But not much happened beyond carrots in the box and happy handshakes. Nor were there people present who supposedly benefit from the donated emergency food and scattershot policies. Note that, two years later, the universal Child Tax Credit is nowhere to be seen.

DANGEROUS PATH TO A CANDY HOUSE

With the advent of our awareness of the climate crisis, we are even more cognizant of how much we waste. Emergency food providers are capitalizing on our newfound disgust with our own garbage.

Philanthropists and environmentalists are converging on food waste by "upcycling." Knowing that in the United States, we waste 40 percent of our food, how can we have hungry people? If only we could get the wasted food into the "mouths" of "the hungry." This is another iteration of the same old dynamic of emergency food as second-class food for second-class people. Now it is food meant to be trash given to people we consider trash.

Despite the dehumanizing rhetoric of food waste for people who are food insecure, there are now national organizations run by young people championing this model and celebrating themselves through the metric of pounds of food. This is well-meaning. But this is yet another way for well-resourced people to absolve themselves of the guilt we feel at wasting food.

To hide the fact that we're overdoing it, we make it a party.

Philadelphia has a local radio station that does this every year. It hosts a live radio show during a multiday food drive in a big parking lot as people unload canned food and bottled water from their minivans. What it winds up looking like is not an awareness-raising event that depicts the experience of hunger. Rather, it is a party for the people who donate. It is a magnified opportunity to show off.

Such showing off and self-congratulation makes it difficult to understand what the press releases from the food banks are about. Philabundance did a contest where, if you gave a certain amount of money to it, you could hear your name on the radio. In response, a woman whose husband died recently thought it would be great to hear her husband's name on the radio. It would help her with her grief. The title of the blog post about it is "All I Want Is to Hear My Husband's Name on the Radio."[18] The story was about how much she is grieving for her husband and giving money to Philabundance so they can provide meals; there was nothing about hunger, the health consequences, or its causes. Capitalizing on this woman's grief and loss, Philabundance created more conceptual confusion.

I know it is hard to read about this because it might make you question your actions in ways that delegitimize your kindness or work. But you are not alone. People like you and me are seduced into this kind of thinking by this false sweetness on the outside walls of the charity industry held up by big food, agriculture, and oil corporations. We're lured inside it the same way that Hansel and Gretel, hungry and lost in an environment of scarcity and starvation, are lured to the candy-coated cottage of a cannibalizing witch. The emergency food system is like a sweet-looking white lady eager to bamboozle us into making us feel nurtured, loved, and full from eating sweet treats on the outside of the house.

But inside this system is corporate greed, the thinly veiled ethos of neoliberalism that will consume us, our kindness, and our well-meaning siblings.

Almost all of us have been lured close enough to lick these walls.

You and me, school districts, colleges, the military, the medical establishment, the "experts" on the National Commission on Hunger, and some of your favorite movie stars.

To recognize it causes heart pain.

I hope you can understand the hurt—most especially for people who must ingratiate themselves to get food from this house.

BACKPACK PROGRAMS: SHAMING KIDS IN THE HALLWAYS

None of us can stand the idea of hungry children.

Let us start with teachers and school nurses, who see kids come to school on Mondays who are ravenous because they had little food on the weekend. Hunger manifests in their behavior. When kids are hungry, they have a hard time paying attention to their teachers, or they have stomachaches or headaches. Many teachers and nurses talk about keeping a stash of food at their desks so if the kids are lethargic or complaining of bellyaches, they can be prepared to support them.

Food banks soon learned that kids' backpacks filled with food are a great way to create a sense of goodwill that drives donations—focusing on children appeals to donors who feel badly for children but not their parents, whom they judge negatively. See it? The separation of children from parents.

Feeding America boasts that it hosts over ten thousand backpack programs across the country. These differ from each other depending on the school district, food bank, and varying ideas of teachers and backpack program administrators. When these efforts got started, school administrators thought they could tell which kids were hungry. They signed up children they thought were struggling and left backpacks stuffed with food neatly lined in a row with kids' names on them in the hallway for kids to pick up on Friday afternoons. As you can imagine, not only were kids made vulnerable to getting teased by their classmates, but they felt ashamed carrying the backpacks home. Other times, teachers privately gave a backpack to students and told them not to share food with siblings or parents.

Nutritionists involved admitted that this created a maelstrom at home over the weekends. School administrators insisted to kids as young as six years old that they should only use the food for themselves. Children were stressed by these instructions and started hiding food under their beds. Or they reported to school administrators that their siblings made requests for food, or there were real family arguments about sharing the food. Children knew they were expected to hide food from their families. In return, their families might reprimand their children for being "greedy." In the meantime, the child might be worried about what their teacher would say if they shared food.

There is little research on the effectiveness of backpack programs. What is published describes the resulting strained social relationships that students have among their families.[19] Many people are also concerned about the quality of food, as some programs stuff backpacks with juice boxes, cookies, Cheez-Its, fruit roll-ups, and cheese sticks. Others suggested that sending home a backpack of food undermines the authority and agency of the parents to feed their kids.

Ultimately, backpack programs shoulder the child with the adult problem of mistreating and devaluing each other. Imagine that every Friday, they're hunching over on their way home with pounds of food.

EMERGENCY FOOD ON COLLEGE CAMPUSES

Without a college degree, it is almost impossible to get a job that pays well enough to feed your family. It's becoming even more impossible to get an education and break out of poverty because tuitions are so high. Many college students today struggle to meet basic needs for clothes, food, shelter, and day care for their young children. College students experience significant rates of food insecurity in all types of colleges and universities—from Hawaii to New York, from rural to urban, from public to private, and from two-year to four-year colleges. Depending on the type and location of the research, these rates range from 9 to 50 percent.[20] Food insecure college students are more likely to struggle to afford textbooks, and often miss or drop classes. The reasons for food insecurity are low wages, the high cost of living, and high tuition.

In 2019, according to the College and University Food Bank Alliance (now part of the organization Swipe Out Hunger), there were over eight hundred institutions of higher education that had launched or were planning to launch food pantry initiatives. Despite the lack of proven success in reducing food insecurity, emergency food provision has now become so popular that it is considered an answer to food insecurity on campus. College students are eager to support each other, and to resist and address food insecurity for themselves and their peers. Swipe Out Hunger has launched a campaign called the Hunger-Free Campus Bill. Through its ingenuity and grit, it has advocated for state governments to provide funds to public universities to develop meal swipe exchanges between students for the campus dining hall (not required for community colleges), establish food pantries, and create SNAP enrollment opportunities. Starting with California, which introduced the bill through the work of assemblyperson Monique Limón, five other states have passed this bill, and it has been introduced in at least twelve more states. This is exciting and important advocacy, but there is something missing from its platform. That is, public education ought to be free. Members of Congress have been fighting for free college tuition since 2015. Bipartisan efforts have made college tuition free for community colleges and people who have low earnings (less than 55 percent of the federal poverty line). More states such as New Mexico are creating broad efforts to expand access to higher education.

As well, it is great in the immediate term to get help signing up for SNAP. But the USDA limits SNAP eligibility to those college students who work over twenty hours per week or are caregivers of a young child.

Before and beyond the efforts of the growing and organized movements, college students from both public and private universities have taken matters into their own hands, creating food pantries on campus or organizing ways to exchange meal card swipes. Not only do colleges and universities seek to help students, but they engage in community-based efforts to reduce food insecurity by working with dining halls to donate leftover foods to soup kitchens and pantries.

The Food Recovery Network, another organization run by and meant to support college students, highlights stories of how college students are doing "their part" to "divert food from the landfill" to get it to those in "need."[21] Harvard University has been in on this too. They were promoting themselves and congratulating their students for collecting leftover food from the Harvard cafeterias to give to MassBay Community College. Between Harvard and Tufts, another prestigious private university and one of the most expensive universities in the country, contributions through an organization called Food for Free churned out over a thousand meals a week. These meals go to the "hungrier" campuses of Bunker Hill and North Shore Community Colleges.[22] Put yourself in the high-tops of the community college students. My guess is you would not have much of an appetite for this hierarchy and celebrated inequity.

Remember, meal swipe exchanges, which seem exciting and important on the surface, are tangled up with Aramark, Sodexo, and other large food companies that have profitable contracts with universities. This is why college students are often required to participate in the cafeteria programs in their first and second years: to guarantee profit for the food company that runs the campus food programs. It is unclear if meal swipe donations are even used by struggling students. When I inquired at my own university two years ago how many students benefited from receiving a donated meal swipe, I learned that the total was three people, and the university could not tell us how many "swipes" were even used, even though dozens of students had donated. Where did those "donations" go? Back to Aramark, the company that is responsible for the massive fires in the Amazon where uncontrolled expansion of ranches continues to destroy the lives and livelihoods of Indigenous people *and* to harm our atmosphere.

Many sustainable and just movements among college students are all around us. Look for the ones that focus on sourcing cafeteria food from local farmers, especially Black and Brown farmers and businesses. Finally, if college students and their families want to support other college students, it might help if they supported the free college movements.

EMERGENCY FOOD FOR ACTIVE-DUTY MILITARY

Aside from being viewed as an opportunity to get a college education, the US military used to be seen as a way to escape poverty. If one survives combat, this can be the case. But we also know many people who served in wars and completed their service may still experience poverty and struggle with food insecurity. Much of the food insecurity and mental health challenges that veterans face is due to untreated, unaddressed trauma from combat and other adversity. A study among veterans of the Iraq and Afghanistan Wars found that 12 percent reported very low food security.[23] When they return from combat, veterans frequently experience many hardships related to post-traumatic stress syndrome, and the US government often fails to provide consistent mental health services along with housing and food assistance supports. Some veterans receive disability pay, but it is often too low, and they run short on money for food. In addition to military veterans, active-duty military struggle with food insecurity. This is true especially for those among the lower enlisted ranks who have multiple dependents.[24]

Almost every military base in the United States has a food pantry. This reveals how low the pay is for active-duty military. The Department of Defense, Veterans Administration, and USDA provide little data on the extent of hunger among active-duty military and veterans. Low-ranking service members can supplement their wages with SNAP. But those who live off the base with their families receive housing subsidies that count toward SNAP income calculations. This prohibits them from receiving SNAP.

We learned about these struggles from Mia Hubbard of MAZON, a large antihunger organization, during her testimony to the National Commission on Hunger. She explained how it related to military ethos:

> The principle of leaving no one behind is deeply embedded in the ethos of the US military. But if we continue to ignore the problem of hunger among service members and veterans and the accompanying policy challenges, we are, in essence, leaving them behind and in the enemy hands of hunger and poverty.[25]

Through repurposed pounds of food, Walmart, Coca-Cola, PepsiCo, and Feeding America pick up what the US government leaves behind.

REFERRALS TO EMERGENCY FOOD FROM HEALTH PROFESSIONALS

The ACA of 2010 required the medical community to wake up to the concept of the social determinants of health. Social determinants are food insecurity, inadequate housing, unsafe neighborhoods, exposure to violence, and low-paying jobs. All contribute to poor health.

The ACA sought to ensure people do not return to the emergency room. Consider that if a person is houseless and living on the streets while trying to manage major mental health challenges, they're likely to go to the emergency room repeatedly. People who use the emergency room excessively are called *high utilizers*. Before the ACA, hospital systems could simply bill Medicaid to get reimbursed for the care provided. People who were homeless were revenue generators. Now everything is about reducing the number of high utilizers, who are likely people without shelter and access to other basic needs. This is why some health systems have found that providing housing and wraparound supports keeps people healthier as well as saves millions of dollars in health care treatment.[26]

My Children's HealthWatch colleagues insisted that if hospitals screened for food insecurity and found ways to treat it, it could prevent health problems and reduce repeat hospital visits. With help from the ACA, it seemed the idea was taking hold.[27] Now many major electronic medical record software companies have inserted the first two questions from the food security scale, and some hospital systems are using this measure to screen for food insecurity and refer people to supports. Administrators and health professionals are trying to figure out what to do once a person screens positive for food insecurity. Of course, one can always help ensure people receive SNAP and WIC. But our research among pediatric practices in Philadelphia found that most people who screened positive for food insecurity were already receiving nutrition assistance.[28]

This creates a quandary. Medical professionals want to prevent and treat food insecurity. Medical providers are trying to figure out how to refer people to the local food pantry and other emergency food providers. What they are discovering is that the pantries are open only a few hours a few times a month. Or that their patients may not be eligible to get food because they do not fit food pantry criteria. Or the food is subpar. Additionally, innovative health care providers who are trying to put these supports in place have come to recognize the social services industry is even more broken and dysfunctional than the health care systems.

Heaven forbid diabetes doctors try to refer someone like Grace to the local food pantry. That just gives her more cans to carry home and throw away herself. Remember that diabetes complications get worse toward the end of the month because SNAP benefits run out and families make do with poor-quality food. Some physicians are savvy. If they are powerful enough in their hospital system, they negotiate for much-needed space to have a prescription food pantry in the hospital. My colleague Deborah Frank launched this decades ago in Boston Medical Center, where people get a food prescription from a hospital doctor. But good luck getting those heavy bags home by bus. At a children's hospital in Chicago, there is a food pantry on every floor. The hospital received a grant to install wireless sensors in all the shelving on each floor to count how many people came. This way, it would not need to have volunteers or staff there. It could also do research and create peer-reviewed publications on what the hospital had learned from the behavior of people in the pantries to see what food they took, how often they came, and at what hours. Fathom this cost compared to providing people with grocery store gift cards or straight up giving them cash.

Millions of dollars in medical and administrative expertise as well as foundation funding are leaching into efforts to make referrals to emergency food providers. Clearly, doctors have no idea what is provided. If they did, they would be horrified by how food charity undermines standard medical practice.

If medical professionals, social workers, schoolteachers, university administrators, military brass, policymakers, and advocates really want to address food insecurity, they must become hungry for something else.

III NOURISHING OUR WORLD

Now that we have come to the truth, let's move on to how to start again.

Remembering that underneath hunger is untreated trauma extending back multiple generations; acknowledging that the systems we have in place help people a little yet keep many people in poverty, and in many cases cause harm; admitting that underneath the trauma and death-dealing superstructure is a culture of domination rooted in white supremacist capitalist heteropatriarchy, part III presents principles and ideas that can reorient our society toward mutuality and equanimity for a more nourishing world.

To evolve toward a world where everyone is nourished requires work in three interdependent domains. First, we need to engage in work that is deeply personal and interpersonal with friends and family. Second, we ought to address political challenges in the realm of public policy and programming. Third, we can allow the spiritual force of love within us to heal our relationships with ourselves, other people, and the natural world. We cannot do the personal work of undoing white supremacy and rape culture that persists in our families and our own bodies without also seeking to shift the systems of our society through policy change. They rely on each other. So even if you are not involved in policy decision-making, you can work on yourself and your family, and show up in support of those who do the policy work. You can imagine, talk about, and share ideas for the kind of world you would want to live in. Maybe it is rooted in care and solidarity. Similarly, if you do policymaking and advocacy, you will not be effective unless you, too, do personal and interpersonal work. This will support you in creating systems and policies that encourage people to transform our society. And we all need spiritual depth rooted in love to survive the hardships ahead. We need each other to join in solidarity to help us survive as a species, support the earth's ecosystems that produce and regenerate food, and end the inequality that drives hunger. Solidarity includes a feeling of mutual care and a willingness to support each other with deep respect in a spirit of collaboration, affection, and interdependence. It is a recognition that our own lives are interwoven with those of others, including those of future generations.

There are four chapters in part III. Chapter 9 focuses on personal and interpersonal work; it is an invitation to stay awake, undo white supremacy culture, and pull the plug on patriarchy and rape culture. Chapter 10 demonstrates how we can also undo the harms of racism and discrimination by creating and supporting policies that implement repair for generations of harm to Indigenous and Black people who have suffered indignity, theft, exploitation, murder, and torture. I propose an abolitionist approach to all state-supported systems along with new federal policy solutions based on equanimity, community care, and solidarity. These universal policies demand an evolution of the human spirit, and willingness to evolve beyond capitalism to embrace a solidarity economy rooted in human rights and the rights of nature, which is explained in chapter 11. Chapter 12 circles back around to the gaping hole at the center. I ask us to look again at the data showing how mothers describing very low food security talked about feeling as if, during their own childhoods, they were not loved. To look into the suffering within that gaping hole takes spiritual courage. I invite us to embrace an ethic of love as well as a deep and abiding accountability to the many generations ahead. To do so demands we work on ourselves to ensure we become ancestors who express loving-kindness, compassion, joy, and equanimity. Our very survival depends on it.

9 THE PERSONAL: UNDOING RACISM AND SEXISM

The invisibility of the one-two punch
that is Blackness and poverty is brutal.
Mix that with being hungry all the damn time
and it becomes combustible.

—VIOLA DAVIS, *FINDING ME*

The condition of truth
is to allow suffering to speak.

—CORNEL WEST, SERMON AT HOWARD UNIVERSITY, 2011

ENTER THE DEPTHS OF THE WOUND

Caution: following my suggestion in "Notes to the Reader," this is a time to take it slow.

Caution (verb): as in *to warn*; to give notice to beforehand especially of danger or risk.

Synonyms: "warn, alert, advise, forewarn, inform, wake."[1]

Consider that violence is a human-generated infection that, if untreated and unacknowledged, creates social, economic, and political chaos. In this chaos, those with all the power can continue to plunder millions of people. Once we understand this, it takes some personal work to understand and take responsibility for how the dynamics of violence have shaped us, and what we can do about it.

People who are victims of violence experience tremendous hurt. But it is also important to recognize that perpetrators of violence hurt themselves in the act of violence. People who hurt other people are very likely people who have, themselves, *already* been hurt. A common refrain in the therapy world is "hurt people hurt people." Whether victim or perpetrator, the trauma continues.

Bayo Akomolafe, Nigerian-born philosopher, writer, and CEO of the Emergence Network, describes this two-way dynamic in visceral terms with attention to the lasting impacts of enslavement on those who were enslaved *and* those who enslaved and tortured others. He writes, "My cells, splintered and traumatized by the fury of your whip, are now stowaway communities hiding in the suburban gloss of your presumably white body. / . . . Every time you hit me, you will harden up or you will break down. / In other words, even you won't remain the same. Even you are torn apart."[2] In other words, the white person will never be free from the harm they or their ancestors caused; the damage done returns to haunt, scar, and stain the perpetrator and their descendants. Psychiatrists, scholars, and historians understand that the perpetrator and victim are always embroiled. Akomolafe's image resonates with W. E. B. Du Bois, who said, "The degradation of men costs something both to the degraded and those who degrade."[3]

Akomolafe contends that we will never be able to find a way forward, nor transform the trauma of today that is rooted in enslavement and genocide, unless we bring ourselves back metaphorically and emotionally to the hull of a slave ship and work through it to destroy or transform our political, economic, and cultural systems.[4] This is a wound. The wound holds wisdom.

He builds on the groundbreaking work of Christina Sharpe, who insists that to be Black in the United States is to be constantly in the wake or hold of the slave ship, or to be the ship itself.[5] Sharpe insists that to be Black is to be constantly affected by the ongoing almost-inescapable harms of enslavement (being stolen, "owned," or otherwise considered dead, almost dead, or killable) and constantly hindered by the "weather," which affects the direction and speed of the ship along with the harshness of its wake. As a "total climate," the weather is the surrounding, penetrating culture of white supremacy; its flip side is anti-Blackness. Making very plain that slavery was and is "the disaster," Sharpe argues that the past is ever present. By extrapolation, all systems in the United States as well as dominant cultural influences entrap, limit, and harm people who are Black, Indigenous, immigrant, disabled, queer, and so on. Ongoing police brutality and murders, mistreatment by people in the medical profession, and regular, persistent racism and bigotry in schools, workplaces, stores, parks, research, and the media, are part of the weather.

Weathering, a term introduced to the world of public health over twenty years ago by researcher Arline Geronimus, is the wearing down of people's bodies and organs due to the stress of structural, institutional, and interpersonal racism, classism, and gender discrimination that Black people and poor people experience on the daily. What Geronimus calls weathering some public health researchers call *allostatic load*, a term used to capture ongoing stress on all human organ systems that can cause poor health. Such stress of racism causes early death and greater health problems among Black people, especially Black women.[6] In her most recent book, covering thirty years of research on systemic oppression by race, class, and gender, Geronimus demonstrates how early death, infant mortality, maternal mortality, and so many more injustices in public health are rooted in oppression, or weathering.

To return to Sharpe's work, *weather* is not mere metaphor nor a medical term; it is *normative*. The weather shapes our bodies, pasts, and futures. In the United States, suffering and oppression is a given—as given as the weather. Knowing that Black death and Black suffering (I'll add hunger and food insecurity) are normative, Sharpe asks, How then does a Black person make a life? How do they breathe freely and deeply? How are they enlivened? How are they nourished?

Giving several meanings to *the wake*—as a track on the water's surface made by a ship, or disturbance of a body swimming, flying, or moved; as a gathering around a loved one recently dead to care for them, and in community with others so as to attend to grief and take joy in their life; as in the line of recoil of a gun; as in being alert, conscious, and wakeful—Sharpe explains the necessity of making a way, tending to and caring for each other, in the wake. Such "thinking needs care"; we must take care in our thinking.

Careful thinking: Juleen's painting, as shared in chapter 1, comes forward through the mist of time and into stark relief.

The barrel is the ship.

She is in the hold.

And we are in her wake.

Though she has since passed on, though her body is in orange, green, and yellow (read weathering, read alloastatic load) and painted in two dimensions, Juleen is very alive, very awake.

She's still staring at us.

What does she ask of us?

Wake work as described by Sharpe is "hard emotional, physical, and intellectual work that demands vigilant attendance." She insists that though the "wake produces Black death and trauma . . . we, Black people everywhere and anywhere we are, still produce in, into and through the wake an insistence on existing, we insist Black being into the wake."[7] To do so is to care for each other with an ethos of mutuality and support.

Though Sharpe is speaking directly to Black people and the Black experience, all of us can learn from this ethic of care and the understanding that the legacy of slavery captures *all* of us in its wake to varying degrees.

The Middle Passage is a profound, terrifying wound that continues to fester, bleed, and infect us in today's world. If we do not contend with the emotional shattering of these experiences, Akomolafe says, then any kind of "reform," any kind of societal "change," will keep us entrapped in the same hierarchical dynamics of the slave ship. The hierarchy of components of the slave ship are like this: food is deep below the hull at the ship's bottom, captured African people suffering in chains are above the food, European and European descendants are the sailors on the deck, and the captain's quarters are up high. Each one of us is on the ship because we are participating (willingly or unwillingly) in the racist, sexist, and capitalist ship of modernity. With this metaphor, Akomolafe outlines our quandary. If we try to be good people and help others through charity or policy change without also working to change our society rooted in enslavement and colonization, then perhaps we have eased some people's pain and eased some of our shame and guilt. But less pain without a complete revolution of traumatizing systems that uphold modernity means that all we have accomplished is moved a few people up to the deck to get fresh air while millions remain in chains below.

Maybe some people have a bit more food or better food and air to breathe on deck. Yet if we are not dismantling the structures that got us to this point—racial capitalism, genocide, patriarchy, whiteness, colonialism, and rape—then we are still on the slave ship or in its wake.

Understanding the dynamics of "the ship" helps us understand how so much "helping" of marginalized and exploited people can often reify the current social structures in place. It is not fully helping. At best it is keeping some people out of trouble and harm's way, and at worst it is reenacting violence.

Reforming our judicial and prison system? It makes the slave ship more comfortable.

Providing housing subsidies? It is a fancy upgrade with traces of the slave ship.

During our interview in summer 2008, a member of Witnesses, a married Black father of five young children and an entrepreneur who lived in public housing, brought me outside to look at the long rows of homes on either side of the street. From the front stoop, he gestured with a sweep of his arm to all the Philadelphia Housing Authority homes—that is, homes made available at low cost to people experiencing poverty—and said,

> Look, Mariana.
> Really, *really* look
> at all these houses in a row
> with Black family after Black family after Black family.
> Public housing is just another slave ship
> in different form.

To not repeat the same patterns of colonialism and enslavement, we must find a way to transform the ship. As a metaphor, the ship is a stand-in for what Treva Lindsey calls a "death dealing superstructure," or what bell hooks refers to as the imperialist, white supremacist, capitalist heteropatriarchy that underlies "the interlocking political systems that are the foundation of our nation's politics."[8] What pushes the ship along is what Sharpe calls, simply, the weather. We are steeped in this culture of domination where Black and Indigenous people, queer people, trans people, immigrants, people with disabilities, poor people (regardless of race and gender), and all women—in other words, the vast majority of people in the United States—are discriminated against. How can we possibly make a life in the wake and in this weather?

In a culture of domination, hooks explains, love cannot flourish.[9]

These are not disembodied systems. They are not outside of us and dismantled easily, as if we are taking apart a ship or home.

Remember how I explained in part II that SNAP's monthly funding shortages appear in people's bloodstreams, where they show higher rates of sugar in the blood due to poor nutrition?

The superstructure enters the bloodstream.

Consider how systemic racism, such as state legislators refusing to expand Medicaid, causes greater risk of preterm birth and early death for Black and Brown people.

The superstructure penetrates the womb.

In part I, I described how malnutrition during childhood caused by falsified food shortages alters the structure of the brain.

The superstructure blunts the brain.

Personal experiences of racism are not only associated with food insecurity, housing insecurity, and other manifestations of disinvestment and disrespect. Racism also causes heart disease.[10]

The superstructure invites itself into the heart.

We embody the death-dealing superstructure. If we are not careful, this "weather" will kill us or we will unwittingly use it to harm others.

INTERSECTIONS OF RACISM, SEXISM, AND CAPITALISM

Understanding that all of us participate in the weather to some degree, we are obligated to do personal work as well as prevent and undo these harms. To do so requires paying deep attention to how it works in various scenarios.

Attorney and scholar Kimberlé Crenshaw reviewed many ways in which Black women are discriminated against. She insisted that US law is incapable of truly comprehending and supporting Black women because it only allows for evidence of racism *or* gender discrimination, without considering both simultaneously. Crenshaw suggested we change our understanding of discrimination as an experience that cannot be parsed out in singular terms. She proposed we take an intersectional approach. *Intersectionality* is the intersecting, inseparable experiences of suffering discrimination because a person is Black *and* female.[11] Many have expanded the context of intersectionality to include poverty, gender expression, and disability.

I provide two examples of how racism and sexism enter people's personal lives and their bodies. The first gets to how interpersonal violence such as child abuse cannot be separated from societal factors that promote or mirror it. The second demonstrates how misogyny and racism intersect, and how our social, political, and economic systems exacerbate and prey on intersectional forms of oppression.

Sarafina, several other members of Witnesses, and I were driving back from recruiting new members of Witnesses in Scranton, Pennsylvania. We were entering another casual conversation over dinner as we had stopped for food during our travel. We regularly exchanged stories about motherhood, child-rearing, and the funny things our kids would do and say. Sarafina and I had a conversation with several others listening in.

> **Sarafina:** Yeah, I pop my son on a regular basis. Teaches him a lesson. Teaches him how to behave.
>
> **Me:** Really? Why do you do that? Why do you have to pop him?
>
> **Sarafina:** Don't tell me you didn't pop Sam when she was younger!
>
> **Me:** Nope. Never.
>
> **Sarafina:** What? That makes no sense. How do you get her to behave? Doesn't she misbehave?
>
> **Me:** Yeah sometimes, but I've never hit her.
>
> **Sarafina:** How do you keep her in line?
>
> **Me:** Uh, I guess through redirecting her or maybe changing my tone. But I would never hit her.
>
> **Sarafina:** (*Eyes wide in shock*.) Unbelievable. Did your parents hit you when you were growing up?
>
> **Me:** Well yes, I got spanked and slapped a few times. But just because my parents did it, doesn't mean I would. I would never hit my kids. No matter what.
>
> **Sarafina:** I got hit all the time. *Hmph*. Black people pop their kids to teach respect.

Me: Really? Why is that a "Black" thing?

Sarafina: O-M-G. Isn't it obvious?

Me: Not really.

I was used to being reprimanded for knowing nothing about Black life. Through my own behavior, I continued to confirm for members of Witnesses the many pitiful habits of white people. These include, but are not limited to, such things as talking in a tight white-sounding tone, missing the point, asking ridiculous questions, always eating salads, and being snooty and clueless, fragile in character, and book smart but otherwise foolish.

I shrugged my shoulders, indicating a willingness to be schooled as usual. At that moment, I was working hard to suspend judgment, though spanking and other forms of humiliating children made me cringe and deflate.

Sarafina: It's just Black parenting, Mariana.

Me: Why is that *Black* parenting? What is Black about it?

Sarafina: (*Exasperated.*) OK, let me break it down to you.

When I was down south,
I stayed with my aunt.
I was a kid, maybe twelve or thirteen.
We were getting ready to go to the mall.
And my aunt grabbed my little cousin,
and she slapped him hard, and yelled,
"Now, YOU BEHAVE!"

I asked my aunt,
"Why d'you whoop him so much?"
She said, "Girl, I hit him inside
my own house
with my own hand,
so he knows how to behave on the outside.
He's got to keep in line.
He's got to behave.
If he steps outta line outside,
they wouldn't just whoop him,
he'd get lynched."
See?

Sarafina broke it down: contemporary violence in the home connects to a deep and ongoing history of brutality rooted in white supremacy. Contemporary racist trends were built up over four hundred years of terror perpetrated by white people. In return, these dynamics have deeply affected the child-rearing practices of many Black and white families. Trauma and violence that occur in the home are perpetrated and upheld by our white-dominated society, collective histories, cultural and economic degradation, and active shaming. This pressure of oppression releases stress into the family and onto the children.

Author and educator Joy DeGruy has a name for these dynamics: post-traumatic slave syndrome.[12] This syndrome is the result of four hundred years of unaddressed trauma in our society that is playing out in the family. Behaviors such as denigrating a child or not lifting them up with praise were adaptive mechanisms to help people survive the brutality of enslavement and ever-present threat of family separation. DeGruy provided an example of a white overseer remarking on the brilliance of an enslaved woman's son. A mother would reply, "No, he's lazy and stupid." In doing so, maybe the enslaver would not put a price on her son and sell him out from under her arms to another enslaver. These ways of being and doing may have been protective during times of enslavement, and may have protected many from lynchings over multiple generations. But as I've mentioned previously, in trauma specialist Menakem's estimation, these behavioral trauma responses begin to take on an accepted sense of culture.[13] This parenting pattern considered to be a cultural norm also slams the trauma deeper into the psyche, into a child's body and our collective body.

My refusal to hit my children is also based in my whiteness. My sense of ease and freedom stems from a confidence that my children will not be killed for simply breathing—for trying to live, go jogging, walk in a park, or sleep in their own bed. This is because my children and I are white. If my children misbehave a little in public, it is unlikely they will be murdered. My children and I are protected by white supremacy culture reflected everywhere, especially in the police's cowardly reliance on race to decide whether they will drag out their gun and pull the trigger.

Here's another illustration that exemplifies how these same dynamics are embroidered into our systems.

Always dead serious, Jewell, a member of Witnesses and a Black mother of two children whom I mentioned before as she talked about the inadequacy of Medicaid, described how she was not allowed to receive Medicaid coverage until she identified the father of her children and provided proof of his paternity. This would supply evidence that Jewell was "poor enough" to receive Medicaid. Caseworkers at the county assistance offices document all sources of income. The children's father is considered an important source of funds. The state relies on this information to garner men's wages to ostensibly be reimbursed for providing "child support." To establish paternity, she would therefore be deemed as telling the truth about her financial conditions. Also, this way the state could garnish his wages.

This was impossible for Jewell, however, as she would be required to get his address, which she did not have. Additionally, she would have to be in contact with him, even though he had assaulted her many times and, as a result, she had filed a formal restraining order on him. She knew well that if her children's father could locate her, he would kill her.

Already, the misogyny and heteronormativity in the system is apparent as it refuses to provide support unless the biological father is identified. This relegated Jewell and her children as disposable unless somehow connected to a man. The man is also suspect—criminalized and made to pay child support to the state.

But Jewell sees it as even more complicated. She recognizes how Black men are mistreated by public systems and actively denied gainful employment opportunities. They feel hemmed in with few options. Out of frustration and built-up rage, they may take their anger out on those closest to them. The same societal forces that keep Black men down may give rise to their willingness to abuse people around them. So it is not just one man or one institution that keeps people unsafe. It is multiple layers of systems and societal processes that mutually reinforce oppression.

For Jewell, it was challenging to find ways to protect herself while utilizing the current systems. She explained,

They have restraining orders.
They try, but what do you do?

It takes the cops so long to arrive.
'Cause the fight I had with my children's father . . .
if he wanted to kill me,
he could've killed me
and then been gone by the time the cops came.
I can only testify . . .
Being a Black man in an urban neighborhood
and not being able to find employment,
they get angry and
they lash out at whoever's near them.
Who is that?
You.

Jewell showed us how public assistance sought to enforce sexist ideas by requiring her to identify the father of the children to establish her "deservingness" and extract money from the father of her children. She needed health coverage for herself and her children, yet under the guise of needing money to support that by extracting it from the father, this also put Jewell in danger. Her life became disposable and unsafe in the very act of applying for health insurance.

In the meantime, her oldest son became damaged by witnessing the abuse she received from his father. Remember, this is an ACE. He manifested severe behavioral problems, including setting his own bed on fire. This caused a house fire that made it unlivable. As a result, not only were she and her family houseless for a while, but it became clear that her son needed residential treatment for significant, debilitating trauma-related symptoms.

The two examples above demonstrate how racism, sexism, and capitalism intersect. The racism and heteropatriarchy are clear. The capitalism is right there in Jewell's experience because she was poor in the first place due to low wages necessary to generate corporate profit. The father's wages were also going to be garnered and sucked back into the state system, thus taking the hard-earned fruits of his low-wage labor. To receive some help and promote her health and right to live, Jewell had to apply for public assistance, which in turn harnessed patriarchal tactics with lethal potential.

As a Black man, Jewell's former partner is far more likely to be imprisoned than a white man; in fact, despite reduced sentencing laws and other attempts to curb mass incarceration, Black men are still far more likely to be imprisoned than white and Latino men. He is at risk for going to jail for unpaid child support too. When one in three Black men are at risk for being ensnared by police and prisons, our carceral society creates more trauma, disenfranchises communities, robs Black people of voting rights, and truncates their ability to build economic security.

INTERSECTIONAL CAPITALISM: THE ECONOMICS
OF RACISM AND MISOGYNY

Capitalism relies on inequality. It gained its global might through three harmful processes: colonization (land theft and genocide), the transatlantic slave trade, and truncating women's rights. Through legal domination, capitalism also relied on criminalizing anyone who resisted or refused to work within this hierarchical structure. It is important to remember that capitalism is not a mere economic structure devoid of social, cultural, and political influences. It *relies* on them. This is why it is important to take an intersectional approach to understanding capitalism. Building on the work of Du Bois, political theorist Cedric Robinson is credited with creating the term *racial capitalism*. His investigations show that capitalism and racism are mutually interdependent. Going deeper, he shows that racism helped give rise to capitalism. That is, capitalism itself was developed through human trafficking, enslavement, and genocide to facilitate the land theft that supplied white settlers with plantations to exploit the labor and bodies of millions for profit. Indeed, if one merely considers who constructed the original buildings in almost any East Coast and southern city, we see the interplay of colonization and enslavement as the foundations of America's supposed economic prowess. This exploitation of people and land was racialized—that is, it was legally justified through the racist lens of white supremacy, where anyone who had a tint in their skin color was deemed subhuman by white people and unworthy of owning land as well as participating in the economy and politics. Their only value to white people was in their service of white people. This racialization was legitimized and strengthened by western European legal systems, which made it possible for people who were exploited in Europe to come to the Americas and build wealth through this hierarchy. Robinson explains that all capital expansion was achieved through the racialization of others to devalue their labor and land, thereby creating the current world economic order.[14]

While many have adopted this stance in their analyses of capitalism, lesser known but growing in influence is the recognition that not only were colonization and racism foundations of capitalism but so is misogyny—the hatred, mistreatment, and abuse of women. Writer and feminist activist Silvia Federici explains the outrageous details of the third form of mass violence forming the three-legged torture stool of modern capitalism: the state domination of women by forcing them from the commons, limiting their ability to earn wages by disappearing them altogether from the workforce so as to subjugate their bodies and labor to reproduction and caregiving only. Through this process they were reduced to simply reproducing more labor.[15] Any woman who lived alone, grew and utilized herbs for healing, including abortion and fertility control, or refused the rising new economic systems was criminalized, and thus under the threat of being tortured to death by burning at the stake or incapacitated through other means. Federici points out that between the 1400s and 1600s as feudalism was breaking down, and many women were joining in social movements in solidarity with serfs, artisans, and merchants to resist feudal lords and protect the commons, the powerful elite were worried about the loss of land, profit, and power. To retain power and profit, they sought to subdue and terrorize women to relegate them to reproduction and housekeeping. Poor women, too, became property, as did slaves. To be property denies one's humanity. Enslaved people were "thingified."[16] That is, they were denied any opportunity to be the sovereign of their bodies, children, present, and futures. They were therefore disposable, commodified, traded, exploited, tortured, and raped to create more property (not people).

The same forces thrive today under different guises: the unpaid labor of housework and child-rearing, no family leave, no sick leave, the criminalization of abortion and family planning, and rampant intimate partner violence. Federici underscores that throughout history, when there is significant economic downturn and population loss (as happened in Europe due to various famines, including the Great Famine of 1315 and the Black Death), women become further subjugated to produce more bodies for the powerful to control and exploit. With this analysis, it becomes clear that the public hand-wringing by US conservatives in 2022 about low birth rates along with the fickle economy, Supreme Court's overturning of *Roe v. Wade*, and concurrent state bans on abortions are a part of this ongoing process. To force women to give birth reduces their power, autonomy, and bodily sovereignty. It simultaneously creates more people for the rich and powerful to plunder.

Overall, the domination and exploitation of Indigenous people, Black people, and women helped capitalism to emerge and to regenerate itself. These intersecting layers of oppression continue to keep women of color down especially. Scholar Susila Gurusami utilizes the term *intersectional capitalism* to drive this point home. She asserts that "during enslavement, the production of white capital required the literal co-optation of Black women's wombs for the reproduction of white profit; enslaved black women were dismissed as hypersexual breeders incapable of being good mothers, while white slaveholders simultaneously leveraged Black children to force their mothers into compliance."[17] This process embedded and obscured within it the legal and moral justification for rape (which I will get to soon).

UNDOING WHITE SUPREMACY CULTURE

Don't let this focus on intersectionality, which makes us focus primarily on the victims of intersectional oppression, let you forget that such experiences are also a reflection of ideas, practices, and beliefs about "whiteness." White people had to be subjugated into these practices as well. As I explained in chapter 5, after the supposed abolition of slavery, white lawmakers installed the Black codes, making it illegal to hire and pay Black people, intermarry with white people, and fraternize or go into business together. So white people were disciplined into this ongoing subjugation. The concept of whiteness justified opportunities to exploit Black and Indigenous people by paying low or no wages, stealing land, restricting educational advancement and health care, and denying access to clean water and air. Concepts of whiteness not only legitimized power and control for white people, especially through the development of the US legal system, but also, in the words of legal scholar Cheryl Harris, today's ideas of whiteness "enshrines the status quo as a neutral baseline, while masking the maintenance of white privilege and domination."[18] That status quo consists of the unchallenged political, economic, and social systems in the United States.

Once you see the exploitative processes of capitalism and racism that rely on inequality, subjugation, and early death, the contours of whiteness or white supremacy culture become visible.[19] Much of the time, white supremacy culture is invisible, most especially to white people who simply consider their way of being as the norm.

White supremacy culture does not just belong to or get harnessed by white people but rather by all kinds of people. It is actually quite common for people of color and marginalized groups to utilize these ways of doing and being to get ahead, or merely survive. The characteristics of white supremacy culture identified by Tema Okun are the tendency toward perfectionism, a sense of urgency, defensiveness, appreciation of quantity over quality, outsized worship of the intellect and written word, conviction that there is only one right way to do something, paternalism, either-or thinking, power hoarding, individualism, love of "progress," insistence on ideas of objectivity, right to comfort, and an emphasis on thinking and writing over emotional wisdom and self-expression.

These characteristics show up in office culture as well as within the culture of politics, business, academia, philanthropy, the judicial system, education, welfare, and health care, and yes, in antihunger spaces. There are many antidotes to whiteness, and hundreds of books and articles developed over decades, along with many organizations that invite people to become more self-aware and get started in changing their assumptions and behaviors about what is appropriate or successful behavior in school, on the job, on the field or court, and in the courtroom.[20]

But let us not fall into that trap of thinking we can read our way out of white supremacy culture. It takes a reorientation to the world with a deep recognition that our patterns of thought are shaped across many generations.

Ultimately, to undo white supremacy culture, it takes a willingness to betray ancestral patterns of owning and controlling other people, and assuming that the way things are at the office, or in government and philanthropy, and so on, are to be accepted and celebrated as professional and socially appropriate. Through discomfort and vulnerability, there is growth and learning; it creates an openness to accepting that all kinds of people have inherent wisdom that should be valued. Undoing whiteness requires solidarity across lines of class, race, ethnicity, gender, and geography to value our common humanity and power. We should also move beyond false notions of objectivity and encourage the concept of both-and along with shared decision-making. We can begin to recognize how defensiveness may be a cover for fear of losing power and credibility, take more time to ensure decisions are thoughtful and inclusive, and be patient with mistakes. Ultimately, dismantling whiteness is about grounding oneself in humility, gentle curiosity, deep listening, and getting out of the way of Black people, Indigenous people, immigrants, and all people of color who are already taking the lead or trying to.

Viewing white supremacy culture as primarily rooted in a racialized trauma response, Menakem, in his book *My Grandmother's Hands*, explains that white supremacy culture keeps us dissociating and disengaging from our emotional depths by staying always busy, running, doing, and thinking rather than feeling what is going on in our bodies.[21] True, harnessing white supremacy culture helps many of us to survive and succeed. But when we do so, we cause harm to many people by devaluing emotions as well as people's desire to be loved and valued, and we do so at tremendous cost to our own emotional well-being.

Those focused on undoing white supremacy culture and its harms insist that we work with our need to express grief; that we build our capacity to feel and express a broad range of emotions without fear and self-loathing. Having depth of emotion allows a person to develop empathy and compassion. It opens us to all sorts of new relationships with different kinds of people. It exposes us to more ways of accepting, empathizing, and having compassion for people who are different from us. Otherwise, we miss out on many nourishing friendships. Almost parallel to the work of Menakem, Larry Ward explains that in order to heal America's racialized way of being and doing, we need to become "whole again by embracing grief. Our grief work is probably the most important thing we can do at this time of awakening as a society, to heal the places in us and in our country that have not known love."[22]

MELTING INDIFFERENCE

The sound you make
upon awakening
in a time like this
is not "Hallelujah!"
It's not, "I get it."
It's not, "Amen."
It's not, "Finally."
It's not, "I'm ready."
It's a sob.
Sob is not nothing.
Sob is not "what you do"
before you do something.
Sob is an act of subversion.

—STEPHEN JENKINSON, INTERVIEW ON *END OF TOURISM* (PODCAST)

We cannot move toward love, compassion, and care for others unless we move beyond our intellect. It has to be done in action, and the action forces us to engage our bodies with meaningful emotional awareness.

If one looks underneath indifference, rage, fear, and avoidance, one is likely to find profound grief—the kind that brings forth the sobs when we wake up to the horrible injustices in front of us. If our ancestors allowed such emotions to emerge, our hearts might be more likely to be open to empathy, compassion, and understanding. We would be able to reach out to each other with kindness, fellowship, and solidarity. If the full depth and breadth of emotional awareness were allowed, the current state of the affairs in the United States, where half of all children are born into poverty, would likely not exist.

But many people who have wealth and power in the United States take no time to assess what is really going on. This is the indifference underneath the death-dealing systems. Indifference to one's own pain and that of others is how people in power have been able to stay "on top" for so long. It is by shutting down their emotions in a traumatic tradition of dissociation. This shuts down their ability to connect with people, especially Black, Indigenous, and Brown people.

It is difficult for many of us to understand when we see and experience indifference around us. I've been trying to get a handle on why people are indifferent by observing and listening deeply to the people in my life. I loved my mother dearly, and she did her best to raise my siblings and me with humor and grace, but she was also emotionally shut down, unwilling and unable to process deep emotions. She taught me to do what she did to survive, which is to keep my emotions tucked tightly away, deep inside. As I explained in the introduction, this can be the trauma response of dissociation.

My mother took great care in her relations with strangers. "Say hello and give a firm handshake," she would coach me. "Look the other person in the eye and stand up straight." This form of greeting was usually a cool encounter that expressed a slight hint of charm, but that also signaled social status, confidence, top of the hierarchy, and a sense of untouchability.

We sometimes attended the Episcopalian church. After the sermon, the minister would say, "Now it's time to pass the peace." Passing the peace is a way of greeting the people around you with a handshake or hug. You say, "Peace" or "Peace be with you," and smile. It was the only time we took your eyes off the minister and hymnal to acknowledge the shared humanity of the people around us.

This was my favorite part of church. It was as if I was given permission to remember that I belonged to a group beyond my own family. I liked it, too, because it felt like transgressing a strange boundary my mother instilled. In passing the peace, I could talk to other people I didn't know. When adults I didn't know smiled at me and shook my hand, saying, "Peace be with you," it felt equalizing and kind. My heart warmed.

But mom felt differently. She would stiffly turn around to one person behind her, give an equally stiff handshake, smile, and turn around to reinhabit a stone face. On the contrary, I'd pass the peace on my mother's other side, to three people behind me, a few behind them, and then a few in front.

I was amazed by my mother's stiffness. Something about touching another stranger and saying "peace" seemed just too intimate for her. It's possible my mother felt that to greet people with "peace be with you" would open an emotional wound deep inside her that she had been protecting all of her life. To say something emotionally caring to another person she did not know well that indicated intimacy and equity was too threatening to her self-defenses. Being vulnerable with her children was also threatening. She protected her heart from everyone.

In my adulthood, I recognized that my mother had been masking a deep depression that was, in many ways, a response to both her parent's alcoholism and her low sense of self-worth. In the rare private moments we shared, my mother sometimes talked about the quality of her depression. She explained that perhaps her own sadness was rooted in how her mother treated her. My mother explained that her mother had unaddressed, unprocessed grief, which was passed on from *her* mother (my great-grandmother). My grandmother, my mother explained, always felt inadequate. She was depressed and devalued because my grandmother's mother was filled with grief at losing her first two children, both boys. One died as a baby from "crib death" or sudden infant death syndrome. The other died at age fifteen from the flu during the pandemic of 1918. He lied about his age so he could drive an ambulance for flu victims, and did so against his parent's wishes. He caught the flu and died quickly, it seems, without reconciliation with his parents.

From that moment, my mother explained, her grandmother always wore black to signal she was in mourning for her boys, and never expressed much care and support for her girl children. Her grandmother always favored boys (perhaps unaddressed grief she felt for having lost her boys or internalized sexism, or both), and made her girl children feel inadequate, worthless, and burdensome. This may have been a major cause of my grandmother's alcoholism, my mother commented. Perhaps this is rooted in my grandmother's low self-worth as well as limited opportunities for self-expression and actualization. This then, my mother theorized, circled back on itself as a form of self-abuse. My mother picked this up as well. In my mother's attempts to prevent passing on her own low self-esteem to us, she worked hard to hide her feelings of grief, loss, and sadness. Most of that original grief was not originally hers, but she made it hers by holding her mother's and grandmother's grief tight to the chest.

"I'm afraid of my depression," she said. "I have a deep gaping hole at my center. It's a dangerous powerful whirlpool that threatens to suck me in if I look at it and try to face it. So to avoid it, what I do is I keep busy, very busy. I do not like to sit down for a second."

This did not surprise me. During my late childhood in the early morning of summertime, when my siblings and I might be languishing over our Cheerios on the front porch, we could hear her coming around the corner. If we couldn't scramble away, we would brace ourselves for the inevitable questions,

What are you going to do today?!
What's your plan?!
Everyone needs a plan!

Not only did it make her nervous to stay in one place or sit still, but anyone else sitting still or simply relaxing without a plan to start running put her on edge. These are the ways she transferred the trauma response in white culture: everything is urgent, so always stay busy to avoid opportunities to feel. Plus always being busy is rewarded by other white people. This makes one feel important and seem important to others.

She continued, "I always stay busy so I can avoid this fear of falling into the hole that has always been there. I am afraid to fall in. So I have to keep running, and running, or stay busy. Because, if I relax and look over the edge, I'm afraid I will get drawn in and never get out. It would be the end of me." My mother knew her problem but had few resources she could muster up to change herself. As well, she relied on my father, a sexist in his own right, for income and companionship. It seems she could not muster the energy and courage to transform without support of those around her.

My mother's constant running and doing naturally kept my siblings and me in a constant state of churning. I was always running, striving, and doing. We were never encouraged to stop, take time to feel our emotions, or just relax. We were certainly never provided the tools for looking over the edge into our own gaping holes.

Here you see at least four generations of white women limited by patriarchy and depression. Where is the racism? It's so embedded in my family's history as to render itself invisible to my family. Only in 2020, long after the death of both of my parents, was I able to get my siblings and cousins to engage in a conversation about enslavement. Interestingly, I was able to begin that conversation after my cousins sent a group email to my siblings and me with a digital image of a letter from that fifteen-year-old boy, my great uncle who, a few weeks after writing the letter, died of the flu in 1918. I knew that was my opening to start a conversation about it—especially since we were all sheltering in place, feeling vulnerable and anxious. Despite my occasional requests to learn more, it never occurred to my siblings and cousins to investigate enslavement in our family history, despite our grandmother's drunken rants about our great ancestors of Virginia while she pointed to the white men in scary-looking portraits on her wall. No one ever mentioned our family's history of enslaving people. Our genteel iciness froze over the deep holes within us and helped us resist attempts to touch that history.

I began the research in earnest in 2020. After a few months of learning how to search the censuses, I found that all four of my grandparents were directly descended from many enslavers. Getting help from an organization called Coming to the Table that supports research, connection, reparations, and many other forms of engagement among descendants of enslavers and people who were enslaved, I built up enough courage to learn how to look. I found more than four hundred people whom my ancestors had enslaved. As I continue to uncover documents, the numbers keep growing. The research is slow and painful, and some of it necessitated talking with my cousins and asking them to go through the dusty boxes they saved with wills and other documents. At the end of my first Zoom meeting with some of my siblings and cousins to discuss our process, my white Virginia cousin, a man around my age, slowly said, "I knew our family had enslaved others, but I guess I never considered till now that our ancestors were rapists."

Many of us white descendants of enslavers keep running and running around so we don't have to confront the truth at the center of our comfortable lives, much less allow ourselves opportunities to touch emotions that go generations deep. What are these emotions? They are likely a complex of unaddressed unbearable grief or horror that can shatter the spirit. That deep hole to the past goes all the way back to the ships with thirty million Africans stolen and entrapped by the transatlantic slave trade. And it goes deeper still, to the embers leftover from tens of thousands of women burned at the stake. Yet for many, as a trauma response, it is frozen over by generations of fear, shame, and self-numbing. This is the ice of indifference.

That deep hole of time travel makes a sound. It's a sob that demands to become a scream.

RAPE CULTURE

Since we're leaning into the sobs and screams, let's get back to food insecurity and name the depth of the trouble that Juleen, Celeste, Tinisha, and Remi made clear. At the center of the depths of this suffering that manifests on the surface as hunger is rape. Rape, and all the associated trauma responses to it, are a taproot that generates and regenerates the experience of hunger. So to put an end to hunger, we must put an end to rape and rape culture.

Rape is a serious harm experienced by people of all races, ethnicities, and genders. Rape wounds a person so profoundly as to damage the soul. The soul is the deepest aspect of self and identity. Harms to the soul last much longer than physical or emotional injury because, as a sexual violation, rape strikes at the core of our own sense of being human and leads to feelings of deep shame. It is a harsh violation of the sacred.

Sarah Deer, a law professor and member of the Muscogee (Creek) nation of Oklahoma, takes on some of the United States's hardest cases of violence against Indigenous women. She asserts that decolonizing and promoting Indigenous sovereignty demands that we put an end to rape itself. From Deer's point of view, colonization is a systemic and complete violation of Indigenous people's identity and sovereignty.[23] Deer explains that colonizers utilized the same tactics that sexual predators use such as humiliation, manipulation, deceit, and physical force. Colonization has the same impact as rape: comprehensive devastation along with the loss of land, place, meaning, and self.

Hence rape is not only an interpersonal act of grave violence and domination but also a political construct that reveals the trauma at the foundation of the United States. Moreover, the reframing of colonization and enslavement as rape brings in the very tangible weight of how patriarchy—the toxic and dangerous ideology as well as actions by men who think and act as if they own the world and everyone in it—wounds the soul. This wound is not metaphoric; it is palpable and real.

Rape culture supports a social, economic, and political environment that allows for and encourages sexual violence against women and children. In the United States, one in four girls and one in thirteen boys have experienced sexual violence.[24] In adulthood, one in six women has been a victim of attempted or completed rape. For Indigenous women, it is one in three.[25] These numbers may be even worse, however, as we know that most women do not report their experiences of rape to legal authorities for fear of being mistreated by the police and judicial system, and for fear of losing their children.

Such fears are rational. Consistent, unrelenting police violence against women and police entanglement with child protective services are well documented. Why would a woman subject herself to reporting the harms against her by calling men in uniform backed by county, state, and federal government with guns and tasers who themselves are known perpetrators of violence? A Buffalo, New York, news report found that every five days, a police officer is charged with committing sexual assault.[26] In their book *Invisible No More: Police Violence against Black Women and Women of Color*, Andrea Ritchie and Angela Davis outline the myriad ways in which the police and judicial system actively engage in violence against women. One of those is legalized rape. There are thirty-five states that allow police to "have sex" with people in their custody—that is, while on duty, and while someone is caged or in handcuffs.[27] This is not consensual; it is legalized rape by state authorities.

The police are just one official entity with extraordinary powers that partakes in rape culture. Predatory exploits by men reach the highest levels of power in the United States to include numerous presidents, members of the Supreme Court, CEOs of large companies, rock and rap stars, gymnastics coaches buoyed by the International Olympic Committee, movie moguls protected by Hollywood agents, and university deans.

This despicable legitimized behavior and sexual exploitation is not new. The rape culture of today is founded on thousands of years of legal rape and violation that have been mandated and encouraged by people in positions of supreme power.

Consider the pope along with the kings and queens he served.

The papal bulls (official decrees from the Vatican) legitimized rape. They justified and endorsed policies to declare the enslavement of others a "divine right." In 1452, Pope Nicholas V gave a "directive" to the king of Portugal to go to the west coast of Africa to invade, subdue, and reduce its people to perpetual slavery and take away all of their property. In 1493, Pope Alexander VI said, "It is pleasing to the divine majesty to subjugate Africans and anyone else who does not believe in the Christian god." In Lenni Lenape historian Steven Newcomb's analysis, the Latin word for subjugation was *deprimanteur*, meaning to reduce, cast down, press down, or hold down. The pope declared, "This is how empires succeed."[28] These enslavement edicts were repeated seven times in the years that followed. Considering this historical and legal dynamic, I cannot help but think of Juleen: pressed, held down, and raped by her father-in-law on the sofa, and who, in order to survive another day, had no choice but to shut down all emotion.

The Spanish, Portuguese, Dutch, English, Swedish, and French were involved in the terror trade. Centuries later, George Washington, Thomas Jefferson, Edmund Randolph (my ancestor), or fill in the list with the white men who signed the US Constitution built this country on rape that was legitimized by racism, patriarchy, and capitalism. These "founding fathers," most of whom enslaved others, had the legal wherewithal and economic incentive to rape women to produce more slaves and more wealth. This wealth is coupled with the soul-wounding violence on which our country was built.[29]

Patriarchy, whiteness, and capitalism rely fundamentally on the idea that men have a right to control, dominate, and own everything—especially women and children.

What happens to white people's souls and the souls of men in this process?

Through more and more domination, they cut themselves off from emotional and spiritual bonds. hooks explains that patriarchy is part of a culture of domination and emotional truncation that forces men to fragment themselves and cut themselves off from feeling deep emotions as well as a sense of love and belonging. How this emotional truncation manifests is often through "psychological terrorism and violence."[30]

Patriarchy, and as an extension heteronormativity, which refuses to accept and embrace nonbinary, trans, and the full array of gender expressions, is upheld through keeping family secrets about violence in the family. This secrecy allows a culture of domination to continue. Additionally, patriarchal culture conditions many of us to somehow become sucked in to believing that love and connection is women's work and a woman's domain. This in turn encourages men to become and remain "emotional cripples," according to hooks, and cut off from their full emotional well-being.[31] As Judith Herman, expert on the trauma of violence against women, explains, there are many men who have committed rape, incest, and other forms of sexual assault who have an utter lack of remorse or tenderness toward the people they harmed.[32]

Healing from hunger and the culture of domination demands that we begin with the truth of the emotional wounding that millions of people seem so eager to ignore or hide. Continuing to hide it only makes the festering more combustible (to use Viola Davis's term) in the family and our body politic.[33] When I say millions of people, I mean regular people who seem to just "go along to get along." This is how the violence of racism, colonization, and patriarchy continue.

To address and heal hunger, the US government and formal institutions not only need to bring forth and reckon with the truth about the terror and harms of enslavement and colonization generally but also specifically about the violence against women and children. Our society enables ongoing racism, discrimination, and violence against women. Herman insists that tyranny in the household is a mere reflection of the tyranny tolerated and facilitated by our society. In tyrannical societies, she argues, the rules are simple. They are governed by the rules of dominance and subordination. "The strong do as they will because they can. The weak and vulnerable submit. Bystanders are fearfully silent, willfully blind, or willingly complicit with those in power."[34] Regardless of representatives of the US government proclaiming that the United States is a democracy, the rules of tyranny still apply when entire groups of people such as women, African American people, and Indigenous people are excluded from the full rights of citizenship. Rape, like hunger, is as American as apple pie.

One of the most important ways to resist and dismantle this tyranny is to change the actions of bystanders. Herman insists that in all of her conversations with survivors, what they want first and foremost is help to recover. Second, they want others to know the truth, and to acknowledge the pain and harm caused by the perpetrators. She pays special attention to the witnesses or bystanders, who oftentimes do nothing, say nothing, and provide no acknowledgment. This isolates sexual violence victims even further. Herman has said, "All the perpetrator asks is that the bystander do nothing. The victim demands action, engagement, and remembering."[35] Our justice system does hardly anything to provide truth, acknowledgment, and repair, so we must seek out alternative approaches to healing that do not follow the rules of tyranny. There are many examples of communities attempting to stop the violence and acknowledge the harm caused by assault while providing alternatives to justice, which I get to in the next chapter. Public efforts also include memorials such as the Survivors Memorial in downtown Minneapolis, making sexual assault visible and allowing survivors to publicly memorialize their stories so people can witness and attend.

Tarana Burke, a survivor of sexual assault, started the #MeToo movement on social media in 2006 to promote empathy toward survivors and ensure they had spaces to feel seen, heard, and validated. As a Black woman, her work is especially important. Black women are far more likely to be ignored and blamed for their victimization than are white women.[36] As well, there is enormous pressure for Black women and girls to not report being raped to protect the collective. That is, to report rape by a Black man, family member, or acquaintance would be considered a form of cultural betrayal, thereby putting Black men at even greater risk in our racist society.[37] The #MeToo movement picked up broad support after Harvey Weinstein, notorious Hollywood producer, was finally publicly called to account for raping and assaulting many women after decades of inside knowledge that he was doing so. One of the reasons the #MeToo movement took off again was because most of the women he harmed are white and have public recognition. Many people recognize and publicly insist that when white women call someone out, the world pays attention. Much less so do people pay attention to the suffering and outcry of Black women and girls. Though Weinstein was clearly causing harm over three decades, as soon as white women broke through the silence of the press, the coverage and legal action was swift. On the other hand, Black women and girls had been publicly calling out R. Kelly for rape and sex trafficking for the same amount of time, but few people paid attention. "We are socialized to respond to the vulnerability of white women," said Burke. "It's a truth that is hard for some people to look in the face, and they feel uncomfortable when I say things like that."[38]

Formerly powerful men like Weinstein and Kelly are in prison now, but that is not the answer, nor is it enough to stem the misogyny in America. Millions of people must publicly denounce this kind of socially sanctioned abuse, speak out against it, and refuse to allow it to happen. And we must do so especially when it comes to the suffering of Black and Indigenous women, even as it makes us uncomfortable and feel exposed.

Herman insists that most of the work that needs to be done to end rape culture is for bystanders to stop being bystanders and instead stand alongside and with victims to help with the truth and healing process. Such action also helps bystanders to reclaim (or claim) their own moral standing. Remember: trauma cannot be faced alone; it is too much for one soul to bear. Having witnesses or bystanders acknowledge and help hold the pain can help relieve it and help make way for healing.

This is hard to do, surely. Yes, it makes us uncomfortable because many of us are afraid to lose family members, financial support, standing in our community, and our sense of belonging. But we can take our cue from thousands of people who have been courageous enough to speak up, resist the tyranny, join with others, and break the chain.

Is this what Juleen asks of us?

10 THE POLITICAL: SOLUTIONS FROM REPARATIONS TO ABOLITION

If you stick a knife in my back nine inches
and pull it out six inches,
there's no progress.
If you pull it all the way out,
that's not progress.
The progress is from healing the wound
that the blow made.
They haven't even begun to pull the knife out,
much less try to heal the wound.
They won't even admit the knife is there.

—MALCOLM X, MARCH 1964 TV INTERVIEW

BREAKING OUT OF BOUNDED JUSTICE

More than fifty years after Malcom X's murder and this country *still* has not evolved. Admitting the knife is there means naming the trauma and harm. Once you name it and tell the truth about it, you can start to heal the wounds from their depths. Without going deep to repair the harms of racism, discrimination, and colonization, any type of change that one makes to improve circumstances may mitigate harm but does not end the systems that cause harm. Violence is not only historical, personal, and interpersonal, it is also systemic. To change systems requires political courage.

In part I, I described our research that demonstrated how the relationship between racial and ethnic discrimination and food insecurity was not reduced when nutrition assistance was figured into the model. So while SNAP can help reduce food insecurity, it cannot touch the deep relationships that food insecurity has with exposure to discrimination and exploitation. SNAP is a helpful program, but by itself and in its current form, it will never eradicate hunger because people participating in SNAP are kept poor, and corporations profit from it. It is embroiled with capitalism and therefore maintains inequality.

This limited programmatic effect of SNAP can be called what health policy professor Melissa Creary describes as "bounded justice."[1] That is, even if we have equity at the center of policy and programmatic decision-making with the hopes of improving health care and other systems that affect health such as nutrition assistance, if we are not seeking to repair the generations of injustice, then the effects of the improvements can only go so far. Inequality may be reduced, but it will continue, and hunger will persist.

If our political leaders publicly and thoughtfully reckoned with the truth of the harms of colonization, slavery, and genocide, this can set the groundwork for *reparations* for the harm of slavery and *rematriation*, the return of land, belongings, human remains, and seeds to Indigenous people who are the original stewards. While policymakers work on making these transformative changes to tell the truth, repair, and heal, the structure of social assistance programs also needs to change (from being targeted only to specific types of people) to become universal. Programs that are only targeted to people who are poor tend to keep people poor and separate people from each other to create a false distinction between people who are worthy or unworthy of receiving support. Finally, ending hunger demands we work to dismantle the systems that separate us from each other and simultaneously envision a new type of society that is rooted in equity, mutuality, and community care. We can begin by envisioning and creating such a world through the abolition of prisons and police, and investing in economies that transcend capitalism to promote solidarity.

Think this is impossible? It is not. There are already movements afoot involving tens of thousands of people, there are congressional bills at the ready, and there are examples of multiple alternatives to capitalism that have been utilized for hundreds of years in the United States. To enact policy change, it takes a different mindset and a willingness to envision a world beyond what we have today. We have to heal the wounds and start again.

REPARATIONS

Reparations means compensating victims. Not only should victims receive financial recompense for harm, but there should be a formal and broadly publicized confirmation that a serious and widespread wrong has been carried out by specific people, institutions, and policies. The United Nations delineated over twenty principles for reparations, which include the fundamental requirement of ensuring victims and their families are involved in designing those processes.[2] Reparations must include opportunities for restitution, rehabilitation (inclusive of mental health care and adequate social services), official truth-telling processes, and a guarantee of nonrepeat.

Many know of the Truth and Reconciliation Commission (TRC) process in South Africa because of the transcendent leadership of Nelson Mandela and Reverend Desmond Tutu. TRCs are formalized processes that reveal and contend with state-supported human rights violations such as torture, abuse, murder, enslavement, genocide, and rape. They hold space for people impacted by the events to share their experiences. These processes are also meant to ensure that perpetrators formally explain what they did, express remorse, and describe the precautions they will take to not repeat offenses. Everything is recorded for the official record, and financial reparations and other types of supports or payments are made to help to repair harms. It is important to name the violence, expose the truth, and ensure there are witnesses and justiciable redress that can create the foundations for new government systems. Worldwide, TRCs are meant to expose the truth and create space for healing by calling individual and state perpetrators to account. They are not always so successful, however, as much depends on commitment for follow through and transparent accountability mechanisms.

Brian Stevenson, the executive director of the Equal Justice Initiative, is the award-winning author of *Just Mercy*, a book (and later movie) based on years of helping people tried and convicted as children to get out of prison and off death row.[3] He explains, "You have to tell the truth first. You have to create a consciousness around the truth before you can have any hopes of reconciliation. And reconciliation may not come, but truth must come. That's the condition."[4]

To solve hunger in America, we must come to account with the truth, no matter how painful. Healing collective trauma demands our collective attention, official and formally recorded processes of truth telling, apologies, reparations, restitution, and repair. Unfortunately, the US government has a long history of only pretending to repair. In its usual duplicitous tradition, it withholds reparations as unremorsefully as Lucy of the *Peanuts* cartoon swipes away the football as Charlie Brown comes up for the kick. This goes as far back as the false treaties set up by supposed leaders in the colonial United States as they stole lands, waters, and entire ecosystems from Indigenous nations. Promises of "forty acres and a mule" for all people who were enslaved became yet another a lie.

Today the US government harbors the same reluctance. H.R. 40, a bill in the US House of Representatives, calls for the establishment of a commission to study and develop a plan for reparations for Black descents of people enslaved by white landowners. It was introduced in 1989. Over thirty-five years later, it has yet to pass. Only in 2019 did the Senate sponsor its first bill on reparations. Before that, nothing on reparations had been considered by the US Senate since the Reconstruction period in the late 1800s.

It is not only the living history of enslavement that demands consideration for reparations to help our society work through collective trauma but also so many injustices that have been carried out since. As an example, author and MacArthur fellow Ta-Nehisi Coates points out 250 years of slavery, 90 years of Jim Crow, 60 years of separate but equal, and 35 years of racist housing policy is a long, violent legacy.[5] He states,

> From 1619 until at least the late 1960s, American institutions, businesses, associations, and governments—federal, state, and local—repeatedly plundered black communities. Their methods included everything from land-theft, to redlining, to disenfranchisement, to convict-lease labor, to lynching, to enslavement, to the vending of children. So large was this plunder that America, as we know it today, is simply unimaginable without it. Its great universities were

founded on it. Its early economy was built by it. Its suburbs were financed by it. Its deadliest war was the result of it.

He goes on to say that "until we reckon with our compounding moral debts, America will never be whole."[6]

Political leaders say the United States in the "richest nation in the world." This is nothing to be proud of, as the riches were gained through enslavement and genocide, and half of all newborns are born into poverty today. So people ought to complete the sentence like this: the United States is the richest nation in the world due to historic and ongoing violence against Black, Indigenous, and Brown people, and through the rape and exploitation of women and children.

Since 2015, the National African American Reparations Commission has upheld a ten-point reparations plan. It includes:

1. Formal Apology and Establishment of an African Holocaust Institute
2. The Right of Repatriation and Creation of an African Knowledge Program
3. The Right to Land for Social and Economic Development
4. Funds for Cooperative Enterprises and Socially Responsible Entrepreneurial Development
5. Resources for the Health, Wellness and Healing of Black Families and Communities
6. Education for Community Development and Empowerment
7. Affordable Housing for Healthy Black Communities and Wealth Generation
8. Strengthening Black America's Information and Communications Infrastructure
9. Preserving Black Sacred Sites and Monuments
10. Repairing the Damages of the "Criminal Injustice System"[7]

Note the inclusion of an apology, attention to the need for health and healing, wealth-building opportunities, repair in the (in)justice system, and education for everyone about enslavement and genocide.

The current backlash against the truth of our history in numerous state legislature bills across the southern states seeking to restrict teaching about enslavement and genocide is deeply harmful. Some people refer to teachings about basic history as "critical race theory." People afraid of basic education about history are making it seem as if trying to understand our history is something new and unfair. White legislators and the white people they represent are filled with fear of the truth, unable to acknowledge the pain and harms of discrimination. They are desperate to stay on that slave ship. Perhaps this is a trauma response of dissociation. Such people deserve compassion, but those of us who have the courage to allow ourselves discomfort need to find ways to help our cousins understand how they are implicated in promoting the early deaths of hundreds of thousands of people if they cannot accept the truth and reckon with their own emotions about it. They may try to ban books and threaten teachers who are doing their jobs, but they cannot fight the tidal wave of truth that millions more people are learning to face. The United States is changing, and those who are fearful of such truths are already outnumbered by people who have depth of feeling, courage, and, yes, lots of books.

Several books have also been written that can guide the United States through a reparations process.[8] For hundreds of years, the US government has long had all the evidence and guidance from Black and Indigenous communities to implement a reparations process. More people need to encourage legislators to take reparations seriously.

But even reparations do not go far enough. The true debt to Black people in the United States can never be repaid proportionate to the damage done. In the words of NYU professor Fred Moten, "What it is that is supposed to be repaired is irreparable. It can't be repaired. The only thing we can do is tear this shit down completely and build something new."[9]

REMATRIATION

Moten is not alone in his assessment. According to Daniel Wildcat, Yuchi member of the Muscogee nation in Oklahoma, reparations do not solve what is at the root. In direct response to Coates, he asks, How do you quantify spiritual and practical connection to land? No amount of money can replace the loss of so much territory. The lands currently referred to as the United States and its territories consist of at least 1.9 billion acres. But this territory is not just acres, soil, forests, waters, the Great Plains, rivers, mountains, and ecosystems. This is the territory of spirit too. No financial repair can be made for the spiritual loss. In Wildcat's words, "For many Native Americans, our land (including the air, water, and biological life on which we depend) is a natural relative, not a natural resource. And our justice traditions require the restoration of our land relationship, not monetary reparations."[10]

Many groups are actively calling for rematriating lands and all that comes with the land. To rematriate is to "restore a people to their rightful place in sacred relationship with their ancestral land."[11] The rematriation of land is a process of restoring or regenerating Indigenous lifeways along with all that has been taken including land, seeds, and food for survival. The Native American Food Sovereignty Alliance is already making way for the rematriation of seeds—through seed exchanges, education, and seed-storing efforts—to restore Indigenous sovereignty. Returning seeds and showing them respect is a way of demonstrating reverence not just for Indigenous people and their food ways but also ancestors and kin. Rowan White, an earth tender and seed keeper of the Mohawk Akwesasne, a part of the Haudenosaunee Confederation, explains their meaning:

> Our life is dependent on that adaptability and that generosity that comes with seeds. [O]ne of the only pathways to a dignified resurgence is to reseed ourselves, to reclaim seeds as part of our bundle and part of our way forward.[12]

Another part of the process of rematriation is the return of cultural artifacts, ceremonial gear, and other forms of sacred art as well as the human remains of people murdered in the massacres and wars carried out by the US military. This includes the return of the remains of Indigenous children who were either murdered or died from neglect at US boarding schools.

While ideas vary widely about rematriation and reparations to support Indigenous people and lands, the Red Nation, a group of Indigenous activists, also have a ten-point plan:

1. The Reinstatement of Treaty Rights
2. The Full Rights and Equal Protection for Native People
3. The End to Disciplinary Violence against Native Peoples and All Oppressed Peoples

4. The End to Discrimination against the Native Silent Majority: Youth and the Poor
5. The End to the Discrimination, Persecution, Killing, Torture, and Rape of Native Women
6. The End to the discrimination, persecution, killing, torture, and rape of Native Lesbian, Gay, Bisexual, Transgender, Queer, and Two-Spirit People (LGBTQ2)
7. The End to the Dehumanization of Native Peoples
8. Access to Appropriate Education, Health care, Social Services, Employment, and Housing
9. The Repatriation of Native Lands and Lives and the Protection of Non-human Relatives
10. The End to Capitalism–Colonialism[13]

These reparations extend far beyond those of the National African American Reparations Commission. They demand land be returned and the end of the concept of ownership itself. The places to start with dismantling colonizing forces are right in front of us. The US government should follow its own laws by acknowledging and restoring treaty rights and openly considering treaties that predate the Constitution. Before the United States became a country, there were many treaties between various Indigenous nations, colonists, and crowns. For instance, the living treaty established in 1613 between the Haudenosaunee and Dutch was a treaty meant to establish friendship and peace while living alongside each other for as "long as the grass is green, as long as the water runs downhill, as long as the sun rises in the East and sets in the West, and as long as our Mother Earth will last." This treaty has been violated continuously by the Dutch and many other people of European descent ever since the land was privatized and waters were polluted. Between 1776 and 1871, the US Congress ratified more than three hundred treaties with Indigenous nations. Yet in 1871, all treaty making was suspended through the Indian Appropriations Act, and all recognition of Indigenous nations as sovereign were destroyed, making way for the US cavalry, buffalo runners, and settlers to steal lands, waterways, and ecosystems. Andrew Jackson, responsible for stopping all nation-to-nation treaty making and the Indian Removal Act, which included the Trail of Tears and many other death walks for Indigenous people, as well as instigating massacres and kidnapping children to boarding schools, remains a hallowed US president whose image still sullies the twenty-dollar bill in our pockets.

Every treaty ratified by the US government and Indigenous nations has been violated by the US government. Restoring treaty rights is a starting point. It is not a good one either, as most of the time, those treaties were signed under threat of invasion, murder, and genocide. Beyond agreements in the treaties, there are hundreds of millions of acres of unceded lands that should be returned that have no treaties associated with them.

Additionally, the restoration of Indigenous lands along with the rematriation of seeds, artifacts, and human remains needs to be ongoing and supported. Most Indigenous people view land, plants, animals, and waters with great respect as nonhuman relatives. All rematriation and repatriation efforts must also seek to restore these lost and violated connections due to toxic dumping, mining, and extraction. Once lands, food, and other objects are returned, going forward, every deliberation with Indigenous nations should have nation-to-nation treaties that are respected. All proposals to use Indigenous land, waters, and other resources should have clearly established and documented free, prior, and informed consent. This is established in the UN Declaration on the Rights of Indigenous Peoples (2007) as well. The US government ought to ratify this international treaty and get to work on repair and restoration (I address this in the next chapter).

In the meantime, it seems that non-Indigenous "settlers" who are not descendants of people who were abducted and enslaved—myself included—ought to be paying a portion of rent or mortgage to nearby Indigenous nations. The precedent for this is already in place in the Seattle area. Through an effort called Real Rent Duwamish, thousands of people are already paying rent to the Duwamish.[14] In the absence of government action, people can engage with this in the meantime as standard practice. Similarly, the Sogorea Te' Land Trust, an Indigenous woman-led organization in the San Francisco Bay Area, laid the groundwork to ensure that people can reconnect with their ancestral lands. The land trust is working with officials to protect sacred shell mounds and ensure land is returned to the Ohlone peoples. Additionally, it creates community-based initiatives that help people prepare for the climate catastrophe. These are only a few examples of a widespread "Land Back" movement that has been ongoing under a variety of names for hundreds of years. As more efforts have success, and "public" and stolen lands are returned to Indigenous stewardship, more people will learn to reconnect with the land, and biodiversity may have a chance at being restored.

This has transformative and unsettling implications.

Eve Tuck and K. Wayne Yang argue that real decolonization means the end of ownership of land, bodies, animals, and plants. Anything short of this in our dialogue and actions is inadequate to restore the lifeways and livelihoods of Indigenous peoples. This seems almost inconceivable in today's world. Tuck and Yang insist on an ethic of incommensurability. This, they say, should unsettle white innocence, and is in direct contrast to the aims of reconciliation. Reconciliation, they maintain, is simply another "settler move to innocence" in an attempt to rescue a sense of future.[15]

With this in mind, we can recognize that to envision a future without hunger requires a complete reorientation of society, with equity, justice, and solidarity at its core.

UNIVERSAL PROGRAMS TO PROMOTE HEALTH AND FLOURISHING

Current social programs meant to help people in poverty discriminate because they rely on the separation of people into deserving and undeserving, and are founded on systems developed through exploitation. When there is separation, especially based on false concepts of deserving and undeserving, some people are always left out, and the boundaries between people can become contentious, stigmatizing, and damaging.[16] This is why it is essential to stop "targeting" people and instead include people by creating universal programs.

Everyone benefits from government assistance—the poorest among the poor and the wealthiest. People who own a home receive a mortgage interest deduction. Wealthy people receive reduced taxes on their investment dividends and capital gains, they can deduct taxes on their yachts and claim gambling loss deductions, and their Social Security calculations are capped, allowing them to pay a smaller proportion of their income to Social Security than people who have lower incomes. Rather than being portrayed as welfare recipients, they are praised and rewarded for building up debt and having a mortgage on their home. On the other hand, people who are exploited through low wages and the long history of discrimination, redlining, exclusion, and disbelonging need to prove they are "worthy" of support. To be worthy means you must be poor and stay poor. It's time to end that nonsense.

Poverty costs the United States at least $1.03 trillion a year. For every dollar spent on reducing childhood poverty, the country would save at least $7 in government spending to address the health and social problems that arise from poverty.[17] These costs are calculated in terms of the need for social programs, increases in medical care costs, and, yes, you guessed it, imprisoning people and taking away people's kids to place them in foster care. To fix this, we need to spend more money to help people avoid poverty; we need to fix the tax code, wage structures, and many other policies that exclude and exploit people who are poor so the wealthy will stop profiting off them. As I demonstrated in part II, government assistance programs facilitate corporate profit, stigmatize people who are poor, and rely on separating and isolating people. Universal programs are rational and can ensure a healthy future for all people, regardless of who they are and the circumstances into which they were born.

Universal basic income (UBI) is a type of social security that guarantees a set amount of money to *every* person. It does not require any specific means test, nor does it require any specific behavior or other requirement such as work. Those who are wealthy will receive it, but then have to give it back at tax time. The program could be paid for by taxing the ultrawealthy. Over time, it could also replace SNAP, TANF, and unemployment. Guaranteed income is a similar concept but is more limited. It is a continuous financial payout based on eligibility criteria such as having a child, like the Child Tax Credit during the COVID-19 pandemic, or it can be a means-tested program.

Research on UBI demonstration projects around the world shows that, compared to similar people who do not receive UBI payments, those who do receive them report major improvements in physical and mental health, school performance of their children, improved life expectancy, and increased entrepreneurship. UBI also has little impact on whether people work. Evidence on the labor market during UBI programs showed that many people who can and will work for others are actively looking for work, or are already working. Many of us might even prefer to simply work for ourselves, create art, be our own bosses, or be a job creator. UBI helps this along.[18]

Experts insist that UBI is the best way to address the onslaught of automation. As more low-wage jobs are being turned over to automated processes, people without relevant marketable skills may not be able to find work.[19] UBI can help support them while they get new training or find other ways to support themselves. Many others promote it because it is more just, egalitarian, and supportive, especially for Black women.[20] Concepts of universal income are not new. Paying attention to the impacts of automation is just a new spin on what many people have been proposing for hundreds of years.

Throughout the ages, many recognized UBI would increase freedom, creativity, and financial generativity. Thomas Moore and Johannes Ludovicus Vives were promoting these ideas in the 1500s. Moore's blunt justification was this: if people had a baseline income, they would not have to steal; then they would not be criminalized and brutalized by the state. Punishing people for being poor and desperate, Moore insisted, simply increases the state-supported murder rate.[21] Up into the 1960s, Martin Luther King Jr. and others insisted that UBI could be the most effective way to prevent poverty, and would reduce the ineffective patchwork of social services and public assistance. Milton Freedman, renowned free market economist, and many others convinced President Richard Nixon to propose a guaranteed income in the early 1970s. But due to political sabotage on the Left and Right as well as Nixon's rightful demise and the failed bid for the presidency of George McGovern, who also proposed a basic income in 1972, enthusiasm for UBI fizzled.

After the onset of COVID-19, UBI returned to the national dialogue due to economic devastation caused by shutting down businesses and schools without immediate public financial support. All around the world, including in the United States, people needed income to pay for housing and food. Canada responded to the COVID-19 pandemic by providing $2,000 a month to all adults. The United States, on the other hand, offered minimally improved processes for accessing unemployment benefits and SNAP; then Congress provided a few sporadic payments of $1,200, $600, and $1,400 for people making less than $75,000 a year. A year later, Congress passed a one-year Child Tax Credit, which it then allowed to expire in January 2022, at the same time that President Biden came to Philabundance to pack up carrots and other pounds of food. Predictably, Children's Healthwatch found that after the Child Tax Credit expired, household food insecurity increased by 25 percent.[22] Guaranteed income and UBI are not pie in the sky ideas. Rather, they offer tangible support that helps people stay healthy and whole.

Guaranteed income pilots are springing up everywhere across the country. Of special note, with support from Mayors for a Guaranteed Income, many cities are following the lead of former Stockton, California, mayor Michael Tubbs, who launched a guaranteed income pilot at $500 per month. The Magnolia Mother's Trust in Jackson, Mississippi, has been providing a small group of Black mothers $1,000 per month. Participants report improved health and well-being for themselves and their children.[23] These efforts are still means tested, however. Which means that not only are they limited in scale but they only reach a certain type of person too. This can start to get mistaken for who is worthy of support and who is not.

UBI can replace means-tested programs that simply exacerbate and even justify stigma against people who are poor. Since it is universal, what happens to some people happens to all. There is no separation nor means test. Witnesses members Tianna Gaines-Turner and Joanna Simmons and I published an article on how SNAP also falls into the trap of excluding many people who could benefit while creating greater stigma. We insist that SNAP could and should be converted into a UBI program to eliminate stigma and ensure that people could spend money how they choose.[24] Moreover, it would cut the problematic ties that millions of people experiencing poverty have through SNAP with C&S Wholesale Grocers Association and the American Beverage Association.

Universal health care has been a topic of decades-long debates in the United States. The failure of our systems to support people in meeting their basic needs such as covering the cost of food, housing, and education makes people sick and costs our health system billions of dollars every year. So not only does being poor make people's health worse but health care costs associated with a serious illness is the primary reason that people who are not originally poor say they fall into poverty.[25] Establishing a ground of economic security for everyone will drive down the need for medical care and reduce health care expenditures. On the flip side, universal health care will ensure that no one becomes poor because they got sick or were disabled. It will also ensure that no one suffers the indignity of starting a GoFundMe page to beg friends and strangers to help them pay their exorbitant medical bills.

Canada, the United Kingdom, Sweden, Germany, and all countries that provide universal health care spend far less per capita than does the United States. Though the United States spends exorbitant amounts on health care, people in the United States are in worse health and have the lowest life expectancy among all wealthy countries. Differences in optimal health within the United States tells an even more sordid truth: Black and Indigenous people have a far lower life expectancy than white people, and life expectancy varies by region, county, and zip code.[26] In Philadelphia, differences by zip code showed inequities greater than fourteen years along the fault lines of racial and ethnic housing segregation. Predominantly Black neighborhoods showed a life expectancy of around seventy-three years whereas in white neighborhoods, the life expectancy was eighty-eight years.[27]

Though heterogeneous, Indigenous life expectancy has consistently been the lowest in the United States. This is a direct reflection of the effects of ongoing genocide, colonization, and land theft. The pandemic caused the highest death rates among Indigenous people. Their overall life expectancy reduced from seventy-two years in 2019 to sixty-five years in 2021. Access to health care is not the only endeavor that will solve health problems; the underlying determinants of health—access to fresh water, safe housing, and clean air—have much to do with overall health. The fact that we spend so much in health care but allow life to be cut short for millions of people should make us wonder if our health systems are death dealing too.

Health care in the United States is also primarily tied to full-time employment. Connecting health care to employment can force people to stay at their jobs despite dissatisfaction or feeling overworked. People in the United States work the longest hours in the world, without any demonstrated increase in productivity or pay. Decision-makers in the federal government know this. The Congressional Budget Office reported that for-profit, employer-based health care is destroying the health of Americans and stymieing economic growth. It calculated major cost savings in health care expenditures and improvements in population health if the US government were to adopt Medicare for All, another form of universal health care that includes both public and private companies. In turn, this would generate more wealth for people, who would then put that money toward their well-being, educational, and entrepreneurial activities.[28]

Universal single-payer health care, paid for with public money without private insurance involvement, would abolish the need for health insurance companies along with the stress people face trying to navigate insurance claims, copays, and exorbitant out-of-pocket expenses, including those for mental health care. Universal health care provides health promotion, disease prevention, access to high-quality as well as culturally appropriate and effective treatment, and rehabilitation and palliation services without causing financial hardship.

Finally, much of the burden of poverty in the United States falls on families with children. This is why *universal school meals* and *universal child care* would immediately relieve financial hardship on families and the health care system alike. Compared to all families across the United States, those with young children reported the highest rates of food insecurity, costing the US government $1.2 billion a year in health care, special education, and lost work productivity.[29]

As I explained in the nutrition assistance chapter, school meal participation promotes child health, improves test scores, and promotes a healthier diet. Many researchers agree that free school meals helps reduce the burden of household food insecurity. Making school meals universally free for all would vastly improve child health *and* reduce meal administrative costs. This would also vastly reduce health care spending and put an end to lunch shaming.[30]

Families with young children among the members of the Building Wealth and Health Network explained to us they participate in TANF not for the paltry sum they receive, nor for the poor advice the state provides to build their résumés. Rather, they do it so they can access affordable childcare. They need childcare to earn income. But they enter a system that disciplines them to low wages, and they can't afford childcare with such low wages they earn on their own. One of the worst scenarios I heard about was from a long-standing advocate with Witnesses named Tina. She is a slight Black Muslim woman who often wore a *khimar*, a head covering for the hair, neck, and shoulders. She lost her mother to cancer when she was eight and became responsible for her younger siblings. To her, this meant she lost most of her own childhood. Tina applied for TANF, like most women I met, in order to get subsidized childcare for her children so she could look for work. Where did her TANF caseworker make Tina start working? Making nine dollars an hour at a local childcare center so she could take care of other people's children, most of whom had mothers who were TANF participants. TANF is a primary example of the many ways our labor laws, public assistance programs, and societal disrespect for women and children keep them trapped in poverty.

A study of childcare workers in Washington State and Texas found that 42 percent of people working in childcare reported food insecurity, and 20 percent reported very low food security.[31] More abysmal than the formal childcare workforce is the situation for domestic workers—people who work in private homes. The vast majority of people who do childcare, eldercare, and cleaning are women. They primarily do so in ways that are informal, where the employers still do not pay Social Security or sick leave. There is a long history of discrimination against domestic workers. After enslavement, Black women frequently had no choice but to work for free (often with their former enslavers). In the 1930s, they and agricultural workers were intentionally excluded from receiving Social Security and forming unions; they were also excluded from the 1970 Occupational Safety and Health Act, which would ensure their right to safety on the job. In the words of Ai-jen Poo, founder of Domestic Workers United, domestic workers "do the work that makes all other work possible," yet they make seventy-four cents on the dollar compared to their peers, like Tina, in the formal sector.[32] Consider how this compounds over the life course: women who worked all of their lives will have less for retirement and Social Security than men. So elderly women will always be in a state of precariousness and poor health without adequate Social Security income.

Universal childcare will solve many problems and bolster the economic power of women across the life course. Universal childcare could boost women's earnings almost $100,000 over their lifetime, for a total of $130 billion for women in the United States. With universal childcare, full-time work for women would increase by 17 percent, and the employment rates for those without an advanced degree would increase by over 30 percent. This would reduce poverty most especially for women of color by helping them to earn more money, have financial freedom, and save more for retirement.[33]

Providing childcare to help women become more financially secure would also help to reduce the rates of imprisonment. The population of women in prison has grown at twice the rate of men in recent decades. The majority of women in prison, 80 percent, are caregivers of children.[34]

ABOLITION AND TRANSFORMATIVE JUSTICE

Having an incarcerated parent is an adverse childhood experience. When kids have a parent in prison, they are more likely to report depression, poor school performance, and behavioral challenges.[35] A 2015 report showed that five million children have or have had a parent in prison. That is one in fourteen children. But for Black families, one in nine children have or have had a parent in jail or prison.[36] Headley's bogus arrest fits this pattern.

Many women in prison have not yet been convicted of a crime, but they are stuck in prison simply because they cannot pay bail. Our bail systems are simply another form of debtors' prison that was banned by federal law in 1833.[37] Up through today, we still see its vestiges, despite a Supreme Court decision in 1983 that being jailed for being unable to pay a debt was found to be unconstitutional under the Fourteenth Amendment's equal protection clauses. Today, many states still have bail systems that penalize those in poverty, destroying people's lives for months and years at a time.

This was the case in Ferguson, Missouri, where Michael Brown was shot and killed and then left in the street for four hours. An external review of the Ferguson police department found that Black people were regularly jailed if they could not pay court fees for routine traffic stops such as rolling through a stop sign. If you go to jail, you risk losing your job; you lose income, and it stains your record. When and if you can get out the other side, you are restricted from receiving housing support and, in many states, your record follows you all the way to the job application, making it extremely difficult to reenter society and pay for your own basic needs. This is the prison system working as designed.

After the abolition of slavery in 1865, prisons became a powerful institution harnessed by states and the federal government to cage Black and Brown people to extract their labor and lands. To control people, white lawmakers created a vast array of crimes to easily imprison or reenslave Black people. In some southern states, Black people had to prove that they were working or they'd be taken to prison; they were not allowed to have certain jobs, children were often taken and forced into apprenticeships, and interracial marriage was illegal. Despite attempts by civil rights activists and the federal government to improve such legal conditions, Jim Crow laws made it a crime to sit in the front of the bus or at a soda fountain counter, and so on. Such ridiculous "crimes" make it easier to keep Black people down or, better yet, disappear them. The "war on drugs" made it especially easy to police Black and Brown people, and the disparate sentencing laws for crack cocaine was another conduit to imprison Black and Brown people. The growth in the prison system has been exponential from the 1980s up through today, as Gilmore, Davis, Kaba, and so many others have pointed out; it is not only founded on racism but is the blunt instrument used to deal with society's socioeconomic struggles and lack of adequate mental health care.[38] The US justice and political systems collude to destroy the lives and humanity of Black and Indigenous people. Gilmore explains that the growth of prisons and of incapacitating large swaths of people in America is a form of "organized abandonment," making Black and Brown communities more fragile and precarious while states pursue profit and economic stability.[39]

The *prison-industrial complex* (PIC) is a term that characterizes the overlapping interests of government and industry that use surveillance, policing, imprisonment, racial control, and makeshift solutions to economic, social, and political problems.[40] The PIC relies on racism, especially anti-Blackness, and desire for property and wealth through harnessing police, prisons, probation services, the courts, and the private companies that profit from transporting, feeding, and exploiting prisoners and people on parole. Even publicly funded prisons have for-profit companies set up to make money from phone calls, video calls, and commissaries.[41]

Through racial profiling and ultramilitarization, police ensnare people into the system. In the words of Phillip Atiba Goff, cofounder and president of the Center for Policing Equity at CUNY, cops are "personal racism concierges."[42] Couple this with the ongoing militarization of the police with surplus military equipment from the Department of Defense, and one can see how dangerous these supposed "peacekeepers" really are.

The US government and our school systems insist that the country's political structure is a democracy. But with the largest prison population in the world, prison becomes a way to destroy people's right to participate in society and their right to vote. Even though prisoners are ineligible to vote, some states allow county population rates to include the prison population. This allows legislators to rely on gerrymandering, primarily in favor of a more conservative voting block because in many states, the prison population counts toward the population needing representation. Since prisoners cannot vote from prison, this process silences entire Black and Brown communities.[43] This is not justice. Nor is it inclusive democracy.

Those who are abolitionists seek alternatives to instilling justice. *Restorative justice* is an attempt to set up meaningful infrastructure where, with a team of support, the perpetrator works with the victim and affected communities to repair and redress the damage done. Restorative justice is a community-based process that seeks reparative justice and moralizing social control. These practices could prevent crime more effectively and create a more meaningful justice experience for victims of crime that could support healing from the trauma of victimization while creating genuine accountability for offenders.

Transformative justice, on the other hand, is a growing movement among sexual assault and childhood sexual abuse survivors who recognize the current US justice system is wholly inadequate to address the traumas associated with sexual abuse and assault. The group Generation Five has engaged in transformative justice processes with an eye toward collective liberation to achieve personal, community, and social transformation as interdependent parts of a larger struggle to build a more loving and respectful society. This includes engagement with the perpetrator(s) to address the challenges that led them to commit the act, and consideration of ways to change those conditions. Note that these layers of involvement do not include "the state." Generation Five, in its *Ending Child Sexual Abuse: A Transformative Justice Handbook*, explains that state-supported systems of oppression in the areas of age, class, race, ethnicity, religion, dis/ability, sexual orientation, and nationality or immigration status demand that transformative justice not involve state actors but rather keep power within neighborhoods and affected communities.[44] The reason to exclude state actors in the process is because the state will most likely harness police and prison as its primary enforcement mechanism. A transformative justice approach focuses on changing the conditions that perpetuate abuse. This takes work to ensure safety, connection, and dignity for all, where every individual can exercise agency. Such efforts to shift from "power over" to "power together" help promote safety, accountability, and collective action.

Effective collective action demands that we get in right relation to each other and work together to create justice without reliance on "the state," without perpetuating violence, and instead promote healing, accountability, resilience, and safety. To do this work demands a certain level of emotional and spiritual maturity; it requires deep internal work and work in community with others.[45]

Prison abolition would allow the funds originally invested in controlling, abandoning, and disappearing Black and Brown people to be redirected toward promoting community safety, beautification, and behavioral health and improving access to affordable housing and healthy food. To achieve community improvements where people can flourish in all aspects of their lives, we should recognize that prison abolition requires making police, those concierges to mass incarceration, obsolete.

Many people have a hard time making sense of police abolition, and can sometimes confuse it with defunding or reforming the police. To *reform* police means to provide them with training in antiracist, trauma-informed policy approaches and conflict resolution. But scholars have found that police reform only expands police budgets and their reach.[46] *Defunding* the police means restricting police budgets to reduce the size and reach of police. This helps to get police out of work they should not be doing and for which they are not trained, such as social services work like responding to mental health crises or loose dogs in the street. This approach, many argue, leaves more money for investing in social services, mental health supports, and neighborhood infrastructure and green spaces. Both approaches may mitigate some harm caused by police, but they do not fundamentally alter the structure of policing.

Policing in the United States follows the model of slave patrols. During times of enslavement, all white people, including children, were required under slave codes to surveil and punish Black people who were not on the plantations of their enslavers. Slave codes were laws that restricted Black people from being off their plantation without papers proving they were given permission, restricted their ability to gather in groups without a white person present, prohibited Black people from learning to read and write, and even to defend themselves if they were attacked by a white person. During this time, men would be hired to do slave patrols, where they were paid to search out people escaping plantations. They were given license to cage and return people to their enslavers and, in other cases, to shoot them dead. After the Civil War, the slave codes turned to Black codes, which created even broader reach to criminalize Black people for not working or not accepting an offer to work at extremely low wages. So white people hired men to enforce the Black codes, thus landing Black people in prison, where the loophole in the US Constitution allowed the enslavement of people in prison. This led to convict leasing, an enormously profitable business that is still in operation today with active support from voters.[47] This institution of policing was made to protect private property and control labor, bully and prevent people from becoming unionized, and ensure the ongoing domination of Black, Brown, and Indigenous people.[48]

The possibilities of abolition are becoming more apparent due to the widespread protests after the murder of George Floyd and the growing political acumen of the Black Lives Matter movement.[49] The popularization of defunding the police and the mainstreaming of abolitionist ideas emerged from many generations of abolitionist work, especially by queer Black women. The most recent endeavors are those such as Critical Resistance, founded by Davis and Gilmore, Project Nia, founded by Kaba, and Interrupting Criminalization, run by Kaba, Ritchie, and many others.[50] These organizations provide resources and many opportunities for people to engage in contemporary abolitionist movements.

Currently, the Breathe Act supported by several members of Congress and made possible by the activism of the Black Lives Matter movement is a bill in the US House of Representatives that proposes to get police or "resource officers" out of schools.[51] Police should be taken out of county assistance offices too. After all, families going to the county assistance office are just trying to get some support to take care of themselves and stay healthy. But as it stands, if you go to the welfare office to try to get childcare or SNAP benefits, there is some likelihood that, like Headley, you could land at Rikers.

Abolition is about dismantling the PIC and simultaneously working toward a world grounded in community care and accountability, mutuality, reciprocity, and kindness—where people would have no need to break the law. Those who do would participate in community processes of accountability circles. These processes require community commitment and solidarity. While they can be difficult to establish, they signify a future worth building.

ABOLITION BEYOND PRISON MAKES WAY FOR A NOURISHING WORLD

But abolition should not only be restricted to envisioning a society without police and prison. Abolition is also about reenvisioning a society with systems in place that promote flourishing and well-being for all people, especially those who are discriminated against.[52] UBI, which would replace TANF and SNAP, and other programs such as all-inclusive childcare and health care, make universal programs a part of that abolitionist stance.

Headley's arrest at a county assistance office when she was trying to get access to subsidized childcare makes it crystal clear that state-supported social services are entangled with the carceral system. Here's another example. When women are released from prison in California, they are required to find work in order to receive benefits and to demonstrate they are earning money formally to get custody of their children again. If they cannot prove they are working, they are likely to be sent back to prison or never get their children back.[53] As a result, their children may end up being sent into or stay in the child welfare system. The trauma to the children, then, may simply continue.

In her new book *Torn Apart: How the Child Welfare System Destroys Black Families—and How Abolition Can Build a Safer World*, Dorothy Roberts maintains that the child welfare system is long past resuscitation or reform. She insists on its abolition. Just as prison destroys communities, so does the child welfare system. The system stems from the long tradition of the US government and white elite separating Indigenous and Black children from their parents. Indigenous children were forced into boarding schools while Black children were stolen, separated, and sold off during enslavement, and afterward, children were forced into unpaid "apprenticeships" picking cotton for white landowners. The same patterns of separating children from Black, Brown, and Indigenous families are playing out today. When one sees the inequities by race and ethnicity, where greater percentages of Black, Brown, and Indigenous families have children taken away than children taken from white homes, it becomes clear that the child welfare system is not a form of "government benevolence" as it is portrayed. Rather, it is by design a form of "state terror."[54]

The threat of taking children away especially forces Black and Indigenous mothers into compliance. I hope you have noted this throughout this book: the constant fear mothers and other caregivers have that if they admit their child is food insecure, the state will swipe away their children. According to Roberts, "Child welfare agencies aim to keep Black mothers submissive by weaponizing their children, while denying the existence of loving ties between them."[55]

The child welfare system, Roberts explains, is supported and helped by police and prisons, exposing how the child welfare system is just one more aspect of America's "carceral web." What distinguishes the child welfare system from policing and prisons is that there is unwarranted surveillance and removal of children without legal oversight. This makes it a useful stealth arm of the "carceral state." Child welfare intervention also asserts itself in response to intimate partner violence. As Roberts points out, caseworkers have far more freedom to extract children in situations where the mother is being abused, while simultaneously, police make it hard to discipline the violent partners. This results in fewer women willing to report intimate partner violence in the home because they know they will be more likely to lose their children.[56]

In some states, imprisonment is statutory grounds for the termination of parental rights. When children are pushed into foster care, they most often become worse off than they were before, with their spirit and well-being crushed. As Roberts asserts, foster care funnels children into the PIC, which is designed to "foreclose their chances for the future."[57]

Adding greater insult, foster caretakers receive higher stipends than families receive through regular TANF. Foster caretakers get these higher stipends *without work requirements*.

We need a new and different system, suggests Roberts, with structures that are not rooted in cruelty, punishment, and destroying Black and Brown families. In a transformed society, there are robust programs that make our society more equal—with equal access to economic security, access to food and housing, and meaningful jobs. When most people who get snagged up in the child welfare system are deeply poor, it is clear that helping people with housing, food, and other basic needs would be far more conducive to families being able to take care of each other and their communities.

Consider that when children were not in school during the shelter-in-place policies during COVID-19, and when there were less caseworkers in New York City, the number of child removals sharply declined, and there were no increases in reports of child abuse. Roberts and others referred to this as a lesson in abolition. In addition to mutual aid societies, stimulus money such as the Child Tax Credit and pandemic EBT helped to financially support families in ways that would not have happened before.

During the COVID-19 shelter-in-place and economic slowdown, so many new ways of offering programs and support were made possible.

Pandemic EBT, universal free breakfasts and lunches, meaningful unemployment benefits, and the Child Tax Credit were investments made without control and domination.

If we had universal programs and publicly funded health care, who would profit? Everyone. That would make new, fertile ground on which we could shift and equalize power.

MOVING TOWARD A SOLIDARITY ECONOMY

When people cannot think beyond the way capitalism works, it shows a lack of imagination, lack of awareness, and lack of drive to struggle for life-giving systems. There are so many alternatives, and many are being utilized today. Solidarity economies have been working alongside capitalism since its inception. In contrast to capitalism, which isolates, separates, and exploits based on hierarchy, a solidarity economy relies on cooperation to create infrastructure for sharing resources based on principles of mutuality and interdependence. A solidarity economy serves as an umbrella term for many types of sharing and mutual aid processes that help people earn a living, share resources, and stay connected. There is no exploitation of humans in sharing economies that have the common good in mind and simultaneous solidarity among workers who can ensure they reap the benefits of their labor.

In the United States, there is a growing movement to make our economy less exploitative. The US Solidarity Economy Network provides support and networking for alternative businesses and cooperatives across the United States.[58] Its principles involve solidarity and cooperation, participatory democracy, sustainability, pluralism, and equity in all dimensions (race, ethnicity, nationality, class, gender, and ability), demonstrating there are multiple ways of creating businesses and other entrepreneurial entities. Well-known collective endeavors are cooperatives. There are three types: *consumer owned* (like your local food co-op), *producer owned* (such as agricultural or craft cooperatives), and *worker owned* (by providing stable employment and profit sharing among workers).

Jessica Gordon Nembhard describes the long history of collective and cooperative practices by African Americans since the earliest days of enslavement.[59] People who were enslaved helped each other through mutual support to survive. These practices continued up through the Reconstruction era, survived in spite of the violence of the Jim Crow era, and continue today in the face of police brutality and mass incarceration. People shared resources from secret gardens and created mutual aid societies that helped to care for the sick. As runaway (maroon) communities started to form, many other types of cooperative venues emerged such as cooperative insurance companies and shared savings to cover burial costs. Gordon Nembhard underscores how cooperatives are defined as much by an interest in collectivism as by oppression. When Black people wanted to start banks and businesses after slavery, they were boxed out, and in the case of Tulsa's "Black Wall Street," hundreds of people were brutalized, murdered, and lynched in the Tulsa Massacre of 1921. Despite these terrifying setbacks, Black people's entrepreneurial spirit prevails. Keeping cooperatives and mutual aid within Black communities and hidden from view was often the only course of action for survival. Picking up on this history, Du Bois suggested that cooperatives were not simply about survival but were also meant to build wealth and dismantle structural racism. As an example, in 1918, the great labor organizer A. Philip Randolph founded the Brotherhood of Sleeping Car Porters Union. This organizing led to the Fair Employment Act banning employment discrimination in 1941.

Carried forward throughout the century, cooperative structures exist not only in worker-owned cooperatives among people who are Black, Brown, and Indigenous but in political activist circles too. The Black Panthers had cooperative housing, cooperative bakeries, and of course their free breakfast programs to grow economic independence and power.

Another important endeavor was Freedom Farm founded by Fannie Lou Hamer in 1969.

"I know what the pain of hunger is about," Hamer told a crowd during a speech in Madison, Wisconsin. "My family was some of the poorest people that was in the state of Mississippi. We were sharecroppers." Hamer had to start work when she was just six years old picking cotton, while her family was trapped in predatory debt created by white landowners. When her parents eked out just enough to purchase livestock when she was thirteen years old, "a white man came onto our property and killed our mules and cows," she said; "they killed everything that we had."[60] The Freedom Farm Cooperative was an effort to resist that kind of predation and exploitation. At its height, the Freedom Farm Cooperative had ten thousand members. The members planted soybeans and cotton as cash crops to pay taxes and administrative expenses. With the cost of membership at one dollar a month, co-op members sowed the rest of the land with cucumbers, peas, beans, squash, and collard greens, all of which was distributed back to those who worked on the co-op. It did not last long, however, as they could not get federal backing nor earn enough revenue to keep going. This did not stop many like-minded people from trying over and again to create cooperative farms, grocery stores, and catering services.[61]

Many more efforts are active today through a resurgence of young people interested in gardening, farming, and food sovereignty. Food sovereignty is a general term to describe collective efforts to keep a food system under local control where growers, workers, distributers, and people who eat the food are engaged in ensuring the food system is responsible to local community needs and desires. It has become mainstream, especially through La Via Campesina, which is an international organization of farmers and other workers who utilize the food sovereignty framework to assert their rights to a healthful standard of living, just food system, and healthy, sustainable, regenerative ecosystem.[62] There is some alignment with Indigenous sovereignty, though the people involved in food sovereignty do not always connect with Indigenous people, nor do they always engage in efforts to decolonize.

Groups such as the national Young Farmers Coalition, Detroit Black Community Food Security Network, Native American Food Sovereignty Alliance, Sankofa Farms in North Carolina, and Leah Penniman and friends of Soul Fire Farm provide training as well as opportunities for people to engage in sustainable agriculture, share technical expertise, and establish food sovereignty and community self-determination.[63] This is only a small sample of a burgeoning movement.

There are also many cooperative buyers' clubs. You may even belong to one. For instance, many people of means are choosing to engage in community-supported agriculture (CSA). This is when communities surrounding a farm sign up and pay for produce and other goods such as eggs, bread, and cheese from a local farm. When communities pay up front, it reduces the time farmers might spend on marketing while spreading the financial risk of farming to community members. This promotes community resilience and social cohesion. There are over 12,500 CSAs across the country. Each of these ensures that food is fresher and stays local. They reduce their carbon footprint and support the local ecosystem by keeping food and animal waste local too. As well, phosphorous is conserved and can be recycled back into the local soil, thereby reducing greenhouse gases. It also keeps economic activity local and strengthens the resilience of the community against both climate catastrophes that could interrupt the global food industry and mass market fluctuations. Young people are drawn to the worker-owned farms because they can define the ethos and share resources. In the end, cooperative farms are more likely to carry out thoughtful land stewardship, conservation, and restoration, which in turn can contribute to reducing harm to the climate.

Finally, I will touch on the stepchild of capitalism: charity. Charity is predicated on a power dynamic where the wealthy bestow kindness and goodness to people who are exploited by the same system that makes people wealthy.[64] In chapter 8, I explained that charity fluffs up the giver and humiliates the receiver, rendering them powerless. There is a common saying in social movements: *solidarity not charity*. Solidarity characterizes the actions and feelings of collective power to create societal and local community structures that support the group. It means joining with all kinds of people with a sense of unity, mutuality, reciprocity, democracy, shared values, and shared power. These ideas are not new. Indeed, in most original societies, gift giving was a way of establishing social cohesion, reciprocity, and mutuality. The largess with which the wealthy are celebrated for giving to charity violates elementary principles of solidarity and merely reifies and celebrates inequality.[65] By extension, it celebrates hunger as a gift to the wealthy.

Food banks and food pantries can adopt a cooperative approach grounded in solidarity that promotes belonging, dignity, and freedom.

Imagine if Feeding America, one of the largest charities in the country, and its entire member network became a giant food cooperative committed to food sovereignty, sustainability, and reciprocity. Feeding America and the other large corporate food banks clearly have the funds and business acumen to create such strategies. That would be powerful and transformative. This way, if a person were a member of the Feeding America food cooperative, pride would begin at the doorway.

11 THE POLITICAL: HUMAN RIGHTS AND RIGHTS OF NATURE

The majority of the world does not find its roots in Western culture or traditions. The majority of the world finds its roots in the Natural World, and it is the Natural World, and the traditions of the Natural World, which must prevail if we are to develop truly free and egalitarian societies.

—HAUDENOSAUNEE DELEGATION TO GENEVA, IN *BASIC CALL TO CONSCIOUSNESS*, ED. AKWESASNE NOTES

THE RIGHT TO FOOD AND TO BE FREE FROM HUNGER

If the United States officially sought to repair harm done to Black and Indigenous people today and in the past, and started to create universal programs, abolished police and prisons, and promoted economies rooted in equity, solidarity, and care, this would begin the transformation of our society. Such new processes and ways of doing may demand new types of codification in law. We should not wait on others to write a new constitution to replace the US Constitution written over 250 years ago. We should call for it now, as Skidmore law professor Beau Breslin, Clay Jenkinson, and others have done.[1] As well, the international nation-state community has an established universal ethics for humanity enshrined in human rights. So before we start lamenting what it would take to write a new constitution, Congress could take up some simple moves to ratify international human rights covenants, and repair or renew its relationship with the international community while simultaneously working to end hunger and promote equity at home.

The United States is the only UN member nation-state that refuses to formally acknowledge the right to food. The right to food and to be free from hunger are fundamental human rights enshrined in the Universal Declaration of Human Rights (1948) and the International Covenant on Economic, Social and Cultural Rights (1966). They incorporate being able to have access to culturally appropriate and healthy food to live a healthy and fulfilling life without fear. The right to food stems from Article 25 of the Universal Declaration of Human Rights, which asserts the right of everyone to an adequate standard of living, including adequate food, clothing, and housing, and to the continuous improvement of living conditions.

The working definition of the right to food is "the right to have regular, permanent and unrestricted access, either directly or by means of financial purchases, to quantitatively and qualitatively adequate and sufficient food corresponding to the cultural traditions of the people to which the consumer belongs, and which ensure a physical and mental, individual and collective, fulfilling and dignified life free of fear."[2]

Much of the language that surrounds the human rights framework includes covenants between governments and their people. Governments must respect, protect, and fulfill fundamental rights to ensure security, dignity and well-being of the people. To *respect* the right to food is to not interfere with people's ability to acquire food. An example of a violation of respect is withholding food during colonization and enslavement or restricting people with a felony from receiving SNAP. To *protect* the right to food is to make sure that others do not interfere with access to food. An example of a violation to protect is when corporations hoard or destroy crops so people cannot access or afford food. To *fulfill* the right to food has two components: to facilitate or create social and economic environments that foster human development, such as supporting living wages so people can buy food, and to provide food to people in an emergency or in circumstances when self-provisioning is beyond their control, such as providing people with food or emergency SNAP benefits after Hurricane Katrina.

The right to food is also dependent on many other rights such as the right to life, health, water, housing, and education. These rights are enshrined in the International Covenant on Economic, Social and Cultural Rights, which the United States has not ratified. This means that the US government refuses to hold itself accountable to its people to ensure that they have their basic needs fulfilled. As well, most of the social, economic, and cultural rights can be characterized as rights that improve the social determinants of health. They are rights to housing, food, education, cultural expression, health and health care, and so on. Almost all countries participating in the United Nations have ratified this standard covenant, but the United States stands alone in its refusal to be held accountable to the right to food.

The right to food is enshrined in other human rights documents too, such as the International Covenant of the Rights of Indigenous Peoples (2007), Convention on the Rights of the Child (1990), and Convention on the Elimination of All Forms of Discrimination against Women (1979). True to form, the United States has not ratified these covenants either. In the meantime, countries such as India, South Africa, Brazil, and twenty other countries have integrated explicit directives on the right to food in their constitutions. There are also United Nations efforts that transcend boundaries of nation-states. Thanks to the leadership of the international organization La Via Campesina and many others, the Declaration on the Rights of Peasants and Other People Working in Rural Areas came into force in 2018.[3] It is the most recent and robust UN covenant that ties the right to food together with land rights, workers' rights, farmers' rights, Indigenous rights, and the rights of the natural world. It is the most comprehensive international covenant for solidarity among poor people around the world. Only eight countries have not ratified it, most of them colonizing nations that actively suppress Indigenous sovereignty such as New Zealand, Australia, and Israel. The United States is among them.

A common misperception about hunger in the United States is that an involuntary lack of access to food ought to be solved with charity. The emphasis on charity for solving food insecurity and hunger is a *needs-based* approach to food. The needs-based approach assumes that people who lack access to food are passive recipients in need of direct assistance. Programs and policy efforts that use this approach tend to provide assistance without expectation of action from the recipient, and without obligation to the recipient. As well, the recipient of emergency food, as I explained in chapter 8, has no legal protections. Providing food in emergency situations for families is not protected by legislation, political will, or coordinated action.

A *rights-based* approach, on the other hand, creates enabling environments that support people in nourishing themselves while providing a structure for legal recourse. A rights-based approach focuses on ways in which conditions and environments can be altered so that people can take an active role in procuring food. It incorporates the idea that good nutrition is not based solely on benevolence but rather is the duty and obligation of a country to its people.

The US government should revisit the opportunity to ratify these documents, where the right to food can be justiciable. This will require strong support in Congress and a clear presidential mandate.

There are other ways to begin to implement the rights-based approach starting with a national strategy to implement the right to food. Structural processes should be put into place whereby agencies, organizations, and citizens are working toward the common goal of actively respecting, protecting, and promoting the right to food. These processes rely on the establishment of a national plan to ensure the right to food and to be free from hunger for everyone, and to do so in ways that rely on widespread democratic participation centered on equity and nondiscrimination. The US National Commission on Hunger recommended this in its report released in 2016.

The finest example of implementation of the right to food is the Brazilian Fome Zero (Zero Hunger) campaign put into place during President Luiz Inácio Lula da Silva's administration starting in 2003. It consisted of a variety of nutrition support programs with a focus on the poorest populations and women, infants, and children, and included conditional cash transfers for school attendance. It was implemented and supported by a newly established Ministry of Food Security and Fight against Hunger that brought together a massive collaboration with nineteen ministries. There was also strong commitment and action to ensure ongoing public and democratic decision-making and transparency. As a result of these efforts, the Lula administration helped to reduce food insecurity by 30 percent and doubled the number of people reached by the program within three years of its start. By 2006, the right to food security was codified in Brazil's National Food and Nutrition Security Law. It defined food and nutrition security as "the realization of everyone's right to regular and permanent access to enough food of good quality that was based on food practices that promote health, respect, and cultural diversity, and are environmentally, culturally, economically, and socially sustainable." Fome Zero became integrated into the government infrastructure, and the Brazilian government codified the right to food into its constitution in 2010. By 2014, these laws and programs had reduced the rates of hunger by 80 percent, and were celebrated by the United Nations World Food Program as a great success.[4]

After that, however, rates of hunger and malnutrition went on the rise over the three next presidencies, and when President Jair Bolsonaro took office in 2019, one of his first actions was to dismantle the Ministry of Food Security. During COVID-19, there was evidence that over 50 percent of the population reported some form of food insecurity.[5] Lula took office again in January 2023. In one of his first speeches he stated, "If at the end of my term in 2026, every Brazilian is having breakfast, lunch and dinner once again I will have fulfilled my life's mission."[6]

Imagine if we had such a president. The United States has presidents who declare "We're going to the moon," "We'll land on Mars," or "Make America great again." How refreshing it would be if a president made a humble and more meaningful pronouncement of making sure everyone has food in a just, sustainable, and nourishing way that is culturally relevant and promotes human well-being and the health of our ecosystems.

While there are sixteen nutrition assistance programs in the United States, there is no coordinated effort to end hunger. Most of the action around the right to food in the United States is through small organizations such as the Detroit Black Community Food Security Network, Southern Rural Black Women's Initiative for Economic and Social Justice, WHY Hunger, and other organizations like the US Human Rights Network. Recently, advocates in the state of Maine were able to get the right to food into their state constitution, though the constitution does not specifically address the right to be free from hunger. Advocates in many other states are seeking to do the same with support from the Food First Information and Action Network, which is the major international organization that helps countries and communities around the world to advance the right to food and nutrition.

More people like you and me should insist that the right to food is the foundation of health and well-being. Anything less is a violation of our humanity and right to live.

FOOD AND CLIMATE

Given our knowledge of food insecurity and what is underneath it, as well as the current climate catastrophe, we can see a massive tidal wave of suffering that is gaining momentum and soon to crash on all of us. It's long past time to lift our heads, adapt, and prepare.

We know there are many people, governments, private militias, and corporations that will seize the chaos ahead and continue to systematically hoard food, water, and wealth. In this book's introduction, I mentioned Mike Davis's treatise on the modern economic system showing how the weather patterns of El Niño facilitated the way for the English to violently withhold food from masses of people who were poor in India, China, and Brazil, leading to the starvation of millions. Capitalizing on weather patterns and the occasional drought is how countries of "the North" colonized nations of "the South." Now the new disasters of today are creating even more ways for governments and corporations to profit.[7]

More famines are on the horizon, but they are preventable.

In May 2019, the United Nations put out an irrefutable report signed by hundreds of scientists warning us that if we do not change the course of human history, a hundred million species will go extinct in the next hundred years; many will go extinct in the next several decades. This includes our mammal friends as well as many fish, mollusks, and other sea life including coral reefs, along with, of course, the bees that pollinate 70 percent of our plant food, and the plants and animals that are food itself. That leaves some of us with some water. But looking at water challenges for the Diné nation, and in Flint, Newark, Jackson, and Dimock, Pennsylvania (where you can light a match and ignite your faucet water due to methane spillage from fracking and the massive failure of our public systems), we see just how our access to potable water may disappear without thoughtful public action and control.

To prepare, we must get into right relationships with our fellow human family, and by doing so, we must do the same with animals, plants, seeds, minerals, and water. If you have friends who are willing to share their wisdom, food, water, housing, friendship, laughter, and care, you are far more likely to survive catastrophes. Evolution of humans and so many other living beings are rooted not in competition but rather cooperation.[8] To have an ethic of responsibility and mutuality supports health and well-being. It is often a neglected and undervalued aspect of the Universal Declaration of Human Rights. Article 29 states, "Everyone has duties to the community in which alone the free and full development of [their] personality is possible."[9]

Demanding rights and freedoms without attention to accountability to the collective can allow people to neglect their fundamental duties and responsibilities to uphold those rights for everyone else. Ignoring such communal responsibilities has also allowed corporations, communities, and individuals to assert their rights without recognizing their inherent obligation to others. In response, the United Nations established an international treaty, the Declaration of Human Duties and Responsibilities (1988), to assert that we are all responsible and have duties to the human family and living world.

The focus on "rights" and "freedoms" often has outweighed our duties and responsibilities for one another. In the years leading up to the creation of the US Constitution, the Haudenosaunee Confederacy, known to colonists as the Iroquois Confederacy, comprised of five nations—the Onondaga, Seneca, Cayuga, Oneida, and Mohawk—worked with the colonists to craft the checks and balances enshrined in the US political systems. Though this history is well documented, many people forget that Indigenous communities in the Northeast inspired the US commitment to democracy. What emerged in the US Constitution, however, was a mangled interpretation of Haudenosaunee values and lifeways, and an outsized focus on protecting property and the rights of landowning white men. The Haudenosaunee Confederacy has long-standing traditions of equality in governance by people of all genders as well as a deep reverence for the land, for the natural world, for the generations before, and for the generations to come. Robin Wall Kimmerer, a Potawatomi author, moss expert, and plant scientist, recalls her conversation with Onandaga elder chief Irving Powless Jr. He claimed the US Constitution was incomplete and inadequate. He said, "If it were up to us, we wouldn't have written the Bill of Rights without a Bill of Responsibilities."[10]

It is time for a new US Constitution rooted in responsibilities to the earth, soil, water, air, food, and each other.

OUR FOOD AS KIN

Let us begin, then, by attending to what all of us should have learned in elementary school about honoring each other, and what Kimmerer describes as the "guidelines for the Honorable Harvest."

> *Know the ways of the ones who take care of you, so that you may take care of them.*
> *Introduce yourself. Be accountable as the one who comes asking for life.*
> *Ask permission before taking. Abide by the answer.*
> *Never take the first. Never take the last.*
> *Take only what you need.*
> *Take only that which is given.*
> *Never take more than half. Leave some for others.*
> *Harvest in a way that minimizes harm.*
> *Use it respectfully. Never waste what you have taken.*
> *Share.*
> *Give thanks for what you have been given.*
> *Give a gift, in reciprocity for what you have taken.*
> *Sustain the ones who sustain you and the earth will last forever.*[11]

Worldwide, Indigenous peoples steward 85 percent of the earth's most biodiverse lands. They have practically no responsibility for the climate crisis, yet they suffer the worst of it. Now the United Nations insists that Indigenous wisdom, such as that of the honorable harvest, is key to the survival of humanity and saving all life on the planet.[12] The terrible irony is that most nation-states that compose the United Nations violently disrespected and forcibly displaced Indigenous communities that warned colonizers and the people who capitalized on colonization of the inevitable catastrophe of environmental destruction.

It is profoundly important that people do not essentialize or commodify Indigenous thought and experiences, as they are quite varied and complicated. Indigenous peoples are complex, diverse, and contain multiple, sometimes conflicting points of view. But it is important to ensure that the original peoples everywhere have their hard-earned expertise, which they developed over thousands of years, respected and valued. Indigenous values, beliefs, and wisdom hold much of the key to everyone's survival.

Let us start with a basic concept rooted in the longtime friend, companion, and relative of many Indigenous peoples in the Americas: corn. Corn or maize, "the Bringer of Life" as the Taino called it, was developed over a ten-thousand-year history in response to cultivation and modification by Indigenous communities that began in the region of Oaxaca, Mexico. Cultivation and reverence for corn spread throughout the continents. Kimmerer identifies some of corn's many names: "Seed of Seeds," "Wife of the Sun," and "Mother of All Things." According to Kimmerer, "These indigenous names honor maize as the center of culture and reflect a deeply respectful relationship between people and the one who sustains them."[13]

In the documentary *Seed: The Untold Story*, Louie Hena of Tesuque and Zuni Pueblos in New Mexico, and organizer of the Indigenous Food and Seed Sovereignty Alliance, described his relationship to corn while holding a handful of kernels.

> Our first mothers were the blue corn and white corn woman.
> This is my grandmother, my grandfather,
> My mom, my dad, my brother, my sister,
> My kids, my grandkids, and myself.
> We all are one.[14]

In this declaration of kinship, there is a common understanding: we are part of earth; we come from the earth; we are all related. Corn participates in everyday life in the United States. Yet we have so little reverence for it. If corn doesn't come to our tummies from the cob, a pot of grits, or warm corn bread, it comes to us through 70 percent of our processed foods, including Coca-Cola and Pepsi, in the form of corn syrup to overload our systems and spill into the liver. Now we pour it as ethanol into our cars.

Kimmerer suggests we need a complete change of mind and spirit to recognize and honor corn as our kin. By extension, our food is our family. The planet is our mutual home that we must share.

The nation of plants agrees.

Stefano Mancuso, internationally renowned Italian botanist, implores people to heed the teachings of plants. In his treatise *The Nation of Plants*, Mancuso created a constitution authored by plants that demands recognition from the United Nations. Beginning with a preamble that admonishes humans for their wrongheaded sense of supremacy, hierarchy, borders, and the ongoing destruction of ecosystems, the constitution has eight articles. It establishes that plants and all living beings have a right to life and to be recognized as sovereign, interconnected, and interdependent; that all plants shall be guaranteed clean water, soil, and atmosphere; that future generations have rights; that there should be no hierarchy of living beings; that every living being should have no borders (here Mancuso gestures to the millions of climate refugees, and explains that trees and plants also migrate to adapt to climate catastrophe); and that all plants shall recognize and foster mutual aid among all living beings.

Plants have no centralized organs, which helps them to adapt and survive. This is clearly evidenced in their existence over billions of years, as opposed to the paltry three hundred thousand years that humans have been around. They have wisdom, longevity, and expertise that humans do not. Recognizing their inherent knowledge, Mancuso uses their voice to insist that "if you do not change right away, the damage for people and for all the natural systems that sustain you will be irreparable." The plants say, "We are the engine of life. . . . We are the basis of your food chain: everything you eat comes from us. Your most important sources of energy come from us. Your medical care depends on us. . . . Now the time has come for you to begin also to use what we can teach you."[15]

HONOR THE PROTECTORS

During the past twenty years, over a thousand people have been murdered as they try to protect their water, air, soil, forests, and food from extraction, exploitation, and pollution. Just in case you think I veered off topic, remember that food and water come from the earth; they need ecosystems, and we need them. Land and water protectors are trying to protect our food, health, and well-being—our very lives. According to a 2019 report by Global Witness, in the Philippines alone, thirty people trying to protect their environment while standing up to the mining, logging, agribusiness, and high-end tourism industries were murdered under Rodrigo Duterte's regime.[16] Throughout the world, government forces, armed militia, private security forces, and hired assassins are murdering, threatening, and criminalizing people—many of them Indigenous—for defending their lands, water, air, and lives.

In Mexico and Central America, the situation is especially frightening. Julián Carrillo, who had already witnessed five of his own family members being murdered in previous years, was trying to defend Indigenous lands in Sierra Tarahumara in Mexico from mining. During this struggle, he was shot dead.[17] In Honduras, the situation is worse; Luis Fernando Ayala, all of sixteen years old, was brutally tortured and then murdered because he was opposing the mining and hydroelectric projects across the region.[18] Ayala was murdered only a few years after Berta Isabel Cáceres Flores, a Lenca woman indigenous to Honduras as well as world-renowned protector of her community's lands and its sacred Gualcarque River, was assassinated because she fought against the illegal construction of the Agua Zarca Dam. Just a few months after being awarded the Goldman Environmental Prize for her work, Berta was murdered in her home by US-trained special forces units of the Honduran military.[19]

Similar violence occurs in the United States. The people of the Oceti Šakowiŋ (the Seven Council Fires, or the Dakota, Lakota, and Nakota people) and people of many other Indigenous nations who carried out non-violent protests to defend their sovereignty in Standing Rock against the Dakota Access Pipeline were threatened, tear-gassed, beaten up, handcuffed, and arrested by government-funded police forces in riot gear. This brutality and the eight hundred arrests were funded by the US government under the Obama administration. Though President Barack Obama finally stalled the construction, the Trump administration overruled that, and the pipeline was finished by force, while dozens are still in jail or dealing with the financial, social, and cultural consequences of having been in prison for trying to defend their own lands, waters, and Indigenous sovereignty. The fight to prevent the construction of the new Line 3, which was built by Enbridge to transport crude oil from the Alberta tar sands through the lands and waterways of the Ojibwe, has led to many more protests and arrests of Indigenous people. Despite Ojibwe resistance, efforts to stop Line 3 were thwarted.

The "man camps" that come along with building oil pipelines are a source of serious trouble and violence in Indigenous communities. According to recent reports in the United States, over six thousand women and girls have been murdered or are missing. Much of these disappearances were a result of the growth of pipeline construction, where men would move in close to Indigenous lands into what are commonly known as man camps constructed by the oil companies.[20] As the pipeline companies continued to plunder the Bakken oil fields in Canada, pipeline construction sites in North Dakota began on and near the Fort Berthold Reservation of the Mandan, Hidatsa, and Arikara nations. Within the first few years of construction, there were over a hundred cases of missing Indigenous women, and many more rapes. While these camps were often on or near reservations in rural areas, due to a 1978 US Supreme Court case, *Oliphant v. Suquamish*, new rules were put in place that Indigenous nation police could not prosecute non-Indigenous people who committed crimes on Indigenous land. It was a grim free-for-all, which has hardly let up even though the Violence against Women Act ensured in 2015 that prosecutions against non-Indigenous people could indeed happen.[21]

Such violence and domination do not occur solely between Indigenous nations on the one hand and corporations and the US government on the other. In Atlanta, Georgia, there are 150 acres of forestlands, originally belonging to the Muscogee and now "property" of the City of Atlanta, that have been designated to be destroyed in order to build a police training facility. The official name is the Atlanta Public Safety Training Center. Most people refer to it as Cop City. Officials asserted that the "state-of-the-art campus would replace substandard offerings and boost police morale." Officials plan to build a fake town in which police can train to subdue, arrest, and imprison people who may be protesting or supposedly trying to cause harm. Thousands of people are horrified at the idea, and in the past few years, many people have been protesting not only the destruction of the forests but also the unconscionable militarization of the police and the intention to train them to carry out urban combat tactics as if they are in a war with their own people in the United States.

Mirroring police tactics in Latin America, Central America, and the Philippines, the US government is now responsible for the senseless and brutal murder of twenty-six-year-old nonbinary climate activist Manual Esteban Páez Terán. Their nickname was "Tortuguita." Tortuguita was camping in the forest with other people who were seeking to prevent the forest from being destroyed. Atlanta police reports said Tortuguita had fired at them. But recent autopsy results corroborate eye-witness accounts and indicate that Tortuguita had no evidence of gunpowder on their body, and that their hands were up when they were shot. Tortuguita was murdered execution style—shot fifty-seven times by the police.[22] Despite this evidence from the autopsy, on October 6, 2023, the local district attorney announced his decision not to charge the Georgia state troopers who shot them.[23]

In response to peaceful actions in support of Tortuguita soon after their murder, twenty-two people were arrested who had been peacefully gathering without any firearms or doing anything illegal. Seeking to protect the forest as well as show up in support of Tortuguita, they were initially arrested for simply having mud on their shoes. But the formal charge? Domestic terrorism.[24]

Investigators, scholars, and activists insist these types of actions constitute standard policing in the United States.[25] Additionally, Atlanta is not the only city looking to build these police combat training centers.

RIGHTS OF NATURE

Before Greta Thunberg came along with her renowned climate strike called Fridays for Future, and her speeches at the UN Swedish Parliament and international meetings, kids in Seattle had already filed a lawsuit against the US government for violating their constitutional right to a future with clean air, fresh water, and land. That suit is still pending, but more young people are joining in.[26]

The events I described above should make it clear that the current US legal system is wholly inadequate to protect the health and well-being of people in the face of corporate resource extraction. People in small towns across America have tried to influence their state legislature or the Environmental Protection Agency (EPA) in attempts to protect their lands, waters, and air from environmental degradation only to find out that there is no law to protect communities from mining and other companies that cause harm. The EPA is not only ineffective but oftentimes it collaborates with polluting corporations.[27]

New laws must be created.

Enter the rights of nature.

It all started with toilets flushing in Philadelphia.

Remember how this book began with a toilet flushing and overflowing? Yes, coming full circle, we're back to the overflowing shit in Philly.

Tamaqua Borough is a small town of about seven thousand people in the middle of coal country in Pennsylvania. This town rests along the Schuylkill River, the same one that flows down through Philadelphia, past the oil refineries (one of which blew up in summer 2019), into the Delaware River, and then into the Chesapeake Bay.

The town was having trouble fighting against a company that was trying to convince it to fertilize its crops with Philadelphia sewage, toxic hospital waste, and something called "fly ash," which is poisonous gunk left over from coal-burning plants. After the coal industry died down in this area, there were two giant pits that were twice the size of the town itself. The "owner" of these pits made them available to the Lehigh Coal and Navigation Company to dump the sludge. In 1994, an eleven-year-old boy named Tony Behun came into direct contact with the sludge and died from a staph infection. Within two years, another teenage boy, Daniel Pennock, also died from a staph infection after exposure to the same sludge. So in 2006, as residents began to fight the company to get rid of the waste, they realized the EPA was not going to help them. They had to develop new laws altogether. The people's strategy was to declare that the natural world around them has a right to personhood and therefore a right to exist. Through arguing that nature has rights, they were able to establish that "residents, natural communities, and ecosystems shall be considered 'persons' for the purposes of the enforcement of the civil rights of those residents, natural communities, and ecosystems."[28] They won the case, protected their land, and the teenagers of the future are safer.

Many other communities across the globe have been inspired by the rights of nature and have begun to find ways to declare that ecosystems, rivers, mountains, and lakes are persons in need of protection. The Whanganui River in New Zealand is a person under domestic law, as is India's Ganges River. In 2019, people in Toledo, Ohio, successfully won a case to grant personhood rights to Lake Erie to help prevent further pollution. This was in response to the three-day shutdown of the city water system in 2014 due to toxic algae blooms. In the same year, Bangladesh granted all of its rivers personhood status, and the Yurok people of California granted personhood to the Klamath River.

This brings us back to Line 3. In 2018, the White Earth Band of Ojibwe (Chippewa) in Minnesota, eager to stop the ongoing construction of Line 3, continued its legal battle by harnessing the rights of nature and declared that *Manoomin* (wild rice) is a person. As a person, Manoomin needs care, and their water source must remain abundant and clean. The law states that "Manoomin, or wild rice, within all the Chippewa ceded territories, possesses inherent rights to exist, flourish, regenerate, and evolve, as well as inherent rights to restoration, recovery, and preservation." Manoomin's rights include "the right to clean water and freshwater habitat, the right to a natural environment free from industrial pollution, the right to a healthy, stable climate free from human-caused climate change impacts, the right to be free from patenting and the right to be free from contamination by genetically engineered organisms."[29]

The struggle of the White Earth Ojibwe and Manoomin continue. Meanwhile, some nation-states have embraced the rights of nature and integrated them into their country's constitution.

Here is an example from Ecuador, via excerpts from its constitution:

Art. 71. Nature . . . where life is reproduced and exists, has the right to exist, persist, maintain and regenerate its vital cycles, structure, functions and its processes in evolution. Every person, people, community or nationality, will be able to demand the recognitions of rights for nature before the public organisms. . . . The State will motivate natural and juridical persons as well as collectives to protect nature; it will promote respect towards all the elements that form an ecosystem.

Art. 73. The State will apply precaution and restriction measures in all the activities that can lead to the extinction of species, the destruction of the ecosystems or the permanent alteration of the natural cycles.

Ecuador has also influenced the United Nations by building on long-standing advocacy and work on environmental justice. In 2009, the United Nations formally acknowledged that the earth and its ecosystems need protection and care in a declaration of the day of Mother Earth. This is also thanks to the leadership of Evo Morales Ayma, former president of the Plurinational State of Bolivia. In his 2009 address to the United Nations, he laid out the seed for the rights of Mother Earth:

The right to life, means the right to exist. It is the right of no ecosystem, species, animal, vegetable, sea, river or lake to be eliminated or pushed to extinction by the irresponsible behavior of human beings. . . .

Right of regeneration for the planet's biocapacity. Mother Earth must be able to regenerate its biodiversity.

Right to a clean life. That means the right of Mother Earth to live without pollution, because not only we humans, but also the fish, animals and trees have the right to live well. The Earth itself has the right to live in a clean environment, free of poisons and toxins.

Since then, the United Nations has been hosting dialogues on the rights of nature and the right to harmony with nature. In 2018, most experts participating declared that the current legal framework of human rights is inadequate to protect life on earth because they do not yet assert the full array of rights of future generations.[30] US legal systems must catch up to the urgent need for a societal shift, where people act on the premise that nature is our kin rather than an endless source of capital.

For humans and other beings to survive, humans must transform our dominant cultural paradigms from greed, competition, and extraction to a culture of solidarity, reciprocity, and humility. Reverence for nature, each other, ourselves, and our food are the places to start.

12 THE SPIRITUAL: ON BECOMING A LOVING LIVING ANCESTOR

When you sit and you council for the welfare of the people,
think not of yourself or your family or even your generation.
Make your decisions on behalf of the seventh generation coming.

> —THE GREAT PEACEMAKER OF THE HAUDENOSAUNEE, TWELFTH
> CENTURY, QUOTED BY OREN LYONS, ONONDAGA COUNCIL OF CHIEFS

Love takes off the masks that we fear we cannot live without and know we cannot live within. I used the word *love* here not merely in the personal sense but as a state of being, or a state of grace—not in the infantile American sense of being made happy but in the tough and universal sense of quest and daring and growth.

> —JAMES BALDWIN, *THE FIRE NEXT TIME*

If all public policy was created in the spirit of love,
we would not have to worry
about unemployment, homelessness,
schools failing to teach children, or addiction.

> —BELL HOOKS, *ALL ABOUT LOVE*

LOVE TODAY AND FOR THE NEXT GENERATIONS

In chapter 3, I brought you into the numerics of lovelessness. I showed the astronomical rates of families reporting food insecurity and emotional neglect, where 56 percent of the people who reported the most severe form of food insecurity said "yes" in response to this question: "Did you often or very often feel that no one in your family loved you or thought you were important or special?" This was almost three times the rate of affirmative responses that people who were food secure reported. The rampant alienation, isolation, and neglect of our children and each other is ripping us apart. Exacerbating this isolation and separation are the current social, economic, and political systems in the United States.

Many cultural commentators and political scientists, including bell hooks, insist that alienation and isolation are upheld by a culture of fear and domination. Love without domination—love that is rooted in care, respect, responsibility, and affection—promotes feelings of belonging. "When we choose to love we choose to move against fear," says hooks. "Against alienation and separation the choice to love is a choice to connect—to find ourselves in each other."[1]

In the studies we did on food insecurity and trauma, we found that lovelessness traveled from generation to generation. In previous chapters, I also demonstrated how we are still reeling from the experiences and actions of people we did not know many generations back in time. Those harms still flow in our blood.

There is a lot of hope, though. Sherita Mouzon, a former member of Witnesses and current staff member of the Center for Hunger-Free Communities, spoke to the press about her view of how it is that people in neighborhoods with high rates of poverty have shorter life spans than people in wealthier neighborhoods. She said it comes as no surprise. "But," she explained, "I always tell my daughter, it's not where you're from, but where you're going."[2]

We should heed Mouzon's wisdom. We can all break that chain.

No matter what our circumstances, we have choice in how we respond to our circumstances and how we treat each other. We have the opportunity to do this in our personal lives. As well, those of us who are writing policy, and those of us calling the shots with nonprofits, small businesses, and big corporations, can muster the courage to talk about love and put love at the center of how we make decisions, write policies, and relate to each other.

Every decision we make affects people around us and multiple generations ahead. We ought to listen to the teachings of the Great Peacekeeper who gifted the Haudenosaunee people with the concept of making decisions not just for the people of today but also for the seventh generation to come—our grandchildren's grandchildren. The way we work to address the gaping holes in our past creates a portal to our future. Our ideas and actions reverberate through time. How we are living, creating, and working today can send discrimination and despair into the future, or we can send forward strength, care, love, resilience, and nourishment.

Humans have a powerful ability to teach each other how to survive throughout the generations. Our ancestors leave tracks, concepts, ideas, instructions, and prophesies. Prophesies are warnings about the future, and they instruct us on how to live today. The Haudenosaunee people or the Onkwehonwe (Real People) have another prophesy: there will be a time when people mistreat their children and when the winds will accelerate. Oren Lyons explains how this is a comment on both the natural world and the human population. Harking to his people throughout the generations, he says that "we're told that the only way to [change] this is to be respectful in your conduct."[3]

But consider our circumstances. In the United States, a child is abused or neglected every forty-seven seconds, and one in five children lives in poverty.[4] Extreme weather events such as hurricanes, blizzards, tornadoes, droughts, wildfires, and high winds are everywhere across the earth, including the United States.

PRACTICING LOVE FOR SELF AND OTHERS

Many people our team has worked with over the years have explained to us that they love so many people. They express loving-kindness for their friends but fail to show that same kindness to themselves. But the capacity to love another person depends on the capacity to love ourselves. People who have a hard time loving themselves may not have received love in ways that make them feel whole, safe, celebrated, and free. This is why low self-esteem—the kinds that Faith, Joanna, or those who want to hurt or kill themselves exhibit—is extremely worrisome.

A few weeks ago, we had a retreat at our center to check on the success of our effectiveness, refine our goals, and check in on each other. One staff member had us go through an exercise as a feelings check. She gave us paper and said, "Draw on your piece of paper how you feel." We did that. Then she said,

OK, flip over the paper,
and draw how you *really* feel.
'Cuz even in a caring work environment like this,
you may not want people to know
or see how you are *really* feeling
deep down inside.

She also referenced that some people, especially Black, Brown, and Indigenous people, or people who have mental illness or another disability, refuse to express emotion because it may put them in harm's way; they may lose their job, lose face, be ridiculed, or invite some other type of trouble.[5]

Having worked with a healing-centered framework, our workplace can occasionally broach emotional depths with deep self-awareness. We were talking about this complexity as a group. A former Network member who coaches new members explained that she often tells people she is fine. She is easy to laugh and express love and appreciation for others. She said she drew a happy and peaceful face on the front side of the paper. But when she was prompted to flip over the paper and draw how she felt underneath that surface emotion, she drew an anxious face and then acknowledged how deep this emotion went. She said that her mother never expressed love for her. In fact, she was always told she was "no good." She noted it makes it hard for her to not only love herself but also trust and love others. "If my own mother could do that to me," she said, "what's to say someone else won't also hurt me? This is why I trust no one with my emotions." Several other staff who had been in either the Network or Witnesses agreed. The staffer who was leading the exercise agreed,

That is the deepest pain,
to not have a mother's love.

But the women who went so deep into that discussion agreed how it is possible to heal their emotional pain. They are breaking the chain, finding ways to love themselves and others, share their joy with others, and work hard to ensure that their own children never feel such a gaping hole in the soul. The Network is a program that has helped bring this forth.

Even if we are not in the Network, however, we can tap in to many types of practices that expand our circle of love. One of the first steps to take is to slow down long enough to look into and understand what's in the "hole" for ourselves. Remember, I described a similar hole in chapter 9 that my mother was afraid to slow down enough to look into and deal with her grief. Sometimes, that hole is due to feelings of being misunderstood and mistreated—as if we do not belong to the world, our family, friends, and community and, by extension, ourselves. It takes practice, stamina, and courage to be resilient enough to withstand the pull of the darkness there.

Buddhist teachings make it clear that much of the world's suffering is rooted in our inability to recognize and heal our wounds. There is a teaching from the Buddha's perspective on how to transform violence that speaks to this directly:

> The whole world is burning with violence. . . . I have looked deeply into the minds of those who are not happy, and I have seen hidden under their suffering a sharp-pointed knife. Because they cannot see the sharp-pointed knife hidden in their mind, they are not able to bear the pain. . . . The pain brought about by the sharp-pointed knife lasts a long time without changing. People hold on to that knife wherever they go, so that their pain spills out into the world. Only when they have a chance to recognize the knife and take it out of their hearts, will their suffering cease, and they will have a chance to stop running.[6]

When I think of my mother and her fear of looking within, I sense that she knew the knife was there in the gaping hole she described, but she was unable to pull it out. Part of that was due to a lack of love for herself that would allow her to hold herself steady. So she just kept running.

A well-known Buddhist practice to help magnify love for self and others is called metta meditation, meaning "loving-kindness" meditation. If we can feel love for our children, lover, or dear friend, then of course we have that capability to love all people, including ourselves. Here is a practice I can share with you. Metta meditation is usually done during a time of being still and quiet, when you can focus on your breathing and feel your own warmth. The structure of such meditation typically begins with yourself and expands outward. You begin by making a quiet proclamation such as

May I be happy,
may I be loved,
may I be healed,
may I be free.

Then you repeat the same loving-kindness stretching outward to people you feel close to. You say, "May you be happy, may you be loved, . . ." and so on. Then you expand the circle of love to people you do not know so well. From there, you send love to people you dislike, and then even to those who have caused you harm. Metta meditations are widely known across the globe, and scientists have found that this practice has profoundly positive effects on emotional, psychological, and physical well-being.[7]

Metta is only a small part of a much broader logic of love known in Buddhist traditions. Thich Nhat Hahn has described four domains of love: *Loving-kindness*, the desire to offer deep listening and understanding while loving everyone, regardless of who they are; *compassion*, the desire to reduce and remove suffering in oneself and others; *joy*, the ability to bring joy and release to those around you; and *equanimity*, to love and treat everyone without discrimination.[8] Buddhist philosophy and practices reach back in time over twenty-six hundred years. Of course, many cultures have similar traditions, but I can only speak to what I've learned over the past few decades of meditation and comradery with people who practice in the Plum Village tradition of Zen Buddhism. A seed of this love practice came from Siddhartha Gautama, or Buddha (the Awakened One), who was sitting under a bodhi tree for many months before he came to the wisdom that founded Buddhism, which branched out through many cultural traditions across the world. The teachings the Buddha passed on came from deep meditation as well as listening to and observing the trees around him. If you remember the previous chapter, where I make it clear that trees and all plant life have much to teach humans, you might recognize this potential for you, yourself, to tap into this ancient and broad wisdom that stems from the natural world.

Loving-kindness is rooted in the capacity to understand another person. We don't even have to express this in person, by email or text, or through social media. We can simply experience this in our hearts and minds. We can feel and send love to people in the way we choose to think, feel, and be. Most of us already do this to some extent. Some of us may be thinking about a loved one faraway; perhaps they are on a trip on the other side of the globe, just in the next room, or getting ready to pick us up from school or work. We wait with great anticipation at seeing them. Or someone we love can be long deceased and we can *still* feel a deep sense of love, affection, and longing. Personally, I can even feel and send love for grandchildren I don't have. There seems to be no limits for how broadly and far we can send loving-kindness.

Compassion is a concept known to most of us, regardless of our spiritual tradition. Many equate compassion with empathy, an ability to feel what another person is feeling (like putting yourself in Maria's pink sneakers as she goes to the ATM machine and, in your heart or mind's eye, attempting to feel what she felt before the father of her kids broke her ribs and stole her money). But it goes beyond that. Over the centuries, many teachers have sought out ways to teach the wisdom of compassion. Patrul Rinpoche, a Buddhist teacher from the nineteenth century, taught people to imagine themselves in the place of others who are in torment—someone about to be murdered or a child who feels unloved. I'd say, remember chapter 1 and think of Juleen in the barrel, where even the nothing she had was falling apart, and her nerves were jumping in orange, green, and yellow, or chapter 10, where it became clear that the barrel was the ship.

Try to get into that barrel. Try to breathe.

If you can't get there, consider this. Patrul Rinpoche asked people to imagine themselves as a mother with no arms whose baby has fallen into a raging river and can do nothing about it. The torment there may be enough to arouse compassion. Yet Buddhist Zen master Thich Nhat Hanh, who passed on from this world in January 2021, explained that compassion is not just to imagine oneself in another's place but rather the *ability to understand that suffering, and then be able to remove pain or transform a person's pain.* So let's stick with that image of an armless woman at the edge of the river. Feel her pain and grief? Got arms? Can you swim? Do you have courage? Then dive in, save the baby, and bring them back to their mother's lap. Then keep them company while you both grieve for all that could have been lost. That is care in the wake.

Removing pain can also mean you can be a kind friend with an open heart who listens deeply as a friend needs to express themselves. Or you can be a doctor, nurse, physician's assistant, therapist, social worker, or spiritual healer who heals pain. In broader ways, this can be helping and healing people through being a legislator who writes policy to improve our political and economic systems of care that help millions of people at a time. Collectively and politically, removal of pain can also take the form of reparations and decolonization.

Let's return to the outset of chapter 10 and consider the image Malcolm X described regarding the nine-inch knife of racially motivated harm. Pulling it out only a little will not help. One must work to remove the entire knife and heal the wound. To do so, one must recognize the knife is there. Consider the mirror image of the spiritual work necessary to pull out the dagger of pain in our own hearts. Both acts of removing pain, politically and spiritually, are interdependent. They are a mirror reflection of what we are called to do.

The other two forms of love—joy and equanimity—also deserve deep attention.

My mother's last summer was 2010, before she died of colon cancer. Her face was ashen from strain and struggle, and not being able to eat. She seemed angry all the time.

Her daily complaint: "Why don't people smile more?"

I viewed her obsession with smiling as a form of oppression. We always had to show eagerness and happiness around her, ever since I could remember. "Stay cheery! Even when you are sad or disappointed." This pressure was a threat. "Laugh and smile, or else!"

On a rainy summer afternoon in 2010, I took my kids for an outing to get away from the emotional storm clouds over the house. I was mad at my mother. I knew she was down, but I was also angry that my children and I were expected to smile on command—not when we were genuinely happy. I was feeling the weight of her suffering; my kids were too.

We walked into a T-shirt shop that sold books as well. While my kids were distracted by the T-shirts, I picked up the book *Being Peace* by Thich Nhat Hanh and read the first few paragraphs:

> Life is filled with suffering, but it is also filled with many wonders, such as the blue sky, the sunshine, and the eyes of a baby. To suffer is not enough. We must also be in touch with the wonders of life. They are within us and all around us, everywhere, anytime.
>
> If we are not happy, if we are not peaceful, we can't share peace and happiness with others, even those we love. . . . If we are peaceful, if we are happy, we can smile and blossom like a flower, and everyone in our family, our entire society, will benefit from our peace.[9]

Tears of shame welled up as I thought of my mother. Of course my mother needs us to smile. She is desperate to experience joy. She cannot find it in herself; she needs joy reflected back to her so she can feel well. I felt that I had begun to experience my own sense of peace and happiness, and I thought that she was ruining it. But I had it backward. I was causing harm by not sharing some of my inner peace with my mother. Recognizing how I can help mirror a sense of peace, healing, and joy, I came home smiling, and have been genuinely smiling more to my kids and everyone around me ever since.

Members of Witnesses also needed more healing, joy, and liberation. Yes, they expressed a lot of grief and sadness; yes, they wanted justice. But most of the time justice was far beyond the horizon, as a distant promise that was losing luster. What lifted Faith, Sarafina, Carla, and Joanna's spirits was everyday kindness, care, respect, and *joy*.

In the absence of money and lack of access to effective policy levers that could increase SNAP and wages, family leave, reparations, and free college education, what could I give? Joy and a sense of ease, peace, and happiness. I started decorating the offices with more joyous colors. We brought in stuffed animals for everyone's kids. We started laughing more and finding ways to help people join in. We focused less on trauma and injustice and began lending more energy to joy, play, fun, dancing, healing, and love. This is the joyous siblinghood we also brought into the healing-centered practices of the Building Wealth and Health Network. The Network became a place of loving friendships. "Loving friendships," hooks states, "provide us with a space to experience the joy of community in a relationship where we learn to process all our issues, to cope with difference and conflict while staying connected."[10]

It's been twenty-two years since I met Juleen, fifteen years since the start of Witnesses to Hunger, twelve years since my mother died, ten years since the start of the Network, and almost seven years since we opened the EAT Café. Through these challenges and projects, I was given the opportunity to build up stamina for unsettling discomfort and pain by generating joy. Suffering is infinite. So must be our joy and sense of happiness to heal it. If the suffering has the energy of a hurricane or tornado, let your love and joy be of equal energy to meet it.

The fourth dimension is equanimity—love without discrimination. This means one cannot decide to love someone based on their behavior, the color of their skin, how much money they have, their gender expression, or their zip code. Hence if a person is addicted to drugs, has hurt someone, or behaves and looks differently than you, you can still offer love with respect and dignity.

This is the deepest and most challenging form of love. It is a form of love that has never been developed on any grand scale in the United States. Lack of equanimity is discrimination. As an antidote to discrimination, equanimity can set new ground from which to heal the pain of not having enough food.

Consider that, if US policies to support people who are poor were rooted in an ethic of love as equanimity, solutions to hunger would be crystal clear: reparations, rematriation, UBI, universal health care, universal childcare, no prisons or police, mutual aid, and the right to food for everyone without the charade of judging someone's worth.

WORTHY OF FOOD AT THE EAT CAFÉ

Our relationships with food can be complex, as they have much to do with our social lives, our perceptions and sensations in our body, where we live, our cultural and spiritual traditions, how much money and time we have, our emotional states, and so much more.

But I want to draw attention to lack of respect for food itself. Remember Akomolafe's depiction of the slave ship. The food was underneath all the humans. Many people view food as a thing, as a simple commodity that can be grown, bought, and sold without consequences or repercussions. How we grow food, care for it, and nurture it should be reflected in the respect for how the food nourishes and cares for us. We are in a mutual relationship. After all, we have a deep intimacy with food as we put it into our mouths, taste it, and swallow it; we invite it into our bodies and expect it to nourish us. Why wouldn't we show food our gratitude and respect?

The way we grow, harvest, sell, buy, and consume food in the United States seems incommensurate with the generosity of plants. Kimmerer wrote about how large and industrial farms plant corn in row after row—as if the corn is part of a military, or worse, as Kimmerer suggests, the corn is "enslaved" to the farmer.[11] The way food is planted, grown, harvested, or gathered is always in a hurry. Migrant farmworkers (many of whom are undocumented and food insecure) have to race the clock in double time because they are only paid by the piece. The same is true for the meatpacking industry. The line for butchering gets faster and more dangerous. Industrial poultry farms shove growth hormones down the throats of chickens and crowd and cage them in giant warehouses without light so they grow faster, and thus we can butcher them faster, wrap them in plastic, and shape them into nuggets for school lunch—for a fee. People love to watch cooking shows where other people run around a grocery store and quickly gather their ingredients, and then they cook meals with speed on time just to get judged and kicked to the side if it's not good enough. The speed matches our greed, and we find this entertaining.

We forget that food is a gift.

Take some time.

Imagine our food talking to us as the plants who are defending their own rights in the face of human onslaught and disrespect.

Millions of people are now losing access to arable land and potable water; tens of millions of climate refugees are leaving their homelands due to the climate catastrophe, war, and tyranny. As a species, humans are in a massive, collective upheaval. If we do not stem the dangers of global warming and begin to heal our relationships and demand equality for all people, many more millions of people will fall victim to military or private militias that will use violent tactics including murder to control food and water. This is already happening. Now that avocados are considered a "superfood" and avocado toast is so popular in the United States, Mexican cartels guard avocado farms with machine guns, while the local communities in the area are losing access to their water because avocado farmers, under protection at gunpoint, are diverting it from non-avocado farms to make a profit.[12]

In the same way we need to heal our relationships with our human family and ourselves, we should engage in more meaningful relationships with plants, animals, soil, water, air, and ecosystems.

Before eating their meal, the monastics and lay community members in the Plum Village tradition recite or listen to the contemplation below. It is an opportunity to slow down to appreciate life and the world around us. It is a meditation on our interconnectedness, our interbeing. It honors our food as a form of self-care and of repairing the world.

1. This food is a gift of the earth, the sky, numerous living beings, and much hard and loving work.
2. May we eat with mindfulness and gratitude so as to be worthy to receive this food.
3. May we recognize and transform unwholesome mental formations, especially our greed and learn to eat with moderation.
4. May we keep our compassion alive by eating in such a way that reduces the suffering of living beings, stops contributing to climate change, and heals and preserves our precious planet.
5. We accept this food so that we may nurture our [siblinghood], build our community, and nourish our ideal of serving all living beings.[13]

Note this concept of gratitude: "so as to be worthy to receive this food." This is not related to the other kind of worthiness on which I previously focused where humans exclude people because they are either poor or not poor enough. Rather, in this framework, to be worthy of our food is to ask ourselves if we are humble enough, and if we have the appropriate respect for our food, land, water, air, soil, and each other. It is a demonstration that we belong to our food and to each other.

The ways that many of us eat—burgers from the drive-through and juicy steaks at the roadside pit stop—are contributing to the sixth great extinction. Agriculture and food production are responsible for about one-quarter of greenhouse gas emissions.[14] The warming of the planet has already surpassed most of its tipping points for sustaining much of life on earth. All living beings—inclusive of trees and shrubs—are trying to migrate to the poles to get to cooler lands and waters. But the food chain along with the food systems on land and water are already depleted—in many cases, in ways beyond repair.[15]

Most of us know this—kids in second grade as well as young and middle-aged adults; even our elders know. But the disrespect continues in our carelessness, hoarding, and waste. One can see the disrespect in the encouragement of throwing a pie in the elementary school principal's face as I highlighted in chapter 8, as a sign of childish victory encouraged by Feeding America if our kids collect record-breaking pounds of food in the form of beef chunks and peanut butter.

If we cannot respect our food, how can we respect all plants, animals, soils, minerals, and waterways? How can we respect our fellow human beings, and how can we have any respect for ourselves? Hunger flourishes in this environment of disrespect.

But we can flip this with equanimity, joy, compassion, and understanding to bring us into right relationship with the planet, each other, and ourselves.

We tried to do this with the EAT Café. We set up the right pay structure and a culture of no judgment. We were trying to stand tall against the winds of capitalism. Even though some people who came to the café were wealthy and could pay triple the amount to supplement other people's meals, many people seemed to go there just to get a good deal. They liked the feeling of participating in something meaningful but neglected to pay the true price.

I will never forget the people who came to the café for food, music, joy, and fellowship, especially one mother of three young children who came in winter 2017. She told the server how grateful she was to have warm food and be in a warm place, as they had been living without water and heat all winter. When the server brought hot chocolate for her and each of the children without anybody asking for it, she was beside herself with tears of grief and gratitude. Loving-kindness, compassion, joy, and equanimity were there. It was meant to be a place of belonging. We were trying to create a place of love and care, and do it through food and companionship. Hot chocolate helps too.

REFLECTING ON WHAT MATTERS

"When we are self-loving," hooks stated, "we attend to the deeper needs of our soul, we no longer feel abandonment or loss of recognition."[16] This self-love is necessary to help plug in to larger networks of solidarity.

We sought to help grow solidarity and love in the programs of Witnesses, the Building Wealth and Health Network, and EAT Café. In the early years of Witnesses, people would ask me, "What's the most challenging thing you have learned from members of Witnesses?" When it felt safe enough to do so, which was never in a public forum, I explained that I was ill prepared for the depths of despair and lack of self-esteem. I could understand how policy interventions could help with income poverty, such as increased wages, housing subsidies for safe and affordable housing, more SNAP benefits and nutrition supports, and laws that ensure equal pay for women. But for the low self-esteem as a result of rape, disrespect, abandonment, or as Treva Lindsey puts it, "unlivable living," I had little idea what to say—I suppose because it would take over two hundred pages of a book to get across the necessary depth of response.[17] I couldn't bear all this pain that people were sharing with me. I could not find a way to articulate its depths. I needed witnesses or bystanders to acknowledge the pain and hold it with me long enough for me to find a way to give it voice. You, dear reader, are witness to this. And by witnessing the pain herein, you are making a way for the healing to come through.

No amount of intellectual thought or "systems change" strategies in the current national policymaking arena can reach the depths of the emotional and spiritual challenges associated with racial trauma, gender-based violence, and child abuse, and with the reflection of all three of these in the violence in our political, cultural, and economic systems. As I listened to the women

I interviewed and worked with over the years, their experiences tapped into a suffering that I did not even know was inside me. They forced me to reckon with hundreds of years of history in the space of a single conversation. I had to expand my heart and deepen my humanity. Larry Ward, a Zen Buddhist and spiritual teacher, asserts that in refusing to address racialized trauma and the devastation of hundreds of years, many people in America "are in sociological despair, meaning we are as a nation out of alignment with our depth of humanity."[18]

What was a person to do to help Joanna feel, deep inside, that she was worth more than one pot, other than constant reassurance, consistent presence, opportunities to speak to legislators as well as be interviewed on the radio and newspaper, and, as I wanted so much, to simply be her friend? Faith, the member of Witnesses whom we had to hospitalize to protect her from killing herself in her laundry room, explained the lack of self-love in a stark way. "I cannot love myself," she remarked when we first met. "I can't even *find* myself to love."

I told her, "Faith, you are so brilliant and you are beautiful and you are such an inspiration to me. Don't you see that?"

She replied,

Mariana, when I look in the mirror,
I literally cannot see myself.
I don't see anything.
I see nothing.

After several years of traveling to Washington, DC, and other places for multiple exhibits and panel functions, Faith and I did a local Philadelphia radio interview about poverty in Philadelphia. She reflected on her relationships with members of Witnesses and the social action in which they participated. "Not until I started doing Witnesses did I feel like I mattered, that people listened. I can see myself now. When I look in the mirror, I see a beautiful woman." Being able to see herself in the mirror was a long, hard struggle that came through developing and acting on feelings of belonging, community care, and joy where she could become involved in struggles beyond herself. In this process, she could begin to see her reflection.

Such a profound gap in the soul is a deeply personal experience. It is also clearly reflected in how US society views Black women and families. Most members of Witnesses understood that this was not simply an experience deep in the body and spirit but instead a reflection of their neighborhoods and communities along with the death-dealing systems of our government and society.

Esther took a photo of trash in the stairwell. She said, "As you go by these abandoned houses in the neighborhood and you see all the trash in the street, you realize no one cares about us, no one cares about me and my children. So then I stop caring about anything." One of her self-portraits was of her face, with tears streaming down both cheeks.

The ongoing disrespect, neglect, and abandonment of primarily Black neighborhoods in Philadelphia is seen in the numerous abandoned factories, boarded-up homes, weeks of uncollected trash in the street, abandoned community centers with fences and barbed wire around them, and more. This is a fractal, again, of what is felt in the body and soul.

Some people may want to say that doing personal work and loving oneself is the wrong focus; it should be protesting against the violent structures in place and taking action to create new ones. I insist, however, that they are one and the same. As I explained in chapter 3, the body keeps the score of traumatic events, just as our social bodies keep the score of ongoing policy and historical violence. The inner and outer are porous and always influence and reflect each other.

So when you see factories abandoned for over forty years, windows broken out, trash in the street, or abandoned homes with caved-in roofs, how can you not read state-sponsored disrespect, abuse, and lovelessness? Bad policy is a form of violence that causes these abuses and abandonments.

After a talk I gave in a Philadelphia church in 2018 about hunger, homelessness, trauma, despair, and how to change it, a white woman from the audience who is at the helm of one of the most powerful philanthropic organizations in the region reprimanded me privately as we stood among the church pews. She said, "You should support the mayor and local leaders. You criticizing the city government takes away from the good they can and will do." But she missed the point. I was talking about the long history of subjugation. I was inviting people to not get complacent just because we have supposedly thoughtful people in charge. I took the long view, deep into the past and far into the future. With our current structures and ways of being, Philadelphia's abandoned factories, neglected streets, dilapidated and unlivable houses, poor health, and household food insecurity simply endure and continue.

After twenty-five years of doing policy-relevant work on hunger, I have little confidence in our current systems. I see how they destroy and abuse. I see no widespread, universal loving-kindness. Rather, I see favoritism for wealthy, white, and powerful people, such as medical, legal, and business professionals, through the billions of dollars invested in Philadelphia center city offices, supplemented by tax breaks that allow for the neglect and disinvestment in schools, neighborhood community centers, libraries, and more. The investments of wealth continue to be directed toward the wealthy who exploit people and keep them impoverished.

Something must change. What's that? Everything.

PREPARE FOR THE END BY ENDING HUNGER

Becoming a loving, more inclusive person is what you and I can do immediately. We owe it to the people around us and those who come after us to spread more love—more kindness, compassion, joy, and equanimity. We also owe it to our more-than-human kin to stop the exploitation and domination. Circling back to what I said at the end of my introduction, I suggest we take our cue from Audre Lorde and make a conscious decision to lean into love with a depth of feeling. It helps us step into our power. This power brings together the personal, political, and spiritual. Lorde said that it is not a "question only of what we do; it is a question of how acutely and fully we can feel in the doing. . . . The aim of each thing which we do is to make our lives and the lives of our children richer and more possible."[19]

Juleen, Joanna, Maria, Celeste, Remi, Faith, Carla, Sarafina, Esther, Sherita, and so many other people who have inspired this book have the courage to speak up and demand transformative change without hesitation, without fear, and full of love for the world and future generations. If you have read this far, I sense you have that fearlessness and love too. Please join in. You are needed for the end of times.

Give yourself some space to evolve and remember that you already know how to end hunger in the United States and around the world. Nothing holds us back from taking action to heal the violences in our past and present. To do so requires us first and foremost to see, hear, acknowledge, and courageously respond to the painful truth expressed by people who know hunger in their gut. From there, we know that if we respond with love and respect in our personal lives, our political work, and our spiritual practice, we can greet the trouble ahead with courage and joy to create a more nourishing world.

Acknowledgments

I owe deepest gratitude to the people of the Southern Cheyenne and Arapaho nations who taught me fundamental values necessary for living a meaningful life. Those values—solidarity not "help," love and companionship, the inter-relatedness of all life, the sacredness of food, reverence for orphans and marginalized people, generating joy amid adversity, and deep humility—have guided me since my early twenties. Specifically, I thank and honor Willie Fletcher Sr. and family, Chester Whiteman, Edwina Medicine Bird, Gerry Hutchinson, Leo Penn, George Old Crow, and their families, and many others who taught me by example. Thank you! *Né-á'eše! Hohóu!* All proceeds from this book are directed to the Cheyenne and Arapaho Language and Culture Department in Concho, Oklahoma.

To all members of Witnesses to Hunger, the Building Wealth and Health Network, participants in Children's HealthWatch, members of the EAT Café advisory board, and participants in other studies that contributed to work on food, justice, and trauma I send my deepest gratitude and love. People involved number in the thousands. Though many must remain anonymous, I especially honor Janon McCreary, Joanna Cruz Simmons, Tianna Gaines-Turner, Imani Sullivan, Myra Young, Angela Sutton, Barbie Izquierdo, Tangela Federick, Myra Maldonado, Marinette and Luis Roman, Crystal Sears, Leticia Ainsley, Tiffany Ross, Whitney Henry, Emily Edwards, Betty Burton, Charlene M., Jean C., Beatriz C., Kim Hart, Susan Harris, Billy Bromage, Kim W., Bonita Cuff, Juell Frazier, Tamara Santiago, Karla Taylor, Leona Brown, Marion Campbell, Charlene Sullivan, April Thompson Harris,

Callalilly Cousar, Ryan Kuck, Mary Seton Corboy, John Kirby, Paulette Adams, Rose Samuel-Evans, James Wright, Kevin Brown, and members of the Black Bottom Association.

Many colleagues in the antihunger social justice spaces shared their wisdom with me. They were generous even when we did not agree. Gratitude goes to people from the Greater Philadelphia Coalition Against Hunger, Community Legal Services, People's Emergency Center, Philabundance, SHARE, Nutritional Development Services, Center on Budget and Policy Priorities, Food Research and Action Center, and Share Our Strength. Specific thanks to Karen Wilson, Steveanna Wynne, Louise Hayes, Anne Ayella, Linda Samost, Wiggy Olson, Kathy Fisher, Glenn Bergman, Kathy Webb, LaDonna Pavetti, Max Finberg, Joel Berg, Jim Weill, Ellen Teller, Billy Shore, Jeremy Everett, and Jessica Bartholow. The Network also owes thanks to people in the federal and state Agency for Children and Families and the Departments of Health and Human Services, with special thanks to Estelle Richman, Ed Zogby, and Tamila Lay. Thank you to Alisha Coleman-Jensen at ERS for constant support with the food security measure, and to Andrea Anatar at Research Triangle Institute, who supported the work of the National Commission on Hunger. Thank you to all commission members, and the congressional staffers and elected officials who helped me keep my head, hone my message, and learn how policy gets developed, destroyed, or patched together. I send sincere gratitude to US Senator Bob Casey Jr., his family and staff, and US Congressman Jim McGovern and staff.

This work required robust financial support. Special gratitude and love to Anonymous, who provided unwavering support and always trusted in the values and risk-taking necessary to try new approaches. Sincere appreciation also to the Robert Wood Johnson Foundation, W. K. Kellogg Foundation, Annie E. Casey Foundation, Merck & Co. Foundation, PEW Charitable Trusts, Claneil Foundation Inc., Philadelphia Health Partnership, Oak Foundation, and Leo and Peggy Pierce Family Foundation. Many people working in print media, radio, and television helped amplify the expertise of members of Witnesses and the Network; of note are Sandy Shae, Marty Moss-Coane, Melissa Harris-Perry, Alfred Lubrano, Greg Kaufman, and filmmakers Kristi Jacobsen and Lori Silverbush. Their courage and witnessing deserve mention and gratitude.

A huge thank you to MIT Press editor Beth Clevenger along with series editors Robert Gottlieb and Nevin Cohen for believing in this project enough to stick with it through several years, many drafts, and a few tears. Thanks to outstanding attention to detail by Virginia Crossman and Cindy Milstein, this book's message is clear. Much gratitude to the author of *Big Hunger*, Andy Fisher, who convinced me to write this book and sent regular encouragement. Thank you to Helen Rubinstein and Stephanie Bize, the 2019 cohort of the Looking Glass Writers Conference, and participants in the 2019 writers retreat at the BANFF Centre for feedback on earlier drafts. Deep appreciation to Janet Poppendieck for her inspiring work and for reading an early draft of chapter 8. Special gratitude to Robin Wall Kimmerer's kind encouragement as I began this work to write with tenderness.

While writing this book, I benefited from belonging to several communities that deepened my resolve to tell the truth. Sending gratitude to the people of Coming to the Table, an organization seeking to promote racial healing among descendants of people who were enslaved and enslavers. I especially thank people in my "writing pod" who aided me in becoming more compassionate. Thank you to the participants in Jem Bendell's sustainable leadership course and Scholar's Warning, and to fellow monster-humans diving into cracks during our course with Bayo Akomolafe. I give the deepest bow of gratitude to the monastics and lay practitioners of Plum Village in the tradition of Thich Nhat Hanh.

Helping me stay true to values of love and equanimity were many dear friends. I especially benefited from *comadres* in the struggle to address food insecurity, doctors Sonya Jones and Katherine Alaimo; friends and Drexel colleagues Rabbi Nancy Epstein and Sandra Bloom, and colleagues of Children's HealthWatch, especially doctors Deborah Frank, John Cook, Maureen Black, Dianna Cuts, Eddie Ochoa, Pat Casey, Stephanie Ettinger de Cuba, and Allison Bovel; spiritual mentors Valerie Brown and Jen Eriksen; and pals Ruth Lopez and Kiki Speidel. Hugs of gratitude to Roberto Castillo Sandoval, whose brilliance and listening heart guided me through my roughest moments.

To my students, thank you for your outstanding work and humor as we explored ideas on human rights, abolition, and the work at the Center for Hunger-Free Communities. Numerous staff and students at the center provided the backbone, brains, brawn, heart, and perseverance to develop the programming, research, and practice described here. Deep gratitude to all who took risks at work, provided wisdom, shared their emotions, and added so much joy. I especially thank Jenny Rabinowich, Christina Council, Ravi Kalwani, Angelo Melendez, Jennifer Breaux, Cizely Kurian, Nijah Famous, Falguni Patel, Kate Scully, Callie Perrone, Rachel Cahill, Lili Dodderidge, Rachel Kirzner, Molly Knowles, Maura Boughter-Dornfeld, Michelle Taylor, Gabriela Grimaldi, Emily Weida, Jing Sun, Pam Phojanakong, and Sabea Evans. Special thank yous to Network coaches Brittany Nelson, Keith Lee, Korah Lovelace, Millie Bass, Molly Baird Ashodian, and Raheem Stevenson. Network leaders Kevin Mansa, Alie Huxta, Jenay Smith, Mike Moody, and Natalie Shaak have the grit, courage, love, compassion, and equanimity to make the Network and all of our programs at the center a joyous place to be, and they help thousands of people in Philadelphia and beyond. I am enormously honored and grateful to be considered their colleague. Many partners and staff made the EAT Café possible, but without the vision of Jeff Benjamin, Marc Vetri, Donnell Jones-Craven, Racquel Williams-Payne, Nia Minard, and the outstanding leadership and magical cooking of Valerie Erwin (@GeecheeGirlCafe), it would not have become such a nourishing and joyous place. Finally, hugs of gratitude to Sherita Mouzon and Victoria Egan for working alongside and guiding me over the last fourteen years. Sherita, you helped me stay humble and gave me courage; Victoria, your generous wisdom kept the Center for Hunger-Free Communities healthy and whole, and your friendship has helped us all to endure.

Everything here became possible with love, joy, and encouragement from my family, most especially Zora, Gabi, Sam, Leonard, and Maude.

Anything here that seems useful should be attributed to the people and groups above.

Finally, thank you, dear reader, for reading to the end.

Peace be with you.

Appendix 1: USDA/ERS Definitions of Food Security for Households with Children, as Measured by the HFSSM

	USDA Designation up through 2005	USDA Designation and Related Questions from HFSSM Current, since 2006	USDA/ERS Definition	Number of Affirmative Responses to HFFSM
Household Food Security Status	Food secure	Food secure *High food security*	No reported indications of food-access problems or limitations	0 of 18
	Food secure	Food secure *Marginal food security* Worried food would run out. Food bought did not last.	Few reported indications—typically of anxiety over food sufficiency or shortage of food in the house. Little or no indication of changes in diets or food intake.	1–2 of 18
	Food insecure *Without hunger*	Food insecure *Low food security* Worried food would run out. Food bought did not last. Could not afford balanced meal. Cut size of meal or skipped meal.	Reports of reduced quality, variety, or desirability of diet. Little to no indication of reduced food intake.	3–7 of 18
	Food insecure *With hunger*	Food insecure *Very low food security* Cut or skipped meal. Ate less than felt should. Hungry but did not eat. Lost weight. Did not eat whole day. Did not eat whole day, 3+ months.	Caregivers report that one or more children in the household lacked adequate, nutritious food at times during the year.	8+ of 18

	USDA Designation up through 2005	USDA Designation and Related Questions from HFSSM Current, since 2006	USDA/ERS Definition	Number of Affirmative Responses to HFFSM
Child Food Security Status	Child food insecure *Without hunger*	Food insecurity *Low food security among children* Children ate only low-variety, low-cost food. Could not feed children balanced meal.	Caregivers reported that children were hungry, skipped a meal, or did not eat for a whole day because there was not enough money for food.	2+ of 8 child-focused questions
	Child food insecure *With hunger*	Food insecurity *Very low food security among children* Children not eating enough. Cut size of children's meals. Children hungry but could not afford food. Children skipped meal. Children did not eat for a whole day.		5+ of 8 child-focused questions

Appendix 2: ACEs' Questions and Scoring

Prior to your 18th birthday:

1. Did a parent or other adult in the household often or very often . . .
    Swear at you, insult you, put you down, or humiliate you? or Act in a
    way that made you afraid that you might be physically hurt?
    a.   No___If Yes, enter 1 __

2. Did a parent or other adult in the household often or very often . . .
    Push, grab, slap, or throw something at you? or Ever hit you so hard that
    you had marks or were injured?
    a.   No___If Yes, enter 1 __

3. Did an adult or person at least 5 years older than you ever . . . Touch or
    fondle you or have you touch their body in a sexual way? or Attempt
    or actually have oral, anal, or vaginal intercourse with you?
    a.   No___If Yes, enter 1 __

4. Did you often or very often feel that . . . No one in your family loved
    you or thought you were important or special? or Your family didn't look
    out for each other, feel close to each other, or support each other?
    a.   No___If Yes, enter 1 __

5. Did you often or very often feel that . . . You didn't have enough to eat,
    had to wear dirty clothes, and had no one to protect you? or Your parents
    were too drunk or high to take care of you or take you to the doctor if
    you needed it?
    a.   No___If Yes, enter 1 __

6. Were your parents ever separated or divorced?
    a.   No___If Yes, enter 1 __

7. Was your mother or stepmother: Often or very often pushed, grabbed, slapped, or had something thrown at her? or Sometimes, often, or very often kicked, bitten, hit with a fist, or hit with something hard? or Ever repeatedly hit over at least a few minutes or threatened with a gun or knife?

    a. No___If Yes, enter 1 __

8. Did you live with anyone who was a problem drinker or alcoholic, or who used street drugs?

    a. No___If Yes, enter 1 __

9. Was a household member depressed or mentally ill, or did a household member attempt suicide?

    a. No___If Yes, enter 1 __

10. Did a household member go to prison?

    a. No___If Yes, enter 1 __

Now add up your "Yes" answers: _____ This is your ACE Score.

Appendix 3: Example of Adversity over Multiple Generations as Explained by Keisha (Interviewed for Child Hunger Study)

CHILD VERY LOW FOOD SECURE

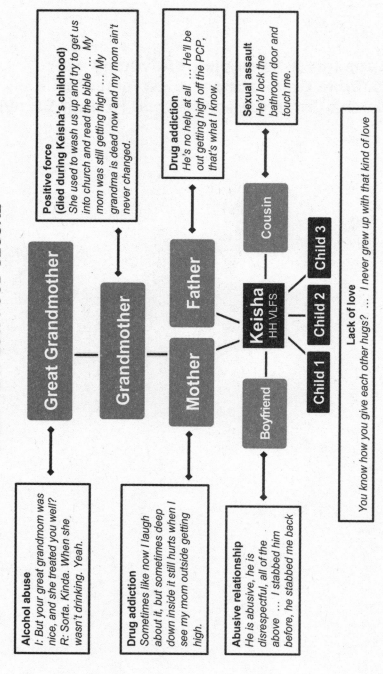

Positive force
(died during Keisha's childhood)
She used to wash us up and try to get us into church and read the bible ... My mom was still getting high ... My grandma is dead now and my mom ain't never changed.

Drug addiction
He's no help at all ...He'll be out getting high off the PCP, that's what I know.

Sexual assault
He'd lock the bathroom door and touch me.

Alcohol abuse
I: But your great grandmom was nice, and she treated you well? R: Sorta. Kinda. When she wasn't drinking. Yeah.

Drug addiction
Sometimes like now I laugh about it, but sometimes deep down inside it still hurts when I see my mom outside getting high.

Abusive relationship
He is abusive, he is disrespectful, all of the above ... I stabbed him before, he stabbed me back

Great Grandmother

Grandmother

Father

Mother

Cousin

Keisha
HH VLFS

Boyfriend

Child 1

Child 2

Child 3

Lack of love
You know how you give each other hugs? ... I never grew up with that kind of love

Appendix 4: Index of Acronyms

ACA	Affordable Care Act
ACES	adverse childhood experiences
AFDC	Aid to Families with Dependent Children
BPP	Black Panther Party
COINTELPRO	Counterintelligence Program of the FBI
C-SNAP	Children's Sentinel Nutrition Assistance Program
DHS	Department of Human Services
EBT	Electronic Benefits Transfer
EITC	Earned Income Tax Credit
EPA	Environmental Protection Agency
ERS	Economic Research Service (of the USDA)
FDPIR	Food Distribution Program on Indian Reservations
FBI	Federal Bureau of Investigation
FNS	Food and Nutrition Service
HFSSM	US Household Food Security Survey Module
PIC	prison-industrial complex
PRWORA	Personal Responsibility and Work Opportunity Act
SNAP	Supplemental Nutrition Assistance Program
TANF	Temporary Assistance for Needy Families
TFP	Thrifty Food Plan
TRC	Truth and Reconciliation Commission
UBI	Universal basic income
USDA	US Department of Agriculture
WIC	Special Supplemental Nutrition Program for Women, Infants, and Children

Notes

PROLOGUE

1. Francis Weller and Michael Lerner, *The Wild Edge of Sorrow: Rituals of Renewal and the Sacred Work of Grief* (Berkeley, CA: North Atlantic Books, 2015).

INTRODUCTION

1. Alisha Coleman-Jensen et al., "Household Food Security in the United States in 2021," Economic Research Report No. ERR-309 (USDA Economic Research Service, September 2022), http://www.ers.usda.gov/publications/pub-details/?pubid=104655.

2. Pëtr Kropotkin, *The Conquest of Bread* (New York: G. P. Putnam's Sons, 1906), 36, https://theanarchistlibrary.org/library/petr-kropotkin-the-conquest-of-bread.

3. Mike Davis, *Late Victorian Holocausts: El Niño Famines and the Making of the Third World*, reissue ed. (London: Verso, 2017), 9.

4. Janet Poppendieck, *Breadlines Knee-Deep in Wheat: Food Assistance in the Great Depression*, rev. and exp. ed. (Berkeley: University of California Press, 2014).

5. Jean Drèze and Amartya Sen, *Hunger and Public Action*, rev. ed. (Oxford: Clarendon Press, 1991).

6. Molly Kinder and Laura Stateler, "Amazon and Walmart Have Raked in Billions in Additional Profits during the Pandemic, and Shared Almost None of It with Their Workers," *Brookings* (blog), December 22, 2020, https://www.brookings.edu/blog/the-avenue/2020/12/22/amazon-and-walmart-have-raked-in-billions-in-additional-profits-during-the-pandemic-and-shared-almost-none-of-it-with-their-workers/.

7. James P. Ziliak, "Food Hardship during the COVID-19 Pandemic and Great Recession," *Applied Economic Perspectives and Policy* 43, no. 1 (March 2021): 132–152, https://doi.org/10.1002/aepp.13099.

8. Kerith Conron et al., "Food Insufficiency among LGBT Adults during the COVID-19 Pandemic" (Williams Institute, UCLA School of Law, April 2022), https://williamsinstitute.law.ucla.edu/wp-content/uploads/LGBT-Food-Insufficiency-Apr-2022.pdf.

9.   Alisha Coleman-Jensen and Mark Nord, "Food Insecurity among Households with Working-Age Adults with Disabilities," Economic Research Report No. ERR-144 (US Department of Agriculture, January 2013), http://www.ers.usda.gov/publications/pub-details/?pubid=45040.

10. Lorie Konish, "This Is the Real Reason Most Americans File for Bankruptcy," CNBC, February 11, 2019, https://www.cnbc.com/2019/02/11/this-is-the-real-reason-most-americans-file-for-bankruptcy.html.

11. Marla Pardilla et al., "High Levels of Household Food Insecurity on the Navajo Nation," *Public Health Nutrition* 17, no. 1 (January 2014): 58–65, https://doi.org/10.1017/S1368980012005630.

12. Jennifer Sowerwine et al., "Reframing Food Security by and for Native American Communities: A Case Study among Tribes in the Klamath River Basin of Oregon and California," *Food Security* 11, no. 3 (June 2019): 579–607, https://doi.org/10.1007/s12571-019-00925-y.

13. Saidiya V. Hartman, *Scenes of Subjection: Terror, Slavery, and Self-Making in Nineteenth-Century America*, rev. and updated ed. (New York: W.W. Norton, 2022), 203.

14. Richard Rothstein, *The Color of Law: A Forgotten History of How Our Government Segregated America* (New York: W. W. Norton, 2017).

15. Mariana Chilton et al., "Food Insecurity and Risk of Poor Health among US-Born Children of Immigrants," *American Journal of Public Health* 99 (2009): 556–562.

16. J. Van Hook and K. S. Balistreri, "Ineligible Parents, Eligible Children: Food Stamps Receipt, Allotments, and Food Insecurity among Children of Immigrants," *Social Science Research* 35, no. 4 (2006): 486–509.

17. Brittany G. Hill et al., "Prevalence and Predictors of Food Insecurity in Migrant Farmworkers in Georgia," *American Journal of Public Health* 101, no. 5 (May 2011): 831–833, https://doi.org/10.2105/AJPH.2010.199703.

18. Mariana Chilton et al., "La alimentación y el bienestar de los ciudadanos Estadounidenses más jóvenes de madres Mexicanas, Centroamericanas, y Caribeñas," *Cahiers Alhim de La Universidad de Paris 8 de Saint-Denis* (January 2008).

19. Sarah Deer, *The Beginning and End of Rape: Confronting Sexual Violence in Native America* (Minneapolis: University of Minnesota Press, 2015).

20. Hartman, *Scenes of Subjection*, 371.

21. bell hooks, *All about Love: New Visions* (New York: William Morrow Paperbacks, 2018), 93.

22. Treva B. Lindsey, *America, Goddam: Violence, Black Women, and the Struggle for Justice* (Oakland: University of California Press, 2022), 9.

23. Maria Yellow Horse Brave Heart et al., "Women Finding the Way: American Indian Women Leading Intervention Research in Native Communities," *American Indian and Alaska Native Mental Health Research* (online) 23, no. 3 (2016): 24–47.

24. Eduardo Duran, Allen E. Ivey, and Derald Wing Sue, *Healing the Soul Wound: Counseling with American Indians and Other Native People* (New York: Teachers College Press, 2006).

25. Joy DeGruy, *Post Traumatic Slave Syndrome: America's Legacy of Enduring Injury and Healing* (Portland, OR: Joy DeGruy Publications, 2017).

26. Silvia Federici, *Caliban and the Witch: Women, the Body and Primitive Accumulation* (Brooklyn: Autonomedia, 2004).

27. Resmaa Menakem, *My Grandmother's Hands: Racialized Trauma and the Pathway to Mending Our Hearts and Bodies* (Las Vegas: Central Recovery Press, 2017), 39.

28. Larry Ward, *America's Racial Karma: An Invitation to Heal* (Berkeley, CA: Parallax Press, 2020), 75.

29. W. E. Burghardt Du Bois and David Levering Lewis, *Black Reconstruction in America, 1860–1880* (New York: Free Press, 1998), 35.

30. David R. Roediger, "The Pursuit of Whiteness: Property, Terror, and Expansion, 1790–1860," *Journal of the Early Republic* 19, no. 4 (1999): 579, https://doi.org/10.2307/3125134.

31. Cheryl I. Harris, "Whiteness as Property," June 10, 1993, https://harvardlawreview.org/1993/06/whiteness-as-property/.

32. Cedric J. Robinson, *Cedric J. Robinson: On Racial Capitalism, Black Internationalism, and Cultures of Resistance* (London: Pluto Press, 2019); Walter Johnson and Robin D. G. Kelley, *Race, Capitalism, Justice* (Boston: Boston Review, 2017).

33. Dallas Goldtooth and Alberto Saldamando, "Indigenous Resistance against Carbon," Indigenous Environmental Network, August 19, 2021, https://www.ienearth.org/indigenous-resistance-against-carbon/.

34. Devon A. Mihesuah and Elizabeth Hoover, eds., *Indigenous Food Sovereignty in the United States: Restoring Cultural Knowledge, Protecting Environments, and Regaining Health* (Norman: University of Oklahoma Press, 2019).

35. Ashanté M. Reese, *Black Food Geographies: Race, Self-Reliance, and Food Access in Washington, D.C.* (Chapel Hill: University of North Carolina Press, 2019).

36. Jessica Gordon Nembhard, *Collective Courage: A History of African American Cooperative Economic Thought and Practice* (University Park: Pennsylvania State University Press, 2014).

37. Michael Twitty, *The Cooking Gene: A Journey through African-American Culinary History in the Old South* (New York: Amistad, 2017); Emily Meggett et al., *Gullah Geechee Home Cooking: Recipes from the Matriarch of Edisto Island* (New York: Harry N. Abrams, 2022).

38. Eve Tuck and K. Wayne Yang, "Decolonization Is Not a Metaphor," *Decolonization: Indigeneity, Education and Society* 1, no. 1 (September 8, 2012), https://jps.library.utoronto.ca/index.php/des/article/view/18630.

39. Red Nation, *The Red Deal: Indigenous Action to Save Our Earth* (Brooklyn: Common Notions, 2021).

40. Keeanga-Yamahtta Taylor, *From #BlackLivesMatter to Black Liberation* (Chicago: Haymarket Books, 2016).

41. Combahee River Collective, "The Combahee River Collective Statement (1977)," statement, April 1977, https://www.blackpast.org/african-american-history/combahee-river-collective -statement-1977/.

42. "Critical Resistance," Critical Resistance, accessed October 14, 2022, https://criticalresistance .org; "Homepage," Project NIA, accessed October 14, 2022, https://project-nia.org/; Taylor, *From #BlackLivesMatter to Black Liberation*.

43. Combahee River Collective, "The Combahee River Collective Statement (1977)"; Angela Y. Davis, *Are Prisons Obsolete?* (New York: Seven Stories Press, 2003); Ruth Wilson Gilmore, *Golden Gulag: Prisons, Surplus, Crisis, and Opposition in Globalizing California* (Berkeley: University of California Press, 2007); Mariame Kaba, Tamara K. Nopper, and Naomi Murakawa, *We Do This 'til We Free Us: Abolitionist Organizing and Transforming Justice* (Chicago: Haymarket Books, 2021); Andrea Ritchie and Angela Y. Davis, *Invisible No More: Police Violence against Black Women and Women of Color*, rep. ed. (Boston: Beacon Press, 2017); Dorothy E. Roberts, *Torn Apart: How the Child Welfare System Destroys Black Families—and How Abolition Can Build a Safer World* (New York: Basic Books, 2022).

44. Chenjari Kumanyika, "Ruth Wilson Gilmore Makes the Case for Abolition," *Intercepted* (podcast), June 10, 2020, https://theintercept.com/2020/06/10/ruth-wilson-gilmore-makes -the-case-for-abolition/.

45. Rebecca De Souza, *Feeding the Other: Whiteness, Privilege, and Neoliberal Stigma in Food Pantries* (Cambridge, MA: MIT Press, 2019).

46. Regina Jackson and Saira Rao, *White Women: Everything You Already Know about Your Own Racism and How to Do Better* (New York: Penguin Books, 2022), 85.

47. Ward, *America's Racial Karma*, 70.

48. Martin Luther King Jr., *Strength to Love* (Boston: Beacon Press, 2019), 162.

49. James Baldwin, "To Crush the Serpent," in *The Cross of Redemption: Uncollected Writings* (New York: Vintage, 2010), 204.

50. hooks, *All about Love*.

51. Thich Nhat Hanh, *Teachings on Love*, rev. ed. (Berkeley, CA: Parallax Press, 2007).

52. Audre Lorde, "Uses of the Erotic: The Erotic as Power, 1978," in *Sister Outsider: Essays and Speeches*, rep. ed. (Berkeley, CA: Crossing Press, 2007), 89.

53. Lorde, "Uses of the Erotic," 89, 90.

54. Lorde, "Uses of the Erotic," 91.

CHAPTER 1

1. Zion Baptist Church was founded in 1882 by Reverend Horace Wayland, a previously enslaved person born in Virginia. Since that time, it has served as a cornerstone in Philadelphia's cultural and spiritual life.

2. L. T. Smith, *Decolonizing Methodologies: Research and Indigenous Peoples* (New York: Zed Books, 2013); Tukufu Zuberi and Eduardo Bonilla-Silva, *White Methods: Racism and Methodology* (Lanham, MD: Rowman and Littlefield, 2008).

3. Jean J. Schensul, Marlene J. Berg, and Ken M. Williamson, "Challenging Hegemonies: Advancing Collaboration in Community-Based Participatory Action Research," *Collaborative Anthropologies* 1, no. 1 (2008): 102–137, https://doi.org/10.1353/cla.0.0009.

4. A hoagie is a deli sandwich on a long roll that usually has meat, vegetables, and cheese.

5. Sue Ann Anderson, "Core Indicators of Nutritional State for Difficult-to-Sample Populations," *Journal of Nutrition* 120, no. supp. 11 (November 1990): 1555–1600, https://doi.org/10.1093/jn/120.suppl_11.1555.

6. The time frame here is twelve months, but this can also be asked about the previous six months or thirty days.

7. Keith Olbermann, "'Worst Person in the World': Mark Nord," NBC News, August 4, 2010, https://www.nbcnews.com/id/wbna15765825.

8. John T. Cook et al., "Welfare Reform and the Health of Young Children: A Sentinel Survey in 6 US Cities," *Archives of Pediatric and Adolescent Medicine* 156, no. 7 (2002): 678–684.

9. Diana B. Cutts et al., "Homelessness during Infancy: Associations with Infant and Maternal and Hardship Outcomes," *Cityscape: A Journal of Policy Development and Research* 20, no. 2 (2018): 119–132.

10. Anne Skalicky et al., "Child Food Insecurity and Iron Deficiency Anemia in Low-Income Infants and Toddlers in the United States," *Maternal and Child Health Journal* 10, no. 2 (November 19, 2005): 177, https://doi.org/10.1007/s10995-005-0036-0.

11. John T. Cook et al., "A Brief Indicator of Household Energy Security: Associations with Food Security, Child Health, and Child Development in US Infants and Toddlers," *Pediatrics* 122, no. 4 (October 2008): e867–e875, https://doi.org/10.1542/peds.2008-0286.

12. David Baker and Natacha Keramidas, "The Psychology of Hunger," *Monitor on Psychology* 44, no. 9 (October 2013): 66, https://www.apa.org/monitor/2013/10/hunger.

13. Molly Knowles, Joanna Simmons, and Mariana Chilton, "Food Insecurity and Public Health," in *Food and Public Health: A Practical Introduction*, ed. Allison Karpyn (New York: Oxford University Press, 2018), 182.

14. Alisha Coleman-Jensen and Mark Nord, "Food Insecurity among Households with Working-Age Adults with Disabilities," Economic Research Report No. ERR-144 (US Department of Agriculture, January 2013), http://www.ers.usda.gov/publications/pub-details/?pubid=45040.

15. Seth A. Berkowitz, Hilary K. Seligman, and Niteesh K. Choudhry, "Treat or Eat: Food Insecurity, Cost-Related Medication Underuse, and Unmet Needs," *American Journal of Medicine* 127, no. 4 (April 2014): 303–310.e3, https://doi.org/10.1016/j.amjmed.2014.01.002.

16. Katherine Alaimo, Christine M. Olson, and Edward A. Frongillo, "Food Insufficiency and American School-Aged Children's Cognitive, Academic, and Psychosocial Development," *Pediatrics* 108, no. 1 (July 2001): 44–53; Diana F. Jyoti, Edward A. Frongillo, and Sonya J. Jones, "Food Insecurity Affects School Children's Academic Performance, Weight Gain, and Social Skills," *Journal of Nutrition* 135, no. 12 (December 2005): 2831–2839, https://doi .org/10.1093/jn/135.12.2831; Larry L. Howard, "Does Food Insecurity at Home Affect Non-Cognitive Performance at School? A Longitudinal Analysis of Elementary Student Classroom Behavior," *Economics of Education Review* 30, no. 1 (February 2011): 157–176, https://doi.org/10.1016/j.econedurev.2010.08.003.

17. Ronald E. Kleinman et al., "Hunger in Children in the United States: Potential Behavioral and Emotional Correlates," *Pediatrics* 101, no. 1 (January 1998): e3, https://doi.org/10.1542 /peds.101.1.e3.

18. Katherine Alaimo, Christine M. Olson, and Edward A. Frongillo, "Family Food Insufficiency, but Not Low Family Income, Is Positively Associated with Dysthymia and Suicide Symptoms in Adolescents," *Journal of Nutrition* 132, no. 4 (April 2002): 719–725, https://doi.org/10 .1093/jn/132.4.719.

19. Maryah Stella Fram et al., "Children Are Aware of Food Insecurity and Take Responsibility for Managing Food Resources," *Journal of Nutrition* 141, no. 6 (June 2011): 1114–1119, https://doi.org/10.3945/jn.110.135988.

20. Elise Gould and Jessica Scheider, "Black and Hispanic Women Are Paid Substantially Less than White Men," Economic Policy Institute, March 7, 2017, https://www.epi.org/publication /black-and-hispanic-women-are-hit-particularly-hard-by-the-gender-wage-gap/.

21. Coleman-Jensen and Nord, "Food Insecurity among Households with Working-Age Adults with Disabilities."

22. "More than Half of All Food-Insecure Households Work Full Time," USDA Economic Research Service, last updated December 7, 2023, https://www.ers.usda.gov/data-products /chart-gallery/gallery/chart-detail/?chartId=108053.

23. Julia Raifman et al., "State Minimum Wage, Paid Sick Leave, and Food Insufficiency during the COVID-19 Pandemic," preprint, submitted March 4, 2021, https://www.medrxiv.org /content/10.1101/2021.03.01.21252723v2.full.

24. Irene Tung, Paul Sonn, and Yannet Lathrop, "The Growing Movement for $15," National Employment Law Project, November 4, 2015, https://www.nelp.org/publication/growing -movement-15/.

25. Jasmine Tucker and Kayla Patrick, "Low-Wage Jobs Are Women's Jobs: The Overrepresentation of Women in Low-Wage Work," National Women's Law Center, Chartbook, August 2017, https://nwlc.org/wp-content/uploads/2017/08/Low-Wage-Jobs-are-Womens-Jobs.pdf.

26. Nancy Krieger et al., "Experiences of Discrimination: Validity and Reliability of a Self-Report Measure for Population Health Research on Racism and Health," *Social Science and Medicine* 61, no. 7 (October 2005): 1576–1596, https://doi.org/10.1016/j.socscimed.2005.03.006.

27. Pam Phojanakong et al., "Experiences of Racial and Ethnic Discrimination Are Associated with Food Insecurity and Poor Health," *International Journal of Environmental Research and Public Health* 16, no. 22 (November 8, 2019): 4369, https://doi.org/10.3390/ijerph16224369.

28. Emily A. Wang et al., "A Pilot Study Examining Food Insecurity and HIV Risk Behaviors among Individuals Recently Released from Prison," *AIDS Education and Prevention* 25 (2013): 112–123.

29. Nancy Krieger et al., "Social Hazards on the Job: Workplace Abuse, Sexual Harassment, and Racial Discrimination—a Study of Black, Latino, and White Low-Income Women and Men Workers in the United States," *International Journal of Health Services: Planning, Administration, Evaluation* 36, no. 1 (2006): 51–85, https://doi.org/10.2190/3EMB-YKRH-EDJ2-0H19.

30. Seth J. Prins et al., "School Health Predictors of the School-to-Prison Pipeline: Substance Use and Developmental Risk and Resilience Factors," *Journal of Adolescent Health* 70, no. 3 (March 1, 2022): 463–469, https://doi.org/10.1016/j.jadohealth.2021.09.032.

CHAPTER 2

1. A hack is an informal cab driver, usually a man. They use their own cars or vans for a small amount of cash to give people rides home from the grocery store or subway or bus stop. Taxis often did not operate in some north Philadelphia neighborhoods, or, if they did so, they did so rarely. Now Uber and Lyft have mostly taken over this informal economy.

2. Mariana Chilton and Sue Booth, "Hunger of the Body and Hunger of the Mind: African American Women's Perceptions of Food Insecurity, Health and Violence," *Journal of Nutrition Education and Behavior* 39, no. 3 (2007): 116–125.

3. Nancy Scheper-Hughes, *Death without Weeping: The Violence of Everyday Life in Brazil* (Berkeley: University of California Press, 2009).

4. Michael Gershon, *The Second Brain: The Scientific Basis of Gut Instinct and a Groundbreaking New Understanding of Nervous Disorders of the Stomach and Intestines* (New York: Harper, 1998).

5. Mihaela Fadgyas-Stanculete et al., "The Relationship between Irritable Bowel Syndrome and Psychiatric Disorders: From Molecular Changes to Clinical Manifestations," *Journal of Molecular Psychiatry* 2, no. 1 (June 27, 2014): 4, https://doi.org/10.1186/2049-9256-2-4.

6. Seth A. Berkowitz et al., "Trends in Food Insecurity for Adults with Cardiometabolic Disease in the United States: 2005–2012," *PLoS ONE* 12, no. 6 (June 7, 2017): e0179172, https://doi.org/10.1371/journal.pone.0179172.

7. Caroline C. Wang, "Photovoice: A Participatory Action Research Strategy Applied to Women's Health," *Journal of Women's Health* 8, no. 2 (1999): 185–192.

8. Molly Knowles et al., "Witnesses to Hunger: Methods for Photovoice and Participatory Action Research in Public Health," *Human Organization* 74, no. 3 (August 2015): 255–265, https://doi.org/10.17730/0018-7259-74.3.255.

9. Ervin Staub, "The Roots of Evil: Social Conditions, Culture, Personality, and Basic Human Needs," *Personality and Social Psychology Review* 3, no. 3 (August 1999): 179–192, https://doi.org/10.1207/s15327957pspr0303_2.

CHAPTER 3

1. Robyn Trappany, Victoria White Kress, and S. Allen Willcoxon, "Preventing Vicarious Trauma: What Counselors Should Know When Working with Trauma Survivors," *Journal of Counseling and Development* 82, no. 1 (Winter 2004): 31–37.

2. Hillary A. Franke, "Toxic Stress: Effects, Prevention and Treatment," *Children* 1, no. 3 (November 3, 2014): 390–402, https://doi.org/10.3390/children1030390.

3. Centers for Disease Control and Prevention, "About the CDC-Kaiser ACE Study," April 6, 2021, https://www.cdc.gov/violenceprevention/aces/about.html.

4. Nadine Burke Harris, *The Deepest Well: Healing the Long-Term Effects of Childhood Trauma and Adversity* (Boston: Mariner Books, 2018).

5. Vincent Felitti et al., "Relationship of Childhood Abuse and Household Dysfunction to Many of the Leading Causes of Death in Adults: The Adverse Childhood Experiences (ACE) Study," *American Journal of Preventive Medicine* 14 (1998): 245–258.

6. Rachel Yehuda et al., "Holocaust Exposure Induced Intergenerational Effects on FKBP5 Methylation," *Biological Psychiatry* 80, no. 5 (September 2016): 372–380, https://doi.org/10.1016/j.biopsych.2015.08.005.

7. Staci Haines, *The Politics of Trauma: Somatics, Healing, and Social Justice* (Berkeley, CA: North Atlantic Books, 2019), 17, 75.

8. Burke Harris, *Deepest Well*, 132–133.

9. Dylan B. Jackson et al., "Adverse Childhood Experiences and Household Food Insecurity: Findings from the 2016 National Survey of Children's Health," *American Journal of Preventive Medicine* 57, no. 5 (September 13, 2019): 667–674.

10. Larry Ward, *America's Racial Karma: An Invitation to Heal* (Berkeley, CA: Parallax Press, 2020).

11. Wendy R. Ellis and William H. Dietz, "A New Framework for Addressing Adverse Childhood and Community Experiences: The Building Community Resilience Model," *Academic Pediatrics* 17, no. 7 (September 2017): S86–S93, https://doi.org/10.1016/j.acap.2016.12.011.

12. Adrian L. Lopresti, "The Effects of Psychological and Environmental Stress on Micronutrient Concentrations in the Body: A Review of the Evidence," *Advances in Nutrition* 11, no. 1 (January 2020): 103–112, https://doi.org/10.1093/advances/nmz082.

13. Haines, *Politics of Trauma.*

14. Mariana M. Chilton, Jenny R. Rabinowich, and Nicholas H. Woolf, "Very Low Food Security in the USA Is Linked with Exposure to Violence," *Public Health Nutrition* 17, no. 1 (February 22, 2013): 73–82, https://doi.org/10.1017/S1368980013000281.

15. Alisha Coleman-Jensen et al., "Household Food Security in the United States in 2020," Economic Research Report (US Department of Agriculture, September 2021), https://www.ers.usda.gov/webdocs/publications/102076/err-298.pdf?v=5244.

16. Mariana Chilton, Molly Knowles, and Sandra L. Bloom, "The Intergenerational Circumstances of Household Food Insecurity and Adversity," *Journal of Hunger and Environmental Nutrition* 12, no. 2 (May 4, 2016): 269–297, https://doi.org/10.1080/19320248.2016.1146195.

17. Usually, researchers describe zero to three ACEs as "low ACEs," and four or more as "high ACEs."

18. Chilton, Knowles, and Bloom, "Intergenerational Circumstances of Household Food Insecurity and Adversity."

19. Jing Sun et al., "Childhood Adversity and Adult Reports of Food Insecurity among Households with Children," *American Journal of Preventive Medicine* 50, no. 5 (May 2016): 561–572, https://doi.org/10.1016/j.amepre.2015.09.024.

20. Many studies that include ACEs simply group the ACEs together. It is commonly understood that each ACE can overlap with others and the cumulative number of ACEs is likely more important than looking at a singular ACE.

21. Centers for Disease Control and Prevention, "About the CDC-Kaiser ACE Study."

22. Cheryl Wehler et al., "Risk and Protective Factors for Adult and Child Hunger among Low-Income Housed and Homeless Female-Headed Families," *American Journal of Public Health* 94, no. 1 (January 1, 2004): 109–115, https://doi.org/10.2105/AJPH.94.1.109.

23. Maria Melchior et al., "Mental Health Context of Food Insecurity: A Representative Cohort of Families with Young Children," *Pediatrics* 124, no. 4 (October 2009): e564–e572, https://doi.org/10.1542/peds.2009-0583.

24. Abraham Kaplan, *The Conduct of Inquiry: Methodology for Behavioral Science* (New Brunswick, NJ: Routledge, 1998).

25. Zenju Earthlyn Manuel, *Opening to Darkness: Eight Gateways for Being with the Absence of Light in Unsettling Times* (Boulder, CO: Sounds True, 2023).

26. Dori Laub and Nanette C. Auerhahn, "Knowing and Not Knowing Massive Psychic Trauma: Forms of Traumatic Memory," *International Journal of Psycho-Analysis* 74, pt. 2 (April 1993): 287–302.

27. Resmaa Menakem, *My Grandmother's Hands: Racialized Trauma and the Pathway to Mending Our Hearts and Bodies* (Las Vegas: Central Recovery Press, 2017).

28. Ward, *America's Racial Karma*, 62.

CHAPTER 4

1. The ethics of carrying out research always inform how research is carried out. All the studies mentioned in this book were approved by the Drexel University Institutional Review Board, which considers the study setup, vulnerability of research participants, amount of money involved to ensure that the amount is not coercive, types of questions asked, management of the data to ensure it is secure, types of outcomes measured, and more.

2. Cecilie Høgh Egmose et al., "The Effectiveness of Peer Support in Personal and Clinical Recovery-Systematic Review and Meta-Analysis," *Psychiatric Services* 74, no. 8 (February 8, 2023), 847–858, https://pubmed.ncbi.nlm.nih.gov/36751908/.

3. Jack Saul, *Collective Trauma, Collective Healing: Promoting Community Resilience in the Aftermath of Disaster* (New York: Routledge, 2013).

4. Michael S. Martin et al., "Food Insecurity and Mental Illness: Disproportionate Impacts in the Context of Perceived Stress and Social Isolation," *Public Health* 132 (March 2016): 86–91, https://doi.org/10.1016/j.puhe.2015.11.014.

5. "Loneliness in America," Cigna, accessed February 17, 2022, https://newsroom.cigna.com/loneliness-in-america.

6. Mark S. Gold, "The Role of Alcohol, Drugs, and Deaths of Despair in the U.S.'s Falling Life Expectancy," *Missouri Medicine* 117, no. 2 (2020): 99–101.

7. Vivek Murthy, *Our Epidemic of Loneliness and Isolation: The U.S. Surgeon General's Advisory on the Healing Effects of Social Connection and Community* (Washington, DC: US Dept. of Health and Human Services, Office of the Surgeon General, 2023), https://www.hhs.gov/sites/default/files/surgeon-general-social-connection-advisory.pdf.

8. Reverend angel Kyodo williams says this phrase often. I heard her encourage this in an antiracism training I participated in during summer 2019.

9. Jerome Dugan et al., "Effects of a Trauma-Informed Curriculum on Depression, Self-Efficacy, Economic Security, and Substance Use among TANF Participants: Evidence from the Building Health and Wealth Network Phase II," *Social Science and Medicine* 258 (August 1, 2020): 113136, https://doi.org/10.1016/j.socscimed.2020.113136; Layla G. Booshehri et al., "Trauma-Informed Temporary Assistance for Needy Families (TANF): A Randomized Controlled Trial with a Two-Generation Impact," *Journal of Child and Family Studies* 27, no. 5 (May 1, 2018): 1594–1604, https://doi.org/10.1007/s10826-017-0987-y.

10. Sandra L. Bloom and Brian J. Farragher, *Restoring Sanctuary: A New Operating System for Trauma-Informed Systems of Care* (Oxford: Oxford University Press, 2013).

11. Shawn Ginwright, "The Future of Healing: Shifting from Trauma-Informed Care to Healing-Centered Engagement," *Medium* (blog), May 31, 2018, https://ginwright.medium.com/the -future-of-healing-shifting-from-trauma-informed-care-to-healing-centered-engagement -634f557ce69c.

12. Booshehri et al., "Trauma-Informed Temporary Assistance for Needy Families (TANF)."

13. Booshehri et al., "Trauma-Informed Temporary Assistance for Needy Families (TANF)."

14. Pam Phojanakong et al., "Trauma-Informed Financial Empowerment Programming Improves Food Security among Families with Young Children," *Journal of Nutrition Education and Behavior* 52, no. 5 (May 1, 2020): 465–473, https://doi.org/10.1016/j.jneb.2020.02.008.

15. Phojanakong et al., "Trauma-Informed Financial Empowerment Programming Improves Food Security among Families with Young Children."

16. Bloom and Farragher, *Restoring Sanctuary*.

PART II

1. Thomas Hübl and Julie Jordan Avritt, *Healing Collective Trauma: A Process for Integrating Our Intergenerational and Cultural Wounds* (Boulder, CO: Sounds True, 2020).

2. Sandra L. Bloom and Brian J. Farragher, *Restoring Sanctuary: A New Operating System for Trauma-Informed Systems of Care* (Oxford: Oxford University Press, 2013).

3. Joan Acker, "Inequality Regimes: Gender, Class, and Race in Organizations," *Gender and Society* 20, no. 4 (August 2006): 441–464, https://doi.org/10.1177/0891243206289499.

4. Gabor Maté and Daniel Maté, *The Myth of Normal: Trauma, Illness, and Healing in a Toxic Culture* (New York: Avery, 2022).

CHAPTER 5

1. This should alert you to how unfair and discriminatory the restaurant industry is. To learn more, see Saru Jayaraman, *Forked: A New Standard for American Dining* (Oxford: Oxford University Press, 2016).

2. This should give a hint as to how most philanthropy works. To learn more, see INCITE! Women of Color Against Violence, *The Revolution Will Not Be Funded: Beyond the Non-Profit Industrial Complex* (Durham, NC: Duke University Press, 2017); Edgar Villanueva, *Decolonizing Wealth: Indigenous Wisdom to Heal Divides and Restore Balance* (Oakland, CA: Berrett-Koehler, 2018).

3. Ann Schimke, "Free Summer Meals for Kids, but What about Hungry Parents?," *Chalkbeat Colorado* (blog), June 30, 2014, https://co.chalkbeat.org/2014/6/30/21107578/free-summer -meals-for-kids-but-what-about-hungry-parents.

4. Ann Collins et al., "Summer Electronic Benefit Transfer for Children (SEBTC) Demonstration: Summary Report" (Abt Associates and Mathematica Policy Research, May 2016), https://fns-prod.azureedge.us/sites/default/files/ops/sebtcfinalreport.pdf.

5. Deborah A. Frank et al., "Heat or Eat: The Low Income Home Energy Assistance Program and Nutritional and Health Risks among Children Less than 3 Years of Age," *Pediatrics* 118, no. 5 (2006): e1293–e1302.

6. Rebecca M. Blank, "Why the United States Needs an Improved Measure of Poverty," *Brookings* (blog), July 17, 2008, https://www.brookings.edu/testimonies/why-the-united-states -needs-an-improved-measure-of-poverty/.

7. Michael Lipsky, *Street-Level Bureaucracy: Dilemmas of the Individual in Public Service*, exp. ed. (New York: Russell Sage Foundation, 2010).

8. "Brian Roberts Net Worth," wallmine.com, accessed October 20, 2022, https://wallmine .com/people/6271/brian-l-roberts.

9. Consolidated Appropriations Act, 2014, H.R. 3547, 113th Cong. (2013–2014), https:// www.congress.gov/bill/113th-congress/house-bill/3547/text.

10. National Commission on Hunger, *Freedom from Hunger: An Achievable Goal for the United States of America: Recommendations of the National Commission on Hunger to Congress and the Secretary of the Department of Agriculture* (Washington, DC: National Commission on Hunger, 2015), https://cybercemetery.unt.edu/archive/hungercommission/20151217000051 /http://hungercommission.rti.org/.

11. Matthew Cortland, "Opinion: Trump's Plan to Cage Kids Indefinitely While Denying Them Vaccines Is Ethnic Cleansing in Plain Sight," *Independent*, August 22, 2019, https://www .independent.co.uk/voices/trump-administration-detention-indefinite-children-cages-flu -vaccine-custody-deaths-a9075181.html.

12. Amy Davidson Sorkin, "The Case of the Missing Immigrant Children," *New Yorker*, May 29, 2018, https://www.newyorker.com/news/daily-comment/the-case-of-the-missing -immigrant-children.

13. Roxanne Dunbar-Ortiz, *An Indigenous Peoples' History of the United States*, rep. ed. (Boston: Beacon Press, 2015).

14. Laura Sullivan and Amy Walters, "Incentives and Cultural Bias Fuel Foster System," NPR, October 25, 2011, NPR News Investigations, https://www.npr.org/2011/10/25/141662357 /incentives-and-cultural-bias-fuel-foster-system.

15. Dorothy Roberts, *Shattered Bonds: The Color of Child Welfare*, rep. ed. (New York: Civitas Books, 2002).

16. Kathryn Joyce, "The Crime of Parenting While Poor," *New Republic*, February 25, 2019, https://newrepublic.com/article/153062/crime-parenting-poor-new-york-city-child-welfare -agency-reform.

17. "Reviews about Philadelphia County Assistance Office Delancey District," Nicelocal, accessed April 8, 2022, https://nicelocal.com/philadelphia/public_services/philadelphia _county_assistance_office_delancey_district/reviews/.

18. I changed her name.

19. Felicia Ann Kornbluh and Gwendolyn Mink, *Ensuring Poverty: Welfare Reform in Feminist Perspective* (Philadelphia: University of Pennsylvania Press, 2019), 123.

20. Alfred Lubrano, "Pa. Uses Federal and State Money to Fight Abortions, Sparking Outrage," *Philadelphia Inquirer*, October 25, 2021, https://www.inquirer.com/news/pennsylvania /abortion-crisis-pregnancy-centers-poverty-tanf-welfare-20211025.html.

21. Frank et al., "Heat or Eat."

22. Diana Romero et al., "State Welfare Reform Policies and Maternal and Child Health Services: A National Study," *Maternal and Child Health Journal* 5, no. 3 (September 2001): 199–206, https://doi.org/10.1023/a:1011352118970.

23. Ashley Southall and Nikita Stewart, "They Grabbed Her Baby and Arrested Her. Now Jazmine Headley Is Speaking Out," *New York Times*, December 16, 2018, New York, https:// www.nytimes.com/2018/12/16/nyregion/jazmine-headley-arrest.html.

24. Sandra Naylor Goodwin, Daniel Chandler, and Joan Meisel, "Violence against Women: The Role of Welfare Reform" (California Institute for Mental Health and National Institute of Justice, April 11, 2003), https://www.ojp.gov/pdffiles1/nij/grants/205792.pdf.

25. Robert Scheer, "Returning to Bad Old Days of Orphanages: Is a Family Valid Only If It Can Survive in the Free Market?," *Los Angeles Times*, December 11, 1994, https://www.latimes .com/archives/la-xpm-1994-12-11-op-7601-story.html.

26. Southall and Stewart, "They Grabbed Her Baby and Arrested Her."

27. Jan Ransom and William K. Rashbaum, "How Brutal Beatings on Rikers Island Were Hidden from Public View," *New York Times*, March 2, 2022, New York, https://www.nytimes.com /2022/03/02/nyregion/nyc-jail-beating-rikers.html.

28. Mariana Chilton, "Jazmine Headley's Arrest Exposes the Punitive Design of Public Assistance," *Nation*, December 14, 2018, https://www.thenation.com/article/archive/jazmine -headley-arrest-public-assistance-poverty-tanf-surveillance/.

CHAPTER 6

1. Sanford Schram, Joe Soss, and Richard C. Fording, eds., *Race and the Politics of Welfare Reform* (Ann Arbor: University of Michigan Press, 2003); Kenneth J. Neubeck and Noel A. Cazenave, *Welfare Racism: Playing the Race Card against America's Poor* (New York: Routledge, 2001).

2. Stephanie Ettinger de Cuba et al., "Loss of SNAP Is Associated with Food Insecurity and Poor Health in Working Families with Young Children," *Health Affairs* 38, no. 5 (May 2019): 765–773, https://doi.org/10.1377/hlthaff.2018.05265.

3. Lisa Ko, "Unwanted Sterilization and Eugenics Programs in the United States," *Independent Lens* (blog), January 29, 2016, https://www.pbs.org/independentlens/blog/unwanted -sterilization-and-eugenics-programs-in-the-united-states/.

4.   Tom Yamachika, "TAX MAN: TANF Hoarding Does No One Any Good," *Garden Island*, January 9, 2022, https://www.thegardenisland.com/2022/01/09/business/tax-man-tanf -hoarding-does-no-one-any-good/.

5.   US Office of Strategic Services, "Simple Sabotage Field Manual," January 17, 1944, 25, 29, 30, https://www.hsdl.org/?view&did=750070.

6.   Felicia Ann Kornbluh and Gwendolyn Mink, *Ensuring Poverty: Welfare Reform in Feminist Perspective* (Philadelphia: University of Pennsylvania Press, 2019).

7.   Ife Floyd et al., *TANF Policies Reflect Racist Legacy of Cash Assistance: Reimagined Program Should Center Black Mothers* (Washington, DC: Center on Budget and Policy Priorities, August 2021).

8.   Neubeck and Cazenave, *Welfare Racism*; Kornbluh and Mink, *Ensuring Poverty*; Mary Corcoran, Sandra K. Danziger, and Richard Tolman, "Long Term Employment of African-American and White Welfare Recipients and the Role of Persistent Health and Mental Health Problems," *Journal of Women's Health* 39, no. 4 (2004): 21–40; Eugenie Hildebrandt and Patricia Stevens, "Impoverished Women with Children and No Welfare Benefits: The Urgency of Researching Failures of the Temporary Assistance for Needy Families Program," *American Journal of Public Health* 99, no. 5 (2009): 793–801; Schram, Soss, and Fording, *Race and the Politics of Welfare Reform*; Janice H. Laakso and Denise J. Drevdahl, "Women, Abuse, and the Welfare Bureaucracy," *Affilia: Journal of Women and Social Work* 21, no. 1 (2006): 84–96.

9.   Kathryn J. Edin and H. Luke Shaefer, *$2.00 a Day: Living on Almost Nothing in America* (Boston: Mariner Books, 2016).

10. Dayanand S. Manoli and Nicholas Turner, "Cash-on-Hand & College Enrollment: Evidence from Population Tax Data and Policy Nonlinearities" (working paper, National Bureau of Economic Research, January 2014), https://doi.org/10.3386/w19836.

11. National Academies of Sciences, Engineering, and Medicine et al., eds., *A Roadmap to Reducing Child Poverty: A Consensus Study Report of the National Academies of Sciences, Engineering, and Medicine* (Washington, DC: National Academies Press, 2019).

12. Douglas J. Besharov et al., eds., *A Safety Net That Works: Improving Federal Programs for Low-Income Americans* (Washington, DC: American Enterprise Institute, 2017).

13. "Policy Basics: The Earned Income Tax Credit," Center on Budget and Policy Priorities, December 10, 2019, https://www.cbpp.org/research/federal-tax/the-earned-income-tax-credit.

14. Kornbluh and Mink, *Ensuring Poverty*, xv.

15. Trefis Team, "McDonald's Stock to Gain after Q3 Earnings?," *Forbes*, November 15, 2021, https://www.forbes.com/sites/greatspeculations/2021/11/15/mcdonalds-stock-to-gain-after -q3-earnings/.

16. Eric Schlosser, *Fast Food Nation: The Dark Side of the All-American Meal*, rep. ed. (Boston: Mariner Books, 2012).

17. Josh Eidelson, "McDonald's Workers Want OSHA to Investigate Pattern of Violence," *Bloomberg*, May 22, 2019, https://news.bloomberglaw.com/daily-labor-report/mcdonalds-workers-want-osha-to-investigate-pattern-of-violence.

18. Deborah Berkowitz, "Behind the Arches: How McDonald's Fails to Protect Workers from Workplace Violence" (National Employment Law Project, May 22, 2019), https://www.nelp.org/publication/behind-the-arches-how-mcdonalds-fails-to-protect-workers-from-workplace-violence/.

19. Annelise Orleck, *Storming Caesar's Palace: How Black Mothers Fought Their Own War on Poverty* (Boston: Beacon Press, 2006).

20. Mike Fillon, "Medicaid Expansion Increases Survival for Patients with Cancer," *CA: A Cancer Journal for Clinicians* 72, no. 5 (September 2022): 407–408, https://doi.org/10.3322/caac.21751.

21. Julia Belluz and Nina Martin, "The Extraordinary Danger of Being Pregnant and Uninsured in Texas," *Vox* (blog), December 19, 2019, https://www.vox.com/science-and-health/2019/12/6/20995227/women-health-care-maternal-mortality-insurance-texas.

22. Chintan B. Bhatt and Consuelo M. Beck-Sagué, "Medicaid Expansion and Infant Mortality in the United States," *American Journal of Public Health* 108, no. 4 (April 2018): 565–567, https://doi.org/10.2105/AJPH.2017.304218; Erica L. Eliason, "Adoption of Medicaid Expansion Is Associated with Lower Maternal Mortality," *Women's Health Issues: Official Publication of the Jacobs Institute of Women's Health* 30, no. 3 (June 2020): 147–152, https://doi.org/10.1016/j.whi.2020.01.005.

CHAPTER 7

1. "WIC Program Overview and History," National WIC Association, accessed October 23, 2022, https://www.nwica.org/overview-and-history.

2. "National and State Level Estimates of WIC Eligibility and Program Reach in 2020," USDA, accessed October 23, 2023, https://www.fns.usda.gov/wic/eligibility-and-program-reach-estimates-2020#:~:text=The%20overall%20WIC%20eligibility%20rate,to%2049%20percent%20in%202020.

3. Laura E. Caulfield et al., *Maternal and Child Outcomes Associated with the Special Supplemental Nutrition Program for Women, Infants, and Children (WIC)* (Rockville, MD: Agency for Healthcare Research and Quality, 2022), http://www.ncbi.nlm.nih.gov/books/NBK579797/.

4. Maureen M. Black et al., "WIC Participation and Attenuation of Stress-Related Child Health Risks of Household Food Insecurity and Caregiver Depressive Symptoms," *Archives of Pediatrics and Adolescent Medicine* 166, no. 5 (May 1, 2012): 444–451, https://doi.org/10.1001/archpediatrics.2012.1.

5. "Special Supplemental Nutrition Program for Women, Infants, and Children (WIC)," USDA, accessed October 23, 2023, http://www.fns.usda.gov/wic/women-infants-and-children-wic.

6. Mia Birdsong, *More Than Enough* (podcast), *Nation*, accessed February 2, 2021, https://www .thenation.com/authors/mia-birdsong/.

7. Victor Oliveira, "Winner Takes (Almost) All: How WIC Affects the Infant Formula Market," USDA Economic Research Service, September 1, 2011, https://www.ers.usda.gov/amber -waves/2011/september/infant-formula-market/.

8. Thomas Ptacek, testimony to the National Commission on Hunger, Portland, ME, July 30, 2015, https://cybercemetery.unt.edu/archive/hungercommission/20151217003316 /https://hungercommission.rti.org/Portals/0/SiteHtml/Activities/PublicHearings /PortlandME/PortlandME_Testimony_Thomas_Ptacek.pdf.

9. Tianna Gaines-Turner, Joanna Cruz Simmons, and Mariana Chilton, "Recommendation from SNAP Participants to Improve Wages and End Stigma," *American Journal of Public Health* 109, no. 12 (December 1, 2019), https://doi.org/10.2105/AJPH.2019.305362.

10. Deborah A. Frank et al., "Nutritional-Assistance Programs Play a Critical Role in Reducing Food Insecurity," *Pediatrics* 125, no. 5 (May 2010): e1267, https://doi.org/10.1542/peds .2010-0808.

11. Colleen Heflin et al., "SNAP Benefits and Childhood Asthma," *Social Science and Medicine* 220 (January 2019): 203–211, https://doi.org/10.1016/j.socscimed.2018.11.001.

12. Seth A. Berkowitz et al., "Supplemental Nutrition Assistance Program (SNAP) Participation and Health Care Expenditures among Low-Income Adults," *JAMA Internal Medicine* 177, no. 11 (2017): 1642–1649; Hilary K. Seligman, "Food Insecurity and Hypoglycemia among Safety Net Patients with Diabetes," *Archives of Internal Medicine* 171, no. 13 (July 11, 2011): 1204, https://doi.org/10.1001/archinternmed.2011.287; Seth A. Berkowitz, Hilary K. Seligman, and Niteesh K. Choudhry, "Treat or Eat: Food Insecurity, Cost-Related Medication Underuse, and Unmet Needs," *American Journal of Medicine* 127, no. 4 (April 2014): 303–310.e3, https://doi.org/10.1016/j.amjmed.2014.01.002.

13. Hilary K. Seligman and Seth A. Berkowitz, "Aligning Programs and Policies to Support Food Security and Public Health Goals in the United States," *Annual Review of Public Health* 40, no. 1 (April 1, 2019): 319–337, https://doi.org/10.1146/annurev-publhealth-040218 -044132.

14. SNAP Participants Collaborative, "Improve SNAP Benefits to Promote Health and Reduce Hunger," policy brief (Center for Hunger-Free Communities, May 2021), https://drexel.edu /hunger-free-center/research/briefs-and-reports/improve-snap-benefits/.

15. Zachary Maxwell, dir., *YUCK! A 4th Grader's Short Documentary about School Lunch* (2012), https://vimeo.com/43793321.

16. Kelsey Kinderknecht, Cristen Harris, and Jessica Jones-Smith, "Association of the Healthy, Hunger-Free Kids Act with Dietary Quality among Children in the US National School Lunch Program," *JAMA* 324, no. 4 (July 28, 2020): 359, https://doi.org/10.1001/jama.2020.9517.

17. Kinderknecht, Harris, and Jones-Smith, "Association of the Healthy, Hunger-Free Kids Act with Dietary Quality among Children in the US National School Lunch Program"; Landon

Evans, "The Effect of Free and Reduced Lunch on Reading and Math Achievement" (master's thesis, Marshall University, 2015).

18. Janet Poppendieck, *Free for All: Fixing School Food in America* (Berkeley: University of California Press, 2010).

19. Elaine Povich, "More States Line Up to Serve Free School Meals to All Kids," *Pennsylvania Capital-Star*, May 30, 2023, https://www.penncapital-star.com/education/more-states-line -up-to-serve-free-school-meals-to-all-kids/.

20. Michelle Lou, "75% of US School Districts Report Student Meal Debt. Here's What They're Doing to Combat the Problem," CNN, May 17, 2019, https://www.cnn.com/2019/05/17 /us/unpaid-school-lunch-debt-trnd/index.html.

21. Nik Heynen, "Bending the Bars of Empire from Every Ghetto for Survival: The Black Panther Party's Radical Antihunger Politics of Social Reproduction and Scale," *Annals of the Association of American Geographers* 99, no. 2 (April 22, 2009): 406–422, https://doi.org/10.1080 /00045600802683767.

22. Heynen, "Bending the Bars of Empire from Every Ghetto for Survival."

23. Mike German, "The FBI Has a History of Targeting Black Activists. That's Still True Today," *Guardian*, June 26, 2020, Opinion, https://www.theguardian.com/commentisfree/2020/jun /26/fbi-black-activism-protests-history.

24. Ward Churchill and Jim Vander Wall, *The COINTELPRO Papers: Documents from the FBI's Secret Wars against Dissent in the United States*, 2nd ed. (Cambridge, MA: South End Press, 2001), 45.

25. Heynen, "Bending the Bars of Empire from Every Ghetto for Survival."

26. Erin Blakemore, "How the US Ended Up with Warehouses Full of 'Government Cheese,'" *History* (blog), July 26, 2018, https://www.history.com/news/government-cheese-dairy -farmers-reagan.

27. PR Newswire, "American Dairy Farmers Depend on Government Subsidies," *Markets Insider*, February 8, 2018, https://markets.businessinsider.com/news/stocks/american-dairy-farmers -depend-on-government-subsidies-1015126442.

28. Callie DiModica, "Cheese Caves and Food Surpluses: Why the U.S. Government Currently Stores 1.4 Billion Lbs of Cheese," *Farmlink Project* (blog), August 19, 2021, https://blog .farmlinkproject.org/stories-and-features/cheese-caves-and-food-surpluses-why-the-u-s -government-currently-stores-1-4-billion-lbs-of-cheese.

29. Paul Wachter, "Nephi Craig, Farm to Table Food, and the Movement to Rediscover Native American Cooking," *Newsweek*, August 23, 2013, https://www.newsweek.com/2013/08/23 /nephi-craig-farm-table-food-and-movement-rediscover-native-american-cooking-237856 .html.

30. Dana Vantrease, "Commod Bods and Frybread Power: Government Food Aid in American Indian Culture," *Journal of American Folklore* 126, no. 499 (2013): 55–69, https://doi.org /10.5406/jamerfolk.126.499.0055.

31. Kathleen Pickering et al., "Written Testimony on Food Insecurity, Plains Indian Tribes, Pine Ridge and Rosebud Indian Reservations" (National Commission on Hunger, July 30, 2015), https://cybercemetery.unt.edu/archive/hungercommission/20151217003520 /https://hungercommission.rti.org/Portals/0/SiteHtml/Activities/WrittenTestimony /InvitedWritten/NCH_Invited_Written_Testimony_Kathleen_Pickering.pdf.

32. Karen Cunnyngham, "Proposed Changes to the Supplemental Nutrition Assistance Program: Waivers to Work-Related Time Limits," issue brief, Mathematica, March 14, 2019, https:// www.mathematica.org/publications/proposed-changes-to-the-supplemental-nutrition -assistance-program-waivers-to-work-related-time.

33. Brynne Keith-Jennings and Raheem Chaudhry, *Most Working-Age SNAP Participants Work, but Often in Unstable Jobs* (Washington, DC: Center on Budget and Policy Priorities, March 15, 2018), https://www.cbpp.org/research/food-assistance/most-working-age-snap -participants-work-but-often-in-unstable-jobs.

34. Stephanie Ettinger de Cuba et al., "Loss of SNAP Is Associated with Food Insecurity and Poor Health in Working Families with Young Children," *Health Affairs* 38, no. 5 (May 2019): 765–773, https://doi.org/10.1377/hlthaff.2018.05265.

35. Josh Levin, *The Queen: The Forgotten Life behind an American Myth* (New York: Little, Brown and Company, 2019).

36. Randy Alison Aussenberg, "Errors and Fraud in the Supplemental Nutrition Assistance Program (SNAP)" (Congressional Research Service, September 28, 2018), https://sgp.fas.org /crs/misc/R45147.pdf.

37. Ashley Lutz, "Wal-Mart Workers Defend Food Drive That Asks Employees to Donate to One Another," *Business Insider*, November 20, 2013, https://www.businessinsider.com/wal -mart-defends-employee-food-drive-2013-11.

38. "Walmart's Fight against a $15 Minimum Wage Could Thrust It into the Inequality Debate," *Bloomberg*, April 27, 2021, https://www.bloomberg.com/news/articles/2021-04-27/walmart -wmt-fights-against-15-minimum-wage-as-inequality-debate-rages.

39. Andy Fisher, *Big Hunger: The Unholy Alliance between Corporate America and Anti-Hunger Groups* (Cambridge, MA: MIT Press, 2017).

40. Hannah Miao, "Walmart and McDonald's Are among Top Employers of Medicaid and Food Stamp Beneficiaries, Report Says," CNBC, November 19, 2020, https://www.cnbc.com /2020/11/19/walmart-and-mcdonalds-among-top-employers-of-medicaid-and-food-stamp -beneficiaries.html.

41. Tom Metcalf, "These Are the World's Richest Families," *Bloomberg*, August 1, 2020, https:// www.bloomberg.com/tosv2.html?vid=&uuid=33b7d301-9410-11ec-aab0-7346496f7341 &url=L2ZlYXR1cmVzL3JpY2hlc3QtZmFtaWxpZXMtaW4tdGhlLXdvcmxkLw==.

42. Kelly D. Brownell and Mark S. Gold, *Food and Addiction: A Comprehensive Handbook* (Oxford: Oxford University Press, 2012).

43. Poppendieck, *Free for All.*

44. Marion Nestle, *Unsavory Truth: How Food Companies Skew the Science of What We Eat* (New York: Basic Books, 2018).

45. Marion Nestle and Michael Pollan, *Food Politics: How the Food Industry Influences Nutrition and Health*, rev. and exp. ed. (Berkeley: University of California Press, 2013).

CHAPTER 8

1. Chances are if you have had a child pass through third grade, you too will recognize this pizza party ruse. It is also covered in Andy Fisher, *Big Hunger: The Unholy Alliance between Corporate America and Anti-Hunger Groups* (Cambridge, MA: MIT Press, 2017). I highlight it here to show how insidious the emergency food marketing tropes are, and how they penetrate the psyches of schoolchildren and their teachers.

2. Fisher, *Big Hunger*; Janet Poppendieck, *Sweet Charity? Emergency Food and the End of Entitlement* (New York: Viking Press, 1998).

3. Beth Osborne Daponte and Shannon Bade, "How the Private Food Assistance Network Evolved: Interactions between Public and Private Responses to Hunger," *Nonprofit and Voluntary Sector Quarterly* 35, no. 4 (December 2006): 668–690, https://doi.org/10.1177/0899764006289771.

4. "Food Drive Toolkit," Philabundance, accessed October 24, 2023, 6, https://www.philabundance.org/wp-content/uploads/2020/11/PHLBFoodDriveToolkitUpdatenov20.pdf.

5. Rebecca De Souza, *Feeding the Other: Whiteness, Privilege, and Neoliberal Stigma in Food Pantries* (Cambridge, MA: MIT Press, 2019).

6. Alfred Lubrano, "First Day of Emergency Food for Federal Workers: 'Grateful' but 'Humiliated,'" *Philadelphia Inquirer*, January 23, 2019, https://www.inquirer.com/news/shutdown-philabundance-federal-workers-philadelphia-emergency-market-hunger-20190123.html.

7. Zoë A. Ginsburg et al., "Unreliable and Difficult-to-Access Food for Those in Need: A Qualitative and Quantitative Study of Urban Food Pantries," *Journal of Community Health* 44, no. 1 (February 2019): 16–31, https://doi.org/10.1007/s10900-018-0549-2.

8. Susan Phillips, "Pa. Charges Energy Transfer with Environmental Crimes over Mariner East Pipeline Project," *State Impact Pennsylvania* (blog), October 5, 2021, https://stateimpact.npr.org/pennsylvania/2021/10/05/pa-charges-energy-transfer-with-environmental-crimes-over-mariner-east-pipeline-project/.

9. Poppendieck, *Sweet Charity?*, 5.

10. Poppendieck, *Sweet Charity?*, 5.

11. Fisher, *Big Hunger.*

12. Denelle Confair, "Local Food Bank's Political Donation Costs Them Funding," KVOA, October 18, 2021, https://www.kvoa.com/news/local-food-banks-political-donation-costs

-them-funding/article_41c80e0a-3065-11ec-8732-1f8780965836.html; "McDonald Leaving Food Bank; Sahuarita Pulled Funding in October," *Green Valley News*, December 13, 2021, https://www.gvnews.com/news/mcdonald-leaving-food-bank-sahuarita-pulled -funding-in-october/article_6336ed1a-5c6e-11ec-8cbe-3bfb4de230fb.html.

13. Alfred Lubrano, "A Digital Effort to Fight Hunger in Montgomery County," *Philadelphia Inquirer*, January 29, 2019, https://www.inquirer.com/news/hunger-montgomery-county -online-grocery-ordering-food-pantry-20190129.html.

14. Philabundance, "Dunkin' Donuts Tweet," Twitter, March 19, 2019, https://twitter.com /philabundance/status/1108013367388717056.

15. David Lazarus, "Millionaire CEOs Should Support a Living Wage for Fast-Food Workers," *Los Angeles Times*, August 4, 2015, https://www.latimes.com/business/la-fi-lazarus-20150804 -column.html.

16. Share Our Strength, "DC No Kid Hungry Dinner," accessed October 20, 2022, https://www .facebook.com/nokidhungry/posts/pfbid02XzJdi5xfvEwmhx6J66qX2pR1Q5arKzSGPkW ppKN1XTcknaStxsniRF7jUSESHwpVl.

17. Mariana Chilton, "Joe Biden's Philabundance Photo-Op Wouldn't Impress Dr. King," *Philadelphia Inquirer*, January 19, 2021, https://www.inquirer.com/opinion/joe-biden -philadelphia-mlk-day-philabundance-hunger-poverty-20210119.html.

18. "All I Want Is to Hear My Husband's Name on the Radio," Philabundance, February 19, 2019, https://www.philabundance.org/all-i-want-is-to-hear-my-husbands-name-on-the -radio/.

19. Maryah S. Fram and Edward A. Frongillo, "Backpack Programs and the Crisis Narrative of Child Hunger—a Critical Review of the Rationale, Targeting, and Potential Benefits and Harms of an Expanding but Untested Model of Practice," *Advances in Nutrition* 9, no. 1 (January 2018): 1–8, https://doi.org/10.1093/advances/nmx008.

20. Kara Cliffords Billings et al., "Food Insecurity among College Students: Background and Policy Options" (Congressional Research Service, June 9, 2021), https://sgp.fas.org/crs/misc /R46817.pdf.

21. "Food Recovery Network: Fight Waste, Feed People," Food Recovery Network, accessed October 23, 2022, https://www.foodrecoverynetwork.org.

22. Food for Free, January 23, 2019, https://foodforfree.org/.

23. Rachel Widome et al., "Food Insecurity among Veterans of the US Wars in Iraq and Afghanistan," *Public Health Nutrition* 18, no. 5 (April 2015): 844–849, https://doi.org/10.1017 /S136898001400072X.

24. Mia Hubbard, "Press Release—Oakland CA," National Commission on Hunger, June 15, 2015, https://cybercemetery.unt.edu/archive/hungercommission/20151218164445 /https://hungercommission.rti.org/Activities/Completed-Public-Hearings/Oakland-CA.

25. Hubbard, "Press Release."

26. Sarah B. Hunter et al., "Evaluation of Housing for Health Permanent Supportive Housing Program" (RAND Corporation, December 5, 2017), https://www.rand.org/pubs/research _reports/RR1694.html.

27. Erin R. Hager et al., "Development and Validity of a 2-Item Screen to Identify Families at Risk for Food Insecurity," *Pediatrics* 126, no. 1 (July 1, 2010): e26–e32, https://doi.org/10 .1542/peds.2009-3146.

28. Molly Knowles et al., "Successes, Challenges, and Considerations for Integrating Referral into Food Insecurity Screening in Pediatric Settings," *Journal of Health Care for the Poor and Underserved* 29 (2018): 181–191.

CHAPTER 9

1. "Caution," *Merriam-Webster*, accessed July 5, 2023, https://www.merriam-webster.com /thesaurus/caution.

2. Bayo Akomolafe, "Crossroads," *Báyò Akómoláfé* (blog), April 18, 2019, https://www .bayoakomolafe.net/post/crossroads.

3. W. E. B. Du Bois, *John Brown* (1909; New York: International Publishers Co., 2014), 16.

4. Bayo Akomolafe, "Grounding VUNJA," February 13, 2020, https://www.bayoakomolafe .net/post/grounding-vunja; Bayo Akomolafe, "The Invisible Constituency of the Slave Ship," February 16, 2022, https://www.bayoakomolafe.net/post/the-invisible-constituency-of-the -slave-ship.

5. Christina Elizabeth Sharpe, *In the Wake: On Blackness and Being* (Durham, NC: Duke University Press, 2016).

6. Arline T. Geronimus, *Weathering: The Extraordinary Stress of Ordinary Life in an Unjust Society* (New York: Little, Brown Spark, 2023); Arline T. Geronimus et al., "'Weathering' and Age Patterns of Allostatic Load Scores among Blacks and Whites in the United States," *American Journal of Public Health* 96, no. 5 (May 2006): 826–833, https://doi.org/10.2105/AJPH .2004.060749.

7. Sharpe, *In the Wake*, 10, 11.

8. Treva B. Lindsey, *America, Goddam: Violence, Black Women, and the Struggle for Justice* (Oakland: University of California Press, 2022); bell hooks, *The Will to Change: Men, Masculinity, and Love* (New York: Washington Square Press, 2004), 17.

9. bell hooks, *Salvation: Black People and Love*, rep. ed. (New York: William Morrow Paperbacks, 2001), 182.

10. LaPrincess C. Brewer and Lisa A. Cooper, "Race, Discrimination, and Cardiovascular Disease," *AMA Journal of Ethics* 16, no. 6 (June 1, 2014): 455–460, https://doi.org/10.1001 /virtualmentor.2014.16.6.stas2-1406.

11. Kimberlé Crenshaw, *On Intersectionality: Essential Writings* (New York: New Press, 2019).

12. Joy DeGruy, *Post Traumatic Slave Syndrome: America's Legacy of Enduring Injury and Healing* (Portland, OR: Joy DeGruy Publications, 2017).

13. Resmaa Menakem, *My Grandmother's Hands: Racialized Trauma and the Pathway to Mending Our Hearts and Bodies* (Las Vegas, NV: Central Recovery Press, 2017).

14. Cedric J. Robinson, *Cedric J. Robinson: On Racial Capitalism, Black Internationalism, and Cultures of Resistance* (London: Pluto Press, 2019).

15. Silvia Federici, *Caliban and the Witch: Women, the Body and Primitive Accumulation* (Brooklyn: Autonomedia, 2004).

16. Martin Luther King Jr., 1967 interview at Ebenezer Baptist Church, Atlanta, Georgia, with NBC News's Sander Vanocur about the "new phase" of the struggle for "genuine equality." NBC News, "MLK Talks 'New Phase' of Civil Rights Struggle, 11 Months before His Assassination," YouTube, April 4, 2018, https://www.youtube.com/watch?v=2xsbt3a7K-8&t=11s.

17. Susila Gurusami, "Working for Redemption: Formerly Incarcerated Black Women and Punishment in the Labor Market," *Gender and Society* 31, no. 4 (August 2017): 436, https://doi .org/10.1177/0891243217716114.

18. Cheryl I. Harris, "Whiteness as Property," June 10, 1993, https://harvardlawreview.org/1993 /06/whiteness-as-property/, 1715.

19. Tema Okun, "(Divorcing) White Supremacy Culture: Coming Home to Who We Really Are," White Supremacy Culture, accessed February 28, 2022, https://www.whitesupremacyculture .info/.

20. Ibram X. Kendi, *How to Be an Antiracist* (New York: One World, 2019); Layla Saad, *Me and White Supremacy* (Naperville, IL: Sourcebooks, 2020); Ijeoma Oluo, *So You Want to Talk about Race* (New York: Seal Press, 2018); Heather C. McGhee, *The Sum of Us: What Racism Costs Everyone and How We Can Prosper Together* (New York: One World, 2021); "Accomplices Not Allies: Abolishing the Ally Industrial Complex," Indigenous Action Media, May 4, 2014, https://www.indigenousaction.org/accomplices-not-allies-abolishing-the-ally-industrial -complex/; "A Home for White People Working for Justice," SURJ, accessed October 23, 2022, https://surj.org/; "Truth, Justice, Healing," Coming to the Table, accessed October 27, 2023, https://comingtothetable.org/.

21. Menakem, *My Grandmother's Hands*.

22. Larry Ward, *America's Racial Karma: An Invitation to Heal* (Berkeley, CA: Parallax Press, 2020), 70.

23. Sarah Deer, *The Beginning and End of Rape: Confronting Sexual Violence in Native America* (Minneapolis: University of Minnesota Press, 2015).

24. "Child Sexual Abuse," Centers for Disease Control and Prevention, December 8, 2021, https://www.cdc.gov/violenceprevention/childsexualabuse/fastfact.html.

25. Michele Black et al., *The National Intimate Partner and Sexual Violence Survey: 2010 Summary Report* (Atlanta: National Center for Injury Prevention and Control, Centers for Disease Control and Prevention, November 2011), https://www.cdc.gov/violenceprevention/pdf /nisvs_executive_summary-a.pdf.

26. "Abusing the Law," *Buffalo News*, December 2016, https://s3.amazonaws.com/bncore /projects/abusing-the-law/data.html.

27. Albert Samaha, "An 18-Year-Old Said She Was Raped While in Police Custody. The Officers Say She Consented," *BuzzFeed News*, accessed October 14, 2022, https://www.buzzfeednews .com/article/albertsamaha/this-teenager-accused-two-on-duty-cops-of-rape-she-had-no.

28. Bill Weiss, "The Doctrine of Discovery—'Domination,'" YouTube, March 30, 2019, https:// www.youtube.com/watch?v=tSfG9YMkxBY.

29. Just because the papal bulls are five hundred year old does not mean that the terror they instilled is not still enacted in today's world. In 2005, Supreme Court justice Ruth Bader Ginsburg ruled in favor of the state of New York when the Oneida nation bought its own land back from the state and insisted that it should not pay taxes because it is a sovereign nation. Again, this land was originally the Oneida peoples'. In her decision in *City of Sherrill v. Oneida Indian Nation of New York*, Ginsburg relied on an 1823 decision by Supreme Court justice John Marshall, which in turn relied on the papal bulls that supported the legality of colonization and land theft. Ginsburg stated that the 1823 decision made sure that the nation could not be capable of "rekindling embers of sovereignty that long ago grew cold." And thus the repurchase of the Oneida nation's original land did not restore its sovereignty. As of February 2022, Pope Frances, despite multiple formal requests by Indigenous nations and Catholic leaders, has yet to rescind the papal bulls. Jack Jenkins, "Bishop Denounces 'Doctrine of Discovery,' Used to Justify Abuse of Indigenous Peoples, and Suggests Pope Francis Do the Same," *America: The Jesuit Review*, July 6, 2021, https://www.americamagazine.org /faith/2021/07/06/bishop-syracuse-doctrine-discovery-indigenous-240986.

30. hooks, *The Will to Change*, 18.

31. hooks, *The Will to Change*, 27.

32. Judith Lewis Herman, *Truth and Repair: How Trauma Survivors Envision Justice* (New York: Basic Books, 2023).

33. Viola Davis, *Finding Me* (New York: HarperCollins and Ebony Magazine Publishing, 2022), 85.

34. Herman, *Truth and Repair*, 26.

35. Quoted in "The Memorial," Survivors Memorial, accessed April 26, 2023, https://www .survivorsmemorial.org.

36. Tayo Bero, "If Society Valued Black Women and Girls, Convicting R Kelly Wouldn't Take So Long," *Guardian*, September 29, 2021, Opinion, https://www.theguardian.com /commentisfree/2021/sep/29/r-kelly-convicting-black-women-girls.

37. Jennifer M. Gómez and Robyn L. Gobin, "Black Women and Girls & #MeToo: Rape, Cultural Betrayal, & Healing," *Sex Roles* 82, no. 1 (January 1, 2020): 1–12, https://doi.org/10.1007/s11199-019-01040-0.

38. Tonya Mosley, "'Me Too' Founder Tarana Burke Says Black Girls' Trauma Shouldn't Be Ignored," NPR, September 29, 2021, Author Interviews, https://www.npr.org/2021/09/29/1041362145/me-too-founder-tarana-burke-says-black-girls-trauma-shouldnt-be-ignored.

CHAPTER 10

1. Melissa S. Creary, "Bounded Justice and the Limits of Health Equity," *Journal of Law, Medicine and Ethics* 49, no. 2 (2021): 241–256, https://doi.org/10.1017/jme.2021.34.

2. United Nations, "Basic Principles and Guidelines on the Right to a Remedy and Reparation," Office of the High Commissioner, December 2005, https://www.ohchr.org/en/professionalinterest/pages/remedyandreparation.aspx.

3. Bryan Stevenson, *Just Mercy: A Story of Justice and Redemption* (New York: Spiegel and Grau, 2015).

4. Brian Stevenson and Sarah Lewis, "Truth and Reconciliation," *Aperture*, April 25, 2018, https://aperture.org/editorial/truth-reconciliation-bryan-stevenson-sarah-lewis/.

5. Ta-Nehisi Coates, "The Case for Reparations," *Atlantic*, June 2014, https://www.theatlantic.com/magazine/archive/2014/06/the-case-for-reparations/361631/.

6. Ta-Nehisi Coates, "Why Is Bernie Sanders against Reparations?," *Atlantic*, January 19, 2016, https://www.theatlantic.com/politics/archive/2016/01/bernie-sanders-reparations/424602/.

7. "What Is NAARC's 10-Point Reparations Plan?," n.d., National African American Reparations Commission, https://reparationscomm.org/reparations-plan/.

8. William A. Darity and A. Kirsten Mullen, *From Here to Equality: Reparations for Black Americans in the Twenty-First Century* (Chapel Hill: University of North Carolina Press, 2020); Roy L. Brooks, *Atonement and Forgiveness: A New Model for Black Reparations* (Berkeley: University of California Press, 2019).

9. Stefano Harney and Fred Moten, *The Undercommons: Fugitive Planning and Black Study* (New York: Minor Compositions, 2013), 152.

10. Daniel Wildcat, "Why Native Americans Don't Want Reparations," *Washington Post*, June 10, 2014, https://www.washingtonpost.com/posteverything/wp/2014/06/10/why-native-americans-dont-want-reparations/.

11. "Purpose and Vision," Sogorea Te' Land Trust, accessed October 19, 2022, https://sogoreate-landtrust.org/purpose-and-vision/.

12. Quoted in Rupa Marya and Raj Patel, *Inflamed: Deep Medicine and the Anatomy of Injustice* (New York: Farrar, Straus and Giroux, 2021), 225, https://www.overdrive.com/search?q=1FBB4766-1309-4A31-B387-A8A1C9C8A662.

13. The Red Nation, *The Red Deal: Indigenous Action to Save Our Earth* (Brooklyn: Common Notions, 2021).

14. Naomi Ishisaka, "The Duwamish People Were Here First. Should Seattleites Pay Them Rent?," *Seattle Times*, January 27, 2020, https://www.seattletimes.com/seattle-news/the -duwamish-people-were-here-first-should-seattleites-pay-them-rent/.

15. Eve Tuck and K. Wayne Yang, "Decolonization Is Not a Metaphor," *Decolonization: Indigeneity, Education and Society* 1, no. 1 (September 8, 2012), https://jps.library.utoronto.ca/index .php/des/article/view/18630.

16. Tianna Gaines-Turner, Joanna Cruz Simmons, and Mariana Chilton, "Recommendation from SNAP Participants to Improve Wages and End Stigma," *American Journal of Public Health* 109, no. 12 (December 1, 2019), https://doi.org/10.2105/AJPH.2019.305362.

17. Neil Schoenherr, "Childhood Poverty Costs U.S. $1.03 Trillion in a Year, Study Finds," *Source* (blog), April 16, 2018, https://source.wustl.edu/2018/04/childhood-poverty-cost-u-s-1-03 -trillion-in-a-year-study-finds/.

18. Juliana Uhuru Bidadanure, "The Political Theory of Universal Basic Income," *Annual Review of Political Science* 22, no. 1 (May 11, 2019): 481–501, https://doi.org/10.1146/annurev -polisci-050317-070954.

19. Annie Lowrey, *Give People Money: How a Universal Basic Income Would End Poverty, Revolutionize Work, and Remake the World* (New York: Crown, 2018); Andrew Yang, *The War on Normal People: The Truth about America's Disappearing Jobs and Why Universal Basic Income Is Our Future* (New York: Hachette Books, 2018).

20. Laura Dwyer-Lindgren et al., "Life Expectancy by County, Race, and Ethnicity in the USA, 2000–19: A Systematic Analysis of Health Disparities," *Lancet* 400, no. 10345 (July 2, 2022): 25–38, https://doi.org/10.1016/S0140-6736(22)00876-5.

21. "A Short History of the Basic Income Idea," BIEN, accessed February 18, 2022, https:// basicincome.org/history/.

22. Allison Bovell-Ammon et al., "Association of the Expiration of Child Tax Credit Advance Payments with Food Insufficiency in US Households," *JAMA Network Open* 5, no. 10 (October 21, 2022): e2234438, https://doi.org/10.1001/jamanetworkopen.2022.34438.

23. "The Magnolia Mother's Trust," Springboard to Opportunities, 2020, http://springboardto .org/index.php/page/the-magnolia-mothers-trust.

24. Gaines-Turner, Simmons, and Chilton, "Recommendations from SNAP Participants to Improve Wages and End Stigma."

25. Lorie Konish, "This Is the Real Reason Most Americans File for Bankruptcy," CNBC, February 11, 2019, https://www.cnbc.com/2019/02/11/this-is-the-real-reason-most-americans -file-for-bankruptcy.html.

26. Rita Giordano, "Where Do You Live? It May Give Clues to How Old You'll Grow, Federal Data Suggest," *Philadelphia Inquirer*, accessed April 8, 2022, https://www.inquirer.com /health/life-expectancy-project-philadelphia-new-jersey-census-tract-20181218.html.

27. "The $1.2 Billion Child Health Dividend," Children's HealthWatch, Policy Action Brief, May 2016, https://childrenshealthwatch.org/wp-content/uploads/FINAL-What-If-brief-for-web.pdf.

28. Jaeger Nelson, "Economic Effects of Five Illustrative Single-Payer Health Care Systems" (working paper, Congressional Budget Office, Washington, DC, February 23, 2022), https://www.cbo.gov/system/files/2022-02/57637-Single-Payer-Systems.pdf.

29. Jennifer J. Otten et al., "The Culture of Health in Early Care and Education: Workers' Wages, Health, and Job Characteristics," *Health Affairs* 38, no. 5 (May 1, 2019): 709–720, https://doi.org/10.1377/hlthaff.2018.05493.

30. Janet Poppendieck, *Free for All: Fixing School Food in America* (Berkeley: University of California Press, 2010); Sarah Martinelli et al., "The Case for Universal Free Meals for All: A Permanent Solution," *Health Affairs Forefront*, accessed October 19, 2022, https://doi.org/10.1377/forefront.20220504.114330.

31. "Life Expectancy of the World Population," Worldometer, accessed November 4, 2023, https://www.worldometers.info/demographics/life-expectancy/.

32. Ai-jen Poo, "The Work That Makes All Other Work Possible," TEDWomen, 2018, https://www.ted.com/talks/ai_jen_poo_the_work_that_makes_all_other_work_possible; Julia Wolfe et al., "Domestic Workers Chartbook: A Comprehensive Look at the Demographics, Wages, Benefits, and Poverty Rates of the Professionals Who Care for Our Family Members and Clean Our Homes," Economic Policy Institute, May 14, 2020, https://www.epi.org/publication/domestic-workers-chartbook-a-comprehensive-look-at-the-demographics-wages-benefits-and-poverty-rates-of-the-professionals-who-care-for-our-family-members-and-clean-our-homes/.

33. National Women's Law Center and Center on Poverty and Social Policy, "A Lifetime's Worth of Benefits: The Effects of Affordable, High-Quality Child Care on Family Income, the Gender Earnings Gap, and Women's Retirement Security," National Women's Law Center, April 12, 2021, https://nwlc.org/resource/a-lifetimes-worth-of-benefits-the-effects-of-affordable-high-quality-child-care-on-family-income-the-gender-earnings-gap-and-womens-retirement-security/.

34. Aleks Kajstura and Wendy Sawyer, "Women's Mass Incarceration: The Whole Pie 2023," Prison Policy Initiative, accessed April 27, 2023, https://www.prisonpolicy.org/reports/pie2023women.html.

35. Joseph Murray, David P. Farrington, and Ivana Sekol, "Children's Antisocial Behavior, Mental Health, Drug Use, and Educational Performance after Parental Incarceration: A Systematic Review and Meta-Analysis," *Psychological Bulletin* 138, no. 2 (March 2012): 175–210, https://doi.org/10.1037/a0026407.

36. "What Happens When Moms Go to Prison," *ChildTrends*, October 28, 2015, https://www.childtrends.org/blog/what-happens-when-moms-go-to-prison.

37. Eli Hager, "Debtors' Prisons, Then and Now: FAQ," Marshall Project, February 24, 2015, https://www.themarshallproject.org/2015/02/24/debtors-prisons-then-and-now-faq.

38. Ruth Wilson Gilmore, *Golden Gulag: Prisons, Surplus, Crisis, and Opposition in Globalizing California* (Berkeley: University of California Press, 2007); Andrea Ritchie and Angela Y. Davis, *Invisible No More: Police Violence against Black Women and Women of Color*, rep. ed. (Boston: Beacon Press, 2017); Mariame Kaba, Tamara K. Nopper, and Naomi Murakawa, *We Do This 'til We Free Us: Abolitionist Organizing and Transforming Justice* (Chicago: Haymarket Books, 2021); Angela Y. Davis, *Are Prisons Obsolete?* (New York: Seven Stories Press, 2003); Combahee River Collective, "The Combahee River Collective Statement (1977)," statement, April 1977, https://www.blackpast.org/african-american-history/combahee-river-collective-statement-1977/.

39. Chenjari Kumanyika, "Ruth Wilson Gilmore Makes the Case for Abolition," *Intercepted* (podcast), June 10, 2020, https://theintercept.com/2020/06/10/ruth-wilson-gilmore-makes-the-case-for-abolition/.

40. Gerry Johnstone and Daniel W. Van Ness, eds., *Handbook of Restorative Justice* (Portland, OR: Willan, 2007).

41. Peter Wagner and Bernadette Rabuy, "Following the Money of Mass Incarceration," Prison Policy Initiative, accessed October 19, 2022, https://www.prisonpolicy.org/reports/money.html.

42. Quoted in Janell Ross, "Segregation Now: #LivingWhileBlack Experiences Are the New Version of 'Whites Only' Signs," NBC News, May 31, 2019, https://www.nbcnews.com/news/nbcblk/segregation-now-livingwhileblack-experiences-are-new-version-whites-only-signs-n1012226.

43. "The Problem," Prison Gerrymandering Project, accessed February 28, 2022, https://www.prisonersofthecensus.org/impact.html.

44. Generation Five, *Ending Child Sexual Abuse: A Transformative Justice Handbook*, n.d., http://www.generationfive.org/wp-content/uploads/2017/06/Transformative-Justice-Handbook.pdf.

45. Shawn Ginwright, *The Four Pivots: Reimagining Justice, Reimagining Ourselves* (Berkeley, CA: North Atlantic Books, 2022).

46. Gilmore, *Golden Gulag*.

47. Gillian Brockell, "La. Voters Keep 'Slavery' at Angola Prison, Once and Still a Plantation," *Washington Post*, November 10, 2022, https://www.washingtonpost.com/history/2022/11/10/angola-prison-louisiana-slave-labor/.

48. Khalil Gibran Muhammad and Chenjerai Kumanyika, "The Origins of Policing in America | Perspective," *Washington Post*, September 24, 2020, https://www.youtube.com/watch?v=eBvo2OE5kqM.

49. Kaba, Nopper, and Murakawa, *We Do This 'til We Free Us*.

50. Critical Resistance, accessed November 5, 2023, http://criticalresistance.org/; Project Nia, accessed November 5, 2023, https://project-nia.org/; Interrupting Criminalization, accessed October 14, 2022, https://www.interruptingcriminalization.com.

51. "The Breathe Act," M4BL, accessed October 14, 2022, https://breatheact.org/.

52. Robin D. G. Kelley, *Freedom Dreams: The Black Radical Imagination*, 20th anniversary ed. (Boston: Beacon Press, 2022).

53. Susila Gurusami, "Motherwork under the State: The Maternal Labor of Formerly Incarcerated Black Women," *Social Problems* 66, no. 1 (February 1, 2019): 128–143, https://doi.org/10.1093/socpro/spx045.

54. Dorothy E. Roberts, *Torn Apart: How the Child Welfare System Destroys Black Families—and How Abolition Can Build a Safer World* (New York: Basic Books, 2022), 88.

55. Roberts, *Torn Apart*, 93.

56. Kathryn Joyce, "She Said Her Husband Hit Her. She Lost Custody of Their Kids," Marshall Project, July 8, 2020, https://www.themarshallproject.org/2020/07/08/she-said-her-husband-hit-her-she-lost-custody-of-their-kids.

57. Roberts, *Torn Apart*, 223.

58. US Solidarity Economy Network, accessed October 23, 2022, https://ussen.org/.

59. Jessica Gordon Nembhard, *Collective Courage: A History of African American Cooperative Economic Thought and Practice* (University Park: Pennsylvania State University Press, 2014).

60. Fannie Lou Hamer, "Until I Am Free, You Are Not Free Either" (speech at the University of Wisconsin at Madison, January 1971).

61. Gordon Nembhard, *Collective Courage*.

62. La Via Campesina, accessed October 23, 2022, https://viacampesina.org/en/.

63. Leah Penniman and Karen Washington, *Farming While Black: Soul Fire Farm's Practical Guide to Liberation on the Land* (White River Junction, VT: Chelsea Green Publishing, 2018).

64. INCITE! Women of Color Against Violence, ed., *The Revolution Will Not Be Funded: Beyond the Non-Profit Industrial Complex* (Durham, NC: Duke University Press, 2017).

65. Gift giving, charity, and solidarity are broad and deep topics. To learn more by starting with a classic anthropology text, see Marcel Mauss, *The Gift: The Form and Reason for Exchange in Archaic Societies*, trans. W. D. Halls (New York: W. W. Norton and Company, 2000).

CHAPTER 11

1. SBS Dateline, "Mexico's Avocado Militia," YouTube, accessed October 14, 2022, https://www.youtube.com/watch?v=oVf3KyPfTjY.

2. United Nations, "About the Right to Food and Human Rights," Office of the High Commissioner, accessed April 4, 2022, https://www.ohchr.org/en/special-procedures/sr-food/about-right-food-and-human-rights.

3. La Via Campesina, accessed October 23, 2022, https://viacampesina.org/en/.

4. Food and Agriculture Organization, "The State of Food Insecurity in the World 2014: Strengthening the Enabling Environment for Food Security and Nutrition," ReliefWeb, September 16, 2014, https://reliefweb.int/report/world/state-food-insecurity-world-2014-strengthening-enabling-environment-food-security-and.

5. Lise Alves, "Pandemic Puts Brazil Back on the World Hunger Map," *New Humanitarian*, July 19, 2021, https://www.thenewhumanitarian.org/news-feature/2021/7/19/pandemic-puts-brazil-back-on-the-world-hunger-map.

6. "Brazil's New President Wants to Reduce the Number of Hungry People," *Economist*, accessed April 24, 2023, https://www.economist.com/the-americas/2023/01/19/brazils-new-president-wants-to-reduce-the-number-of-hungry-people.

7. Naomi Klein, *The Shock Doctrine: The Rise of Disaster Capitalism* (New York: Picador, 2008).

8. Roberto Cazzolla Gatti, "A Conceptual Model of New Hypothesis on the Evolution of Biodiversity," *Biologia* 71, no. 3 (March 1, 2016): 343–351, https://doi.org/10.1515/biolog-2016-0032.

9. UN General Assembly, Resolution 217 A, Universal Declaration of Human Rights, Art. 29 (Dec. 10, 1948), https://www.un.org/en/about-us/universal-declaration-of-human-rights#:~:text=Article%2029,of%20his%20personality%20is%20possible.

10. Clay S. Jenkinson, "Is It Time for a New Constitutional Convention?," Governing, July 24, 2022, https://www.governing.com/context/is-it-time-for-a-new-constitutional-convention.

11. Robin Wall Kimmerer, *Braiding Sweetgrass: Indigenous Wisdom, Scientific Knowledge and the Teaching of Plants* (Minneapolis: Milkweed Editions, 2013), 183; emphasis in original.

12. United Nations, "On Climate Change Frontline, Indigenous Provide Pointers to Save Planet," *UN News* (blog), June 25, 2021, https://news.un.org/en/story/2021/06/1094812.

13. Robin Wall Kimmerer, "Corn Tastes Better on the Honor System," *Emergence Magazine*, 2018, https://emergencemagazine.org/feature/corn-tastes-better/.

14. Taggart Siegel and Jon Betz, dir., *Seed: The Untold Story* (Portland, OR: Collective Eye Films, August 22, 2016), 9:34–9:57, https://www.seedthemovie.com.

15. Stefano Mancuso and Gregory Conti, *The Nation of Plants* (New York: Penguin Random House, 2021), 9.

16. Global Witness, *Enemies of the State? How Governments and Business Silence Land and Environmental Defenders* (London: Global Witness, 2019).

17. Aristegui Noticias, "Julián Carrillo Defended the Forest with His Life," Amnesty International, November 28, 2018, https://www.amnesty.org/en/latest/news/2018/11/la-mortal-defensa-del-bosque-por-julian-carrillo/.

18. Alberto Pradilla, "Defensores ambientales en Honduras: Una imagen terrible en el celular de Marta Raquel," La mula, April 10, 2018, https://mongabay-latam.lamula.pe/2018/04

/10/defensores-ambientales-en-honduras-una-imagen-terrible-en-el-celular-de-marta-raquel
/mongabaylatam/.

19. Nina Lakhani, "Who Killed Berta Cáceres? Behind the Brutal Murder of an Environment Crusader," *Guardian*, June 2, 2020, World News, https://www.theguardian.com/world/2020
/jun/02/who-killed-berta-caceres-behind-the-brutal-of-an-environment-crusader.

20. Annita Lucchesi and Abigail Echo-Hawk, "Missing and Murdered Indigenous Women & Girls," Urban Indian Health Institute, November 24, 2018, https://www.uihi.org/resources
/missing-and-murdered-indigenous-women-girls/.

21. Acee Agoyo, "'What She Say, It Be Law': Tribes Protected Their Women before Being Stripped of Sovereignty," *Indianz*, March 25, 2019, https://www.indianz.com/News/2019/03/25
/what-she-say-it-be-law-tribes-protected.asp.

22. Natasha Lenard, "Police Shot Atlanta Cop City Protester 57 Times, Autopsy Finds," *Intercept*, accessed April 24, 2023, https://theintercept.com/2023/04/20/atlanta-cop-city-protester
-autopsy/.

23. Kate Brumback and R. J. Rico, "Troopers Who Fatally Shot a 'Cop City' Activist near Atlanta Won't Be Charged, Prosecutor Says," AP News, last updated October 6, 2023, https://apnews.com/article/cop-city-atlanta-activist-shot-no-charges-421f6fe392a920252
3ea154b2ddabb7d.

24. Natasha Lenard, "Atlanta Cop City Protesters Charged with Domestic Terror for Having Mud on Their Shoes," *Intercept*, March 8, 2023, https://theintercept.com/2023/03/08
/atlanta-cop-city-protesters/.

25. Elena Novak, "Why Tortuguita's Murder Is Only the Tip of the Iceberg," *Waging Nonviolence*, April 7, 2023, https://wagingnonviolence.org/2023/04/tortuguita-cop-city-azacualpa
-soa/.

26. "Youth v Gov: 11-Year-Old Levi Knows Climate Change Is No Hoax; Sues Government for His Future," Impact Fund, April 19, 2019, https://www.impactfund.org/social-justice-blog
/youthvgov.

27. Kai Huschke, "The EPA Has Abandoned Its Duty to Protect the Environment. 'Rights of Nature' Laws Can Fill the Void," *In These Times*, April 16, 2020, https://inthesetimes.com
/article/trump-epa-covid-19-environmental-law-rights-of-nature-air-water-pollution.

28. "Tamaqua Borough, Pennsylvania," Community Environmental Legal Defense Fund, August 31, 2015, https://celdf.org/2015/08/tamaqua-borough/.

29. Winona LaDuke, "The White Earth Band of Ojibwe Legally Recognized the Rights of Wild Rice," *YES! Magazine*, February 1, 2019, https://www.yesmagazine.org/environment
/2019/02/01/the-white-earth-band-of-ojibwe-legally-recognized-the-rights-of-wild-rice
-heres-why.

30. "Programme," Harmony with Nature, United Nations, accessed April 25, 2023, http://www
.harmonywithnatureun.org/.

CHAPTER 12

1. bell hooks, *All about Love: New Visions* (New York: William Morrow Paperbacks, 2018), 6.

2. Rita Giordano, "Where Do You Live? It May Give Clues to How Old You'll Grow, Federal Data Suggest," *Philadelphia Inquirer*, accessed April 8, 2022, https://www.inquirer.com /health/life-expectancy-project-philadelphia-new-jersey-census-tract-20181218.html.

3. Tree Media, "Oren Lyons on the Indigenous View of the World," YouTube, September 16, 2016, https://www.youtube.com/watch?v=kbwSwUMNyPU.

4. "Child Abuse Statistics," Children's Advocacy Centers of Tennessee, n.d., http://www.cactn .org/child-abuse-information/statistics.

5. Shawn Ginwright, *The Four Pivots: Reimagining Justice, Reimagining Ourselves* (Berkeley, CA: North Atlantic Books, 2022).

6. Thich Nhat Hanh, "The Art of Transforming Suffering," *Mindfulness Bell*, no. 88 (Autumn 2021): 20.

7. Xianglong Zeng et al., "The Effect of Loving-Kindness Meditation on Positive Emotions: A Meta-Analytic Review," *Frontiers in Psychology* 6 (November 3, 2015): 1693, https://doi.org /10.3389/fpsyg.2015.01693.

8. Tree Media, "Oren Lyons on the Indigenous View of the World."

9. Thich Nhat Hanh, *Being Peace*, 2nd ed. (Berkeley, CA: Parallax Press, 2005).

10. hooks, *All about Love*, 133–134.

11. Robin Wall Kimmerer, "Corn Tastes Better on the Honor System," *Emergence Magazine*, accessed October 14, 2022, https://emergencemagazine.org/feature/corn-tastes-better/.

12. bell hooks, *Communion: The Female Search for Love* (New York: William Morrow Paperbacks, 2002).

13. "New Contemplations before Eating," Plum Village, January 15, 2014, https://plumvillage .org/articles/news/new-contemplations-before-eating/.

14. "Food Production Is Responsible for One-Quarter of the World's Greenhouse Gas Emissions," Our World in Data, accessed May 2, 2023, https://ourworldindata.org/food-ghg-emissions.

15. Duncan Williamson, Kate Munro, and Monica Carlotti, "Climate Change: A Hunger Crisis in the Making," ReliefWeb, October 26, 2021, https://reliefweb.int/report/world/climate -change-hunger-crisis-making.

16. hooks, *Communion*, 139.

17. Treva B. Lindsey, *America, Goddam: Violence, Black Women, and the Struggle for Justice* (Oakland: University of California Press, 2022).

18. Quoted in Kimmerer, "Corn Tastes Better on the Honor System."

19. Audre, Lorde, "Uses of the Erotic: The Erotic as Power, 1978," in *Sister Outsider: Essays and Speeches*, rep. ed. (Berkeley, CA: Crossing Press, 2007), 89.

Index

Page references followed by *f* and *t* indicate figures and tables, respectively.

EPA (Environmental Protection Agency), 284

Epidemiology, xv

Epigenetics, 88

Equanimity, 292, 296

Erotic power and knowledge, 25–26

ERS (Economic Research Service), 43–44. *See also* HFSSM

Erwin, Valerie, 20

Esther (case study), 149, 302

Ethnography, xiv–xv

Extinctions, 276

Fair Employment Act (1941), 266

Faith (case study), 106–110, 133, 301

Family leave, 57, 148

Famines, 6–7, 276

Farm Bill (1933), 165, 180

Fast-food workplaces, 157–158

FBI (Federal Bureau of Investigation), 170–172

FDPIR (Food Distribution Program on Indian Reservations), 175–177

Federal poverty line, 129–130

Federici, Silvia, 225–226

Feeding America, 27, 190–193, 195, 199, 202–203, 207, 269

Felitti, Vincent, 86–87

Feudalism, 225

Fight, flight, or freeze responses, 86–87

Fisher, Andy, 181, 195

Fletcher, Willie, 11

Floyd, George, 262

FNS (Food and Nutrition Services), 167–168

Fome Zero (Zero Hunger), 274–275

Food and Nutrition Services (FNS), 167–168

Food banks, 190–192, 195–196, 199–200, 268–269. *See also* Emergency food systems; Food pantries; Philabundance

Food Distribution Program on Indian Reservations (FDPIR), 175–177

Food drives, 191, 201

Food First Information and Action Network, 275

Food for Free, 205

Food insecurity. *See also* Hunger
and ACEs, 99–101
and addiction, 94–95
and caregivers' health, 49
charity as a solution to, 273
among children, 99–101, 101*f*
and children's development, 48–49
and the climate crisis, 276–278, 280
during the COVID-19 pandemic, 7–8
definition of, xi, 8, 43–45
and depression, 49–52, 65, 99–101
and disabilities, 52–53
and discrimination, 58–59
and domination, 13–14
and emotional neglect, 100–101, 101*f*
and employment, 57–58
and family stress, 53
across generations, 93, 98–99, 314*f*
health professionals' referrals for, 207–208
and housing insecurity, 48–50
hunger as, 43–46
among Indigenous peoples, disproportionate, 4, 10–12
inequities in, 4–5, 8–13
levels of, 44–45, 309–310*t*
mapping of, 199
measuring, 42–48, 92–93, 309–310*t*, 321n6
and the monetization of meals, 198–199
during pregnancy, 48
after prison, 59
quantitative vs. qualitative research on, 74
rates of, 8–13
and violence, 90–93, 96, 101–102, 119
and wages, 57

Food pantries. *See also* Emergency food systems; Food banks
on college campuses, 204–205
as cooperatives, 268–269

Hispanic people. *See* Latinx people

Hoarding food and resources, 6–7, 151, 181–182

Holocaust, 88, 103, 147–148

Homelessness
  and caregivers' health, 49
  and emergency room use, 207
  and housing support, 54
  during pregnancy, 48

hooks, bell
  on the culture of domination, 14, 24, 218, 288
  on the imperialist, white supremacist, capitalist heteropatriarchy, 217
  on love and spirituality, 24–25, 288, 300
  on patriarchy, 236–237

Hoopa people, 11–12

Hoover, J. Edgar, 170–171

Household Food Security Survey Module. *See* HFSSM

Household Pulse Survey, 8

Housing insecurity, 48–50

H.R. 40 (reparations bill), 244

Hubbard, Mia, 206

Human rights, 9, 271–276, 296

Humility, 37

Hunger. *See also* Food insecurity
  among children, 92–97
  and community gardens, 4
  as created by people in power, 5–7 (*see also* Capitalism)
  definitions of, xi
  and depression, 49–52, 65, 69
  and disbelonging, 2
  discomfort of, 39–42
  discrimination as causing, 9
  domains of healing, 14–15
  as entitlement failure, 9, 135–136, 193
  and feelings of disrespect, 90
  and the focus on food, 3–4, 7–10
  as food insecurity, 43–46
  across generations, 91–92, 94

  grief about, xiii–xiv
  and gut bacteria, 71–72
  initiatives on, 3, 10 (*see also specific programs*)
  measuring, 42–48, 309–310*t*, 321n6
  physical vs. mental/emotional, 68–70, 72
  quantitative vs. qualitative research on, 74
  the right to freedom from, 271–272, 274–275
  solutions to, 10, 14–15
  trauma of, 15, 119
  and violence, 90–93, 96, 101–102, 119
  and wages, 5, 9

Hunger-Free Campus Bill, 204

Immigrants
  children separated from parents, 137–138, 160
  denied health insurance coverage, 160
  disproportionate food insecurity among, 12–13

Impoverishment. *See* Poverty

Incommensurability, ethic of, 250

India, 6

Indian Appropriations Act (1871), 248

Indian Child Welfare Act (1978), 139

Indian Removal Act (1830), 248–249

Indifference. *See* Emotional numbness

Indigenous Environmental Network, 20

Indigenous peoples. *See also specific peoples*
  boarding schools for children of, 11, 138, 263
  capitalism's domination of, 226
  collective trauma among, 16
  diabetes among, 11
  disproportionate food insecurity among, 4, 10–12
  disproportionate hunger among, 4
  food assistance among, 173–177
  food insecurity among, 174
  food sharing with, 37
  food viewed as kin by, 278–280
  forced relocation of, 248–249

Seeds, returning, 242, 247
Segregation, residential, 12, 56
SELF (safety, emotions, loss, and future), 115–116
Self-esteem, low, 56, 97–98, 231–232, 289, 300–302
Sen, Amartya, 6–7, 9
Sesame Street, 194–195
Sexism
  personal work on, 218–224
  and the pleasure of domination, 18
  in public assistance, 223
  and racism, 219–224
Sex work, 70, 79
Shandra (case study), 156
Share Our Strength, 199
Sharpe, Christina, 214–216, 218
Shelters, 54
Shirley (case study), 128, 130, 156–159, 194
Sicangu Oyate Lakota communities, 176
Simmons, Joanna, 253
Slager, Michael, 160
Slavery
  abolition of, 12, 226, 258
  bans on teaching about, 245–246
  and Black codes, 123–124, 226, 261
  collective trauma caused by, 16
  harm across generations caused by, 214–215
  legacy of, personal work on, 214–218, 221, 233–234
  and the pleasure of domination, 18
  as rape, 234–235
  slave codes/patrols under, 261
SNAP (Supplemental Nutrition Assistance Program), xvi
  and ACEs, 100
  benefit calculation by, 167
  benefits of, 127–128
  college students participating in, 204
  corporate exploitation of, 120, 179–183
  demonstrating worthiness for, 2

effectiveness of, 59, 166
eligibility for, 130
as an entitlement program, 135–136, 165
establishment of, 163–164
and the focus on food, 3–4
food choices under, 165–166
funding for, 134–137, 165
health benefits of, 166
immigrants' access to, 13
importance of, 73
Indigenous peoples participating in, 175, 177
ineligible items for purchase under, 165
limitations of, 242
participation rates for, 165
recommendations for improving, 134–137
separation from Medicaid and TANF, 143
stigma created by, 253
tax credits for participants, 156–157
veterans participating in, 165–166, 206
work requirement for, 177–179
Social determinants of health, 207
Social Security, 9, 141, 250–251, 256–257
Soda, 182
Sodexo, 205
Sogorea Te' Land Trust, 249
Solidarity
  vs. charity, 268–269
  economies of, 20, 28, 265–269
  healing power of, 106–108, 115–116
  between researchers and the researched, 36–37
Soul, harm to, 234
Soul Fire Farm, 267
Soup kitchens, 2, 199–200
South Dakota, 138–139
Southern Rural Black Women's Initiative for Economic and Social Justice, 275
Special Supplemental Nutrition Program for Women, Infants, and Children. *See* WIC
Spirituality, 24–25

Spiritual work, 211–212, 287–304
loving others, 292–296
loving ourselves, 289–291, 300–301
removing pain, 293–294
respecting food, 297–299
on self-esteem, 300–302
smiling, 294–295
for surviving throughout generations,
288–289
Starbucks, 195
Starvation amid plenty, 6–7
Starvation studies, 49
Staub, Irvin, 75
St. Christopher's Hospital for Children
(Philadelphia), 47
Sterilization, forced, 150
Stevenson, Brian, 243–244
Stop & Shop, 182
Stress. *See also* Trauma
fight, flight, or freeze responses to, 86
of racism, 215
toxic, 85–86
Stunting, 163
Subsidized housing, 54
Sugar, 182–183
Suicide and suicidal ideation, 53, 65, 83, 86,
96–97, 106–107, 109–110
Summer EBT (Electronic Benefits Transfer),
126–127
Summer Food Service Program, 124
Sunoco, 193
Survivors Memorial (Minneapolis), 238
Swipe Out Hunger, 204

Taino people, 279
Tamaqua Borough (Pennsylvania), 284
TANF (Temporary Assistance for Needy
Families)
and the Building Wealth and Health
Network, 113–114
caseworkers, interactions with, 130, 144,
151, 155

childcare benefits, 148–149, 151–152,
256
eligibility and work requirements for,
130–133, 135, 143–144, 148–149,
151
family cap in, 150
as financial apartheid, 153–154
funding diverted by, 142–143, 151
funding for, 135, 142
goals of, 142, 151
grant amounts by, 143, 148, 153
income reportable to, 155
marriage promoted by, 142
participation rates for, 152–153
as racist and misogynistic, 148, 153
rent allowance by, 154
sabotage by, 152–156
as separating and isolating people, 120
separation from Medicaid and SNAP, 143
systemic discrimination, 132–133
tax credits for participants, 156–157
Taylor, Linda, 179–180
Temporary Assistance for Needy Families.
See TANF
Tewa (Pueblo) people, 174
Texas, 159–160
TFP (Thrifty Food Plan), 167–168
Thunberg, Greta, 283
Tina (case study), 256
Tinisha (case study), 63–64, 72
Tortuguita (Manual Esteban Páez Terán), 283
Trail of Tears, 248–249
Transformative justice, 260
Trauma. *See also* Breaking the chain of trauma
and oppression; Rape; Stress
appeasement response to, 88–89
behavioral responses to, 88
biological/physical responses to, 87–88,
119
among children (toxic stress), 85–86
(*see also* ACEs)
definition of, 17

Keith Douglass Warner, *Agroecology in Action: Extending Alternative Agriculture through Social Networks*

Christopher M. Bacon, V. Ernesto Méndez, Stephen R. Gliessman, David Goodman, and Jonathan A. Fox, eds., *Confronting the Coffee Crisis: Fair Trade, Sustainable Livelihoods and Ecosystems in Mexico and Central America*

Thomas A. Lyson, G. W. Stevenson, and Rick Welsh, eds., *Food and the Mid-Level Farm: Renewing an Agriculture of the Middle*

Jennifer Clapp and Doris Fuchs, eds., *Corporate Power in Global Agrifood Governance*

Robert Gottlieb and Anupama Joshi, *Food Justice*

Jill Lindsey Harrison, *Pesticide Drift and the Pursuit of Environmental Justice*

Alison Alkon and Julian Agyeman, eds., *Cultivating Food Justice: Race, Class, and Sustainability*

Abby Kinchy, *Seeds, Science, and Struggle: The Global Politics of Transgenic Crops*

Vaclav Smil and Kazuhiko Kobayashi, *Japan's Dietary Transition and Its Impacts*

Sally K. Fairfax, Louise Nelson Dyble, Greig Tor Guthey, Lauren Gwin, Monica Moore, and Jennifer Sokolove, *California Cuisine and Just Food*

Brian K. Obach, *Organic Struggle: The Movement for Sustainable Agriculture in the U.S.*

Andrew Fisher, *Big Hunger: The Unholy Alliance between Corporate America and Anti-Hunger Groups*

Julian Agyeman, Caitlin Matthews, and Hannah Sobel, eds., *Food Trucks, Cultural Identity, and Social Justice: From Loncheras to Lobsta Love*

Sheldon Krimsky, *GMOs Decoded: A Skeptic's View of Genetically Modified Foods*

Rebecca de Souza, *Feeding the Other: Whiteness, Privilege, and Neoliberal Stigma in Food Pantries*

Bill Winders and Elizabeth Ransom, eds., *Global Meat: The Social and Environmental Consequences of the Expanding Meat Industry*

Laura-Anne Minkoff Zern, *The New American Farmer: Immigration, Race, and the Struggle for Sustainability*

Julian Agyeman and Sydney Giacalone, eds., *The Immigrant-Food Nexus: Food Systems, Immigration Policy, and Immigrant Foodways in North America*

Benjamin R. Cohen, Michael S. Kideckel, and Anna Zeide, eds., *Acquired Tastes: Stories about the Origins of Modern Food*

Karine E. Peschard, *Seed Activism: Patent Politics and Litigation in the Global South*

Jennifer Gaddis and Sarah Robert, eds., *Transforming School Food Politics around the World*

Mariana Chilton, *The Painful Truth about Hunger in America: Why We Must Unlearn Everything We Think We Know—and Start Again*